Music
Reference and Research
Materials

Music
Reference and Research
Materials

AN ANNOTATED BIBLIOGRAPHY

Second Edition

Compiled by VINCENT DUCKLES

The Free Press, *New York*
Collier-Macmillan Limited, *London*

Introduction to the Second Edition

THE PLEA for corrections and additions that concluded the *Introduction* to the first edition of this work has not gone unheeded. Responses have come from a wide group of music students, teachers, and librarians. The chagrin at having ones oversights pointed out has been more than balanced by the pleasure at finding that this bibliography has been extensively and searchingly used. I am particularly grateful for suggestions made by my own students at the University of California, and to my colleague Daniel Heartz. John Davies, Music Librarian of the British Broadcasting Corporation, London, made many helpful comments, as did Jan La Rue, New York University, Frederick Crane, Lousiana State University, and George Skapski of San Fernando Valley State College. For assistance in the preparation of the manuscript of this edition, I am indebted to Lee Rosen.

Apart from the correction of old entries and the addition of new, no major changes have been introduced in this edition. A few minor revisions in organization should be noted however. These include: (1) an added section on *Jazz and Popular Music* under *Bibliographies of Music*; (2) the printed and manuscript sources of early music have been combined under one alphabet rather than two; and (3) *Catalogs of Private Collections* have been extracted from the general list of music library catalogs and entered in a section of their own. A substantial number of new book reviews have been added, and much attention has been given to making the *Index* more usable from a subject point of view.

The bibliography of music is an actively growing field. This is reflected not only in the fact that more than 200 new entries have been added to this edition, but also in the high quality of the work that is being done. The International Inventory of Musical Sources has been progressing slowly but surely toward its goal. The publication of the catalogs of major Italian music libraries has been moving ahead under the direction of Claudio Sartori in the series *Bibliotheca Musicae*. In this country we have the exemplary bibliography of *Instrumental music printed before 1600* by Howard Brown (see no. 749) and the long-awaited *Index of Festschriften* by Walter Gerboth (no. 426). Our control over the materials of popular song has been greatly enhanced by the appearance of Richard Wolfe's bibliography of *Secular music in America, 1801–25* (no. 809) and by the work of James Fuld (no. 718) and Nat. Shapiro (no. 720). Two new series devoted exclusively to music bibliography are off to a promising start: the Detroit Studies in Music Bibliography (see nos. 1329–37) and the Music Library Association Index Series (nos. 1353–58). In an effort to incorporate such new developments until the last moment before going to press, we have added a number of items outside of the regular numbered series. These are identified by a letter following the given number (e.g. 200a).

Vincent Duckles

1966

Introduction to the First Edition

A BIBLIOGRAPHY can be regarded as the relatively inert by-product of scholarly activity, or it can be treated as an active ingredient in the learning process. The latter perspective has been adopted in this guide to *Music Reference and Research Materials*. While no one but a professional bibliographer may be expected to come for his leisure reading to a list of books, most of us can respond with interest to an organized survey of the literature of a particular field. A bibliography, in fact, offers one of the best means of gaining an over-all impression of a subject area. It throws the essential patterns of a discipline into relief, casting light on what has been accomplished and drawing attention to the shadows where work still needs to be done. This guide has been designed to illuminate the bibliographical resources for musical scholarship. It is, above all, intended to serve a teaching purpose. Implicit in its organization is the concept that bibliography is an approach to knowledge, a way in which the student can progress toward mastery in his chosen field of specialization within the larger dimensions of the field of music. The guide was developed, through a series of editions beginning in 1949, as a text for a graduate seminar entitled "An Introduction to Musical Scholarship" given in the Music Department of the University of California at Berkeley. If its pattern has been determined to some extent by the way in which music bibliography is taught in a specific institution, its structure is still flexible enough to permit other teachers to use it in their own way.

The work is actually intended to fulfill the requirements of two groups: graduate students who need to become acquainted with the resources for musical research, and music reference librarians whose job it is to help others find the information they want. While the needs of the two have much in common, there are points at which their interests diverge. Much more is listed here than will be required for reference services in any but a large music research library, and there is material included which the scholar would rarely need to consult unless he moved outside of the traditional framework of historical musicology.

The present volume is much larger than any of its predecessors, yet it remains a selective list. One limitation in coverage, strictly enforced, is the selection of titles that pertain directly or exclusively to *music*. This criterion eliminates a great deal of valuable reference material, particularly important in areas that lie on the borderline between musicology and other disciplines: liturgics, the theater arts, literature, the dance, etc. No musicologist can afford to neglect such general reference tools as the *Encyclopedia of Religion and Ethics*, or Cabrol's *Dictionnaire d'archéologie chrétienne et de liturgie*, or, in another area, the *Census of Medieval and Renaissance Manuscripts in the U.S. and Canada*, by Seymour de Ricci, or Paul O. Kristeller's valuable survey of the catalogs of *Latin Manuscript Books before 1600*. The fact that these tools are indispensable only serves to demonstrate that musicology is far from being a self-sufficient and self-contained discipline. But an attempt to list all of the peripheral resources would inflate the present work and destroy its focus. There are excellent bibliographies of general reference works currently available. Perhaps the best service to be offered to the young musicologist here is to direct him to Constance M. Winchell's *Guide to Reference Books* (7th ed., 1951, and later supplements) or to Theodore Besterman's *World Bibliography of Bibliographies* (3rd ed., 1955–56). If all else fails, he should be urged to rely on that universal repository of fact and resource, *the reference librarian*, who sits behind a desk in every large library, prepared to guide the inquiring student through the complex paths of information retrieval. But there is a distinct advantage to be gained in approaching the general reference tools from the musician's point of view. Recently Keith E. Mixter has furnished such an approach in his manual on *General Bibliography for Music Research* (1962), published as Number 4 in the Detroit Studies in Music Bibliography. It is a pleasure to be able to point to that work as a useful complement to this one.

A few further statements should be added to make clear what ground this guide is, and is not, intended to cover. It does not represent the well-rounded library of musical literature; it contains no entries for biography, no local histories, no monographs or studies devoted to most of the subject areas into which the field of music can be subdivided. It is certainly not a basic list of titles which every music library should acquire; but it does provide a list from which the essential materials for a music reference collection can be selected. It can best be described as a bibliography of music bibliographies, its emphasis being on those works which themselves serve as points of departure for further investigations: lists, inventories, alphabetized compilations of facts about music. The one section which falls most conspicuously outside of this pattern of bibliographical emphasis is the section on "Histories and Chronologies." This is the only category in which books are listed for what they contain intrinsically rather than for their function as guides to further information.

In its preliminary forms this book has been put to use in a number of courses in music bibliography throughout the country, and as a result has benefited from the suggestions of several generous-minded critics. I am particularly indebted to Professor Albert T. Luper of the State University of Iowa, and to Professor Otto Albrecht of the University of Pennsylvania for their help in this respect. The form of the annotations owes much to Richard Angell of the Library of Congress, who placed his notes at my disposal. My colleagues in the Music Library of the University of California at Berkeley, Harriet Nicewonger and Minnie Elmer, have made their influence felt on nearly every page in matters that have to do with the selection of titles, the framing of the annotations, and the reading of proof.

One feature which has been introduced for the first time in the current edition is the citation of book reviews. These are offered as practical aids to the evaluation of the items. No effort has been made to achieve complete coverage: reviews are cited only for the more recent items, and are confined largely to those published in the English-language journals.

The entries are numbered throughout this book, and, for the most part, each title is entered once. There are some instances of duplicate entries, however, when the content of the item calls for its listing in more than one category. Eitner's *Quellen-Lexikon* is a case in point. This title is entered once as a dictionary of biography, and again as a bibliography of early music.

Abbreviations are used sparingly. What they save in space in a work of this kind is rarely commensurate to the inconvenience caused to the user. They are confined to the standard symbols for the dictionaries and journals most frequently cited in reviews: *Grove's* for *Grove's Dictionary of Music*

[ix]

and Musicians, 5th edition; *MGG* for *Die Musik in Geschichte und Gegenwart; Acta M* for *Acta musicologica; JAMS* for *Journal of the American Musicological Society; MQ* for *The Musical Quarterly;* and *Notes* for *Music Library Association Notes*, 2nd series.

A bibliographer's work is never done. Even as this edition goes to press, I am troubled by the submerged voices of would-be entries which may have been overlooked, and entries which may have been misplaced or misrepresented. Other music bibliographers proceed, unconcerned, with their work, the results of which will eventually call for supplements, or even substantial revisions in our present pattern of organization. But if one were too attentive to such considerations a work of this kind would never reach the point of publication. Now that it has made its appearance, I hope that it will attract collaboration, in the form of corrections, additions, or suggestions for improvement, from all who have occasion to use it.

Vincent Duckles

1964

Contents

Guides to Systematic and Historical Musicology *93*

Bibliographies of Music Literature *99*

Bibliographies of Music *143*

Dictionaries
and Encyclopedias

THE MOST comprehensive bibliography of music dictionaries and encyclopedias is found in James B. Coover's *Music lexicography*, Denver, 1958 (no. 1327), which offers some 1,335 entries. Other convenient listings appear in the article "Lexika der Musik," by Hans Heinrich Eggebrecht, in *MGG*, Vol. 8; in A. Hyatt King's survey in *Grove's*, 5th edition, Vol. 2; and in the *Harvard dictionary of music*. A useful chronological approach is found in a list by Richard Schaal, printed in the *Jahrbuch der Musikwelt*, 1949, p. 104–11, and also in *Hinrichsen's music book*, Vol. 7, p. 594–601, under the title "The fore-runners of the Grove-Blom."

A growing recognition of the value of early dictionaries as historical documents has brought many out-of-print titles into current availability through the efforts of such reprint publishers as Frits A. M. Knuf of Hilversum, Georg Olms of Hildesheim, Dover Publications of New York, and the Akademische Druck-und Verlagsanstalt of Graz.

The present list includes the most important music dictionaries and encyclopedias in current use, in all modern languages, cited as far as is possible under their latest editions. It also includes a selection of titles of those earlier works available in modern reprints, or of continuing value for reference purposes.

General

Those works in which both terms and biography are treated in the same alphabet are cited as "general" dictionaries and encyclopedias. The prototype for such works is Johann Walther's *Musikalisches Lexicon*, published in 1732 (see no. 48). From this important work two lines of descent may be traced, one leading through a series of concise dictionaries, usually in one volume and intended for quick reference; the other moving in the direction of multivolume, large-scale works with extended articles, more properly described as encyclopedias.

1

Abert, Hermann J., ed. Illustriertes Musik-Lexikon. Stuttgart, J. Engelhorns Nachf., 1927. 542 p.

A popular general dictionary, based on *Riemann* (no. 38) and *Das neue Musiklexikon* (no. 73). 503 pictures on 72 plates, and numerous short musical examples. Contributing editors: Hermann Abert, Friedrich Blume, Rudolf Gerber, Hans Hoffmann, and Theodor Schwartzkopff.

2

Algemene Muziekencyclopedie, onder leiding van A. Corbet en Wouter Paap. Redactiesecretaris: J. Robijns. Antwerpen, Zuid-Nederlandse Uitg. [1957–63] 6 v.

Comprehensive coverage of all aspects of music, including ethnomusicology, popular music, jazz. Brief biographies include performers, musicologists, composers, dancers. Major articles signed by contributors from England, Israel, United States, U.S.S.R., etc. Subject bibliographies and discographies, and brief lists of works for composers and musicologists. Valuable for its wide biographical range. Illustrated.

3

Allorto, Riccardo e Alberto Ferrari. Dizionario di musica. Milano, Casa Editrice Ceschina [1959] 576 p.

A popular dictionary of terms and biography. Brief biographical entries, mentioning representative works of minor composers, giving full tabulations of works of major composers. Well printed and illustrated, 8 plates in color. No bibliographical references.

4

Arma, Paul et Yvonne Tiénot. Nouveau dictionnaire de musique. Paris, Éditions Ouvrières [1947] 285 p.

A "pocket" dictionary, comprising some 2,000 biographical entries and 6,000 terms. 365 illustrations and short musical examples. Brief articles and summary listings of composers' works. Table of abbreviations.

5

Blom, Eric. Everyman's dictionary of music. Further rev. ed. London, Dent; New York, Dutton, 1958. 687 p.

First pub. in 1946; U.S. ed., 1948; rev. ed., 1954.

A popular, quick-reference book of terms, titles, biographies. Small in size but exceptionally rich in information. Excludes living performers. Summary listings of composers' works.

Review of 1954 ed. by Vincent Duckles in *Notes*, 13 (1955) p. 70–72.

6
Blume, Friedrich, ed. Die Musik in Geschichte und Gegenwart. Allgemeine Enzyklopädie der Musik . . . Kassel u. Basel, Bärenreiter-Verlag, 1949– . 14 v. 1949 - 1968.
Published in fascicles: No. 126/127 as of November 1966. Vols. 1–13: A-VERZ.

A comprehensive music reference work of the highest scholarly merit. In the German language, but international in scope and coverage. Articles contributed by specialists throughout the world. Gives complete listings of composers' works and detailed bibliographical references. Many of the articles are full-scale monographs, and all attempt to embody the latest research. Abundant illustrative material.

Reviewed by Willi Apel in *JAMS*, 3 (1950) p. 142–45; 5 (1952) p. 56–57 and p. 138–39. By Charles Warren Fox in *Notes*, 7 (1950) p. 466–67; 10 (1953) p. 451–52; 12 (1954) p. 92–93. By Paul Henry Lang in *MQ*, 36 (1950) p. 141–43; 38 (1952) p. 477–79. Reviewed in *Die Musikforschung* by Rudolph Steglich in 6 (1953) p. 260–64; by Hans Ehinger in 8 (1955) p. 92–96; by Kurt von Fischer in 9 (1956) p. 331–36; 10 (1957) p. 423–28; by Hellmut Federhofer in 12 (1959) p. 338–41.

Publication of the 5th ed. of *Grove's dictionary* in 1954 provided the occasion for some critical comparisons between *Grove's* and *MGG*. See Richard S. Hill in *Notes*, 12 (1954) p. 85–92, and A. Hyatt King, "Grove V and MGG," in *The monthly musical record*, 85 (1955) p. 115–19, p. 152–57, p. 183–85.

7
Bonaccorsi, Alfredo. Nuovo dizionario musicale Curci. Milano, Curci [1954] 557 p.

Emphasis on terms, forms, but with essential biographies. Brief bibliographies for most articles, including references to modern republications for composers.
Review in *Rassegna musicale*, 24 (1954) p. 389–91.

8
Borba, Tómas [e] Fernando Lopes Graça. Dicionário de música, ilustrado. Lisboa, Edições Cosmos, 1956. 2 v.

9
Bottenheim, Sam. Prisma encyclopedie der muziek. Bewerkt en ingeleid door Wouter Paap. [2. druk] Utrecht, Het Spectrum [1957] 2 v.

[3]

10

Coeuroy, André. Dictionnaire critique de la musique ancienne et moderne. Paris, Payot, 1956. 413 p.

Primarily biographical, its chief value is in the section "Écoles moderne" (p. 92–191): chronological lists by country, giving brief stylistic characteristics and one or two works for each composer. Important modern composers are entered in the main alphabet. Appropriate cross references.

Collins Encyclopedia of Music. See no. 49.

11

Cooper, Martin, ed. The concise encyclopedia of music and musicians. New York, Hawthorn Books [1958] 516 p.

English edition: London, Hutchinson, 1958.

> It is [the] "average music lover" for whom the present work is designed. The expert and connoisseur are already well catered for with twelve-volume dictionaries and detailed studies of particular musical fields, but my task has been to present in a concise, easily digestible form the history and technical rudiments of an art which plays an increasing part in our life (Foreword).

Biographical entries are brief. Longer discussions of major terms and forms. No bibliographies. Well illustrated with 16 color plates and more than 100 in monochrome. 17 contributors apart from the editor.

12

Corte, Andrea Della e G. M. Gatti. Dizionario di musica. 6. ed. Torino, G. B. Paravia [1959] 724 p.

First published in 1925.

Includes personal names, subjects, instruments, cities, covering all countries and periods, but with emphasis on Italian names and topics. Brief biographies list major works, with fair coverage of republications of old music, especially for Italian composers.

13

Diccionario Enciclopédico de la Música. [Dirección general: A. Albert Torrellas] Barcelona, Central Catalana de Publicaciones [1947]–52. 4 v.

Supersedes *Diccionario de la música ilustrado*, 1927–29. 2 v.

Contributors include composers and musicologists from Spain, Portugal, and Latin America.

Vol. 1: "Terminología, tecnología, morfología, instrumentos." Technical terms in all languages, including Greek and Oriental (transliterated). No bibliography or documentation.

Vols. 2–3: "Biografías, bibliografía, monografías, historia, argumentos de operas." Biographies of composers, performers, musicologists, with emphasis on Spanish and South American musicians. Lists of works for major composers, classified listing for minor figures. Historical articles under names of countries. Extended articles for Spanish provinces, covering folk music, history, composers, institutions, etc. No bibliographical references.

Vol. 4: "Apéndice, por A. Albert Torrellas . . ."

14

Dizionario Ricordi della Musica e dei Musicisti. [Direttore: Claudio Sartori; redattori: Fausto Broussard, et al. Milano] Ricordi, 1959. 1,155 p.

Wide biographical coverage, including living performers, important composers of light music, musicologists. Concise articles, excellent bibliographies and lists of compositions.

Review by Jack A. Westrup in *Music and letters*, 41 (1960) p. 80–81; by James B. Coover in *Notes*, 17 (1960) p. 564–66.

15

Dunstan, Ralph. A cyclopaedic dictionary of music . . . 4th ed., greatly enl. and rev. London/Philadelphia, Curwen [1925] 632 p.

First published in 1908.

Terms and biography. Very brief entries, numerous short musical illustrations. Intended for amateurs. Suffers from an excess of misleading and useless information. Numerous appendices of vocabulary, pronunciation, music theory, etc. The "Musical bibliography" (p. 618–31) is chiefly of 19th-century works in English.

16

Enciclopedia della Musica. Direttore: Claudio Sartori; Vice-direttore: Riccardo Allorto. Milano, Ricordi [1963–64] 4 v.

The major modern Italian encyclopedia of music. Well printed and illustrated, including color plates. Contributions by some 232 international specialists. Long articles signed. Good bibliographical coverage.

17

Encyclopédie de la Musique. [Publié sous la direction de François Michel en collaboration avec François Lesure et Vladimir Fédorov, et un comité de rédaction composé de Nadia Boulanger, et al.] Paris, Fasquelle [1958–61] 3 v.

Preceding the dictionary proper is a series of essays (vol. 1, p. 1–238)

[5]

devoted to general information about music in society: festivals, concerts, radio, the music press, education in France, copyright laws, institutions and associations. A "Livre d'Or," p. 35–76, gives portraits and facsimile pages from the manuscripts of leading contemporary composers. Chronological table of music history, p. 203–38.

Much emphasis on ideas and principles rather than on individuals and works. Biographical articles are short. Bibliographical references, many to *MGG*. Lists of works for major composers; fuller treatment of subjects. Many signed articles. Excellent illustrative material, musical and pictorial. Especially valuable for its coverage of modern music.

Review by James B. Coover in *Notes*, 16 (1959) p. 381–83.

18

Encyclopédie de la Musique et Dictionnaire du Conservatoire. Fondateur, Albert Lavignac; Directeur, Lionel de La Laurencie. Paris, C. Delagrave, 1913–31. 2 parts in 11 v.

Originally published in fascicles.

Part I: "Histoire de la musique." Part II: "Technique, esthétique, pédagogie."

The work was designed, in the tradition of the French encyclopedists, as a universal repository of musical knowledge. International in scope, although most of the contributors are French. Many of the studies, particularly in the history part, are full-scale monographs and still rank among the most important surveys of their fields. History is treated by country. Some of the chief contributors are Maurice Emmanuel, Amédée Gastoué, Oscar Chilesotti, Romain Rolland, Henry Expert, and Rafael Mitjana. Part II deals with music theory, instruction, and aesthetics in all aspects, including acoustics, notation, instrument making, choreography, institutions. Major articles by Charles Koechlin, Paul Rougnon, and Vincent d'Indy. Illustrated; numerous musical examples.

The *Encyclopédie* lacks an index, and for this reason the detailed tables of contents at the end of each part are most useful as a guide to its contents. A partial index, compiled by Robert Bruce, in *Notes*, ser. 1 (May 1936), is not generally available.

19

Encyclopédie Methodique, ou par ordre de matières; par une société de gens de lettres, de savans et d'artistes . . . *Musique,* publiée par MM. Framery et Ginguené. Paris, Chez Panckoucke, 1791–1818. 2 v.

Vol. 1: A–G, 760 p. Vol. 2: H–Z, 558 p.

Publisher varies. Tome II, Paris, Chez Mme. veuve Agasse. In this volume the name of De Momigny is added to that of the two other compilers. Vol. 1 contains a musical appendix of 74 p., vol. 2, of 114 p.

The *Encyclopédie methodique* is a large general reference work of which the two volumes cited are concerned with music. These volumes are of considerable historical importance since they incorporate articles from Rousseau's *Dictionnaire de musique* (no. 217) and from the Diderot-d'Alembert *Encyclopédie*, along with more recent commentary. Articles are signed.

20

Encyclopedie van de Muziek. Hoofdredactio: Louis M. G. Arntzenius, et al. Met bijzondere medwerking van J. Kunst, et al. Amsterdam, Elsevier, 1956–57. 2 v.

Vol. 1: A–H. Vol. 2: I–Z.

21

Enťsiklopedicheskiĭ Muzykalnyi' Slovar' [Edited by I. V. Keldysh, B. S. Shteinpress, I. M. IAmpol'skiĭ] Moscow, 1959. 326 p.

22

Grove, Sir George, ed. Grove's dictionary of music and musicians. 5th ed., edited by Eric Blom. London, Macmillan; New York, St. Martin's Press, 1954. 9 v.

Supplementary volume, edited by Eric Blom; associate editor, Denis Stevens, 1961. 493 p.

First published in 1879–89; 2nd ed., 1904–10, ed. by J. A. Fuller-Maitland; 3rd ed., 1927–28, ed. by H. C. Colles; 4th ed., 1940, ed. by H. C. Colles. A supplementary volume to the 3rd edition appeared in 1940, covering the period from 1928 to 1940, with new information pertaining to earlier entries. An American supplement, ed. by W. S. Pratt, published in 1920, and again in 1928, containing material on the U.S., Canada, and Spanish America.

Grove's dictionary is the standard comprehensive music encyclopedia in English. It includes information on music history, theory and practice, instruments, terms, and biographies in one alphabet. Signed articles, bibliographies, useful lists of works for composers since Bach.

Although the 5th edition was completely reset, expanded, and brought up to date, it falls short of *MGG* as a tool for scholarship; however, it holds an undisputed place as the major music reference work in English.

Review of the 5th edition by Richard S. Hill in *Notes*, 12 (1954) p. 85–92; by William Glock in *The score*, no. 11 (Mar. 1955) p. 53–56; by Paul Henry

[7]

Lang in *MQ*, 41 (1955) p. 215–22; in *The Times literary supplement*, Dec. 3, 1954, p. 778 (anon). See also A. Hyatt King, "Grove V and MGG", in *The monthly musical record*, 85 (1955) p. 115–19, p. 152–57, p. 183–85; also corrections and additions in the *Musical times*, 96 (1955) p. 591–96, p. 643–51. Review of *Supplementary volume* by Vincent Duckles in *Notes*, 19 (1962) p. 246–47.

23

Gurvin, Olav og Ø. Anker, eds. Musikkleksikon. Ny revidert utg. Oslo, Dreyer [1959] 902 columns.

First published in 1949.

Biography, including jazz musicians, performers, and composers. Title entries for dramatic works, familiar art songs, and folk songs. Terms, short articles, partial lists of works, occasional bibliographical references. Popular.

24

Hughes, Rupert. Music lovers' encyclopedia, containing a pronouncing and defining dictionary of terms, instruments, etc. . . . including a key to the pronunciation of sixteen languages, many charts; an explanation of the construction of music for the uninitiated; a pronouncing biographical dictionary; the stories of the operas, and numerous biographical and critical essays by distinguished authorities. Completely revised and newly edited by Deems Taylor and Russell Kerr. Garden City, N.Y., Garden City Books [1954] 897 p.

First published in 1903 under the title *The musical guide;* subsequent editions in 1912, 1939.

25

Jacobs, Arthur. A new dictionary of music. [Harmondsworth, Middlesex] Penguin Books [1958] 416 p.

Hardcover edition with new introduction and corrections, London, Cassell, 1961; Chicago, Aldine Publishing Co., 1961.

Another pocket dictionary "for the inquiring music-lover," with brief identifications of people (mostly composers and performers), terms, operatic and other specific titles, and all sorts of musical topics. It may be well worth the money, though one wonders whether a pocket music dictionary isn't below the point of diminishing returns from excessive brevity and over-generalization. Quoted from *Notes*, 16 (1958) p. 68.

Review by Harold Samuel in *Notes*, 20 (1963) p. 657–58.

26

Keller, Gerard en P. Kruseman. Geïllustreerd muzieklexicon, onder redactie van G. Keller en Philip Kruseman, met medewerking van Sem Dresden, Wouter Hutschenruijter, Willem Landré . . . 's-Gravenhage, J. P. Kruseman, 1932. 966 p.

Brief articles, bibliographical references, and lists of major works for composers. Similar to Abert (no. 1) in form and content, but useful in connection with contemporary Dutch names.

27

Larousse de la Musique. [Dictionnaire encyclopédique] en 2 volumes. Publié sous la direction de Norbert Dufourcq, avec la collaboration de Félix Raugel, Armand Machabey. Paris, Larousse [1957] 2 v.

A handsome, beautifully illustrated dictionary. Brief but authoritative articles by international contributors. Biographies (composers, performers, musicologists, choreographers); title entries (operas, ballets, manuscripts); subjects (terms, places). Some emphasis on ethnomusicology. Bibliographies given in an appendix to each volume under the same headings as the articles.

Special features: Discography and analysis (vol. 1, p. 587–626; vol. 2, p. 537–640). Musical examples in analytical section. Two phonorecords, "Illustrations sonores," issued with the encyclopedia: (1) Les instruments de musique (with vol. 1); (2) Principaux termes du langage technique (with vol. 2).

Review by Paul Henry Lang in *MQ*, 45 (1959) p. 120–23; by James B. Coover in *Notes*, 16 (1959) p. 381–83.

28

Mendel, Hermann. Musikalisches Conversations-Lexikon. Eine Encyklopädie der gesammten musikalischen Wissenschaften. Für Gebildete aller Stände, unter Mitwirkung der Literarischen Commission des Berliner Tonkünstlervereins. . . . Berlin, L. Heimann; New York, J. Schuberth, 1870–79. 11 v.

2nd edition with supplementary volume, "Ergänzungsband," Berlin, R. Oppenheim, 1880–83. 3rd edition, "Neue wohlfeile Stereotyp-Ausgabe," Leipzig, List & Francke [1890–91].

Founded by Mendel, continued (vols. 7–11) by August Reissmann. One of the major 19th-century general music encyclopedias. Superseded in most respects, but still useful for obscure names and earlier concepts and criticism. Partial lists of works; few bibliographical references.

29

Meyers Handbuch über die Musik. Herausgegeben und bearbeitet von der Fachredaktion Musik des Bibliographischen Instituts. 2nd ed. Mannheim, Bibliographisches Institut, 1961. 1,062 p.

A miscellaneous assemblage of facts about music, musicians, and musical institutions. Lists of libraries, societies, research institutes, performers, etc. Wide in scope but superficial. The emphasis is on European musical activities and persons.

P. 493–993: a biographical dictionary of musicians. Combined index of subjects and persons.

30

Moore, John W. Complete encyclopaedia of music, elementary, technical, historical, biographical, vocal and instrumental. Boston, J. P. Jewett, 1854 [copyright notice, 1852] 1,004 p.

Appendix . . . containing events and information occurring since the main work was issued. Boston, Oliver Ditson, 1875. 45 p.

Reprinted by Ditson in 1880.

The first comprehensive American musical dictionary, containing more than 5,000 terms, 4,000 biographical citations, 200 articles, much of which drawn from Gerber, Choron and Fayolle, Burney, Hawkins, Hogarth, Calcott, Gardiner, Busby, Hamilton, Schilling, and Fétis. Substantial additional material from *Dwight's musical journal* and the *New York musical times.* Especially rich in notices of 18th- and 19th-century musicians, although somewhat weak in early Americana.

31

Moser, Hans J. Musik Lexikon. Vierte, stark erweiterte Aufl. Hamburg, H. Sikorski, 1955, 2 v.

First published in 1932–35; 2nd, ed., 1943; 3rd ed., 1951. *Ergänzungs Band,* 1964.

Brief, authoritative articles, with special emphasis on bibliographies and lists of early music in new editions. Addressed to German readers, but increasingly international in scope with the later editions. The 4th edition, first to appear in 2 volumes, is extensively revised, with many new articles and bibliographical additions.

32

Musiikin Tietokirja. Toimituskunta: Tiovo Haapanen, et al. Helsingissä, Kustannusoskeyhtiö Otava [1948] 573 p.

Terms, subjects, operas, biographies (including performers, publishers, musicologists, many contemporary composers). Emphasis on Scandinavian musicians. Partial lists of works.

33
Muzička Enciklopedija. [Glavni redaktor: Josip Andreis] Zagreb, Izdanje i naklada leksikografskog zavoda, 1958–63. 2 v.

Vol. 1: A–J. 760 p. Vol. 2: K–Z. 855 p.

Contributors: Yugoslavian musicologists. Major articles signed. Condensed biographical, extended subject entries. Well organized bibliographies and lists of works. Living performers excluded. International coverage, with emphasis on Slavic composers. Excellent in content and appearance.

Review by Josef Brozek in *Notes*, 21 (1963–64) p. 128–29.

34
Norlind, Tobias. Allmänt musiklexikon. 2. omarbetade uppl. Stockholm, Wahlström & Widstrand [1927–28] 2 v.

First published in parts, 1912–16.

Many biographies, with full lists of compositions, including information as to dates and publishers.

35
Panum, Hortense og William Behrend. Illustreret musikleksikon. Nyudgave under redaktion af Povl Hamburger, under medvirken af William Behrend, O. M. Sandvik, Jürgen Balzer. København, Aschehoug, 1940. 735 p.

First published in parts, 1924–26.

Designed for popular use. International in coverage, but with emphasis on Scandinavian names and subjects. Based principally on the 1st edition of *Norlind* and the Schytte translation of *Riemann*.

36
Pena, Joaquín. Diccionario de la música Labor; iniciado por Joaquín Pena, continuado por Higinio Anglés, con la colaboración de Miguel Querol y otros distinguidos musicólogos españoles y extrajanos. Barcelona, Labor, 1954. 2 v.

Begun in 1940 as an adaptation of *Riemann*, but developed as a new dictionary of music for Spanish-speaking countries. Contributors are Spanish and Spanish-American. Foreign biographies drawn from *Riemann*, *Grove*, *Baker*, *Schmidl*, etc. Covers bio-bibliography, technique, and history. Designed for professional musicians and for general use.

37
Pratt, Waldo S. The new encyclopedia of music and musicians. New and rev. ed. New York, Macmillan, 1929. 969 p.

[11]

First published in 1924.

Originally planned as an abridgement of the 2nd edition of *Grove's*, but developed as an independent work. Arranged in 3 main alphabets: terms, biography, institutions and organizations. Appendices for bibliography: musicians before 1700, and operas and oratorios produced since 1900. Covers primarily the 18th- to 20th-centuries, with emphasis on living musicians and the American scene. Excellent definitions of musical terms.

38

Riemann, Hugo. Musik-Lexikon. 12. völlig neubearbeitete Auflage in drei Bänden. Hrsg. von Wilibald Gurlitt. Mainz, B. Schott's Söhne, 1959– .

Vol. 1: Personenteil, A–K, 1959. 986 p. Vol. 2: Personenteil, L–Z, 1961. 976 p.

Gurlitt's edition is the latest in the series based on Riemann's work, first published in 1882. The 12th edition is the first in which terms and biography are in separate alphabets: Vols. 1 and 2. "Personenteil". Vol. 3. "Sachteil" (not yet published as of 1966). Alfred Einstein was editor of the 9th, 10th, and 11th editions, and added much to the scope and authority of the work.

The Riemann *Lexikon* is a universal dictionary of music, covering all times and places, and incorporating the achievements of German musical scholarship. Superior to *Moser* (no. 31) in typography and organization, and to *Baker* (no. 51) in bibliographical coverage. Lists of works are included in the bodies of the articles; modern editions of early works, and bibliographical references, in separate paragraphs.

Riemann has been widely translated, and most of the translators have incorporated new material of national interest. The principal translations are as follows:

> *Dictionnaire de musique*. Traduit d'après le 4me édition par Georges Humbert. Paris, Perrin, 1895–1902. 2me éd., Paris, Perrin, 1913. 3me éd., entièrement refondue et augm. sous la direction de A. Schaeffner, avec la collaboration de M. Pincherle, Y. Rokseth, A. Tessier. Paris, 1931.

> *Dictionary of music*. New edition, with many additions by the author. Trans. by J. S. Shedlock. London, Augener, 1893. Later editions in 1902 and 1908.

> *Muzykal'nyi slovar'* . . . Moskva, P. Iurgenson, 1901–1904. A Russian translation from the 5th German edition.

> *Nordisk musik-lexikon*, udarbeidet af H. V. Schytte, 1888–92. 2 v.

Reviews of the 12th edition by Vincent Duckles in *Notes*, 16 (1959)

p. 240–42; by Paul Henry Lang in *MQ*, 45 (1959) p. 563–66; by Hans H. Eggebrecht in *Die Musikforschung*, 12 (1959) p. 221–23; by Charles Van den Borren in *Revue belge de musicologie*, 14 (1960) p. 137–38.

39

Rubertis, Victor de. Pequeño diccionario musical, tecnológico y biográfico. 6. ed., corregida y aumentada. Buenos Aires, Ricordi Americana, 1962. 349 p.

40

Schilling, Gustav. Encyclopädie der gesammten musikalischen Wissenschaften, oder, Universal-Lexikon der Tonkunst . . . Stuttgart, F. H. Köhler, 1835–38. 6 v.

Supplement-Band, hrsg. von Gustav Schilling, 1842.

One of the leading 19th-century repositories of musical knowledge. A comprehensive work with emphasis on the subject aspects, but including numerous biographies displaced or reduced in later reference works.

41

Scholes, Percy A. The concise Oxford dictionary of music. 2nd edition. London/New York, Oxford Univ. Press, 1964.

First published in 1952.

Primarily a reduction of the *Oxford companion* (no. 42). Includes "some hundreds of short biographical entries for vocal and instrumental performers and conductors . . . and some hundreds of entries concerning individual compositions." About 10,000 entries, 3,500 biographical.

Review of the first edition by Charles Warren Fox in *Notes*, 9 (1952) p. 605–606.

42

Scholes, Percy A. The Oxford companion to music. 9th ed., completely rev. and reset and with many additions to text and illustrations. London/New York, Oxford Univ. Press, 1955. 1,195 p.

First published in 1938.

Intended for the general reader. The *Companion* is a unique one-man encyclopedia, unified by the compiler's opinions, tastes, and interests, which are always stimulating but occasionally provincial. Especially strong in articles on the sociology of music and in a number of entries overlooked in most music reference works (e.g. "Misattributed compositions," "Nicknamed compositions"). Detailed cross references, but no bibliographies. A bibliographical supplement issued with the 1940 edition has not been reprinted. (See no. 437.)

[13]

Review of the 8th edition by Charles Warren Fox in *Notes*, 8 (1950) p. 177–78; of the 9th edition by Vincent Duckles in *Notes*, 13 (1955) p. 70–72.

43
Sohlmans Musiklexikon. Nordiskt och allmänt uppslagsverk för tonkonst, musikliv och dans. Redaktion: Gösta Morin, Carl-Allan Moberg, Einar Sundström. Stockholm, Sohlmans Förlag [1948–52] 4 v.

The major modern Swedish music encyclopedia. Contributions by leading Scandinavian musicologists. Biography, title entries for operas, ballets, etc., subject entries for persons, places, institutions. Good lists of works; bibliographies somewhat uneven. Wide biographical coverage, especially for living performers. Many portraits.

44
Svensson, Sven E. E. Bonniers illustrerade musiklexikon. Under medverkan av Erik Noreen. Stockholm, A. Bonnier [1946] 1,379 p.

Popular, well-illustrated, universal in coverage, but with emphasis on Scandinavian names, especially performers. Bibliographical references.

45
Thompson, Oscar, ed. The international cyclopedia of music and musicians. 9th ed., edited by Rcbert Sabin. New York, Dodd, Mead, 1964. 2,476 p.

First published in 1939. 8th ed. (1958) edited by Nicolas Slonimsky.

The best one-volume general dictionary of music in English. Strong list of contributors, with extended signed articles for major persons and subjects. Large number of title entries. Particularly valuable for detailed lists of works by major composers, given in tabulated form. Through the 8th edition the work carried an appendix of opera plots and an extensive bibliography of music literature.

Review of the 5th edition by Charles Warren Fox in *Notes*, 7 (1950) p. 291–92; of the 9th edition by Irene Millen in *Notes*, 22 (1965) p. 733–35.

46
Tonkonsten; Internationellt musiklexikon. Stockholm, Nordiska Uppslagsböcker [1955–57] 2 v.

Popular, illustrated dictionary giving pronunciations of foreign names, lists of works and bibliographies for major composers, bibliographical references on important topics. Covers popular music. Signed articles by Scandinavian contributors.

47
Tschierpe, Rudolph. Kleines Musiklexikon. Mit systematischen Übersichten und zahlreichen Notenbeispielen. [5. durchgesehene und ergänzte Auflage.] Hamburg, Hoffmann und Campe [1955] 412 p.
First published in 1946.
An excellent small general dictionary. Brief but inclusive. Representative works listed for major composers. Bibliographical references. Tables illustrating dance forms, theory, and history. An appendix lists major writers on music, with their fields of specialization; another lists titles of operas, operettas, oratorios, choral and orchestral works.

48
Walther, Johann G. Musikalisches Lexicon, oder musikalische Bibliothek (1732). Faksimile-Neudruck, hrsg. von Richard Schaal. Kassel und Basel, Bärenreiter, 1953. 659 p., 22 fold. plates. (Documenta musicologica. Erste Reihe, 3.)
A facsimile edition of the prototype for all general dictionaries of music. Walther's *Lexicon* (1732) established the pattern later developed in *Riemann, Moser,* and other modern dictionaries, and, in itself, constitutes a primary source of information about late baroque musical knowledge and practice.

49
Westrup, Jack A. and F. L. Harrison. The new college encyclopedia of music. New York, Norton [1960] 739 p.
Published in England, 1959, under the title *Collins music encyclopedia.*
A "popular" student dictionary. Detailed summaries of works for major composers, fields of activity for minor ones. References to early works published in the standard historical editions or anthologies. Technical articles with musical illustrations. Title entries for repertory works. Selective bibliographies, primarily English. British pronunciations.
Review by James B. Coover in *Notes,* 17 (1960) p. 564–66.

50
Zenei Lexikon, a zenetörténet és zenetudomány enciklopédiája . . . szerkesztették Szabolcsi Bence és Tóth Aladár. Budapest, Gyözö Andor, 1930–31. 2 v.
A general music encyclopedia of high quality. Major articles signed by outstanding musicologists, Hungarian and foreign. Long articles on national music, forms, music for various instruments. Biographical articles discuss major works and list others by category. Short bibliographies.
The first volume of a revised and expanded edition of this work, edited

[15]

by Dénes Bartha, has been issued (Budapest, Zenemükiadó Vállalat, 1965) A–F, 687 p.

Biography, International

Listed here are dictionaries and encyclopedias, international in coverage, in which the emphasis is exclusively or mainly on persons engaged in activities related to music: composers, performers, scholars, critics, impresarios, etc. The line that separates biographical dictionaries from volumes of collected biography is a rather arbitrary one. The distinction is essentially between works that contain numerous brief entries, alphabetically arranged, and works that consist of collections of essays on a fairly limited group of musicians. Works in the latter category have been excluded, and for this reason the user should not expect to find entries for such titles as Donald Brook's *Masters of the keyboard* (London, 1947), or his *Singers of today* (London, 1949), David Ewen's *Dictators of the baton* (New York, 1943), or Madeleine Goss's *Modern music-makers* (New York, 1952).

51

Baker, Theodore. Baker's biographical dictionary of musicians. 5th ed. Completely revised by Nicolas Slonimsky. New York, G. Schirmer [1958] 1,855 p.

First published in 1900; subsequent editions in 1905, 1919, and 1940. Reprinted in 1965, with a 143-page *Supplement* providing biographical information on some 700 new names, as well as updating numerous old entries.

Baker's is by far the best biographical dictionary in English; a standard work from its beginning. Through the 3rd edition early figures were treated briefly, with references to Grove and Eitner. For the 4th edition, these biographies were rewritten as independent articles (by Gustave Reese, Gilber Chase, and Robert Geiger). The 5th edition was greatly enlarged and checked carefully for accuracy. Treats musicians in all categories. Long lists of works. Outstanding bibliographical coverage.

Review of the 5th edition by Brooks Shepard Jr. in *Notes*, 16 (1959) p. 239–40; by Philip L. Miller in *MQ*, 45 (1959) p. 255–58.

52

Choron, Alexandre É. et F. J. M. Fayolle. Dictionnaire historique des musiciens, artistes et amateurs, morts ou vivans, qui se sont illustrés en une partie quelconque de la musique et des arts qui y sont relatifs. . . . Paris, Valade, 1810–11. 2 v.

Another printing, 1817.

[16]

The first French biographical dictionary of importance. International in scope. Partial lists of works for major composers. A valuable guide to early 19th-century musical opinion. The dictionary proper is preceded by an 81-page "Sommaire de l'histoire de la musique" by Choron.

Translated and expanded in the English *A dictionary of musicians*, 1824. (See no. 54.)

53

A Dictionary of Modern Music and Musicians. Ed. by Arthur Eaglefield Hull. London, J. M. Dent, 1924; New York, E. P. Dutton, 1924. 543 p.

Primarily biographical, although there are entries for terms related to modern music. For the period *c*. 1880–1920, the best international coverage of any dictionary of its time. Written with the aid of numerous foreign collaborators. Comprehensive lists of works and bibliographies about composers. Also includes publishers, musicologists, organizations, new instruments, etc.

For a German translation and expansion by Alfred Einstein, see no. 73.

54

A Dictionary of Musicians, from the earliest ages to the present time, comprising the most important biographical contents of the works of Gerber, Choron and Fayolle, Count Orloff, Dr. Burney, Sir John Hawkins, etc. Together with upwards of a hundred original memoirs of the most eminent living musicians and a summary of the history of music. London, Sainsbury, 1824. 2 v.

Reprinted in 1827. Reprint by Da Capo Press, New York, 1966. 2 v.

Largely a translation of Choron and Fayolle (no. 52), including the "Summary of the history of music," but with substantial additions of English musicians. The first major biographical dictionary of musicians in English. The tone is popular and anecdotal but furnishes an excellent picture of contemporary taste and opinion. The compiler is not identified, but the work has been attributed to its publisher, John Sainsbury.

55

Eitner, Robert. Biographisch-bibliographisches Quellen-Lexikon der Musiker und Musikgelehrten der christlichen Zeitrechnung bis zur Mitte des 19. Jahrhunderts . . . Leipzig, Breitkopf & Härtel, 1898–1904. 10 v.

Eitner's *Quellen-Lexikon* is mainly a bibliography of primary sources, but it does contain much useful biographical information, often helpful with respect to obscure names.

[17]

For fuller information on this important reference work, see under *Bibliographies of music*, no. 760.

56

The Etude Music Magazine. Portraits of the world's best-known musicians, an alphabetical collection of notable musical personalities of the world, covering the entire history of music. Compiled and edited by Guy McCoy. Philadelphia, Theodore Presser [1946] 251 p.

Portraits and brief identifications of 4,748 composers, performers, and other musicians, largely reprinted from *Etude*, 1932–40. Geographical index of American names.

One of the few dictionaries of its kind. Of limited value, however, since the portraits are reproduced at little more than postage-stamp size.

57

Ewen, David. Composers of today, a comprehensive biographical and critical guide to modern composers of all nations. 2nd ed. New York, H. W. Wilson, 1936. 332 p.

First published in 1934. The work has been superseded by nos. 59 and 137.

Brief biographies, critical discussion, and classified lists of the principal works for about 200 living composers. Portraits. Lists of recordings.

58

Ewen, David. Composers of yesterday, a biographical and critical guide to the most important composers of the past. New York, H. W. Wilson, 1937. 488 p.

Biographies, lists of works, bibliographies, lists of recordings, and portraits of about 200 composers from Dunstable to the end of the 19th-century. Selected on the basis of current acceptance or importance in music history.

59

Ewen, David. European composers today; a biographical and critical guide. New York, H. W. Wilson, 1954. 200 p.

A companion volume to the previously published *American composers today* (no. 137). Together, these two volumes replace *Composers of today* (no. 57) above.

Review by Frank C. Campbell in *Notes*, 11 (1954) p. 476.

60

Ewen, David. Living musicians. New York, H. W. Wilson, 1940. 390 p.

First supplement . . ., 1957.

A dictionary of performers, especially American or active in America. Portraits. The supplement contains biographies of 147 musicians who have come into prominence since 1940.

61

Fétis, François J. Biographie universelle des musiciens et bibliographie générale de la musique. 2me éd. Paris, Firmin Didot Fréres, 1866–70. 8 v.

First published in 1835–44. *Supplément et complément*, pub. sous la direction de M. Arthur Pougin. Paris, 1878–80. 2 v.

Fétis' work set the standard for modern biographical research in music. A tremendous scholarly achievement for its time, it contains a vast amount of biographical and bibliographical information, complete lists of works, and occasionally, annotated lists of books about composers. Although outdated and marred by the author's personal critical bias, it remains a useful starting point for research and serves as a record of the earlier stages of musicology.

62

Gerber, Ernst Ludwig. Historisch-biographisches Lexicon der Tonkünstler, welches Nachrichten von dem Leben und Werken musikalischer Schriftsteller, berühmter Componisten, Sänger, etc. . . . enthält. Leipzig, J. G. I. Breitkopf, 1790–92. 2 v.

(See no. 63 below.)

63

Gerber, Ernst Ludwig. Neues historisch-biographisches Lexikon der Tonkünstler . . ., Leipzig, A. Kühnel, 1812–14. 4 v.

The Gerber *lexika* are early biographical dictionaries of great historical importance. The compiler expanded the biographical content of Walther's *Lexicon* (no. 48) and produced the first major self-contained dictionary of musical biography. The 4-volume edition of 1812–14 supplements but does not supersede the earlier 2-volume edition (no. 62 above). Both compilations must be used for complete coverage.

64

Le Grandi Voci. Dizionario critico-biografico dei cantanti, con discografia operistica. Roma, Istituto per la collaborazione culturale, 1964. 1,044 columns.

Published under the direction of Rodolfo Celletti; consultants for the discographies, Raffaele Vegeto and John B. Richards; editor, Luisa Pavolini.

[19]

An illustrated dictionary of opera singers, historical and contemporary, with discographies of the major artists.

65

Hughes, Rupert. The biographical dictionary of musicians. Originally compiled by Rupert Hughes, completely revised and newly edited by Deems Taylor and Russell Kerr. Over 8,500 entries, together with a pronouncing dictionary of given names and titles and a key to the pronunciation of sixteen languages. New York, Blue Ribbon Books, 1940. 481 p.

A popular reference work. Brief entries with representative works for composers mentioned. Useful for the abundance of obscure performers entered.

66

The International Who is Who in Music. Fifth (mid-century) edition. J. T. H. Mize, editor-in-chief. Chicago, Who is Who in Music [1951] 576 p.

Biographies, with portraits, of persons active in music, including educators, musicologists, private teachers, performers. Not strictly international, since the emphasis is on musicians active or well known in the U.S. Contains a number of supplementary lists and directories, e.g. the principal symphony orchestras in the U.S., Canada, and other countries. Strongly directed toward the commercial aspects of music.

67

International Who's Who in Music and Musical Gazetteer, a contemporary biographical dictionary and a record of the world's musical activity, edited by César Saerchinger. New York, Current Literature Pub. Co., 1918. 861 p.

The geographical index and directory of schools and organizations are now only of historical interest, but the biographical section is still useful for minor figures of the first two decades of the century. Composers, performers, critics, musicologists, teachers—their education, activity, principal works, addresses.

68

Kutsch, K. J. Unvergängliche Stimmen; kleines Sängerlexikon [von] K. J. Kutsch [und] Leo Riemans. Bern, Francke [1962] 429 p. (Sammlung Dalp, Bd. 92).

69

Mattheson, Johann. Grundlage einer Ehren-Pforte, woran der tüchtigsten Capellmeister, Componisten, Musikgelehrten, Tonkünstler, etc. erscheinen sollen. Zum fernern Ausbau angegeben von Mattheson, Hamburg, 1740. Vollständiger, originalgetreuer Neudruck mit gelegentlichen bibliographischen Hinweisen und Matthesons Nachträgen, hrsg. von Max Schneider. Berlin, Leo Liepmannssohn, 1910. 428 p., with *Anhang* of 51 p.

A "diplomatic" edition of the original printing of 1740.

Mattheson's work is, strictly speaking, a volume of collected biography rather than a biographical dictionary. But the volume stands first, chronologically, among all self-contained works of musical biography, establishing the precedent for Gerber's *Lexikon* (no. 62) and subsequent dictionaries of musical biography. Most of the essays were contributed by the subjects themselves.

70

Merseburger, Carl W. Kurzgefasstes Tonkünstlerlexikon für Musiker und Freunde der Musik. Begründet von Paul Frank [pseud.] Neu bearbeitet und ergänzt von Wilhelm Altmann. 14. stark erweiterte Auflage. Regensburg, G. Bosse, 1936. 730 p.

First published in 1860 as P. Frank's *Kleines Tonkünstlerlexikon*. Title varies slightly in subsequent editions.

One of the most popular of the prewar German dictionaries of musical biography. Extremely wide coverage but with minimum data. Over 18,000 entries, including composers, librettists, performers, musicologists. Many minor figures. No lists of works or bibliographical references. Useful for quick reference.

71

Les Musiciens Célèbres. [Publié sous la direction de Jean Lacroix . . .] [Genève] L. Mazenod, 1946. 385 p.

Also published in German under the title *Die berühmten Musiker.* Genève, 1946.

An "art" publication, chiefly valuable for its fine full-page portraits of musicians. 66 individual biographies and several group articles, chronologically arranged. P. 293–349: brief identifications of other composers.

72

Musikens Hven-Hvad-Hvor. Udarbejdet af Nelly Backhausen og Axel Kjerulf. København, Politikens Forlag, 1950. 3 v.

Vol. 1: "Musikhistorie." Chronology from antiquity to 1900, with composer index. Vols. 2–3: Biographies (composers, performers, musicologists) indicating field of activity and principal works. Vol. 3: p. 141–414. Title list of 15,000 entries, including operas, repertory works, popular and musical-comedy songs, folk-songs. For each, identification, composer, and date if known.

73

Das Neue Musiklexikon, nach dem *Dictionary of modern music and musicians*, hrsg. von A. Eaglefield Hull, übersetzt und bearb. von Alfred Einstein. Berlin, M. Hesse, 1926. 729 p.

A German translation of no. 53, with many additions and corrections by Einstein. Most of the information in this revision is incorporated in the 11th edition of the Riemann *Musik-Lexikon*.

74

Prieberg, Fred K. Lexikon der neuen Musik. Frieburg & München, K. Alber, 1958. 495 p.

Primarily biographical, but with a few articles on aspects of and trends in contemporary music (film music, radio operas, polytonality, 12-tone music, *musique concrète*, etc.). Factual rather than critical, covering education, activities, and principal works of 20th-century composers.

75

Schäffer, Bogusław. Leksykon kompozytorów XX wieku. v. 1– . Kraków, Polskie Wydawnictwo Muzyczne, 1965– .

Vol. 1: A–L.

A Polish-language dictionary of 20th-century composers. International in coverage but particularly strong in Slavic musicians. Portraits; bibliographies.

76

Schmidl, Carlo. Dizionario universale dei musicisti. Milano, Sonzogno [1928?–29] 2 v.

Supplemento, 1938. 806 p.

The major bio-bibliography in Italian, and best general biographical source for Italian musicians. Emphasis on native composers, librettists, and performers, with full articles on well-known persons and brief accounts of minor ones. Dates of first productions of dramatic works. Lists of works, including modern republications. Particularly valuable for articles on Italian literary figures and their relations to music. All forenames are Italianized.

77

Schnoor, Hans. Oper, Operette, Konzert. Ein praktisches Nachschlagebuch für Theater- und Konzertbesucher, für Rundfunkhörer, Fernsehteilnehmer und Schallplattenfreunde. Güttersloh, C. Bertelsmann, 1963. 575 p.

First printed in 1955.

A handbook for the musical amateur and concertgoer. Organized biographically, but with emphasis on the composers' works in the current repertory. Some 347 musical examples and numerous illustrations. With an appended glossary and indexes of persons and subjects.

Who's Who in Music . . . See no. 90.

78

Young, Percy M. Biographical dictionary of composers, with classified list of music for performance and study. New York, Crowell, 1954. 381 p.

Published in England under the title *A critical dictionary of composers and their music.* London, Dobson, 1954.

Selective list of 500 composers. Brief critical surveys of each, titles of representative works, and references to further sources of information, usually in English. Intended for the general student rather than the specialist.

Biography, National

Any dictionary of musical biography may be expected to be strong in names within its own language group. There are also numerous specialized dictionaries of biography devoted specifically to the musicians' particular countries. Only the most important of such dictionaries are listed here, with emphasis on the recent, currently available publications. They are tabulated in the following list for quick reference.

Austria

79
Steirisches Musiklexikon. Im Auftrage des Steirischen Tonkünstler-bundes unter Benützung der "Sammlung Wamlek" bearb. und hrsg. von W. Suppan. Graz, Akademische Druck- und Verlagsanstalt, 1962– .
Lieferung 1–5. A–ROSEGGER, completed by 1965.
A biographical dictionary of musicians associated with Graz and other parts of Steirmark. Comprehensive for pre-1800 names, selective for post-1800. Good bibliographical coverage for composers' works and writings on the musicians.

Belgium

80
Centre Belge de Documentation Musicale. Music in Belgium; contemporary Belgian composers. Brussels, Published in co-operation with the CeBeDeM by A. Manteau, 1964. 158 p.
A publication designed to stimulate interest in contemporary Belgian music. Biographical sketches of 48 modern Belgian composers, with lists of their major works. Portraits. Index of names and brief list of recordings.

81
Hemel, Victor Van. Voorname Belgische toonkunstenaars uit de 18de, 19de, en 20ste eeuw. Derde bijgewerkte druk. Antwerpen, Cupido-Uitgave [1958] 84 p.
Short biographies of 101 musicians of Belgian descent.

82
Vannes, René. Dictionnaire des musiciens (compositeurs) . . . avec la collaboration de André Souris. Bruxelles, Maison Larcier [1947] 443 p.
Belgian composers from the 15th century to 1830, with comprehensive lists of works, published or in manuscript, and references to other sources of information.
Comments by Richard S. Hill in *Notes*, 6 (1949) p. 607–608.

Canada

83
Canadian Broadcasting Corporation. Catalogue of Canadian composers; edited by Helmut Kallmann. Rev. and enl. ed. [Ottawa, 1952?] 254 p.

356 brief biographical sketches, giving activities, education, addresses. Listings of works as complete as possible, giving titles, dates of publication, medium, duration, publisher. Works in manuscript included. List of Canadian publishers and composers' organizations.

84

Canadian Broadcasting Corporation. Thirty-four biographies of Canadian composers. Prepared and distributed by the International Service of the Canadian Broadcasting Corp. English and French text. Montreal, Canadian Broadcasting Corp., 1964. 110 p.

Czechoslovakia

85

Československý Hudební Slovník, osob a institucí. Praha, Státní hudební vydavatelství, 1963–65. 2 v.
Editors: Gracian Černušák, Bohumír Štědroň, Zdenko Nováček.
Czech bio-bibliographical dictionary. Also includes entries under names of places and institutions.
Review by Camillo Schoenbaum in *Die Musikforschung*, 18 (1965) p. 347–49.

86

Dlabač, Jan Bohumir. Allgemeines historisches Künstler-Lexikon für Böhmen und zum Theil auch für Mähren und Schlesien. Auf Kosten der hochlöblichen Herrenstände Böhmens hrsg. Prag, Gedruckt bei G. Hasse, 1815. 3 v.
An early dictionary of Czech musicians.
Reprint projected by Frits A. M. Knuf, Hilversum, Holland, as vol. 7 in the series *Facsimile-reprints of early music dictionaries.*

87

Gardavsky, Čenek, ed. Contemporary Czechoslovak composers. Prague, 1965. 562 p.
Biographies and bibliographical information on more than 300 Czech composers. English text.

England

88

Brown, James D. and Stephen S. Stratton. British musical biography: a dictionary of musical artists, authors, and composers born in Britain and its colonies. Birmingham, Stratton, 1897. 462 p.

Emphasis on composers living at the time of publication. Great masters treated briefly to afford room for the obscure. Includes a large number of English musicians who cannot be found elsewhere, with excellent bibliographies.

Humphries, Charles and William C. Smith. Music publishing in the British Isles. . . .
See no. 1208.

Kidson, Frank. British music publishers. . . .
See no. 1211.

89
Palmer, Russell. British music. London, Skelton Robinson, 1948. 283 p.
"Biographical index of contemporary British musicians and musical organizations," p. 17–255. Portraits.

90
Pulver, Jeffrey. A biographical dictionary of old English music. London, Kegan Paul; New York, Dutton, 1927. 537 p.
English musicians active from about 1200 to the death of Purcell (1695). Cites manuscript sources, contemporary publications, and occasionally modern editions. Somewhat discursive in style, with lists of works scattered through the bodies of the articles, but a useful starting point for the study of early English musicians. See also the author's companion volume covering old English musical terms (no. 216).

91
Who's Who in Music. Edited by David Simmons and Peter Townend. London, Burke's Peerage, 1962. 331 p.
First published in 1935; 2nd edition, 1937, edited by Sir Landon Ronald; 3rd edition edited by L. G. Pine, 1949–50.
Primarily devoted to British music and musicians. Includes articles on various British musical organizations and many helpful lists (publishers, periodicals, etc.) in the "directory" section. "Overseas section," p. 311–28, is devoted to foreign music publishers, festivals, retailers, wholesalers, manufacturers, agents, orchestras, opera companies. In the 3rd edition the "Overseas section" is much more extensive, containing biographical notices of foreign musicians, p. 315–87.
Review by Fred Blum in *Notes*, 19 (1962) p. 442–43.

France

92

Brossard, Yolande de, ed. Musiciens de Paris, 1535–1792. Actes d'état civil d'après le fichier Laborde de la Bibliothèque Nationale. Préface de Norbert Dufourcq. Paris, Éditions A. et J. Picard, 1965. 302 p. (Vie Musicale en France sous les Rois Bourbons, 11).

A directory of early Parisian musicians based on a card file compiled by Léon de Laborde (d. 1869), comprising some 6,624 cards listing musicians of all kinds active in Paris during the period covered. Index of musicians arranged chronologically under their specialties.

93

Dictionnaire des Musiciens Français. [Paris] Seghers, 1961. 379 p. (Dictionnaires Seghers, 3.)

A pocket, illustrated dictionary of French musicians. Coverage is selective, particularly as regards contemporary figures. Brief summaries of the major works of composers; no full listings; no bibliographies.

94

Favati, Guido, ed. Le biografie trovadorische, testi provenzali dei secc. XIII e XIV, edizione critica . . . Bologna, Libreria Antiquaria Palmaverdi, 1961. 523 p. (Biblioteca degli "studi mediolatine e volgari," 3.)

Not a French biographical dictionary in the ordinary sense, but a critical edition of the original 13th- and 14th-century biographical descriptions of the troubadour composers.

For specialists in Romance philology and Medieval music; to be used in connection with Gennrich (no. 767) and Pillet (no. 785).

Germany

95

Fellerer, Karl G. ed. Rheinische Musiker. 1. Folge-Köln, Arno Volk-Verlag, 1960– (Beiträge zur rheinischen Musikgeschichte, 43, 53, 58– .)

1. Folge (1960): 91 names. 2. Folge (1962): 58 names. 3. Folge (1964): 62 names.

The first three in a series of volumes giving biographical and biblio-graphical information on musicians of the Rhineland. Each volume is alphabetically complete in itself, but the indexing is cumulative. The work follows the pattern established in Mattheson's *Grundlage einer Ehren-Pforte* (1740) in that most of the biographies of living musicians are self-compiled.

[27]

96
Fey, Hermann. Schleswig-Holsteinische Musiker, von den ältesten Zeiten bis zur Gegenwart; ein Heimatbuch. Hamburg, C. Holler [1922] 126 p.

Dictionary arrangement. Full bibliographies of compositions, with authority references. "Quellennachweis," p. 125–26.

97
Kossmaly, Karl und C. H. Herzel. Schlesisches Tonkünstler-Lexikon, enthaltend die Biographieen aller schlesischen Tonkünstler, Componisten, Cantoren, Organisten, Tongelehrten, Textdichter, Orgelbauer, Instrumentenmacher . . . hrsg. von Kossmaly und Carlo [pseud.] Breslau, E. Trewendt, 1846–47. 332 p.

Issued in 4 parts, each in a separate alphabet. Long articles, giving classified lists of compositions, roles for performers, concert programs.

98
Kürschners Deutscher Musiker-Kalender. 2. Ausg. des Deutschen Musiker-Lexikons. Herausgeber: Hedwig und E. H. Müller von Asow. Berlin, W. de Gruyter, 1954. 1,702 columns.

First edited in 1929. See no. 102.

Biographies of living German, Austrian, and Swiss musicians in all categories and German-born musicians in foreign countries. Entries give essential biographical information and detailed lists of works. Excessive use of abbreviations. Index by date of birth (1854–1939) and death (1929–54).

99
Kürschners Biographisches Theater-Handbuch. Schauspiel, Oper, Film, Rundfunk: Deutschland, Österreich, Schweiz. Hrsg. von Herbert A. Frenzel und Hans J. Moser. Berlin, W. de Gruyter, 1956. 840 p.

Names, addresses, activities of singers, music directors, actors, critics, dancers, choreographers, composers, librarians of theater collections, etc. Entries are for persons living as of 1956.

100
Ledebur, Carl F. H. W. P. J., Freiherr von. Tonkünstler-Lexikon Berlins von den ältesten Zeiten bis auf die Gegenwart. Berlin, L. Rauh, 1861. 704 p.

An important early dictionary of Berlin musicians. Entries for composers, publishers, performers, amateurs, born or active in Berlin, with detailed bibliographies of compositions.

Reprint projected by Frits A. M. Knuf, Hilversum, Holland, as volume 5 in the series *Facsimile-reprints of early music dictionaries*.

101
Lipowsky, Felix J. Baierisches Musik-Lexikon. München, J. Giel, 1811. 338 [i.e. 438] p.

An early dictionary of some historical importance of Bavarian composers and performers. Lists of major compositions. Occasional title-page transcriptions.

Reprint projected by Frits A. M. Knuf, Hilversum, Holland, as volume 6 in the series *Facsimile-reprints of early music dictionaries.*

102
Müller, Erich H., ed. Deutsches Musiker-Lexikon. Dresden, W. Limpert, 1929. [862] p. 1,644 columns.

Preceded *Kürschners . . .*, no. 98.

Living German musicians and foreign musicians active in German concert life: composers, performers, conductors, teachers, scholars. Full lists of works, published and unpublished.

103
Verband Deutscher Komponisten und Musikwissenschaftlicher. Komponisten und Musikwissenschaftlicher der Deutschen Demokratischen Republik. Kurzbiographien und Werkverzeichnisse. Berlin, Verlag Neue Musik, 1959. 199 p.

Brief biographical sketches of 85 East German composers and musicologists, with listings of their major works. Preceded by a group of short essays on musical life and institutions in the Eastern zone. Portraits.

Holland

104
Gregoir, G. J. Biographie des artistes-musiciens néerlandais des XVIIIe et XIXe siècles, et des artistes étrangers résidant ou ayant résidé en Néerlande à la même époque. Anvers, L. Dela Montagne, 1864. 238 p.

Brief biographies of Netherland musicians. Careers summarized, major works mentioned for composers, but no full listings.

105
Letzer, J. H. Muzikaal Nederland, 1850–1910. Bio-bibliographisch woordenboek . . . 2. uitgaff met aanvullingen en verbeteringen. Utrecht, J. L. Beijers, 1913. 201 p., with 10 p. of additions.

Composers, musicologists, performers, etc., active in Holland 1850–1910. Biographies, lists of works, occasional dates of first performances.

[29]

106

Straeten, Edmond vander. La musique aux pays-bas avant le XIXe siècle. Documents inédits et annotés. Compositeurs, virtuoses, théoriciens, luthiers; opéras, motets, airs nationaux, académies, maîtrises, livres, portraits, etc. Bruxelles, C. Muquardt, 1867–88. 8 v.

Vols. 2–7 published by G. A. Van Trigt; Vol. 8 by Schott.

Not strictly a biographical dictionary, but an invaluable collection of documents, transcripts of records, biographical and bibliographical notes related to the activities of Flemish musicians (Dutch and Belgian). Vol. 6 is devoted to Flemish musicians in Italy; Vols. 7–8, to Flemish musicians in Spain. Rich in information of the greatest interest to students of early European music.

Reprint edition announced for publication by Frits A. M. Knuf, Hilversum, Holland.

Hungary

107

Molnár, Imre. A magyar muzsika könyve, szerkesztette Molnár Imre. . . . Budapest, Merkantil-Nyomda, 1936. 632 p.

Institutions, organizations, and biographical entries for composers, performers, and other musicians.

India

108

Sambamoorthy, P. A dictionary of South Indian music and musicians. Madras, The Indian Music Publishing House, 1952– .

In progress. Vol. 1: A–F. Vol. 2 (1959): G–K.

Portraits of composers and performers.

Israel (and Jewish Musicians in General)

109

Gradenwitz, Peter. Music and musicians in Israel; a comprehensive guide to modern Israeli music. Tel Aviv, Israeli Music Publications, 1959. 226 p.

Biographies, varying in length, of about 60 composers, grouped by school or tendency. Appendix, p. 133–63, contains an alphabetical listing of composers and their works, but without reference to the biography section. Also given is a list of publishers, and a group of publishers' catalogs.

110
Saleski, Gdal. Famous musicians of Jewish origin. New York, Bloch, 1949. 716 p.
Informal biographies, classified according to type of activity: composers, conductors, violinists, etc. About 400 entries. No bibliographies, but major works are mentioned in the articles. Portraits. P. 679–716: Israeli musicians.

111
Stengel, Theodore und Herbert Gerigk. Lexikon der Juden in der Musik, mit einem Titelverzeichnis jüdischer Werke. Berlin, B. Hahnefeld, 1941. 404 p. (Veröffentlichungen des Instituts der NSDAP. zur Erforschung der Judenfrage . . . 2.)
First published in 1940. 380 p.
Among the more shameful products of German National Socialism were dictionaries of Jewish musicians compiled to further the purposes of anti-semitism. This and the item following may be cited as examples of their kind.

112
Girschner, Otto. Repetitorium der Musikgeschichte. Elfte Auflage. Köln, P. J. Tonger, 1941. 438 p.
A question-answer survey of music history.
P. 350–411: "Juden in der Musik," a biographical supplement first introduced in the 9th ed., 1936.

Italy

113
Angelis, Alberto de. L'Italia musicale d'oggi. Dizionario dei musicisti: compositori, direttori d'orchestra, concertisti, insegnanti, liutai, cantanti, scrittori musicali, librettisti, editori musicali, ecc. 3. ed., corredate di una appendice. Roma, Ausonia, 1928. 523, 211 p.
Earlier editions: 1918, 1922.
Living Italian musicians, with comprehensive lists of works.

[31]

114

Damerini, Adelmo. Misicisti toscani; scritti di G. Barblan et al, settembre 1955, a cura di Adelmo Damerini e Franco Schlitzer. Siena [Ticci] 1955. 81 p.

A publication of the *Accademia musicale chigiana*.

Latin America

115

Mariz, Vasco. Dicionário bio-bibliográfico musical (brasileiro e internacional). Pref. de Renato Almeida. Rio de Janeiro, Livraria Kosmos, 1948. 246 p.

Brief biographies of the best-known musical figures since the Renaissance, including performers. Useful for Brazilian musicians. Living persons included.

116

Mayer-Serra, Otto. Música y músicos de Latinoamérica. Mexico, Editorial Atlante, 1947. 2 v.

Primarily biographical, although terms, dance forms, instruments are included. Listings of composers' works vary from brief resumes to full tabulations for major composers. Portraits.

117

Pan American Union. Music Section. Composers of the Americas, biographical data and catalogs of their works. [Washington, D.C., 1955–].

7 volumes to 1964. Each volume contains from 4 to 16 names, alphabetically arranged, with brief biographies in English and Spanish, portraits, pages from scores, sometimes autographs. Works are given chronologically within principal mediums, with date of composition, timing, publisher, and recordings if any. Unpublished works also listed.

Poland

118

Chybiński, Adolf. Słownik muzyków dawnej polski do roku 1800. Kraków [Polskie wydawnictwo muzyczne, 1949] 163 p.

Biographical dictionary of musicians (composers and performers) active in Poland to 1800. Brief articles mentioning principal works. List of references for each entry. Preface discusses sources of information: *Fétis*, *Eitner*, many Polish publications and official records.

119

Sowiński, Wojciech. Les musiciens polonais et slaves, anciens et modernes; dictionnaire biographique. . . . Précédé d'un résumé de l'histoire de la musique en Pologne. . . . Paris, A. Le Clere, 1857. 599 p.

Another edition, in Polish, published in 1874.

"Résumé de l'histoire de la musique en Pologne," p. 1–44. "Anciens instruments de musique chez les polonais et les slaves," p. 45–58. Long biographical articles, with full bibliographies for major composers.

Portugal

120

Amorim, Eugénio. Dicionário biográfico de musicos do norte de Portugal. [Porto] Edições Maranus [1935] 110 p.

Chiefly 19th-century and living musicians. Some extended articles, with compositions listed in body of text.

121

Mazza, José. Dicionário biográfico de musicos portugueses, com prefácio e notas do José Augusto Alegria. . . . [Lisboa, 1945?] 103 p.

"Extraido da revista, *Ocidente*, 1944/45."

A dictionary compiled around 1790 and preserved in a manuscript in the Biblioteca Publica de Évora. Arranged by Christian names; many names of members of religious orders. The dictionary occupies p. 13–40; additional biographical information supplied by the editor from other sources, p. 41–103.

122

Vasconcellos, Joaquim A. da Fonseca E. Os músicos portuguezes. Biographia-bibliographia. Porto, Imprensa portugueza, 1870. 2 v.

Long biographical articles, lists, and discussions of compositions. Useful for early names, library locations of manuscripts, etc. Discussions of operas include dates and places of first performances.

123

Vieira, Ernesto. Diccionário biográphico de músicos portuguezes; historia e bibliographia da música em Portugal. Lisboa, Moreira & Pinheiro, 1900 [i.e. 1900–1904] 2 v.

More inclusive than Vasconcellos, above. Comprehensive lists of works for major composers. Vol. 2 includes supplementary material and a chronological index.

Rumania

124

Lexiconul Compozitorilor si Muzicologilor Români. (Lexicon of Rumanian composers and musicologists.) Bucharest, Musical Publishing House, 1965. 388 p.

Biographical data and information on the works of the most prominent Rumanian composers and musicologists. Treats musicians of earlier times but stresses contemporary activities. Portraits and discographies.

Russia

125

Boelza, Igor F. Handbook of Soviet musicians. London, Pilot Press [1944] 101 p.

First printing, 1943.

40 short biographies. Portraits. Separate bibliographical section listing each composer's works. English titles; dates given when known.

126

Sovetskie Kompozitory, kratkiĭ biograficheskiĭ spravochnik. Sostaviteli: G. Bernandt i A. Dolzhanskiĭ. Moskva, Sovetskii Kompozitor, 1957. 695 p.

Biographical sketches of 1,072 composers, with a full listing of their compositions arranged by medium, with dates of first performance for large works. Also lists literary works by the musicians.

Review by Fred K. Prieberg in *Musical America*, 78 (July, 1958) p. 28–29.

127

Vodarsky-Shiraeff, Alexandria. Russian composers and musicians, a biographical dictionary. New York, H. W. Wilson, 1940. 158 p.

Brief biographies of outstanding figures: composers, performers, teachers, critics. Classfied lists of major works, bibliographical references. Cross references to variant spellings of Russian names.

Scandinavia

128

Kappel, Vagn. Contemporary Danish composers against the background of Danish musical life and history. [2nd rev. ed., Copenhagen] Det Danske Selskab, 1950. 116 p.

[34]

First published in 1948.

Designed for public relations purposes. Biographical sketches of 14 contemporary Danish composers. Representative works cited but no full lists. List of records of Danish music, p. 97–113.

129
Sundelin, Torsten. Norrländskt musikliv. Uppsala, Almqvist & Wiksell, 1946. 358 p.

Spain

130
Alcahali y de Mosquera, José Maria Ruiz de Lihori y Pardines, Baron de. La musica en Valencia. Diccionario biográfico y crítico. . . . Valencia, Domenech, 1903. 445 p.

Biographies of widely varying length, with summary lists of works for major composers. Under "Anónimos," p. 39–170, the compiler introduces long literary digressions concerning liturgical drama, dance music, military music, etc., with extensive musical examples.

Switzerland

131
Refardt, Edgar. Historisch-biographisches Musikerlexikon der Schweiz. Leipzig/ Zürich, Hug & Co., 1928. 355 p.

Comprehensive biographical coverage for names connected with Swiss music from the Middle Ages to the end of the 16th-century; musicians and instrument makers of the 17th- and 18th-centuries; composers only for the 19th- and 20th-centuries. Lists of works.

132
Schweizer Musiker-Lexikon. Dictionnaire des musiciens suisses, 1964. Im Auftrag des Schweizerischen Tonkünstlervereins bearbeitet von . . . Willi Schuh [et al.] Zürich, Atlantis Verlag [1964] 421 p.

The expansion of a biographical dictionary of Swiss musicians that appeared originally as V. 2 of the *Schweizer Musikbuch* (Zürich, 1939). Treats Swiss musicians of all periods, as well as foreign musicians resident in Switzerland or associated with the music of the country. Articles in French and German. Excellent bibliographical coverage.

[35]

133

Swiss Composers' League. 40 contemporary Swiss composers. Bodensee, Verlag Amriswil, 1956. 222 p.

Brief biographies and critical comment. A few representative works are described and a larger selection listed, with imprints and instrumentation given. Recordings. Portraits. Text in English and Spanish.

United States

134

American Society of Composers, Authors, and Publishers. The ASCAP biographical dictionary of composers, authors, and publishers. Ed. by Daniel I. McNamara. 2nd ed. New York, Crowell [1952] 636 p.

First published in 1948.

"Includes sketches of 2171 writers of lyrics and composers (1400 of whom are writers and popular musicians) and 402 publishers" (cf. *Winchell*, 1953). All members and former members of ASCAP. Major works listed.

135

Boone, Charles. The Composers' Forum index of Bay Area composers. Berkeley, Calif., The Composers' Forum [1964] [typescripts, unpaged].

Brief biographical sketches and lists of representative works for 46 composers residing in the San Francisco Bay area. An index prepared for the Composers' Forum and deposited in 23 libraries throughout the country.

136

California. Governor's Committee to Encourage Selection, Performance and Publication of Music of Merit by Western Composers. A directory of contemporary California composers. V. 1– [Sacramento, Calif., Governor's Committee . . .] 1961. 33 leaves (typescript).

No more published?

Lists composers alphabetically, with their addresses. Cites published works and commercially available recordings. Committee chairman: Agnes Booe.

137

Ewen, David, comp. American composers today, a biographical and critical guide. New York, H. W. Wilson, 1949. 265 p.

Composers active in the U.S. and Latin America, 1900–1946. Principal works and recordings listed. Bibliographical references to books and periodicals.

Review by Lee Fairley in *Notes*, 6 (1949) p. 615–16.

See also no. 59.

138

Feather, Leonard. The encyclopedia of jazz. Completely revised, enlarged and brought up to date. New York, Horizon Press, 1960. 527 p.

First published in 1955.

P. 13–90: introductory material, essays on the history, sociology, and structure of jazz. P. 96–473: biographies of jazz musicians, outlining their careers and summarizing their recording activities. Addresses given.

139

Gentry, Linnell. A history and encyclopedia of country, western, and gospel music. [Printed for the author by McQuiddy Press, Nashville, Tenn., 1961] 380 p.

A most important reference tool in its own field.

Part II, p. 3–167: anthology of magazine articles on country, western, and gospel music since 1904. Part III, p. 168–75: country musical shows since 1924. Part IV, p. 176–351: biographies of country, western, and gospel singers, musicians, and comedians.

140

Historical Records Survey. District of Columbia. Bio-bibliographical index of musicians in the United States of America from colonial times . . . sponsored by the Board of Commissioners of the District of Columbia. 2nd ed. Washington, D.C., Music Section, Pan American Union, 1956. 439 p.

Reprint of the 1941 edition.

An index to biographical information contained in 66 works (dictionaries, histories, etc.) on American music, with page references to the volumes indexed.

141

Lawless, Ray McKinley. Folksingers and folksongs in America; a handbook of biography, bibliography, and discography. Illustrated from paintings by Thomas Hart Benton and others, and from designs in Steuben glass. New rev. ed. with special suppl. New York, Duell, Sloan and Pearce, [1965] 750 p.

First published in 1960.

A general book of knowledge for folk song enthusiasts, with information

[37]

pertaining to singers, song collecting, sources and recordings. The major part of the work is devoted to biographical information on American folk singers.

Review of first edition by Rae Korson in *Notes*, 18 (1960) p. 62.

142

McCarty, Clifford. Film composers in America; a checklist of their work. Foreword by Lawrence Morton. Glendale, Calif., John Valentin [1953] 193 p.

163 names, with film scores listed by date. Index of film titles; index of orchestrators.

Review by F. W. Sternfeld in *Notes*, 11 (1953) p. 105.

Also entered as no. 625.

143

Mangler, Joyce Ellen. Rhode Island music and musicians, 1733–1850. Detroit, Information Service, Inc., 1965. 90 p. (Detroit studies in music bibliography, 7.)

Primarily a directory of early Rhode Island musicians; indexed by profession and by chronology.

Supplement I: Organ builders and installations in Rhode Island churches. Supplement II: Membership in the Psallonian Society 1816–32. Bibliography of primary and secondary sources.

144

Music and Dance in California, compiled by William J. Perlman. Edited by José Rodriguez. Hollywood, Bureau of Musical Research, 1940. 467 p.

Earlier edition, 1933, published under the title *Who's who in music and dance in Southern California.*

This and the following six titles (nos. 144–50) are a series of regional reference works covering different sections of the U.S. Long articles on the development of musical and dance activities. Biographical sketches of composers, performers, conductors, educators, etc. Portraits. Pronounced emphasis on the commercial aspects of music.

145

Music and Dance in the Central States. Edited by Richard D. Saunders; compiled by William J. Perlman. Hollywood, Bureau of Musical Research [1952] 173 p.

146

Music and Dance in the New England States. . . . Sigmund Spaeth, editor-in-chief; William J. Perlman, director and managing editor. New York, Bureau of Musical Research [1953] 347 p.

147

Music and Dance in New York State. Sigmund Spaeth, editor-in-chief; William J. Perlman, director and associate editor. . . . 1952 ed. New York, Bureau of Musical Research [1951] 435 p.

148

Music and Dance in Pennsylvania, New Jersey and Delaware. Sigmund Spaeth, editor-in-chief; William J. Perlman, director and managing editor. . . . New York, Bureau of Musical Research [1954] 339 p.

149

Music and Dance in the Southeastern States. . . . Sigmund Spaeth, editor-in-chief; William J. Perlman, director and managing editor. New York, Bureau of Musical Research [1952] 331 p.

150

Music and Dance in Texas, Oklahoma and the Southwest. Edited by E. Clyde Whitlock and Richard D. Saunders. Hollywood, Bureau of Musical Research [1950] 256 p.

151

North Carolina Federation of Music Clubs. North Carolina musicians; a selective handbook. Chapel Hill, Univ. of North Carolina Library, 1956. 82 p. (Univ. of North Carolina Library Extension Pubn., V. 21, No. 4.)

152

Reis, Claire R. Composers in America; biographical sketches of contemporary composers with a record of their works. Rev. and enl. ed. New York, Macmillan, 1947. 399 p.

First published in 1930 under the title *American composers*. . . .

A survey of music written by American serious composers, 1915 to 1947. Biographies of 332 composers, with a classified listing of their works, manuscripts included (date, publisher, duration). Supplementary list of 424 names without biographical data.

Review by Lee Fairley in *Notes*, 4 (1947) p. 458–59.

[39]

153
Works Projects Administration. Northern California. Celebrities in El Dorado, 1850–1906. Cornel Lengyel, editor. San Fransisco, prepared with [the] assistance of the Work Projects Administration of California; sponsored by the City and County of San Francisco, 1940. 270 leaves (typescript). (History of music in San Francisco, 4.)

> A biographic record of 111 prominent musicians who have visited San Francisco and performed here from the earliest days of the gold rush era to the time of the great fire, with additional lists of visiting celebrities (1909–40), chamber music ensembles, bands, orchestras, and other music-making bodies (Editor's Note).

Yugoslavia

154
Kovačević, Krešimir. Hrvatski kompozitori i njihova djela. Zagreb, Naprijed, 1960. 553 p.
Biographies of 50 Croatian composers, for the most part contemporary, with descriptive accounts of their principal works. Summaries in English. Classified index of works analyzed; general index.

Musical Instruments, Makers and Performers

There is a substantial group of reference books concerned with the construction, performance, and iconography of musical instruments. A great deal of work has been done with respect to the violin, and there is an increasing number of reference tools devoted to keyboard and to wind instruments.

For specific descriptions, prices, and illustrations of individual instruments, particularly those of the string family, the student should not neglect the catalogs of various dealers: Hamma, Herrmann, Hill, Lyon & Healy, Wurlitzer, etc. These are not included in our listing.

For the iconography of musical instruments, see *Buchner* (no. 161), *Besseler* (no. 295), *Kinsky* (no. 330), and *Komma* (no. 331).

See also "Bibliographies of Music Literature" (no. 539 ff.) and "Catalogs of Musical Instrument Collections" (no. 1139 ff.).

155
Avgerinos, Gerassimos. Lexikon der Pauke. Frankfurt am M., Verlag Das Musikinstrument [1964] 105 p. (Das Musikinstrument, 12.)
A dictionary of terms, chiefly German, connected with drums and drum playing.

156

Bachmann, Alberto A. An encyclopedia of the violin. Translated by Frederick H. Martens. New York, D. Appleton, 1925. 470 p.

Reissued, with a preface by Stuart Canin, New York, Da Capo Press, 1966.

Contains a series of alphabets: violin makers in Europe, violin makers in America, European bow makers, American bow makers, string quartets (groups), terms, violinists, music for the violin. Portraits.

157

Bachmann, Alberto A. Les grands violinistes du passé. . . . Paris, Fischbacher, 1913. 468 p.

Biographies of 40 violinist-composers, varying in length, but with lists of works and a number of full or partial thematic catalogs (i.e. Corelli, Kreutzer, Leclair, Rode, Sarasate, Tartini, Viotti, Vivaldi, etc.).

158

Bechler, Leo und Bernhardt Rahm. Die Oboe und die ihr verwandten Instrumente, nebst biographischen Skizzen der bedeutendsten ihrer Meister. Anhang: Musikliteratur für Oboe und englisch Horn, zusammengestellt von Dr. Philipp Losch. Leipzig, C. Merseburger, 1914. 98 p., 32 p. (Anhang).

A history of the oboe and related instruments, with brief biographical sketches of famous players. Supplementary list of works for oboe and English horn, solo and with other instruments.

159

Boalch, Donald H. Makers of the harpsichord and clavichord, 1440 to 1840. London, G. Ronald [1956] 169 p.

Lists 820 makers of early keyboard instruments and describes more than 1,000 of their instruments, giving dates, registers, compasses, histories, and present ownership. 32 photo plates.

Review by Frank Hubbard in *Notes*, 14 (1957) p. 572–73. Review in *The Times literary supplement*, Dec. 21, 1956.

160

Bone, Philip James. The guitar and mandolin: biographies of celebrated players and composers. [2nd ed., enl.] London, New York, Schott, 1954. 388 p.

First published in 1914.

Performers and composers, including "standard" composers who have written for guitar or mandolin. Major works are mentioned, but there are no complete listings. Portraits.

Review by Richard Capell in *Music and letters*, 35 (1954) p. 254.

161

Buchner, Alexander. Musical instruments through the ages. Trans. by Iris Urwin. London, Spring Books [1956].

First published, with the text in Czech, by Artia, Prague. German edition: *Musikinstrumente im Wandel der Zeiten.*

Not a dictionary or encyclopedia, but important as a collection of beautifully reproduced plates, some 323 in number, of musical instruments and representations of musical performance in painting, engraving, and sculpture.

162

Clarke, A. Mason. A biographical dictionary of fiddlers, including performers on the violoncello and double bass. . . . London, W. Reeves [1895] 360 p.

Anecdotal accounts.

163

Fairfield, John H. Known violin makers. [New York, Bradford Press, 1942] 192 p.

Separate listings of European makers from the 16th-century, and American makers. For each, a brief biography, description of works, and the current price range of the instruments.

164

Gorgerat, Gérald. Encyclopédie de la musique pour instruments à vent. Lausanne, Éditions Rencontre [1955] 3 v.

A pretentious work which attempts to cover all information pertaining to the making and performance of wind instruments, and much more that has no particular relevance. Useful fingering charts for all winds. Several special lists:

Vol. 3, p. 243–83: Principal works for wind instruments, solo and ensemble. Vol. 3, p. 285–340: Dictionary of composers cited in the text. Brief identifications; no page references. Vol. 3, p. 341–524: Table of French terms, with their equivalents in Italian, German, English, and Spanish.

165

Hamma, Fridolin. German violin makers; a critical dictionary. . . . translated by Walter Stewart. London, W. Reeves, [1961] 49 p., 80 pl.

Translated from the 1948 German edition, *Meister deutscher Geigen-baukunst*. Stuttgart, 1948.

Alphabetical listing of 550 names of important German makers, with plates illustrating their work.

Review by Cynthia L. Adams in *Notes*, 19 (1962) p. 261–62.

166

Hamma, Walter. Meister italienischer Geigenbaukunst. (Zum 100 jähr. Bestehen der Firma Hamma & Co., Stuttgart, im Jahre 1964. Engl. Übers.: Walter J. Stewart. Franz. Übers.: Aristide Wirsta.) Stuttgart, Schuler, 1965. 728 p.

Revision and expansion of a work first published in 1931.

Describes more than 300 instruments made by Italian masters. Descriptions arranged alphabetically by makers, with biographical information and photographic plates of details.

167

Haupt, Helga. "Wiener Instrumentenbauer von 1791 bis 1815," in *Studien zur Musikwissenschaft*, Beihefte der Denkmäler der Tonkunst in Oesterreich. Bd. 24. Graz, Hermann Böhlaus, 1960. P. 120–84.

Alphabetical listing of Viennese instrument makers, in all categories. Addresses, dates of activity. Well documented.

168

Henley, William. Universal dictionary of violin and bow makers. [Managing ed., Cyril Woodcock. Brighton, Sussex, Amati Pub. Co., 1959–60] 5 v.

Continued in *Dictionary of contemporary violin and bow makers*, by Cyril Woodcock. Brighton, 1965. 96 p.

Biographies of varying length. Long accounts of important figures, with descriptions and prices of famous instruments. Labels transcribed but no facsimiles. Rather subjective and literary in style.

169

Hirt, Franz Josef. Meisterwerke des Klavierbaus. Geschichte der Saitenklaviers von 1440 bis 1880. Olten, Urs Graf Verlag, 1955. 521 p.

Beautifully illustrated book, with information about the history, design, construction, makers, etc., of keyboard instruments. Full-page photographic plates, useful sections of biography and bibliography.

170

Irwin, Stevens. Dictionary of pipe organ stops. Detailed descriptions of more than 600 stops, together with definitions of many other terms

[43]

connected with the organ, and an examination of the acoustical properties of many types of pipes and the various divisions of the organ. New York, G. Schirmer [1962] 264 p.

Illustrated. Includes a short bibliography.

171

Jacquot, Albert. Dictionnaire pratique et raisonné des instruments de musique anciens et modernes. 2nd ed. Paris, Fischbacher, 1886. 280 p.

Many names of Eastern instruments included. Some illustrations. Brief definitions. No bibliography.

172

Jahnel, Franz. Die Gitarre und ihr Bau. Technologie von Gitarre, Laute, Mandoline, Sister, Tanbur und Saite. Frankfurt am Main, Verlag Das Musikinstrument, 1963. 250 p.

A compendium of information on the construction of the guitar and other fretted instruments. Bibliography, numerous tables and lists, detailed plans and technical data. A handsomely designed and printed volume, invaluable for the musical instrument maker or interested performer.

173

Jalovec, Karel. Enzyklopädie des Geigenbaues. Leiden, E. J. Brill, 1965. 2 v.

Vol. 1: 940 p., 51 colored illustrations on 24 plates. Vol. 2: 405 illustrations on 595 plates; 3,000 reproductions of violin makers labels.

174

Jalovec, Karel. Italian violin makers. Rev. ed. London, P. Hamlyn, 1964. 445 p.

First published in Prague, 1952; published in London, 1958, with text in Czech and English.

Accounts of Italian violin makers, with descriptions and dimensions of important instruments. Many illustrations, some in color. Index by place; scale plans and facsimiles of labels.

175

Jalovec, Karel. The violin makers of Bohemia; including craftsmen of Moravia and Slovakia. London, Anglo-Italian Pubns. [1959] 129 p., 392 plates.

Originally published in Czech under the title *Cesti houslari*. Prague, 1959. German ed., 1959.

Covers the work of some 1,200 Czech violin makers. Photographs of instruments, and a section of makers' labels in facsimile.

176
Langwill, Lyndesay G. An index of musical wind-instrument makers. 2nd and enlarged ed. Edinburgh [1962] 202 p.

First published in 1960.

Alphabetical index of some 3,000 makers of mouth-blown woodwind and brass instruments, including all forms of bagpipes, ocarinas, etc. Detailed entries for the most important makers. Locations of examples of early instruments in museums and private collections.

P. 131–34: bibliography; p. 135–39: list of instrument collections.

Review by Josef Marx in *Notes*, 18 (1961) p. 234–36; by Georg Karstädt in *Die Musikforschung*, 18 (1965) p. 90–91.

177
Lütgendorff, Willibald Leo, Freiherr von. Die Geigen- und Lautenmacher vom Mittelalter bis zur Gegenwart, nach den besten Quellen bearbeitet. . . . 4. mit der 3. übereinstimmende Aufl. Frankfurt am Main, Frankfurter Verlags-Anstalt, 1922. 2 v.

First published in 1904, in 1 volume.

Vol. 1: History of the making of stringed instruments by country. Index of manufacturers by city, with dates of birth and death. Bibliography, p. 403–20. Many illustrations.

Vol. 2: Biographical dictionary of makers of stringed instruments. P. 583–668: facsimiles of trademarks and labels.

178
Marcuse, Sibyl. Musical instruments; a comprehensive dictionary. New York, Doubleday, 1964. 608 p.

Intended to serve English readers as Sachs *Real-Lexikon* (no. 190) does German. World coverage, although the author acknowledges incompleteness with respect to non-European and folk instruments.

P. 603–608: listing of 206 sources of information about instruments.

179
Michel, Norman E. Historical pianos, harpsichords and clavichords. Pico Rivera, Calif. [1963] 209 p.

A volume of photographs of pianos. P. 1–46: photos of pianos, birthplaces, family homes and historical societies related to 35 presidents of the U.S. P. 47–86: pianos and homes of statesmen, actors, etc. P. 77–135: photos from libraries, historical societies, museums, and other institutions. P. 136–209: photos of musical instruments from all over the world. A curious exercise in bibliographical name-dropping.

[45]

180

Michel, Norman E. Michel's piano atlas. Contains names of pianos, dates of manufacture, and serial numbers. Pico Rivera, Calif. [1961] 272 p.
First published as *Pierce piano atlas*, 1947– .
6,580 names of pianos. For some of these, there is no information other than name; for others, complete lists of serial numbers.

181

Möller, Max. The violin-makers of the low countries (Belgium and Holland). Amsterdam, M. Möller, 1955. 165 p.
A historical survey of violin making in Belgium and Holland.
P. 23–129: photographic plates, chiefly of instruments in detail. P. 131–53: "Alphabetical Register," brief critical comments on the makers and their work. Glossary of terms in English, French, German, and Flemish.

182

Morris, W. Meredith. British violin makers, a biographical dictionary of British makers of stringed instruments and bows, and a critical description of their work. 2nd ed., rev. and enl. London, R. Scott, 1920. 318 p.
First published in 1904.
P. 87–259: alphabetical dictionary of violin and bow makers. Some labels in facsimile. P. 261–94: "A list of present-day makers, and a few old makers recently discovered."

183

Niemann, Walter. Klavier-lexikon: Elementarlehre für Klavierspieler, Anleitung zur Aussprache des italienischen, Tabelle der Abkürzungen in Wort und Notenschrift, Literaturverzeichnis, ausführliches Fremdwörter-, Sach- und Personallexikon. 4. völlig umgearb. und reich verm. Aufl. . . . Leipzig, C. F. Kahnt, 1918. 365 p.
First published in 1912 as *Taschen-Lexikon für Klavierspieler*.

184

Norlind, Tobias. Systematik der Saiteninstrumente. Stockholm [Emil Kihlströms Tryckeri] 1936–39. 2 v.
At head of title: Musikhistorisches Museum, Stockholm.
Vol. 1: *Geschichte der Zither* (1936). Vol. 2: *Geschichte des Klaviers* (1939).
Detailed classification and description of stringed instruments, based on the archive in the Musikhistorisches Museum in Stockholm where records of some 40,000 instruments are maintained. Illustrated. Bibliographical references and locations given for specific instruments in European and American collections. The work was projected in 4 parts, only 2 of which were completed.

[46]

185

Poidras, Henri. Critical and documentary dictionary of violin makers old and modern, translated by Arnold Sewell. . . . Rouen, Imprimerie de la Vicomté, 1928–30. 2 v.

Originally published in French, 1924, with a 2nd ed. in 1930. There is also a one-volume English edition, 1928.

Brief biographical notices, with critical comments, arranged alphabetically under national schools: Italian, French, English, German, etc. Photographic plates of instruments; facsimiles of labels.

186

Prat Marsal, Domingo. Diccionario biográfico, bibliográfico, histórico, crítico de guitarras (instrumentos afines), guitarristas (profesores, compositores, concertistas, lahudistas, amateurs), guitarreros (luthiers), danzas y cantos, terminología. Buenos Aires, Casa Romero y Fernández [1934] 468 p.

The main alphabet contains biographies and lists of compositions.

P. 423–52: dance forms; p. 453–64: terminology.

187

"Provisional Index of Present-day Makers of Historical Musical Instruments (Non-keyboard)." In *Galpin Society journal*, 13 (July, 1960) p. 70–97.

Makers of historical keyboard instruments listed in an appendix, p. 86–87.

A useful guide to sources of modern replicas of historical musical instruments.

188

Roda, Joseph. Bows for musical instruments of the violin family. Chicago, W. Lewis & Son, 1959. 335 p.

Brief history and description of the bow, including statistics as to dimensions and weight.

P. 119–325: biographical list of bow makers, with 47 excellent plates of their work.

189

Sachs, Curt. Handbuch der Musikinstrumentenkunde. Leipzig, Breitkopf u. Härtel, 1920. 412 p. (Kleine Handbücher der Musikgeschichte nach Gattungen, Bd. 12.)

Not precisely a dictionary, but a systematic and historical description of musical instruments classified according to type: idiophones, membranophones, chordaphones, aerophones, etc. Much of the same ground is covered in Sachs' *The history of musical instruments* (New York, Norton, 1940), in which the approach is chronological and by cultural areas.

190

Sachs, Curt. Real-Lexikon der Musikinstrumente, zugleich ein Polyglossar für das gesamte Instrumentengebiet. [Rev. and enl. ed.] New York, Dover Publications [1964], 451 p.

First published in Berlin, 1913; unaltered reprint of the original edition issued by G. Olms, Hildesheim, 1962.

A technical and historical dictionary of instruments of all periods and countries. Names of instruments and parts of instruments in some 120 languages and dialects, European, African, and Asian. Locations of examples in instrument collection. Illustrations; some bibliographies. This is Sachs' great work in this field, and one of the best sources of information on instruments.

For a recent English-language dictionary inspired by the *Real-Lexikon*, see no. 178.

191

Straeten, Edmund S. J. van der. The history of the violin, its ancestors and collateral instruments from [the] earliest times to the present day; with 48 plates and numerous illustrations in [the] text. London, Cassell [1933] 2 v.

Vol. 1, p. 55–416, and the whole of Vol. 2 consist primarily of biographies of violinists, grouped by period, and under period by country. Biographical index, Vol. 2, p. 443–73. Information on many obscure violinist-composers not elsewhere readily accessible, with lists of works by catagory.

192

Thornsby, Frederick, W., ed. Dictionary of organs and organists. Bournemouth, H. Logan [1912] 364 p.

Chiefly concerned with 19th-century British organs and organists.

P. 111–231: "Brief specifications of the principal organs in the British Isles." P. 239–352: "The organist's *who's who*: Brief biographical notes of the leading British organists."

193

Valdrighi, Luigi Francesco. . . . Nomocheliurgografia antica e moderna; ossia, elenco di favvricatori di strumenti armonici con note esplicative e documenti estratti dall'archivio di stato in Modena. . . . Modena, Coi tipi della Societa tipografica, 1884. 327 p.

P. 2–106: an alphabetical listing of 3,516 instrument makers, giving name, nationality, dates of birth and death, name of special instrument, and the school, style, or system. Many of these names are given fuller biographical treatment in the section following, p. 107 to end.

194
Vannes, René. Dictionnaire universel des luthiers. 2nd éd. revue et augmentée. Bruxelles, Les Amis de la Musique, 1951. 408 [163] p.
Tome second. Tome additif et correctif. Bruxelles, 1959. 198, lviii p.
First published in 1932, Paris, Fischbacher, under the title *Essai d'un dictionnaire universel....*
Most comprehensive of all dictionaries of violin makers. Each volume has its own alphabet of biographical entries. Bibliographical references. Both volumes combined give 3,400 facsimiles of makers' labels. Vol. 2, p. 67–198: index of makers by place of birth or center of activity.
Review by Doris Commander in *Violins and violinists,* 12 (Nov., 1951) p. 326; review of *Tome second* by Albert Van der Linden in *Revue belge de musicologie,* 14 (1960) p. 144, and by William Lichtenwanger in *Notes,* 17 (1960) p. 577.

195
Vercheval, Henri. Dictionnaire du violoniste. . . . Paris, Fischbacher, 1923. 192 p.
Part I, p. 9–141, includes terms of interest to violinists, history of stringed instruments, etc. Part II, p. 143–92, is a biographical dictionary of violinists, composers, teachers, violin and bow makers, giving dates and nationalities.

196
Wörthmüller, Willi. "Die Nürnberger Trompeten- und Posaunenmacher des 17. und 18. Jahrhunderts." In *Mitteilungen des Vereins für Geschichte der Stadt Nürnberg.* Bd. 46 (1955) p. 372–480.
Also published separately.
A musicological study the major portion of which is a dictionary of 40 Nuremberg brass instrument makers of the baroque period, with a listing of their surviving instruments. Tracing of monograms and other makers' devices. 5 plates.

197
Wright, Rowland. Dictionnaire des instruments de musique; étude de lexicologie. London, Battley Bros., 1941. 192 p.
An etymological dictionary of names for musical instruments mentioned

in French writings from ancient times to the end of the 19th-century. Extremely well documented; precise bibliographical references. One of the few dictionaries of terms to employ a thoroughly etymological approach.

198

Zuth, Josef. Handbuch der Laute und Gitarre. Wien, Verlag der Zeitschrift für die Gitarre, 1926. 297 p.

Terms, biographies of performers, instrument makers, and composers, giving titles of compositions, publishers, and dates. International coverage for all periods, including many early names. A scholarly work, with supported statements and bibliographical references.

Terms

Dictionaries of terms have a longer history than any other form of music lexicography. Their prototype is Johannes Tinctoris' *Terminorum musicae diffinitorium* (no. 224), a work compiled in the late 15th-century. Almost equally significant is Sébastian de Brossard's *Dictionnaire de musique*, 1701 (no. 204), one of the first in the long line of "modern" dictionaries of music.

A few specialized dictionaries of terms will be found under other headings in this volume. See no. 170 (pipe organ stops); no. 178 (names of musical instruments); no. 229 (liturgical music terms).

199

Apel, Willi. Harvard dictionary of music. Cambridge, Mass., Harvard Univ. Press, 1947. 833 p.

First printed in 1944.

The standard reference work in English for nonbiographical information, designed to provide accurate and pertinent information on all musical topics. Emphasis on the historical approach. Good bibliographies; excellent brief historical articles.

The fifth printing (1947) contains a section of "Addenda and corrigenda to original entries," p. 825–33.

200

Apel, Willi and Ralph T. Daniel. The Harvard brief dictionary of music. Cambridge, Mass, Harvard Univ. Press, 1960. 341 p.

Paperback edition: New York, Washington Square Press, 1961.

Review by James B. Coover in *Notes*, 18 (1961) p. 239–40.

201

Baker, Theodore. Dictionary of musical terms . . . with a supplement containing an English-Italian vocabulary for composers. New York, G. Schirmer [1923] 257 p.

First published in 1895.

Useful small manual, with brief definitions of English and foreign words, especially those used in performance. More extended articles on topics such as pitch, notation, instruments. More than 9,000 terms treated.

202

Bobillier, Marie (Michel Brenet, pseud.). Dictionnaire pratique et historique de la musique. Paris, A. Colin, 1926. 487 p.

2nd edition appeared in 1930.

The standard French dictionary of terms, including terms from Greek and medieval music theory, historical sketches of musical forms. Fairly long articles, excellent small illustrations. No bibliographies.

203

Bobillier, Marie (Michel Brenet, pseud.). Diccionario de la musica, histórico y técnico. Traddución de la última edición francesa, revisada y notablemente ampliada con multitud de artículos nuevos . . . por José B. Humbert, J. Ricart Matas & Aurelio Capmany. Barcelona, Iberia, J. Gil [1946] 548 p.

Translation of the 2nd edition of the preceding, revised and with special emphasis on Spanish terms, Latin and South American terminology and folklore. Profusely illustrated.

204

Brossard, Sébastien de. Dictionnaire de musique contenant une explication des termes grecs, latins, italiens & françois les plus usitez dans la musique . . . Facsimile of the first folio edition, Paris, 1703. Amsterdam, Antiqua, 1964.

First printed in 1701, in octavo; 2nd edition, 1705.

Brossard's *Dictionnaire* is the prototype for all modern dictionaries of musical terms. It also contains a listing of more than 900 authors who have written about music. For an early English musical dictionary based on Brossard, see no. 209.

205

Carter, Henry H. A dictionary of Middle English musical terms. Bloomington, Indiana, Indiana Univ. Press, [1961] 655 p. (Indiana University humanities series, 45.)

[51]

Terms are not only defined but quoted in their original contexts with citation of their sources. P. 569–604: bibliography of works quoted; p. 605–49: works consulted but not quoted.

Review by Leonard Ellinwood in *Notes*, 19 (1962) p. 262–63.

206
Dolzhanskiĭ, A. Kratkiĭ muzykalnyi slovar. 3rd ed. Moskva, 1959. 517 p.

First published, Leningrad, 1952.

207
Elsevier's Dictionary of Cinema, Sound and Music, in six languages: English/American, French, Spanish, Italian, Dutch, and German. Compiled and arranged on an English alphabetical base by W. E. Clason. Amsterdam/New York, Elsevier Publishing Co., 1956. 948 p.

One of a series of polyglot technical dictionaries relating to special fields of science and industry. 3,213 terms, with brief definitions and the equivalent phrases in French, Spanish, Italian, Dutch, and German. Indexes in each of the five languages.

208
Gerigk, Herbert. Fachwörterbuch der Musik. [Münchberg i. Bayern] B. Hahnefeld [1954] 206 p.

A small, useful dictionary of German definitions of the most common musical terms, in French, Italian, Latin, with some in English.

Review by Richard Schaal in *Die Musikforschung*, 8 (1955) p. 245.

209
Grassineau, James. A musical dictionary; being a collection of terms and characters, as well ancient as modern; including the historical, theoretical, and practical parts of music. . . . London, Printed for J. Wilcox, 1740. 347 p.

Reprint projected by Frits A. M. Knuf, Hilversum, Holland, as Vol. 2 of the series *Facsimile reprints of early music dictionaries.*

Largely an adaption of Brossard (no. 204), but with some additions. A later edition, 1769, has an appendix containing additional terms from Rousseau's *Dictionnaire de musique* (no. 217).

210
Janovka, Tomas Baltazar. Clavis ad thesaurum magnae artis musicae, seu elucidarium omnium ferè rerum av verborum, in musica figurali tam vocali, quàm instrumentali abvenietum. Consistens potissimum in definitionibus & divisionibus; quibusdam recentioribus de scala, tono, cantu, &

genere musicae & c. sententijs, variísque exquisitis observationibus . . . alphabetico ordine compositum à Thoma Balthasare Janovka. Vetero-Pragae, in Magno collegio Carolino typis Georgij Labaun, 1701. 324 p.

Scheduled for reprint publication by Frits A. M. Knuf, Hilversum, Holland, as Vol. 3 of the series *Facsimile reprints of early music dictionaries.*

This work shares with Brossard (no. 204) the distinction of being one of the first modern dictionaries of musical terms. The two compilers worked simultaneously but independently of each other.

211

Katayen, Lelia and Val Telberg. Russian-English dictionary of musical terms. New York, Telberg Book Corp., 1965. 125 leaves. (Typescript.)

Russian-English equivalents in musical terminology. No definitions. Short bibliography.

212

Koch, Heinrich Christoph. Musikalisches Lexikon, welches die theoretische und praktische Tonkunst, encyclopädisch bearbeitet, alle alten und neuen Kunstwörter erklärt, und die alten und neuen Instrumente beschreiben, enthält. . . . Frankfurt am Main, A. Hermann dem Jüngern, 1802. 2 v.

One of the first of a long line of German dictionaries of terms. Particularly important for definitions and concepts pertaining to late baroque and classic music and instruments.

A revised edition, by Arrey von Dommer, printed in Heidelberg, 1865, has very little resemblance to the original.

Reprint publication by Georg Olms, Hildesheim, 1964.

213

Lichtenthal, Pietro. Dizionario e bibliografia della musica. Milano, A. Fontana, 1826. 4 v.

The first 2 volumes of this work are a dictionary of terms, the last 2, a bibliography of music literature based on Forkel's *Allegemeine Literatur der Musik* (see no. 425). A French edition of the dictionary of terms, "traduit et augmenté par Dominique Mondo," appeared in Paris in 1839.

See also no. 432.

214

Limenta, Fernando. Dizionario lessicografico musicale italiano-tedesco-italiano. Milano, Hoepli, 1940. 391 p.

Designed to provide precise Italian equivalents for German technical terms not adequately treated in most dictionaries.

215
Padelford, Frederick M. Old English musical terms. Bonn, P. Hanstein, 1899. 112 p. (Bonner Beiträge zur Anglistik, 4.)

216
Pulver, Jeffrey. A dictionary of old English music and musical instruments. London, Kegan Paul; New York, E. P. Dutton, 1923. 247 p.

Terms used by Tudor and early Stuart musicians. Fairly long articles, with references to early literary and musical sources for the terms. 10 plates of early English instruments.

217
Rousseau, Jean J. Dictionnaire de musique. Paris, Duchesne, 1768. 548 [i.e. 556] p. 13 folded plates.

Several editions published in Paris and Amsterdam during the 18th-century. An English edition, translated by William Waring, published under the title *A complete dictionary of music*, 2nd edition, London, 1779.

Based on articles written by Rousseau for the Diderot and d'Alembert *Encyclopedia* but not included in that work. Reflects the stimulating and highly personal views of an 18th-century man of letters. Wide influence and considerable historical importance.

218
Sacher, Jack, ed. Music A to Z. Based on the work of Rudolf Stephen. [Translators: Mieczyslaw Kolinski and others] New York, Grosset & Dunlap, 1963. 432 p.

A translation, with additions and corrections, of Rudolf Stephen's music dictionary in the Fischer Lexikon series, see no. 222.

Review by Theodore Karp in *JAMS*, 17 (1964), p. 394–95; by Harold Samuel in *Notes*, 20 (1963), p. 658–59.

219
Sinzig, Pedro. Dicionário musical. Rio de Janeiro, Kosmos, 1947. 613 p.

A modern Portuguese-language dictionary of terms. Based largely on Apel and Riemann. Bibliographical references.

220
Smith, W. J. A dictionary of musical terms in four languages. London, Hutchinson [1961] 195 p.

English terms with equivalents in French, Italian, and German. Pronunciations given in phonetic symbols. No definitions.

221
Stainer, Sir John and W. A. Barrett. Dictionary of musical terms.
New and rev. ed. London, Novello, 1898. 464 p.

Terms in Italian, French, Latin, German, Hebrew, Greek, Russian,
Spanish, Arabic, with brief definitions in English.

222
Stephen, Rudolf. Musik. [Frankfurt am Main] Fischer Verlag [1957]
382 p. (Das Fischer Lexikon, Enzyklopädie des Wissens, 5.)

General articles cover major topics, with more detailed information
approached through an index. Topical bibliographies, p. 355–64. 10 plates.
A scholarly summation of musical knowledge for the general reader.

223
Thiel, Eberhard. Sachwörterbuch der Musik. Stuttgart, Alfred
Kröner Verlag, 1962. 602 p. (Kröners Taschenausgabe, 210.)

Review by Harold Samuel in *Notes*, 20 (1963) p. 658.

224
Tinctoris, Johannes (Jean). Dictionary of musical terms. An English
translation of *Terminorum musicae diffinitorium* together with the Latin text.
Translated and annotated by Carl Parrish [with a bibliographical essay by
James B. Coover] New York, Free Press [1963] 108 p.

A 15th-century dictionary of musical terms, and one of the first books on
music to be printed. 291 terms defined. Important for an understanding of
Renaissance music theory and practice. The Latin text was reprinted in
Coussemaker's *Scriptorum* (1867), in Forkel's *Allgemeine Literatur der Musik*
(1792), and with a German translation in Chrysander's *Jahrbuch der
Musikwissenschaft*, I (1863). It appeared in a French translation with intro-
duction and commentary by Armand Machabey (Paris, 1951), and in an
Italian translation by Lionello Cammarota (Rome, 1965).

225
Tovey, Donald F. Musical articles from the *Encyclopaedia britannica*.
London, New York, Oxford Univ. Press, 1944. 256 p.

Paperback edition: New York, Meridian Books, 1956, as *The forms of
music*.

28 articles on the larger aspects of music. Shorter ones (madrigal, sonata,
etc.) are briefly historical; others (harmony, sonata forms, etc.) are comprehensive and analytical. Reprinted from Tovey's contributions to the 11th
edition of the *Britannica*.

[55]

226
Vannes, René. . . . Essai de terminologie musical. Dictionnaire universel comprenant plus de 15,000 termes de musique en italien-espagnol-portugais-français-anglias-alleman-latin et grec. . . . Thann, "Alsatia," ca. 1925. 230 p.

Most extensive manual of its kind, containing 15,000 entries in 8 languages. Includes forms, terms, instruments in current use. Brief definitions given under the original or characteristic language, with equivalents in other languages. No explanatory or historical material.

227
Wotton, Tom S. A dictionary of foreign musical terms, and handbook of orchestral instruments. Leipzig, Breitkopf u. Härtel, 1907. 226 p.

Less comprehensive than Vannes (no. 226). Designed as an aid to score reading, including orchestral terms, instruments, tempo indications, etc. Primarily in French, German, and Italian.

Church Music

This section begins with a list of several general dictionaries relating to church music. This is followed by a list of handbooks on the hymnology of various Protestant groups, with citations under the denominations represented. Such handbooks are essentially bibliographies of sacred music, but most of them contain enough biographical and factual information to justify listing them among the encyclopedias and dictionaries of church music.

228
Carroll, J. Robert. Compendium of liturgical music terms. Toledo, Ohio, Gregorian Institute of America, 1964. 86 p.

An attempt to provide a single source for information most frequently requested by students and working church musicians (Preface).

229
Hughes, Anselm. Liturgical terms for music students; a dictionary. Boston, McLaughlin & Reilly [1940] 40 p.

Concise definitions of terms likely to occur in the literature of ancient ecclesiastical music of the West. Tables give structure of mass and office. Includes terms from the church calendar, terms referring to notation, texts with explanations of their places in the liturgy.

[56]

230
Julian, John. A dictionary of hymnology, setting forth the origin and history of Christian hymns of all ages and nations. Rev. ed. with new suppl. London, J. Murray, 1907. 1,768 p.
Unaltered reprint in 2 volumes, New York, Dover, 1957.
First published in 1892.
Entries under authors, titles, and subjects of hymn texts. Brief but adequate biographical notices. Long articles on American, English, Latin, etc. hymnody. For individual hymns gives original publication and location in other hymnals. Contains a vast amount of information on musical and literary aspects of Christian hymnody.

231
Kornmüller, P. Utto. Lexikon der kirchichen Tonkunst. . . . 2. verb. und verm. Aufl. Regensburg, A. Coppenrath, 1891–95. 2 v. in 1.
First published in 1870.
Vol. 1: Dictionary of subjects, terms, instruments connected with Catholic church music, with a subject index of topics discussed in extended articles.
Vol. 2: Biographical dictionary of church musicians. Published works cited for early names, categories of compositions for recent ones.

232
McCutchan, Robert G. Hymn tune names, their sources and significance. Nashville, Tenn., Abingdon Press [1957] 206 p.
Alphabetical listing of tunes, giving their metrical structures and thematic incipits in letter notation. Commentary related to authors, composers, and sources. Numerous cross references. Melodic index. First line index of texts, with author, translator, and tune name.

233
Kümmerle, Salomon. Encyklopädie der evangelischen Kirchenmusik. Gütersloh, E. Bertelsmann, 1888–95. 4 v.
Originally published in Lieferungen, 1883–95.
Terms and biographies related to Protestant church music. Entries for chorale titles, with full musical quotations of the melodies. The author was responsible for basic research on the melodies of the Lutheran chorale.
Review by Friedrich Spitta in *Vierteljahrschrift für Musikwissenschaft*, 1 (1885) p. 235–38.

234
Ortigue, Joseph Louis d'. Dictionnaire liturgique, historique et théorique de plain-chant et de musique d'église, au moyen âge et dans les

temps modernes. Paris, J. P. Migne, 1853. 1,563 p. (Nouvelle encylopédie théologique, Tome 29.)

A pioneer reference work on liturgical music, of considerable historical importance. Documented with frequent references to the works of the leading 18th- and early 19th-century specialists in church music.

235
Stubbins, George W. A dictionary of church music. London, Epworth Press [1949] 128 p.

A practical reference book for the use of church organists and choir directors. Short explanations of technical terms and concise information on topics related to church music.

236
Weissenbäck, Andreas. Sacra musica; Lexikon der katholischen Kirchenmusik. Klosterneuburg, Augustinus Druckerei, 1937, 419 p.

Biography, terms, and subjects in one alphabet. Articles on religious organizations and music publishing houses. More comprehensive in coverage than Kornmüller (no. 231) but the articles are briefer.

Congregational

237
Companion to Congregational Praise. Edited by K. L. Parry, with notes on the music by Erik Routley. London, Independent Press [1953] 580 p.

P. 1–336: notes on the words and music for 884 hymns and chants. P. 337–550: biographical notes on hymn writers and composers. Chronological listing of 396 musical sources. Index of tune names and first-line index of hymns.

Episcopal

238
Protestant Episcopal Church in the U.S.A. The Hymnal 1940 companion. [3rd ed. rev.] New York, Church Pension Fund, 1956. 741 p. First published in 1949.

Contains historical essays on texts and tunes; biographies of authors, composers, translators, and arrangers. List of organ works based on hymn tunes, with publishers. Index of scriptural tests; general index; melodic index; index of tunes; first-line index.

239
Protestant Episcopal Church of England. Historical companion to hymns, ancient and modern. Edited by Maurice Frost. London, Printed for the Proprietors by William Clowes & Sons, 1962. 716 p.

The latest revision of a work compiled in 1909 by W. H. Frere, under the title *Historical edition of hymns ancient and modern*; revised in 1950.

P. 1–124: Introduction, with contributions by Egon Wellesz, Ruth Massenger, C. E. Pocknee, and Lowther Clarke, covering the history of hymnody and of the Anglican hymnal. P. 125–478: Texts and commentary for 636 hymns, including the language of the original if translated. Index of first lines, brief biographies of hymn writers, chronological list of authors and translators, alphabetical index of tunes, index of plainsong, notes on the composers, with chronology, list of publications and tunes, metrical index.

Evangelical and Reformed

240
Haeussler, Armin. The story of our hymns: the handbook to the hymnal of the Evangelical and Reformed Church. St. Louis, Eden Publishing House, 1952. 1,088 p.

Commentrary on 561 hymns and other liturgical pieces. Biographies of hymn writers and notes on sources. Bibliography. Index of scriptural texts, topical index, metrical index, indexes of tune names, composers, arrangers, and sources. First line index.

Lutheran

241
Polack, William G. The handbook of the Lutheran hymnal. 2nd and rev. ed. St. Louis, Concordia [1942] 681 p.

Texts of and commentary on 660 Lutheran hymns. Biographical and historical notes on the authors and composers. Index of biblical references, table of hymns for feasts and festivals, first-line index, including stanzas of hymns; index of tunes, metrical index, topical index, index of authors and translators.

Mennonite

242
Hostetler, Lester. Handbook to the Mennonite hymnary. Newton, Kansas, General Conference of the Mennonite Church of North America, Board of Publications, 1949. 425 p.

[59]

Commentary on 623 Mennonite hymns and other liturgical pieces. Bibliography. Indexes.

Methodist

243

McCutchan, Robert G. Our hymnody, a manual of the Methodist hymnal. 2nd ed. New York, Abingdon Press, 1942. 619 p.

First published in 1937.

Commentary on 664 hymns and other liturgical pieces. Hymn calendar, bibliography, and 9 special indexes.

Mormon

244

Cornwall, J. Spencer. Stories of our Mormon hymns. 2nd edition, revised and enlarged. Salt Lake City, Utah, Deseret Book Co., 1963. 302 p.

A popular companion to the Mormon hymnal, giving information on composers and writers of texts for approximately 311 hymns used in the Mormon church.

Presbyterian

245

Handbook to the Hymnal. Philadelphia, Presbyterian Board of Christian Education, 1935. 566 p.

Unitarian

246

Foote, Henry W. American Unitarian hymn writers and hymns. Compiled for the Hymn Society of America for publication in the Society's proposed *Dictionary of American hymnology*. Cambridge, Mass. [Author] 1959. 270 leaves (typescript).

Contains an historical sketch of American Unitarian hymnody, a catalog of American Unitarian hymn books, alphabetical list of hymn writers, biographical sketches, and first-line index of published hymns.

[60]

Opera and Theatre Music

Dictionaries of opera and theater music are of two principal kinds: (1) they are compilations of facts related to the history or to the production of musical dramatic works (*The Opera directory*, no. 273, is a good example); or (2) they are listings of operatic works, often chronological or associated with a particular place (e.g., Loewenberg's *Annals of opera*, no. 263, or Bauer's *Opern und Operetten in Wien*, no. 248). Titles in the latter category might be regarded properly as bibliographies of music, but we have entered them here in order to concentrate materials on the musical theater in one section.

Listeners' guides to opera and collections of opera plots have been excluded.

One encyclopedia of theater arts demands mention at this point, although its coverage extends far beyond the realm of music. This is the *Enciclopedia dello spettacolo*. Roma, Casa Editrice le Maschere, 1954–62, 9 v.) published under the auspices of the Cini Foundation. It is an illustrated reference work covering all aspects of the theater, with contributions by outstanding authorities in the field.

See also *Le Grandi Voci*, no. 64, a biographical dictionary of opera celebrities.

247

    Altmann, Wilhelm. Katalog der seit 1861 in den Handel gekommenen theatralischen Musik (Opern, Operetten, Possen, Musik zu Schauspielen, usw.). Ein musikbibliographischer Versuch . . . Wolfenbüttel, Verlag für musikalische Kultur und Wissenschaft, 1935. 384 p. (incomplete).

This work was published in *Lieferungen*, of which four appeared carrying the entries through "Siegmund, Josef."

Operas, ballets, and incidental music since 1861, arranged under composer with references from librettist, etc. Gives brief titles of works, type, librettist, date of first performance if known, type of score, language of text, and publisher. There is no key to the abbreviations of publishers' names, but most of these can be readily identified.

248

    Bauer, Anton. Opern und Operetten in Wien; Verzeichnis ihrer Erstaufführungen in der Zeit von 1629 bis zur Gegenwart. Graz-Köln, Hermann Böhlaus Nachf., 1955. 156 p. (Wiener musikwissenschaftliche Beiträge, 2.)

4,856 stage works, listed by title, with indexes by composer, author, and chronology.

249

    Bernandt, Grigoriĭ B. Slovar' oper. Vpervye postavlennykh ili izdannykh v dorevoliŭtsionnoĭ Rossii i v SSSR. Moskva, Sovetskiĭ Kompozitor, 1962. 554 p.

[61]

A dictionary of operas first performed or first published in Russia during the period 1736–1959. Entries are alphabetical by title. Information includes genre of the work, composer, first performance, librettist, and literary source, and many details that relate to production. Indexed by composer, librettist, and author of the original literary source.

250

Bignami, Luigi. Cronologia di tutti gli spettacoli rappresentati al Teatro Comunale di Bologna della sua apertura 14 Maggio 1763 a tutto l'autunno 1881. Bologna, Mattiuzzi, 1882. 248 p.

The entries consist in transcriptions of theater bills for the period under consideration. All types of dramatic works are included, but by far the largest part of the repertory is opera. Numerous indexes of performers, composers, authors, and other categories of theater personnel.

251

Burton, Jack. The blue book of Broadway musicals. Watkins Glen, N.Y., Century House [1952] 320 p.

Lists title, date, composer, author, principals, and musical numbers for more than 1,500 operettas, musical comedies, and reviews from the 1890s to 1951. Arranged by decades, with a general introduction to each period.

252

Burton, Jack. The blue book of Hollywood musicals; songs from the sound tracks and the stars who sang them since the birth of the talkies a quarter-century ago. Watkins Glen, N.Y., Century House [1953] 296 p.

Complementing *The blue book of Tin Pan Alley* (1951) and *The blue book of Broadway musicals* (1952), this present anthology completes a trilogy on popular music (Introduction).

See also *The blue book of Tin Pan Alley* (1962) entered under "Bibliographies of Music: Jazz and Popular," no. 714.

253

Clemént, Félix et Pierre Larousse. Dictionnaire des opéras (Dictionnaire lyrique) contenant l'analyse et la nomenclature de tous les opéras, opéras-comiques, opérettes et drames lyrique représentés en France et à l'étranger depuis l'origine de ces genres d'ouvrages jusqu'à nos jours. . . . Rev. et mis à jour par Arthur Pougin. Paris, Libraire Larousse [1905] 1,203 p.

First published in 1869 under the title *Dictionnaire lyrique*.

Title entries (frequently under the French form, with references to other forms) for operas and comic operas presented in France and elsewhere from the beginnings to the date of publication. For each entry: language of text, number of acts, authors of words and music, place and date of first performance, brief sketch of plot, occasional criticism. Index of composers. A comprehensive work.

254

Dassori, Carlo. Opere e operisti (dizionario lirico 1541–1902). . . . Genova, Tipografia editrice R. Istituto Sordomuti, 1903. 977 p.

Includes 15,406 operas by 3,628 composers. Author and title lists only, no descriptive and critical matter.

Part I: Alphabetical list of composers, with dates of birth and death, chronological list, under composer, of operas, with dates and places of first performances.

Part II: Title list of all operas that have been performed in Italy.

255

Eaton, Quaintance. Opera production: a handbook. Minneapolis, University of Minnesota Press, 1961. 266 p.

Contains uesful information on 224 "long" and 148 "short" operas, including timings, difficulty of leading roles, instrumentation, source and cost of scores and parts, photographs of productions, lists of performing groups.

256

Filippis, Felice de et R. Arnese. Cronache del Teatro di S. Carlo (1737–1960). Napoli, Edizioni Politica Popolare, 1961. 466 p.

P. 25–112: chronological listing, by year, of first performances of operas given at the San Carlo Opera in Naples from 1737 to 1960.

P. 113–304: a biographical dictionary of opera composers, with lists of their major works.

Indexes of librettists and singers; summary of the seasons in which each work was performed. 76 full-page illustrations.

257

Fog, Dan. The Royal Danish Ballet, 1760–1958, and August Bournonville. A chronological catalogue of the ballets and ballet-divertissements performed at the Royal Theatres of Copenhagen, and a catalogue of August Bournonville's works. Copenhagen, Dan Fog, 1961. 79 p.

Lists 516 ballet works performed by the Royal Danish Ballet, citing the choreographer, composer, and publisher of the music if available. Index of titles and of persons. Facsimile plates of music title pages.

258

Galvani, Livio Niso. I teatri musicali di Venezia nel secolo XVII (1637–1700). Memorie storiche e bibliografiche. Milano, Ricordi, 1878. 193 p.

Operas performed in Venice during the 17th-century, listed chronologically under 16 different theaters or opera houses. Entries listed by title, with composer, librettist, publication data of libretti, dedicatee, and much useful information. Indexes of names, titles, librettists, and composers.

259

Gatti, Carlo. Il teatro alla Scala, nella storia e nell'arte (1778–1963). Milano, Ricordi, 1964. 2 v.

A handsome set, the second volume of which contains the chronicles of La Scala, complete inventories of the opera, ballet, and concert performances from 1778 to the present, and an analytical index. The chronologies were compiled by Giampiero Tintori.

260

Johnson, H. Earle. Operas on American subjects. New York, Coleman-Ross Co., 1964. 125 p.

An alphabetical listing, by composer, of operas from the 17th-century to the present based on American subject matter or involving American characters. The entries supply much interesting information related to plot, performance, and estimates by contemporary critics. Topical, title, and general indexes.

See also Julius Mattfeld's *A handbook of American operatic premieres*, no. 265.

261

Lessing, G. E. Handbuch des Opern-Repertoires. [Neubearbeitung] London, New York, Boosey & Hawkes, 1952, 393 p.

An organized compilation of facts related to the performance of 392 operas in the current repertoire, including casts of characters, locales of action, instrumentation, duration of acts, dates of first performance, and publishers of the music.

A work of reference intended for the use of theatrical managers, conductors, dramatists and in libraries (Author's Preface).

262

Lewine, Richard and Alfred Simon. Encyclopedia of theater music: a comprehensive listing of more than 4,000 songs from Broadway and Hollywood, 1900–60. New York, Random House [1961] 248 p.

[64]

A guide to the song repertory of the American musical theater.

Part I: Theater songs 1900–24. Part II: Theater songs 1925–60. Part III: Motion picture songs. Part IV: Show chronology 1925–60.

Songs are listed alphabetically by title, with composer, lyricist, show, and year given. List of published vocal scores and index of shows.

263

Loewenberg, Alfred. Annals of opera, 1597–1940, compiled from the original sources; with an introduction by Edward J. Dent. 2nd ed., rev. and corrected. Genève, Societas Bibliographica [1955] 2 v.

First published in 1943 by W. Heffer, Cambridge. 879 p.

Vol. 1: chronological listing of operas by dates of first performance, including (with a few exceptions) only works known to have been produced. The list is limited to older operas that are extant and modern ones that have created interest outside their countries of origin. Each entry includes composer's name, original title of the work, English translation for all languages except German, French, and Italian. Librettist identified; place and date of first performance given.

Vol. 2: indexes by title, composer, librettist, and a general index for other names, places, and subjects.

A work of distinguished scholarship; essential for the historical study of opera.

Review of 2nd edition by Edward N. Waters, in *Notes*, 13 (1956) p. 285–86.

264

Manferrari, Umberto. Dizionario universale delle opere melodrammatiche. Firenze, Sansoni, 1954–55. 3 v. (Contributi alla biblioteca bibliografica italica, 4, 8, 10.)

One of the most comprehensive of all listings of opera. Entries under composer, giving title, librettist, place and date of first performance, and first performances in other opera houses.

265

Mattfeld, Julius. A handbook of American operatic premieres, 1731–1962. Detroit, Information Service, Inc., 1963. 142 p. (Detroit studies in music bibliography, 5.)

This guide to operatic performances in the United States attempts to present a record of the premieres of nearly 2,000 operas and related works from 1731 to the end of 1962. . . . Included are operas by native and naturalized composers, which have been performed outside the country (Preface).

Works listed alphabetically by title, with a composer index.

266

Moore, Frank L. Crowell's handbook of world opera. New York, Crowell, 1961. 683 p.

Contains brief information on individual operas, "people in opera," "characters in the operas," "first lines and titles of famous numbers," chronological list of important operas, glossary of terms used in opera, themes, recordings, and indexes of singers by voice range.

267

Mooser, Robert-Aloys. Opéras, intermezzos, ballets, cantates, oratorios joués en Russie durant le XVIIIe siècle. . . . Essai d'un répertoire alphabétique et chronologique. 3e édition revue et complétée. Bale, Bärenreiter, 1964. 177 p.

First published in 1945; 2nd edition, 1955.

Gives librettist, translators of work, date and place of first performance, language of performance, date of publication of the libretto, etc. Sources of information are well documented. Indexes.

Review by Anna A. Abert of the 2nd ed. in *Die Musikforschung*, 9 (1956) p. 106.

268

Opera Manual: a handbook of practical operatic information. Edited by Mrs. Charles A. Matz and Marguerite Wickersham. New York, Central Opera Service, 1956.

Contains lists of operas in modern translation; chamber operas, citing voices and instruments needed, sets, duration, source of music. Information on costume and scenery rentals. Bibliography of stagecraft materials; lists of awards for singers; opera activity in the U.S., 1955–56; addresses of publishers, opera groups; unpublished translations, sources of chamber operas, etc.

269

Richard Rodgers Fact Book. New York, the Lynn Farnol Group, Inc., 1965. 582 p.

A compendium of facts related to the career of Richard Rodgers. Largest section devoted to his stage, film, and television scores; works entered chronologically from 1920 to 1965, with production information, story, cast, musical numbers, and excerpts from contemporary reviews. General bibliography and discography; indexes of musical compositions and productions.

270

Rieck, Waldemar. Opera plots, an index to the stories of operas, operettas, etc., from the sixteenth to the twentieth century. New York, The New York Public Library, 1927. 102 p.

> Over 200 books and editions published in English, French, German and Danish during the past 80 years have been indexed; 998 composers are represented by more than 2,775 works in operatic form (Introduction).

271

Riemann, Hugo. Opern-Handbuch. Repertorium der dramatisch-musikalischen Litteratur (Opern, Operetten, Ballette, Melodramen, Pantomimen, Oratorien, dramatische Kantaten, usw.). Leipzig, H. Seemann Nachfolger [n.d.] 862 p.

Originally published by C. A. Koch, Leipzig, 1887. Intended as an opera supplement to Riemann's *Lexikon*.

Title articles give genre, number of acts, composer, librettist, first performance. Composer articles give dates, chronological list of operas. Librettist entries give dates and chief activity.

272

Rosenthal, Harold and John Warrack. Concise Oxford dictionary of opera. London, Oxford Univ. Press, 1964. 446 p.

A richly informative pocket dictionary of opera. Special emphasis laid on the growth of opera in Eastern Europe, on literary backgrounds and relationships, and on singers. Includes a brief bibliography for further study.

273

Ross, Anne. The opera directory. London, John Calder; New York, Sterling Pub. Co., [1961] 566 p.

A source book of current opera facts and figures. Introductions and headings in 6 languages (English, French, German, Italian, Spanish, Russian). Material organized under 13 headings, the most important of which are: opera singers, conductors, producers and designers, technical staff, theaters and producing organizations, festivals, living composers, works by living composers, librettists, colleges and schools of music, casting index, glossary.

The identical volume is issued with various foreign title pages under the imprints of publishers in Paris, Geneva, Berlin, London, New York, etc.

274

Seltsam, William H. Metropolitan opera annuals. New York, H. W. Wilson Co., 1947. 751 p.

Chronological listing of Metropolitan Opera performances, with casts, from the initial season (1883–84) through 1946–47. Coverage for each season includes roster, excerpts from press reviews of noteworthy performances. Indexed by artist, opera. Supplements issued annually in the final issue of each volume of the periodical *Opera news. First supplement*, 1957, cumulates information for 1945–57.

275

Smith, William C. The Italian opera and contemporary ballet in London, 1789–1820; a record of performances and players with reports from the journals of the time. London, The Society for Theatre Research, 1955. 191 p.

Cites 618 works produced in the London theaters during the period under consideration, with commentary by the author and quotations from contemporary sources. Indexes of operas, burlettas, cantatas; of ballets and divertissements; of singers, ballet personnel, composers, and instrumentalists.

276

Towers, John. Dictionary-catalogue of operas and operettas which have been performed on the public stage. Morgentown, W. Va., Acme Pub. Co. [1910] 1,045 p.

Title list of 28,015 operas, giving for each composer his nationality, and birth and death dates. Alternative or translated titles included. Composer index. No information on librettists, no historical or descriptive material.

277

Wolff, Stéphane. Un demi-siècle d'opéra-comique (1900–50): les oeuvres, les interprètes. Paris, Éditions André Bonne, 1953. 339 p.

I, p. 15–231: the works arranged alphabetically by title, with much detailed information as to cast, production, etc. II, p. 233–339: the interpreters and their roles, a series of biographical sections treating the singers, dancers, conductors and other personnel involved in opéra-comique productions.

278

Wolff, Stéphane. L'Opéra au Palais Garnier, 1875–1962: les oeuvres, les interprètes. Paris, "L'Entr'acte," 1963. 565 p.

A book of facts related to the Paris opéra and its productions from 1875 to the present.

I, p. 23–378: productions listed in several alphabets according to type ("oeuvres lyriques et oratories," "oeuvres chorégraphiques, oeuvres dramatiques," etc.). II, p. 379–552: persons affiliated with the opéra (singers, conductors, dancers, composers, administrative personnel).

Miscellaneous

279
Barlow, Harold and S. Morgenstern. A dictionary of musical themes. New York, Crown [1948] 642 p.
Contains 10,000 themes from instrumental works, arranged alphabetically by composer. Indexed by scale degrees in letter notation, with all themes transposed to C major or minor. Title index.

280
Barlow, Harold and S. Morgenstern. A dictionary of vocal themes. New York, Crown [1950] 547 p.
Reissued, 1966, under the title: *A dictionary of opera and song themes.*
Contains themes from operas, cantatas, oratorios, art songs, and miscellaneous vocal works, arranged alphabetically by composer. Indexed by scale degrees as in the preceding work. Title and first-line index.
Review by Harold Spivacke in *Notes*, 8 (1951) p. 334–35.

281
Berger, Kenneth W. Band encyclopedia. [Evansville, Ind., Distributed by Band Associates, 1960] 604 p.
A compendium of information useful to band directors. Includes revisions of the author's earlier publications: *Band bibliography, Band discography*, and *Bandmen*, a biographical dictionary, of band musicians.
Review by Keith Polk in *Notes*, 18 (1961) p. 424–26; by J. M. Lundahl in *Journal of research in music education*, 10 (1962) p. 81–82.

282
Burrows, Raymond M. and Bessie C. Redmond. Concerto themes. New York, Simon and Schuster [1951] 296 p.
More inclusive than Barlow and Morgenstern (no. 279) for concertos. Arrangement alphabetical by composer. Indexed by concerto titles, keys, solo instruments.

283
Burrows, Raymond M. and Bessie C. Redmond. Symphony themes. New York, Simon and Schuster [1942] 295 p.

284

Cobbett, Walter W., ed. Cyclopedic survey of chamber music. 2nd ed. London, Oxford Univ. Press, 1963. 3 v.

First published in 2 volumes, 1929–30.

Cobbett's *Cyclopedia* is a biographical and subject dictionary of chamber music, giving full lists of works in this category under composer. Solo works and piano compositions included. The main emphasis is critical and analytical. Excellent critical and bibliographical material, with signed articles by outstanding authorities.

The second edition is a reissue of the original two volumes with minor corrections, plus a third volume which brings the work up to date.

Vol. 3 of the 1963 edition is composed of extended articles surveying chamber music since 1929 in Europe, Great Britain, Russia, and America. Editor and principal contributor is Colin Mason. Chapter on "Chamber music in America" by Nicolas Slonimsky; on "Soviet chamber music," by I. I. Martinov. Classified bibliography on chamber music; index of composers.

Review of 2nd edition by Homer Ulrich in *Notes*, 21 (1963–64) p. 124–26.

285

Gammond, Peter and Peter Clayton. Dictionary of popular music. New York, Philosophical Library [1961] 274 p.

A dictionary of names, terms, titles of major popular songs. Listings of works and recordings for principal composers of popular music. Pronounced British slant.

286

Gold, Robert S. A jazz lexicon. New York, Knopf, 1964. 363 p.

A dictionary of terms from the world of jazz. Both musical and sociological interest. Date of usage is specified where possible. Informative introduction and bibliography.

287

Heinzel, Erwin. Lexikon historischer Ereignisse und Personen in Kunst, Literatur und Musik. Wien, Verlag Brüder Hollinek [1956] 782 p.

A dictionary treating the artistic, literary, and musical works based on the lives of historical persons or events as designated by place names. Entries arranged alphabetically with persons and events interfiled. The information includes a summary of the historical details followed by a classified listing of the art works in which the person or event is represented.

287A
Heinzel, Erwin. Lexikon der Kulturgeschichte in Literatur, Kunst und Musik, mit Bibliographie und Ikonographie. Wien, Brüder Hollinek, 1962. 493 p.

A sequel to the author's *Lexikon historischer Ereignisse und Personen* . . . (above). This work is concerned with significant personalities in literature, art, and music as subjects for creative work in the various media. Bibliographies and inconographies included.

288
Read, Gardner. Thesaurus of orchestral devices. New York, Pitman [1953] 631 p.

> Intended to be a lexicon of instrumentation which will serve the student and/or professional orchestrator in the same manner and to the same degree that Bartlett's *Familiar quotations*, Roget's *Thesaurus* . . . aid both the student of literature and the established writer (Preface).

Nomenclature in English, Italian, French, and German, with ranges of instruments, lists of devices with reference to the page and measure number of the score. List of music publishers and their U.S. agents. Index of nomenclature and terminology.

289
Slonimsky, Nicolas. Thesaurus of scales and melodic patterns. New York, Coleman-Ross, 1947. 243 p.

> A reference book . . . for composers in search of new materials.

Contains nearly 1,000 scales, both traditional and contrived.

290
Stambler, Irwin. Encyclopedia of popular music. New York, St. Martin's Press, 1965. 359 p.

Terms, biography, and titles in one alphabet. Special articles: "Tape recorder tips" by Vern Bushway (p. 259–64); "Stereophonic sound" by W. P. Hopper, Jr. (p. 265–68); "New popular song" by Hal Levy (p. 269–71). Appendix lists recipients of awards issued by radio, TV, and motion picture industries. Discography. Bibliography.

H*istories*
and Chronologies

WE have been particularly selective in this area. The titles include only the standard general histories of music in the major European languages, together with some of the more recent outline histories. Excluded are all histories devoted to the music of a particular national group, most early histories (pre-1850) unless, as in the case of Burney, Hawkins, Forkel, or Martini, they are of extraordinary interest and are currently available, and histories of special periods, or forms, except as they occur as part of a comprehensive series. Music histories come and go, and few of those designed for the general reader, or for the music student, may be expected to outlive their time. This will account for the fact that some of the familiar occupants of library shelves, such as Dommer, Naumann, Rowbotham, and Rockstro, are missing from this list.

It is true of the early histories as it was of the early dictionaries that a number of titles have been restored to availability through modern reprint publication. Mention of this fact will be made in the annotations that follow, even though publication may still be in the projected stage as of 1966.

Those who want a comprehensive, chronological listing of music histories will find one in the appendix to Warren Allen's *Philosophies of music history* (no. 1318) under the title "Bibliography of literature concerning the general history of music in chronological order." See also the article "Histories" by S. T. Worsthorne, in *Grove's* 5th edition, Vol. 4, p. 296–306, for both a chronological and a systematic listing.

Histories

291

Abbiati, Franco. Storia della musica. 2nd ed. [Milano] Garzanti [1943–46] 5 v.

A general history of music for Italian readers. Numerous pictorial and musical illustrations. Each major section is followed by an anthology of

[73]

excerpts from the writings of modern authorities on the period under consideration.

Vol. 1: Roma. Medio Evo. Rinascimento. Vol. 2: Seicento. Vol. 3: Settecento. Vol. 4: Ottocento. Vol. 5: Novecento.

292

Adler, Guido, ed. Handbuch der Musikgeschichte. . . . 2. vollständig durchgesehene und stark ergänzte Aufl. Berlin-Wilmersdorf, H. Keller, 1930. 2 v.

Unaltered reprint of the 2nd edition, Schneider, Tutzing, 1961.

First printed in 1924 in 1 volume. Adler's *Handbuch* is the standard compendium of music history, representing the fruits of German scholarship in its most flourishing and influential period. Major articles contributed by such authorities as Alfred Einstein, Wilhelm Fischer, Robert Haas, Friedrich Ludwig, Curt Sachs, Arnold Schering, Peter Wagner, and Egon Wellesz.

293

Ambros, August Wilhelm. Geschichte der Musik. . . . 3. gänzlich umgearb. Aufl. Leipzig, Leuckart, 1887–1911. 5 v.

Republication, by subscription, announced by Georg Olms, Hildesheim, 1966.

One of the last major one-man histories of music. The author did not live to carry the 4th volume past the beginning of the 17th century. Based on original research, the work is particularly important for its coverage of the sources of Medieval and Renaissance music.

Bd. I: Ancient music. 1862. 2nd ed., 1880. 3rd ed., 1887 (B. v. Sokolowsky, ed.).

Bd. II: Music of the Middle Ages. 1864. 2nd ed., 1880 (Otto Kade). 3rd ed., 1891 (Heinrich Riemann).

Bd. III: The Renaissance to Palestrina. 1868. 2nd ed., 1893 (Otto Kade).

Bd. IV: (not completed by Ambros) Italian music, 1550–1650. 1878 (Gustav Nottebohm). 2nd ed., 1881. 3rd ed., 1909 (Hugo Leichtentritt).

Bd. V: "Eine Beispielsammlung zu dem dritten Bande." 1882 (Otto Kade). 2nd ed., 1887. 3rd ed., 1911.

The work by Wilhelm Langhans (see no. 350) was intended to complete the Ambros history from the 17th- through the 19th-century.

294

Bernard, Robert. Histoire de la musique. [Paris] Fernand Nathan, 1961–63. 3 v.

A history of music distinguished for its fine printing and rich illustrative material, including numerous plates in full color. The work lacks bibliography or other documentation. Vol. 1 treats the history of European music to the end of the 18th century; Vols. 2 and 3 are concerned with 19th- and 20th-century developments in Europe and the Americas, with brief discussions of Oriental music.

295
Besseler, Heinrich and Max Schneider, eds. Musikgeschichte in Bildern. v. 1– . Leipzig, Deutscher Verlag für Musik, 1961– .

A large-scale work projected to cover all periods of the history of music in pictures. Publication of the volumes and their subsections (Lieferungen) will not necessarily follow in chronological order. The Kinsky *A history of music in pictures* (no. 330) is taken as a point of departure, but the scope is greatly expanded. Each issue contains numerous plates with commentary, a bibliography, chronological tables, and indexes. Publication to date is as follows:

Band I. *Musikethnologie.* Lieferung 1, Ozeanien (by Paul Collaer) 1965. Lieferung 2, Amerika (by Paul Collaer) 1966.

Band II: *Musik des Altertums.* Lieferung 1, Ägypten (by Hans Hickmann) 1962. Lieferung 4, Greichenland (by Max Wegner) 1963. Lieferung 5, Etrurien und Rom (by Günter Fleischhauer) 1964.

Band III: *Musik des Mittelalters und der Renaissance.* Lieferung 2, Islam (by Henry George Farmer) 1966.

Review by Caldwell Titcomb in *JAMS*, 17 (1964) p. 386–91; by Fritz Bose in *Die Musikforschung*, 17 (1964) p. 184–85.

296
Bonnet, Jacques. Histoire de la musique, et de ses effets, depuis son origine jusqu'à present. . . . Paris, J. Cochart, 1715. 487 p.

One of the first histories of music, it was begun by Pierre Bourdelot, continued by his nephew, Pierre Bonnet, and finally completed and published by the brother of the latter, Jacques Bonnet.

Reprinted by the Akademische Druck- und Verlagsanstalt, Graz, as part of the series, *Die grossen Darstellungen der Musikgeschichte in Barock und Aufklärung*, 1966.

297
Bücken, Ernst, ed. Handbuch der Musikwissenschaft. Wildpark-Potsdam, Akademische Verlagsgesellschaft Athenaion [1927–31] 13 v. in 10. First issued serially in parts.

A series of monographs on various periods and aspects of music history

[75]

by the leading German musicologists of the period between World Wars I and II. Well printed and profusely illustrated, including plates in color. Reprinted by Musurgia, New York, 1949. 13 v. in 9.

298

[Vol. 1] Besseler, Heinrich. *Die Musik des Mittelalters und der Renaissance* [1931] 337 p.

299

[Vol. 2] Blume, Friedrich. *Die evangelische Kirchenmusik* [1931] 171 p. Has been reedited under the title, *Geschichte der evangelischen Kirchenmusik* . . . Herausgegeben unter Mitarbeit von Ludwig Finscher, Georg Feder, Adam Adrio und Walter Blankenburg. Kassel, Bärenreiter, 1965. 465 p.

300

[Vol. 3] Bücken, Ernst. *Geist und Form im musikalischen Kunstwerk* [1929] 195 p.

301

[Vol. 4] Bücken, Ernst. *Die Musik des 19. Jahrhunderts bis zur Moderne* [1929] 319 p.

302

[Vol. 5] Bücken, Ernst. *Die Musik des Rokokos und der Klassik* [1927] 247 p.

303

[Vol. 6] Haas, Robert. *Aufführungspraxis der Musik* [1931] 298 p.

304

[Vol. 7] Haas, Robert. *Die Musik des Barocks* [1929] 290 p.

305

[Vol. 8] Pt. 1. Heinitz, Wilhelm. *Instrumentenkunde* [1929] 159 p.

306

[Vol. 8] Pt. 2. Lachmann, Robert. *Die Musik der aussereuropäischen Natur- und Kulturvölker* [1929] 33 p.

307

[Vol. 8] Pt. 3. Sachs, Curt. *Die Musik der Antike* [1928] 32 p.

308

[Vol. 8] Pt. 4. Panóff, Peter. *Die altslavische Volks- und Kirchenmusik* [1930] 31 p.

309

[Vol. 9] Mersmann, Hans. *Die moderne Musik seit der Romantik* [1928] 225 p.

310

[Vol. 10] Ursprung, Otto. *Die katholische Kirchenmusik.* [1931] 312 p.

311

Burney, Charles. A general history of music, from the earliest times to the present period. With critical and historical notes by Frank Mercer. London, Foulis; New York, Harcourt, 1935. 4 v. in 2.

Originally published in London, 1776–89, 4 v. Burney's history stands with that of John Hawkins at the starting point of modern historical writing in the music field. Of outstanding literary value, its present significance is that of a document of 18th-century musical taste and learning.

A reprint of the Mercer edition by Dover Publications, New York, 1957, 2 v. Reprint of the original edition projected by the Akademische Druck- und Verlagsanstalt, Graz, in the series *Die grossen Darstellungen der Musikgeschichte* . . .

312

Cannon, Beekman C., Alvin H. Johnson and William G. Waite. The art of music, a short history of musical styles and ideas. New York, Crowell [1960] 484 p.

Designed as an introduction to the history of music, presupposing little background. The "basic principles of music" are covered in an appendix. No bibliography. Brief musical examples in the text.

Review by Warner Imig in *Journal of research in music education,* 9 (1961) p. 172.

313

Collaer, Paul and Albert Van der Linden. Atlas historique de la musique, avec la collaboration de F. van den Bremt. . . . Préface de Charles van den Borren. Paris, Elsevier [1960] 179 p.

An illustrated survey of music history. 15 full-page maps relating to various aspects of musical culture and development. More than 700 illustrations. A delight to the eye and a stimulant to the mind.

Review by Robert E. Wolf in *MQ,* 47 (1961) p. 413–16.

314

Combarieu, Jules. Histoire de la musique des origines au début du XXe siècle. Paris, A. Colin, 1946–60. 5 v.

Vols. 1–3 originally published 1913–19.

I: Des origines à la fin du XVIe siècle. II: Du XVIIe siècle à la mort de Beethoven. III: De la mort de Beethoven au début du XXe siècle. IV: L'aube du XXe siècle (by René Dumesnil, 1958). V: La première moitié du XXe siècle (by René Dumesnil, 1960).

315

Confalonieri, Giulio. Storia della musica. Milano, Nuova accademia editrice [1958] 2 v.

A popular general history, lavishly printed on glossy paper, with 34 plates in full color and hundreds of black and white illustrations. No musical examples. Essential bibliography listed by chapter at the end of the second volume, where there is also a general index and an index of illustrations.

316

Corte, Andrea della. Antologia della storia della musica, dalla Grecia antica all'ottocento. 4. ed., rinnovata in un volume. Torino, G. B. Paravia [1945] 491 p.

First published in 1926 in 2 volumes.

An anthology of writings on music history, chiefly by modern European scholars but with a few early documents (excerpts from Zarlino, Galilei, Caccini, Peri, etc.). Italian text.

317

Corte, Andrea della e Guido Pannain. Storia della musica. 2. ed. Torino, Unione Tipografico-Editrice Torinese, 1944. 3 v.

First published in 1935; 2nd edition, 1942, reprinted, 1944.

The standard general history of music for Italian readers.

I: Dal medioevo al seicento. II: Il settecento. III: L'ottocento e il novecento.

318

Crocker, Richard L. A history of musical style. New York, McGraw-Hill, 1966. 573 p.

One of the few histories of music to focus attention consistently on musical style.

319

Dufourcq, Norbert, ed. La musique des origines à nos jours. Préface de Claude Delvincourt. Nouv. éd., rev., augm. Paris, Larousse, 1954. 591 p.

The reprinting of a work first published in 1946.

Richly illustrated compendium of music history and related fields, the work of 44 scholars, chiefly French. Organized in 5 books, of which the

3rd (p. 83–431) deals with the history of Western music. Other books treat of the voice and instruments, ancient and near-Eastern music, non-European music, musical aesthetics. A series of 17 appendixes cover special topics such as notation, music theory, criticism, music libraries and other institutions. 6 colored plates, and numerous black-and-white illustrations.

320
 Einstein, Alfred. A short history of music. 3rd American edition. New York, Knopf, 1947. 438 p.
 Also issued as a paperback. Originally published in German, 1934.
 One of the most perceptive and authoritative concise histories of music. Published in numerous editions and translations. Most editions incorporate a useful anthology of 39 musical examples, originally issued in 1917 as "Beispielsammlung zur älteren Musikgeschichte." A handsome illustrated edition (London, Cassell, 1953) edited by A. Hyatt King unfortunately does not contain the musical supplement.

321
 Ferguson, Donald N. A history of musical thought. 3rd ed. New York, Appleton-Century-Crofts [1959] 675 p.
 First published in 1935; 2nd ed., 1948.
 An influential one-volume work designed for music history courses at the college level. One of the first to propagate the results of German scholarship in America.

322
 Finney, Theodore M. A history of music. Rev. ed. New York, Harcourt, 1947. 720 p.
 First published in 1935. A well organized student's history.

323
 Forkel, Johann Nikolaus. Allgemeine Geschichte der Musik. Leipzig, im Schwikertschen Verlage, 1788–1801. 2 v.
 Reprint projected by the Akademische Druck- und Verlagsanstalt, Graz, in the series *Die grossen Darstellungen der Musikgeschichte* . . .
 The first full-scale history of music in German, by the scholar who has been called "the father of modern musicology." The work is incomplete, covering only as far as the early 16th century.

324
 Gleason, Harold. Music literature outlines. Series 1–5. Rochester, N.Y., Levis Music Stores, 1949–55.

Ser. 1: Music in the Middle Ages and Renaissance. 2nd ed., 1951.
Ser. 2: Music in the Baroque.
Ser. 3: American music from 1620–1920.
Ser. 4: Contemporary American music (mimeographed).
Ser. 5: Chamber music from Haydn to Ravel.

Historical outlines with copious bibliographical references, including recordings. The organization of Series 1 and 2 follows closely that of the works by Reese and Bukofzer in the *Norton history of music series*. (See nos. 354, 356.)

325
Grout, Donald J. A history of Western music. New York, Norton, 1960. 742 p.

Also published in a shortened edition.

Intended for undergraduate college music students or for the general reader. "An elementary knowledge of musical terms and of harmony . . . has been assumed." Based on a stylistic approach. Contains numerous musical and pictorial illustrations. Annotated bibliography for further reading, a chronology of musical and historical events, and a glossary of terms.

Review by Albert T. Luper in *Notes*, 18 (1960) p. 47–48; by Warren Allen in *Journal of research in music education*, 8 (1960) p. 124–26; by Alec Harman in *Musical times* (Dec., 1962) p. 845–47.

326
Gruber, Roman Il'ich. Istoriia muzykal'noĭ kyl'tury. Moskv, Gosudarstvennoe muzykal'noi izdatel'stvo, 1941–59. 2 v.

A general history of music from antiquity to the beginning of the 17th century, for Russian readers. Vol. 1, Part 1, deals with Egypt, Mesopotamia, India, China, etc., as well as Greece and Rome. The final chapter of Vol. 2 is concerned with the musical culture of the Western Slavs to the 17th century.

327
Handschin, Jacques. Musikgeschichte in Überblick. Hrsg. von Franz Brenn. 2. ergänzte Auflage. Luzern, Räber, 1964. 442 p.

First published in 1948.

A stimulating short history weighted in the direction of Medieval and Renaissance music. Chronological tables and a classified bibliography.

Review of the 2nd edition by Joseph Müller-Blattau, in *Die Musikforschung*, 18 (1965) p. 441.

328
Harmen, Alec and Wilfrid Mellers. Man and his music, the story of musical experience in the West. New York, Oxford Univ. Press, 1962. 1,172 p.

First published in 1957–59 in 4 separate volumes. Vol. 1: Medieval and early Renaissance music (up to *c.* 1525). Vol. 2: late Renaissance and Baroque music (*c.* 1525–*c.* 1750). Vol. 3: the sonata principal (from *c.* 1750). Vol. 4: Romanticism and the 20th century.

A history designed for the intelligent layman and stressing the social and cultural backgrounds. Comparative chronology and list of recommended books and music.

Review of Vol. 2 by J. Merrill Knapp in *Notes*, 17 (1960) p. 569–70; of Vols. 3 and 4 by William S. Newman in *Notes*, 15 (1957) p. 99–101; of the composite volume by Jack A. Westrup in *Music and letters*, 43 (1962) p. 265–66.

329
Hawkins, Sir John. A general history of the science and practice of music. London, Payne and Son, 1776. 5 v.

New edition, "with the author's posthumous notes," published by Novello, London, 1853, 3 v. (Vol. 3 is an "atlas" of portraits); reprinted by Novello in 1875.

Unabridged republication of the 1853 Novello edition, with a new introduction by Charles Cudworth, New York, Dover, 1963. 2 v.

A reissue of the same edition has been announced by the Akademische Druck- und Verlagsanstalt, Graz.

Hawkins' history appeared in the same year that the first volume of Burney's history (no. 311) was published. The two works inevitably invited comparison, largely to Hawkins' disadvantage. His history, however, has much to recommend it, particularly the extensive translations of excerpts from early theory works and the inclusion of many examples of early music.

330
Kinsky, Georg. A history of music in pictures. New York, Dutton, 1937. 363 p.

Originally published in German in 1929; first English edition, 1930; reprint, New York, Dover, 1951. There is also a French edition.

Pictures include musicians' portraits; music in painting, drawing, and sculpture; facsimile pages of early musical and theoretical works; plates of early instruments. Arranged chronologically from antiquity to the early

20th century. Index to instruments, place names, and personal names.

331
Komma, Karl Michael. Musikgeschichte in Bildern. Stuttgart, Alfred Kröner [1961] 332 p.

743 well reproduced illustrations concerned with the history of music from antiquity to the 20th century; detailed commentary on each illustration.

Review by Hans Engel in *Die Musikforschung*, 18 (1965) p. 440–41.

332
Kretzschmar, Hermann, ed. Kleine Handbücher der Musikgeschichte nach Gattungen. Leipzig, Breitkopf & Härtel, 1905–22. 14 v. in 15.

Vols. 1–5, 8, 10, 11, and 13 have been announced for reprint publication by Georg Olms, Hildesheim.

A series of historical monographs dealing with the development of particular musical forms or disciplines. Although superseded in many respects, the volumes remain basic studies in the areas with which they are concerned.

333
Vol. 1: Schering, Arnold. Geschichte des Instrumentalkonzerts . . . 1905. 226 p. 2. Aufl., 1927.

334
Vol. 2: Leichtentritt, Hugo. Geschichte der Motette. 1908. 453 p.

335
Vol. 3: Schering, Arnold. Geschichte des Oratoriums. 1911. 647 p. Notenanhang, 39 p.

336
Vol. 4: Kretzschmar, Hermann. Geschichte des neuen deutschen Liedes. I. Von Albert bis Zelter (all published). 1911. 354 p.

337
Vol. 5: Schmitz, Eugen. Geschichte der Kantate und des geistlichen Konzerts. I. Geschichte der weltlichen Solokantate (all published). 1914. 327 p. 2. Aufl., 1955.

338
Vol. 6: Kretzschmar, Hermann. Geschichte der Oper. 1919. 286 p.

339

Vol. 7: Kretzschmar, Hermann. Einführung in die Musikgeschichte. 1920. 82 p. (See no. 404.)

340

Vol. 8: Wolf, Johannes. Handbuch der Notationskunde. I. Tonschriften des Altertums und des Mittelalters . . . II. Tonschriften des Neuzeit, Tablaturen, Partitur, Generalbass und Reformversuche. 1913–19. 2 v.

341

Vol. 9: Botstiber, Hugo. Geschichte der Ouvertüre und der freien Orchesterformen. 1913. 274 p.

342

Vol. 10: Schünemann, Georg. Geschichte des Dirigierens. 1913. 359 p.

343

Vol. 11: Wagner, Peter. Geschichte der Messe. I. Bis 1600 (all published). 1913. 548 p.

344

Vol. 12: Sachs, Curt. Handbuch der Musikinstrumentenkunde. 1920. 412 p.

345

Vol. 13: Aber, Adolf. Handbuch der Musikliteratur . . . 1922. 696 cols. (See no. 411.)

346

Vol. 14: Nef, Karl. Geschichte der Sumphonie und Suite. 1921. 344 p.

347

Laborde, Jean Benjamin de. Essai sur la musique ancienne et moderne. Paris, Impr. de P. D. Pierres, et se vend chez E. Onfroy, 1780. 4 v.

Reprint projected by Akademische Druck- und Verlagsanstalt, Graz, in the series *Die grossen Darstellungen der Musikgeschichte* . . .

Laborde's is the major French contribution to music historiography of the 18th century. The *Easai* is a vast assemblage of information on musical ethnology, organology, history, and biography. Much attention is directed toward French lyric poetry and the chanson.

348

Lang, Paul Henry. Music in Western civilization. New York, Norton [1941] 1,107 p.

Music in the context of the social, political, and cultural currents of Western civilization. One of the most influential of all music histories produced in America, it coincided with, and to a large extent contributed to, the general acceptance of music history in American higher education.

Comprehensive bibliography in all languages, one alphabet, p. 1,045–65.

German edition, Augsburg, 1947. Translated into Spanish, Portuguese, Czech, and Japanese.

349

Lang, Paul Henry and Otto Bettmann. A pictorial history of music. New York, Norton [1960] 242 p.

Text based on Lang's *Music in Western civilization*, above, with selected illustrations. Inferior reproduction technique.

350

Langhans, Wilhelm. Die Geschichte der Musik des 17. 18. und 19. Jahrhunderts in chronologischem Anschlusse an die Musikgeschichte von A. W. Ambros. Leipzig, F. E. C. Leuckart, 1884. 2 v.

Written as a continuation of Ambros' unfinished history, no. 293.

Manuel, Roland. See **Roland-Manuel.**

351

Nef, Karl. An outline of the history of music. Trans. by Carl Pfatteicher. New York, Columbia Univ. Press [1935] 400 p.

Originally published as *Einführung in die Musikgeschichte*, in 1920. An augmented French edition by Yvonne Rokseth appeared in 1931.

An excellent outline history for use in college or university music courses. "Brief, yet comprehensive; readable, yet scholarly" (translator's foreword). Rich in bibliographical references and musical examples in the text. General bibliography, p. 355–59.

352

The Norton History of Music Series. New York, Norton, 1940– .

A publisher's series consisting of independent works on different periods in the history of music. It was at one time announced that the volumes would be reissued as a set. In that case, some of the titles listed below may not be included.

The volumes by Reese and Bukofzer are particularly rich in bibliographical content.

353

Sachs, Curt. The rise of music in the ancient world, East and West. [1943] 324 p.

354

Reese, Gustave. Music in the Middle Ages. [1940] 502 p. Also published in an Italian edition under the title *La musica nel medioeve*, Florence, Sansoni, 1964. 642 p. Much new illustrative material has been added to this edition.

355

Reese, Gustave. Music in the Renaissance. [1954] 1,022 p. Rev. ed. [1959].

Review by Denis Stevens in *Music and letters*, 36 (1955) p. 70–73; by Edgar H. Sparks in *Notes*, 17 (1960) p. 569.

356

Bukofzer, Manfred. Music in the Baroque era; from Monteverdi to Bach. [1947] 489 p.

357

Einstein, Alfred. Music in the Romantic era. [1947] 371 p.

358

Austin, William W. Music in the 20th century; from Debussy through Stravinsky. [1966] 708 p.

359

Blume, Friedrich. Music in the classic era. (In preparation, 1967.)

360

The New Oxford History of Music. London, New York, Oxford Univ. Press, 1954– .

Each volume is a composite work made up of contributions by scholars of international repute and edited by a specialist in the period. The set has been planned in 10 volumes plus a volume of chronological tables and general index. There is an accompanying set of recordings issued under the title *The history of music in sound*, with illustrated booklets designed for teaching purposes. All recordings and pamphlets have appeared.

361

Vol. 1: Ancient and oriental music, ed. by Egon Wellesz. 1957. 530 p.

Review by Curt Sachs in *Notes*, 16 (1957) p. 97–99; by Roy Jesson in *MQ*, 44 (1958) p. 245–53; by Charles Seeger in *Ethnomusicology*, 3 (1959) p. 96–97.

362

Vol. 2: Early medieval music up to 1300, ed. by Anselm Hughes. 1954. 434 p.

Review by Charles Warren Fox in *MQ*, 41 (1955) p. 534–47; by Jeremy Noble in *Music and letters*, 36 (1955) p. 65–70.

363

Vol. 3: Ars Nova and the Renaissance (1300–1540), ed. by Anselm Hughes and Gerald Abraham. 1960. 565 p.

Review by Richard H. Hoppin in *MQ*, 47 (1961) p. 125; by Thurston Dart in *Music and letters*, 42 (1961) p. 57–60.

The following volumes are in preparation:
Vol. 4: The age of humanism (1540–1630).
Vol. 5: Opera and church music (1630–1750).
Vol. 6: The growth of instrumental music (1630–1750).
Vol. 7: The symphonic outlook (1745–90).
Vol. 8: The age of Beethoven (1790–1830).
Vol. 9: Romanticism (1830–90).
Vol. 10: Modern music (1890–1950).
Vol. 11: Chronological tables and general index.

364
The Oxford History of Music [2nd ed.] London, Oxford Univ. Press, 1929–38. 7 v. (plus an introductory volume).

First printed in 1901–1905 in 6 volumes. Volumes 4–6 of the 2nd edition are reprints of the original volumes.

365

Introductory volume, edited by Percy C. Buck. 1929. 239 p.

A symposium by 9 scholars, covering Greek and Hebrew music, notation, musical instruments, theory to 1400, plainsong, folk song, social aspects of music in the Middle Ages. Chapter bibliographies, p. 233–39.

366

Vols. 1–2: Wooldridge, H. E. The polyphonic period. 2nd rev. ed. by P. C. Buck. 1929–32. 2 v.

367

Vol. 3: Parry, C. and Hubert, H. The music of the seventeenth century. 1938. 486 p.

368

Vol. 4: Fuller-Maitland, J. A. The age of Bach and Handel. 2nd ed. 1931. 362 p.

369

Vol. 5: Hadow, W. H. The Viennese period. 1931. 350 p.

370

Vol. 6: Dannreuther, Edward. The romantic period. 1931. 374 p.

371

Vol. 7: Colles, H. C. Symphony and drama, 1850–1900. 1934. 504 p.

372

Pincherle, Marc. An illustrated history of music. Ed. by Georges and Rosamond Bernier. Trans. by Rollo Myers. New York, Reynal [1959] 221 p.

Published in France under the title *Histoire illustrée de la musique.* Paris, Gallimard, 1959.

A magnificently designed volume, with 200 illustrations in black and white, 40 in full color. The text is planned as an introduction to music history, but maintains a high standard in accuracy and critical comment. Traces the history of music from antiquity to modern times, but lacks documentation apart from the illustrations.

Review by Denis Stevens in *The musical times,* 101 (Aug., 1960) p. 493; by Emanuel Winternitz in *Notes,* 18 (1960) p. 48–50; by Jack A. Westrup in *Music and letters,* 41 (1960) p. 388.

373

The Prentice-Hall History of Music Series. Englewood Cliffs, N. J., Prentice-Hall, 1965– .

A publisher's series, for which H. Wiley Hitchcock serves as general editor. Short, one-volume surveys of music history by leading American scholars, covering the major historical periods as well as folk and non-Western music. The series is projected in 9 volumes.

374

[Vol. 1]: Nettl, Bruno. Folk and traditional music of the Western continents. 1965. 213 p.

375

[Vol. 2]: Pauly, Reinhard. Music of the classic period. 1965. 214 p.

376

[Vol. 3]: Seay, Albert. Music in the Medieval world. 1965. 182 p.
The following volumes are in preparation:
  Palisca, Claude. Baroque music.
  Salzman, Eric. An introduction to 20th-century music.

[87]

Malm, William P. Music cultures of the Pacific, the Near East, and Asia.

Hitchcock, H. Wiley. Music in the United States, a historical introduction.

[Author unannounced] 19th-century Romanticism in music.

Newman, Joel. Renaissance music.

377

Printz, Wolfgang Caspar. Historische Beschreibung der edelen Sing- und Kling-kunst . . . Dresden, 1690. Faksimile-Nachdruck. Herausgegeben und mit neuen Registern versehen von Othmar Wessely. Graz, Akademische Druck- und Verlagsanstalt, 1964. 240 p. (Die grossen Darstellungen der Musikgeschichte in Barock und Aufklärung, 1.)

A facsimile edition of a work that has often been described as the first history of music. Printz's observations are based largely on biblical authority and legend, but his work exercised considerable influence on the 18th-century music lexicographers and historians.

The editor's introduction and revised index occupy 120 p.

378

Prunières, Henry. A new history of music; the Middle Ages to Mozart. Trans. and ed. by Edward Lockspeiser. New York, Macmillan, 1943. 413 p.

Originally published as *Nouvelle histoire de la musique.* Paris, 1934–36. 2v.

Valuable for its emphasis on the earlier periods.

379

Riemann, Hugo. Handbuch der Musikgeschichte. 2nd ed. [edited by Alfred Einstein] Leipzig, Breitkopf & Härtel, 1920–23. 2 v. in 4.

First published in 1904–13.

A product of one of the most vigorous and stimulating minds in German musicology, always provocative, frequently misleading. Extensive chapter bibliographies and sections devoted to brief biographies of musicians. Numerous transcriptions of early music, all of which must be viewed in the light of Riemann's unorthodox editorial methods.

380

Roland-Manuel, ed. Histoire de la musique. Paris, Gallimard, 1960–63. 2 v. (Encyclopédie de la Pléiade, 9 and 16).

Vol. 1: Des origines à Jean-Sébastien Bach. 2,238 p. Vol. 2: Du XVIIIe siècle à nos jours. 1,878 p.

An important work. The language is French but the approach is international, comprising contributions by specialists from many different countries. Vol. 1 begins with a chapter on "Elements et geneses," followed by surveys of the music of non-European cultures, of ancient and oriental music, and of the music of the Moslem world. Thereafter the organization is chronological according to countries. At the end of Vol. 2 there are chapters devoted to contemporary music, to the history of musicology and criticism. Each volume has a chronological table and index and an analytical table of contents.

381

Sachs, Curt. Our musical heritage, a short history of music. 2nd ed. Englewood Cliffs, N.J., Prentice-Hall, 1955. 351 p.

First published in 1948.

Designed as a textbook for an introductory course in music history. References to essential bibliography and recordings.

382

Salazar, Adolfo. La música en la sociedad europea. [México] El Colegio di méxico [1942–46] 9 parts in 4 v.

A general history for Spanish readers, from antiquity to the end of the 19th century.

383

Smijers, Albert, ed. Algemeene muziekgeschiedenis; geïlustreerd overzicht der Europeesche muziek van de oudheid tot heden. 4. bijgewerkte druk. Utrecht, W. de Haan, 1947. 518 p.

2nd edition, 1940.

A composite history in 8 books, each written by a different Dutch or Flemish scholar. Short bibliographies after each book. Plates and numerous musical illustrations.

384

Strunk, W. Oliver. Source readings in music history from classical antiquity through the romantic era. New York, Norton [1950] 919 p.

87 items excerpted from the writings of theorists, composers, teachers, critics, and practical musicians, arranged roughly in chronological order under topics. Each item is introduced by a few concise and illuminating comments by the editor. The translations are excellent, the editorial work exemplary. An indispensable volume in any library of music history. Also published in a 4-vol. paperback, by Norton, New York, 1965.

Review by Manfred Bukofzer in *Notes*, 8 (1951) p. 517–18; by Erich Hertzmann in *MQ*, 37 (1951) p. 430–32; by Leo Schrade in *JAMS*, 4 (1951) p. 249–51.

385
Subirá, José. Historia de la música. 3. ed., reformada, ampliada, y puesta al dia. Barcelona, Editorial Salvat, 1958. 4 v.
First published in 1947; 2nd edition, 1951.
Handsomely printed and lavishly illustrated, musically and pictorially. Some emphasis on ethnomusicology. The approach is generally chronological, but with chapters on the development of notation, 17th-century theory and performance practice.

386
Ulrich, Homer and Paul Pisk. A history of music and musical style. New York, Harcourt, [1963] 696 p.

The authors' purpose in writing this history of music has been to offer a clear, straightforward presentation of historical developments in musical style (Preface).

Review by Susan Thiemann in *Notes*, 20 (1963) p. 638–42.

387
Wörner, Karl H. Geschichte der Musik; ein Studien- und Nachschlagebuch . . . 4. Aufl., stark erweiterte und ergänzte Neufassung. Göttingen, Vanderhoeck & Ruprecht, 1965. 554 p. First published in 1954; 2nd edition, 1956; 3rd edition, 1961. A well organized outline history with excellent bibliographical references, somewhat in the manner of *Nef* (no. 351).

Chronologies

388
Chailley, Jacques. Chronologie musicale en tableaux synoptiques. Paris, Centre de documentation universitaire et S.E.D.E.S. réunis, 1955– 140 p.
1re partie: De 310–1,600.
A workbook of musical chronology, with parallel tables of political, literary, and artistic events. Most detailed for the period prior to the 15th century.

389
Detheridge, Joseph. Chronology of music composers. Birmingham, J. Detheridge, 1936–37. 2 v.
Vol. 1: 820–1810. Vol. 2: 1810–1913.

More than 2,500 names of composers arranged chronologically by date of birth. Brief comments on their activity, fields of composition, nationality. Numerous inaccuracies and misleading statements, but valuable as one of the most comprehensive works of its kind. Alphabetical index of names.

390

Mattfeld, Julius. Variety music cavalcade, 1620–1961: a chronology of vocal and instrumental music popular in the United States. . . . With an introduction by Abel Green. Revised edition. Englewood Cliffs, N.J., Prentice-Hall, 1962. 713 p.

First issued in 1952 as *Variety music cavalcade, 1620–1950.*

Originally appeared in a modified form as *Variety radio directory 1938–39,* supplemented in weekly issues of *Variety.*

Lists popular music chronologically, with a brief account of the parallel social and historical events occuring each year. The index lists all musical works by title, with date of first publication.

Review by Irving Lowens in *Notes,* 20 (1963) p. 233–34.

Also entered as no. 719.

391

Mies, Paul and N. Schneider. Musik im Umkreis der Kultur-geschichte. Ein Tabellenwerk aus der Geschichte der Musik, Literatur, bildenden Künste, Philosophie und Politik Europas. Köln, P. J. Tonger [1953] 2 v.

Vol. 1: chronological tables of musical periods and events. Vol. 2: parallel tables of history, philosophy, literature, art, and architecture.

392

Schering, Arnold. Tabellen zur Musikgeschichte, ein Hilfsbuch beim Studium der Musikgeschichte. Fünfte Auflage bis zur Gegenwart ergänzt von Hans Joachim Moser. Wiesbaden, Breitkopf & Härtel, 1962. 175 p.

First published in 1914; 3rd edition, 1921; 4th edition, 1934.

Chronological tables outlining the important events in music history from antiquity to 1962, including birth and death dates of musicians, the principal events of their lives, significant publications and performances, and dates marking the activity of important music centers and stylistic developments. Parallel historical and cultural events given. The 4th edition contains a 30-page supplement giving a detailed listing of the contents of the major *Denkmäler* and *Gesamtausgaben* published by Breitkopf & Härtel. This is omitted from the 5th edition, which offers an index of names and subjects.

393
Slonimsky, Nicolas. Music since 1900. 3rd ed., rev. and enl. New York, Coleman-Ross, 1949. 759 p.

First published in 1937, N.Y., Norton. 2nd edition, 1938.

Contains a "Tabular view of stylistic trends in music: 1900–1948," (p. xxvii–lxii); "Descriptive chronology: 1900–1948," (p. 1–626); "Letters and documents," (p. 627–712). There is an index to the descriptive chronology (p. 713–59). The earlier editions contained a "Concise biographical dictionary of 20th-century musicians," omitted in the 3rd edition.

The chronology records significant events in the development of contemporary music: dates of composition and first performance, the founding of institutions and societies, births and deaths of contemporary musicians. International in scope, but with increased emphasis on American music for the decade from 1937 to 1948. The appendix quotes many of the major documents in the history of contemporary music.

Guides to
Systematic and Historical Musicology

THIS section lists a group of works designed to introduce the student to the methods and materials of musical research. The works vary widely in pattern and approach, some concerned with the content, others with the method of the discipline. Some emphasize the historical aspects of research, others, the systematic. The present list is not intended to be exhaustive. The reader will find a useful bibliography of writings on musicology by Ernst C. Krohn as *Appendix I* to Spiess' *Historical musicology* (see no. 409 below).

More than a century has passed since the term "Musikwissenschaft" was introduced by Friedrich Chrysander(*Jahrbücher für musikalische Wissenschaft*, 1863), and ever since that time musicologists have been attempting to define their field, to plot its structure and clarify its relationship to other areas in the humanities. For a general discussion of the history of musical scholarship, and a comprehensive bibliography on the subject, see the article "Musikwissenschaft" by Walter Wiora and Hans Albrecht in *MGG*, Vol. 9, col. 1,192–1,220. For a recent consideration of the underlying concepts and scope of the field, see "Musicology reconsidered," by Lloyd Hibberd, in *Acta M*, 31 (1959) p. 25–31.

394
Adler, Guido. Methode der Musikgeschichte. Leipzig, Breitkopf & Härtel, 1919. 222 p.

This, as is the author's *Der Stil in der Musik* (1929), is a basic study of the content and method of historical musicology. Contains a bibliographical supplement, "Verzeichnis von bibliographischen Hilfswerken für musik-historische Arbeiten," now outdated but of interest as a listing of music reference resources prior to World War I.

395
Broeckx, Jan L. Methode van de muziekgeschiedenis, met een inleiding door Prof. Dr. Fl. Van der Mueren. Antwerpen, Metropolis, 1959. 368 p.

A comprehensive survey of the methods and content of historical musicology. The three major divisions of the work are concerned with (1) basic concepts, (2) working procedures, and (3) terminology. Numerous bibliographical references in the text and a bibliographical appendix, p. 329–39.

396

Chailley, Jacques, ed. Précis de musicologie. Paris, Presses Universitaires de France, 1958. 431 p.

A syllabus published under the auspices of the Institute of Musicology of the University of Paris. Contributions by 25 French musicologists covering varied aspects of musical research. The emphasis is historical. Main approach is chronological, but there are chapters devoted to music bibliography, ethnomusicology, instruments, dance, philosophy and aesthetics, etc. Bibliography is stressed throughout.

397

Fellerer, Karl G. Einführung in die Musikwissenschaft. 2. neubearb. und erweiterte Aufl. [Münchberg] B. Hahnefeld [1953] 190 p.

First published in 1942.

Historical musicology plays a comparatively minor role in this survey of the content of musical knowledge. Emphasis is on the systematic areas: acoustics, aesthetics, psychology, sociology, and pedagogy. Extensive bibliographies for each chapter.

Review by Glen Haydon in *Notes*, 11 (1953) p. 111–12; in *Die Musikforschung*, 8 (1955) p. 96–97.

398

Garrett, Allen M. An introduction to research in music. Washington, Catholic University of America Press, 1958. 169 p.

A rather superficial attempt to survey the content and methods of musicology in a course intended for first-year graduate students in music.

Review by Donald J. Grout in *Notes*, 16 (1959) p. 246–47.

399

Harrison, Frank L., Mantle Hood, and Claude V. Palisca. Musicology. Englewood Cliffs, N.J., Prentice-Hall, 1963. 337 p. (The Princeton studies: humanistic scholarship in America.)

Harrison writes on "American musicology and the European tradition," Palisca on "American scholarship in Western music," and Hood on "Music, the unknown." Stimulating, thoughtful statements on the place of musicology in the world of learning. The work has already exercised a wide influence on discussions of the nature and purpose of American musicology. See Joseph Kerman, "A profile for American musicology," in *JAMS*, 18 (1965) p. 61–69; and the reply by Edward Lowinsky, "Character and purposes of American musicology," in the same journal p. 222–34.

Review by Jan La Rue in *JAMS*, 17 (1964) p. 209–14; by Vincent Duckles in *Notes*, 21 (1964) p. 368–69. The subject of an editorial by Paul Henry Lang in *MQ*, 50 (1964) p. 215–26. Joint review by Charles Seeger, Lincoln B. Spiess, and David McAllester in *Anuario, Inter-American Institute for Musical Research*, 1 (1965) p. 112–18.

400

Haydon, Glen. Introduction to musicology: a survey of the fields, systematic and historical, of musical knowledge and research. New York, Prentice-Hall, 1941. 329 p.

Unaltered reprint by the Univ. of North Carolina Press, Chapel Hill, 1959.

Systematic musicology (acoustics, psychology, aesthetics, theory, and pedagogy) occupy the major part of this work (243 p.). Historical musicology is treated in the last 54 pages. Each section has a special bibliography, with a general bibliography, p. 301–13.

401

Husmann, Heinrich. Einführung in die Musikwissenschaft. Heidelberg, Quelle & Meyer [1958] 268 p.

An introduction to systematic musicology. Much attention is given to acoustical and psychological aspects of the subject. The approach embraces all musical phenomena in all cultures. Extensive bibliography organized by chapter headings, p. 235–55.

Review by Werner Korte in *Die Musikforschung*, 13 (1960) p. 340–42.

402

Irvine, Demar B. Methods of research in music. Part I: Methods. Seattle, Washington, 1945. 69 p. (typescript).

A syllabus for music research students at the college level. Emphasis on methodology, with chapters covering "the field," "the problem," "the sources," "the facts," "the report." No bibliography.

403

Irvine, Demar B. Writing about music; a style book for reports and theses. [Seattle, Univ. of Washington Press, 1956] 74 p.

A guide for the preparation of the research report in music, with detailed instructions regarding the preparation of the manuscript, documentation, use of illustrations, and abbreviations.

404

Kretzschmar, Hermann. Einführung in die Musikgeschichte. Leipzig, Breitkopf & Härtel, 1920. 82 p. (Kleine Handbücher der Musikgeschichte, 7.)

A brief, narrative account of the content of and sources for the historical study of music. Relevant literature is mentioned in context. Chapter I traces the development of music historiography through the 19th century. Also cited as no. 339.

405

Machabey, Armand. La musicologie. Paris, Presses Universitaires de France, 1962. 128 p. (Que Sais-je, 978).

Brief survey of the scope, content, and methods of musicology treated under five headings: "Sources," "Les éléments," "Les formes," "Les instruments," "Diffusion." Highly selective bibliography.

406

Morgan, Hazel B. Music research handbook, for: music education, music theory, music history, music literature, musicology . . . in collaboration with Clifton A. Burmeister. Evanston, Ill., The Instrumentalist, 1962. 110 p.

A compendium of devices and methods intended to assist students in writing "research" papers. What is implied by "research" rarely extends beyond the requirements of a student's term report.

407

Riemann, Hugo. Grundriss der Musikwissenschaft. 4. Aufl., durchgesehen von Johannes Wolf. Leipzig, Quelle & Meyer, 1928. 160 p. (Wissenschaft und Bildung, 34.)

408

Schiedermair, Ludwig. Einführung in das Studium der Musikgeschichte: Leitsätze, Quellen, Übersichten und Ratschläge. 4. umbearb. und erweiterte Aufl. Bonn, F. Dümmlers Verlag, 1947. 167 p.

First published in 1918.

Brief surveys, with bibliographies, of the major historical periods. Concluding chapters deal with methodology, institutions, advice to students, and career possibilities, all pertaining to the German scene. A useful appendix lists major *Gesamtausgaben* and the contents of several publishers' series devoted to early music.

409

Spiess, Lincoln B. Historical musicology, a reference manual for research in music . . . with articles by Ernst C. Krohn, Lloyd Hibberd, Luther A. Dittmer, Tsang-Houei Shu, Tatsuo Minagawa, Zdeněk Novaček. Brooklyn, Institute of Mediaeval Music [1963] 294 p.

A text and reference book of musical research, includes lists of suggested topics for class and seminar reports, term papers, and dissertations; with a copious bibliography, index of publishers, etc. (quoted from the publisher's prospectus).

The bibliography consists of 1,980 numbered items, in all categories, distributed throughout the text. Ernst C. Krohn's essay, "The development of modern musicology," p. 153–72, provides a useful bibliography of the history of the discipline.

Review by Vincent Duckles in *Notes*, 20 (1963) p. 469–71.

410

Westrup, Sir Jack A. An introduction to musical history. New York, Harper and Row, 1964. 174 p.

First published in London by the Hutchinson University Library, 1955. A short, practical introduction to the study of music history.

This is not a history of music. It is simply an attempt to outline some of the problems which historians and students have to face, and to give some idea of the conditions in which music has come into existence (Author's Preface).

Although intended as a layman's guide, this little book is one of the few clear treatments of the problems of music historiography in English.

Review by Allen P. Britton in *Journal of research in music education*, 3 (1955) p. 154.

Bibliographies
of Music Literature

THE term "music literature" as applied here refers to writings on music, as opposed to musical scores. Such writings may appear as periodical articles or monographs; they may be cited in complete, self-contained bibliographical works, or in serial publications; and they can be organized in terms of a variety of subject fields. Nearly every dissertation or research study will have its appended bibliography of relevant literature, and most of the authoritative dictionaries or encyclopedias have subject bibliographies connected with their articles. It would be impossible to cite all of these resources, but the titles selected are numerous enough to form a substantial section of the present book. Following is an outline of the subdivisions employed:

> Bibliographies of Music Literature
> General
> Current or Annual
> Lists of Music Periodicals
> Special and Subject
> > Contemporary music
> > Dissertations
> > Ethnomusicology
> > Instruments
> > Jazz
> > Medieval and Renaissance Music
> > Music Education
> > National Music
> > Opera and Theater Music
> > Primary Sources
> > Sacred Music

See also "Catalogs of Music Libraries and Collections." Most of the published library catalogs provide separate sections for holdings in books on music.

General

411

Aber, Adolf. Handbuch der Musikliteratur in systematisch-chronologischer Anordnung. Leipzig, Breitkopf & Härtel, 1922. 696 cols. (Kleine Handbücher der Musikgeschichte, 13.)

Scheduled for republication by Georg Olms, Hildesheim.

A classified bibliography for students of music history. International coverage, although strongest in German materials. Entries from at least 13 important musicological journals are included. Subject and author indexes.

Also listed as part of the *Kretzschmar* series of music history, no. 345.

412

Adlung, Jacob. Anleitung zu der musikalischen Gelahrtheit, 1758. Faksimile-Nachdruck hersg. von H. J. Moser. Kassel, Bärenreiter, 1953. 814 p. (Documenta Musicologica, Erste Reihe, 4.)

2nd ed., revised by J. A. Hiller, 1783.

Chronologically one of the first important critical bibliographies of music literature. The author proposed to list all works on musical subjects necessary to "educated music lovers, and particularly to lovers of keyboard music," as well as to builders of organs and other instruments.

See the description of this work in Gustav Reese's *Fourscore classics of music literature* (no. 601) New York, Liberal Arts Press, 1957. P. 74–75.

413

Azhderian, Helen Wentworth. Reference works in music and music literature in five libraries of Los Angeles County. Los Angeles, Published for the Southern Calif. Chapter of the Music Library Association, by the University of Southern Calif., 1953. 313 p.

A partial supplement of holdings in the USC Library, January 1952–June 1962. Prepared by Joan M. Meggett. 1962. 13 p.

A bibliography of musicological literature, approx. 4,500 entries. International coverage. Full bibliographical citations. Classified listing with author index. The libraries represented are: The Henry E. Huntington Library, The William Andrews Clark Memorial Library, The Los Angeles Public Library, and the libraries of the University of Southern California and the University of California at Los Angeles.

Review by Otto Albrecht in *Notes*, 11 (1954) p. 468–69; by Vincent Duckles in *JAMS*, 7 (1954) p. 242–43.

414

Becker, Carl F. Systematisch-chronologische Darstellung der musikalischen Literatur von der frühesten bis auf die neueste Zeit. . . . Leipzig, R. Friese, 1836. 571 cols. and 34 p.

Nachtrag, 1839.

Modern reprint by Frits A. M. Knuf, Hilversum, 1966.

Becker presents a classified bibliography of many now obscure works. His work fills the gap, chronologically, between Lichtenthal (no. 432) and Eitner's *Bücherverzeichniss*, 1885, (no. 424). Includes newspaper and periodical articles. Gives place of publication, date, pagination, with brief annotations. 33-page index by subject, author, etc. by subject, author, etc.

415

Belknap, Sara Y. Guide to the musical arts. New York, Scarecrow Press, 1957. (not paginated)

Indexes 11 English-language and 2 foreign music and theater journals for the period 1953–56. Two major sections: I: Articles; II: Illustrations. The *Guide* has serious shortcomings as a reference tool: unnumbered pages, confused entries, much space devoted to ephemera. Its chief value lies in the section on illustrations.

See also the author's *Guide to the performing arts*, no. 443.

416

Blechschmidt, Renate. "Bibliographie der Schriften über Musik aus der Deutschen Demokratischen Republik, 1945–59." In *Beiträge zur Musikwissenschaft*, Jahrg. 1 (1959) Heft, 3 p. 51–75; Jahrg. 2 (1960) Heft 1, p. 50–68; Heft 2, p. 64–78.

Classified list covering the writings on music produced in Germany (East zone) for the 15-year period.

417

Blom, Eric. A general index to modern musical literature in the English language, including periodicals for the years 1915–26. London, Philadelphia, Curwen [1927] 159 p.

Entries for books by author, for parts of books by catchword subject, in one alphabet.

418

Blum, Fred. Music monographs in series; a bibliography of numbered monograph series in the field of music current since 1945. New York, Scarecrow Press, 1964. 197 p.

Gives contents of more than 250 monographic series in the music field originating in some 30 countries.

Over one-third of them may best be described as broadly musicological in content, many issued under the auspices of universities or scholarly societies; others, ranging in tone from the academic to the popular, cover the gamut of musical subject matter . . . (Preface).

Review by Thomas Watkins in *Current Musicology* (Fall, 1965) p. 227–29.

419

Breitkopf & Härtel (Publishers). Das Musikbuch, eine nach Gruppen und Gattungen geordnete Zusammenstellung von Büchern über Musiker, die Musik und Instrumente, mit erläuternden Einführungen . . . aus dem Verlage von Breitkopf & Härtel. Leipzig, Brektkopf & Härtel, 1913. 390 p.

Nachtragsband, 1926. 149 p.

A trade catalog of Breitkopf & Härtel books on music. Illustrated. Gives detailed descriptions of the works and their content. The book provides a useful survey of German music literature as issued by the leading music publisher of the first third of the 20th century.

420

Briquet, Marie. La musique dans les congrès internationaux (1835–1939). Paris, Heugel, 1961. 124 p. (Publications de la Société Française de Musicologie, 2èm sér. Tome X.)

A bibliographical survey of the contributions on music made at international congresses from 1835 to 1939. Classified listing of 164 congress reports with the papers on music itemized. Indexed by place of meeting, by chronology, by author, and by subject.

Review by Richard Schaal in *Die Musikforschung*, 17 (1964) p. 183.

421

Büchting, Adolf. Bibliotheca musica. Verzeichnis aller in Bezug auf die Musik . . . 1847–66, im deutschen Buchhandel erschienenen Bücher und Zeitschriften. Nebst Forssetzung 1: die Jahre 1867–71 umfassend. Nordhausen, A. Büchting, 1867–72. 2 v.

A bibliography of music literature covering German publications from 1847 to 1871. The work takes its place chronologically after that of Becker (no. 414) in the history of music bibliography. The gap of 8 years in coverage between Becker and Büchting has been filled by Robert Eitner. See no. 424.

422

Carl Gregor, Duke of Mecklenburg. Bibliographie einiger Grenz-
gebiete der Musikwissenschaft. Baden–Baden, Librairie Heitz, 1962. 200 p.
(Bibliotheca bibliographica Aureliana, 6.)

A bibliography devoted to areas peripheral to the traditional emphasis of
historical musicology. Includes books and periodical articles on aesthetics;
psychology; sociology of music; relations between music and the other
arts; musical interests of poets, writers, philosophers, etc. 3,519 entries,
alphabetical by author, with indexes of subjects and of persons as subjects.

423

Darrell, Robert D. Schirmer's guide to books on music and musicians;
a practical bibliography. New York, G. Schirmer, 1951. 402 p.

A bibliography of currently available (in 1951) books in English.
Detailed subject classifications, numerous annotations. Full bibliographical
information, including publisher's prices.

Appendix I, p. 346–77: selected books in French, German, Italian, and
Spanish. Appendix II, p. 378–84: juvenile literature. Key to publishers,
chiefly American.

Review by Raymond Kendall in *Notes*, 9 (1951) p. 119–20; by Richard S.
Angell in *JAMS*, 5 (1952) p. 60–61.

424

Eitner, Robert. Bücherverzeichnis der Musikliteratur aus den Jahren
1839 bis 1846 im Anschluss an Becker und Büchting . . . Leipzig, Breitkopf
& Härtel, 1885. 89 p. (Monatshefte für Musikgeschichte. Beilage. 17.
Jahrgang.)

Intended to bridge the gap between Becker's bibliography, no 414, and
Büchting's, no. 421.

425

Forkel, Johann N. Allgemeine Litteratur der Musik, oder Anleitung
zur Kenntniss musikalischer Bücher, welche von den ältesten bis auf die
neusten Zeiten bey den Greichen, Römern und den meisten neuern
europäischen Nationen sind geschreiben worden. Leipzig, Schwickert,
1792. 540 p.

Reprint of the original edition by Georg Olms, Hildesheim, 1962.

The first comprehensive bibliography of music literature, and still a
work of great utility. Classified listing of some 3,000 works on all aspects
of musical knowledge, with brief biographical notices of the authors and
descriptive annotations. Complete tables of contents are given for the most
important books.

[103]

Forkel's classification system has served as the model for many sub-sequent bibliographies. See Scott Goldthwaite, "Classification problems, bibliographies of literature about music," in *Library Quarterly* (Oct., 1948), p. 255 ff.

Forkel's work was expanded and translated into Italian by Pietro Lichtenthal in 1826. See no. 432.

426

Gerboth, Walter. "Index of Festschriften and some similar publications." In *Aspects of Medieval and Renaissance music, a birthday offering to Gustave Reese.* New York, W. W. Norton, 1966. p. 183–307.

The most comprehensive treatment of music *Festschriften* available. In three parts: A. List of Festschriften, under the name of the individual or institution honored. B. Subject listing of 2,710 articles. C. Author and secondary-subject index.

427

Institute for Computer Research in the Humanities. New York University. Writings on the use of computers in music. Compiled by Gary Berlind in collaboration with Barry S. Brook, Lejaren A. Hiller Jr., Jan P. LaRue, and George W. Logemann. New York University, Institute for Computer Research in the Humanities [1965] 21 p. (typescript).

A demonstration bibliography prepared for distribution at the national meeting of the American Musicological Society at Ann Arbor, Michigan, December, 1965.

> It reflects the state as of 20 December, 1965 of an automated bibliographic file maintained and continually updated by the Institute . . . The Institute plans to print annual cumulations, the first as part of the Proceedings of the New York Chapter of the American Musicological Society (Preface).

428

Kahl, Willi und Wilhelm-Martin Luther. Repertorium der Musikwissenschaft. Musikschrifttum, Denkmäler und Gesamtausgaben in Auswahl (1800–1950) mit Besitzvermerken deutscher Bibliotheken und musikwissenschaftlicher Institute. Kassel, Bärenreiter, 1953. 271 p.

A comprehensive bibliography of music literature, broadly classified, including useful lists of Festschriften, conference reports, and critical editions. International in scope. Prepared as a union list of musicological holdings in postwar German libraries. Some 2,795 items. Indexed by persons, subjects, and geographical locations.

Review by Otto Albrecht in *Notes*, 11 (1954) p. 468–69; by Vincent Duckles in *JAMS*, 7 (1954) p. 242–45.

429
Krohn, Ernst C. The history of music: an index to the literature available in a selected group of musicological publications. St. Louis, Washington University, 1952. 463 p. (Washington University Library Studies, 3.)

Reissued by Baton Music Co., St. Louis, 1958.

Classified index of articles on music history in 39 leading musicological publications—chiefly German and English periodicals. The general arrangement is chronological, with subdivisions by subject. Includes book reviews.

Review by Richard Appel in *Notes*, 10 (1952) p. 105–106; by Scott Goldthwaite in *JAMS*, 6 (1953) p. 250–51; by Wolfgang Schmieder in *Die Musikforschung*, 6 (1953) p. 278–80.

430
Krohn, Ernst C. "Musical Festschriften and related publications." In *Notes*, 21 (Winter-Spring, 1963–64) p. 94–108.

A useful listing of *Festschriften*, cited chronologically under four headings: A. works of major musicological interest; B. works compiled in homage to individual musicians, living or of the past; C. commemorative volumes consisting of original music; and D. those celebrating a particular institution, school, society or performing group.

431
Leguy, Jean. Catalogue bibliographique des livres de langue française sur la musique. . . . Paris, E. Ploix, 1954. 59 p.

Fascicule complémentaire au catalogue général de 1954, et supplément 1954–59. Paris, 1959. 33 p.

Classified listings of French books on music in print or available through E. Ploix-Musique, Paris. Primarily a dealer's catalog, but a useful source of bibliographical information. Gives author, title, place of publication, pagination, size, and price. No publishers given.

432
Lichtenthal, Pietro. Dizionario e bibliografia della musica. Milano, A. Fontana, 1826. 4 v.

Vols. 3, 4 are a translation of Forkel's *Allgemeine Litteratur der Musik* (no. 425) with additions to 1826. Vols. 1, 2 are the dictionary of musical terms cited as no. 213.

433

McColvin, Lionel R. and Harold Reeves. Music libraries, including a comprehensive bibliography of music literature and a select bibliography of music scores published since 1957. . . . Completely re-written, revised and extended by Jack Dove. London, Andre Deutsch, 1965. 2 v.

First published in 1937–38.

The bibliography of writings on music is found in Vol. 2, p. 79–454. Classified according to a modified Dewey schedule; devoted chiefly to works in English. It is somewhat uneven, overdeveloped in topics of particular British interest, incomplete and inconsistant in citation form.

The work is also cited as no. 1349.

Review by J. P. S. in *Recorded Sound*, 20 (1965) p. 394–95.

434

Materiały do Bibliografii Muzyki Polskiej. [Redaktor serii: Tadeusz Strumiłło, Kraków] v. 1– Polskie Wydawnictwo Muzyczne [1954]- .

Tom III: Bibliografia Polskiego piśmiennictwa muzycznego, opracowal Kornel Michałowski, 1955. 280 p.

Classified bibliography of books on music in Polish. Lists of theses and dissertations, 1917–54. Index.

A supplement to Tom III (published as Tom IV of the series) contains classified listings of new Polish books on music published between 1955 and 1963, with some addenda from earlier years. Kraków, 1964.

For other volumes of this set, see no. 580, 581.

435

Matthew, James E. The literature of music. London, E. Stock, 1896. 281 p.

Essays on the literature of music, in historical sequence to the 18th century, thereafter by topics: histories, biographies, dictionaries, sacred music, opera, instruments, music as a science, bibliography. Narrative style. Matthew, although out of date, provides the only self-contained study of music bibliography available in print. It still presents a useful survey of the earlier literature of music.

436

Refardt, Edgar. Verzeichnis der Aufsätze zur Musik in den nicht-musikalischen Zeitschriften der Universitätsbibliothek Basel. Leipzig, Breitkopf & Härtel, 1925. 105 p.

A classified list of writings on music in over 500 nonmusical newspapers and periodicals, arranged alphabetically by author. One of the few efforts to compile a bibliography of musical literature in journals outside of the music field.

437

Scholes, Percy A. A list of books about music in the English language, prepared as an appendix to the *Oxford companion to music*. London, New York, Oxford Univ. Press, 1940. 64 p.

A subject list which derives chiefly from the compiler's own library. Bibliographical information uneven, frequently lacking in place of publication. An informal preface; some annotations.

438

Uspenskaĩa, S. L. Literatura o muzyke, 1948–53. Moskva, Izdatel'stvo Vsesoĩuznoĭ knizhnoĭ palaty, 1955. 343 p.

Classified list of books and periodical articles in Russian, 1948–53. Name index, list of periodicals (including nonmusical journals).

Two further volumes in this series have appeared: 1958, covering the years 1954–56; and 1959,covering 1957. The latest is: *Sovetskaya literatura o muzyke; bibliograficheskiĭ ukazatel za 1957 god.* [By S. Uspenskaĩa and B. Yagolim.] Moskva, Sovetskiĭ Kompozitor, 1959. 191 p. 1,967 numbered entries. (See *Notes*, 18 (1960) p. 82.)

Current or Annual
(including periodicals that offer regular listings of music literature)

The only way to keep abreast of publication in the field of music literature is to consult a variety of current listings. Many of these treat special subject areas within the field: ethnomusicology, music theory, sacred music, etc. Periodicals that carry regular listings of music literature are cited in this section by title, with annotations directing attention to the relevant departments. Several of the current bibliographies of music (scores) are also concerned with music literature; see nos. 644, 650.

439

Acta Musicologica. V. 1–   Internationale Gesellschaft für Musik-wissenschaft, 1928– .

"Index novorum librorum," a department appearing in most issues of this journal, is one of the best sources of bibliographical information for the period between 1930 and 1950. It gives a classified listing of books on music in all languages. The department was discontinued after 1952.

440
African Music. Journal of the African music society, v. 1– . Roodepoort, Transvaal, Union of South Africa, 1954– .

Each annual issue has a section of "books and pamphlets received," as well as reviews of current publications in ethnomusicology.

441
American Bibliographic Service. Quarterly check-list of musicology. An international index of current books, monographs, brochures and separates. V. 1– . Darien, Connecticut, American Bibliographic Service, 1959– .

An unclassified numbered listing of current writings on music. The selection is broad and rather uncritical. Full bibliographical information, including prices. Indexed by authors, editors, and translators in the last issue of each volume.

442
"Articles Concerning Music in Non-Musical Journals *1949-64*." In *Current musicology* (Spring, 1965) p. 121–27; (Fall, 1965) p. 221–26.

The first installment stresses articles on historical subjects; the second, articles under various systematic headings: acoustics, philosophy and aesthetics, music in literature, psychology, sociology, etc.

443
Belknap, Sara Y. The guide to the performing arts, 1957– , v. 1– . New York, Scarecrow Press, 1960– .

An annual periodical index to the performing arts. Began as a supplement to the *Guide to the musical arts* (no. 415). Contains a "general" section and a "television arts" section. References to performers, performing groups, as well as general subject headings. As of 1963, 5 volumes have appeared, covering 1957–61.

444
"Bibliographie der Aufsätze zur Musik in Aussermusikalischen Italienischen Zeitschriften." In *Analécta musicologica*, Veröffentlichungen der Musikabteilung des deutschen historischen Instituts in Rom. Bd. I (1963) p. 90–112. Bd. II (1965) p. 144–228.

A bibliography of writings on music in Italian nonmusical journals. Part 1 by Paul Kast. Part 2 by Ernst-Ludwig Berz. The two installments are organized somewhat differently and indexed independently. The first contains 237 entries, the second, 1,074.

445

Bibliographie des Musikschrifttums. Jahrgang 1936– . Leipzig, Frankfurt a. M., F. Hofmeister, 1936– . (Herausgegeben im Auftrage des Instituts für Musikforschung, Berlin.)

Editors: 1936–37, Kurt Taut; 1938–39, Georg Karstädt, (1940–49, suspended publications); 1950– . Wolfgang Schmieder.

A bibliography of books and an index to periodical literature in all European languages. A large number of nonmusical journals included. Classified by broad subjects, with an index of names (author and subject) and places. The emphasis is on "serious" music.

This bibliography follows in a direct line of descent from the listings in the *Peters Jahrbuch*, no. 453.

Review of *Jahrgang 1950–51* by Richard Schaal in *Die Musikforschung*, 8 (1955) p. 371–72; by Richard S. Hill in *Notes*, 11 (1954) p. 555–57; by Scott Goldthwaite in *JAMS*, 8 (1955) p. 55–57. Review of *Jahrgang 1952–53* by Richard Schaal in *Die Musikforschung*, 10 (1957) p. 440.

446

A Bibliography of Periodical Literature in Musicology . . . Nos. 1–2 (1938–39, 1939–40) Washington, D.C., American Council of Learned Societies, 1940–43. 2 v.

Indexes approximately 240 periodicals, all European languages, musical and nonmusical, from Oct., 1938 through Sept., 1940. Signed abstracts or annotations for most of the articles. Vol. 1 contains a list of graduate theses accepted in American colleges, universities, and conservatories, Oct. 1, 1938—Sept. 1, 1939.

Vol. 1 compiled by D. H. Daugherty. Vol. 2, added compilers: Leonard Ellinwood and Richard S. Hill.

447

Bulgarski Muzikalen Knigopis: trimesechen bioliografski biuletin za novoizliazla literatura po muzika i noti. Sofiia, 1958– . (Bulgarski Bibliografski Institut "Elin Pelin.")

Quarterly, classified list of books and periodical articles on music and publications in musical notation issued in Bulgaria. Cumulative index, the October–December issue containing index for the entire year.

448

Deutsche Musikbibliographie. Jahrgang 1– . Leipzig, F. Hofmeister, 1829– .

Title varies: 1829–1942, *Hofmeisters musikalisch-literarischer Monatsbericht.*

Lists German, Swiss, and Austrian publications of music and music literature. Alphabetical by author, giving date and place of publication, pagination, and price. A monthly publication useful chiefly for its listings of music. Indexed by publisher. Entries are cumulated in Hofmeister's *Jahresverzeichnis* . . . (no. 455).

Also cited as no. 649.

449

Deutsche Staatsbibliothek (Berlin). Neuerwerbungen ausländischer Musikliteratur. Vol. 1– . Berlin, Deutsche Staatsbibliothek, 1956– . (Bibliographische Mitteilungen, Nr. 12, 1954–55; Nr. 16, 1956–75; Nr. 19, 1958–60.)

Classified lists of books on music, foreign publications, acquired by the Deutsche Staatsbibliothek (East Berlin). Issued at irregular intervals as part of the library's series of *Bibliographische Mitteilungen*. The three volumes appeared in 1956, 1958, and 1962 respectively.

450

Ethnomusicology. Journal of the Society for Ethnomusicology. V. 1– . Middletown, Conn., Wesleyan Univ. Press, 1953– .

Title varies: 1953–57, *Ethno-Musicology Newsletter*.

Prints a "current bibliography" section in each issue listing books and periodical articles related to the field. Organized by geographical areas and topics. The journal also publishes from time to time special bibliographies devoted to the work of leading ethnomusicologists.

451

Fontes Artis Musicae. Review of the International Association of Music Libraries. V 1– . Paris, International Association of Music Libraries, 1954– .

Each issue contains a "Liste internationale sélective" of music publications classified by country. Music literature appears under the subheading "Ouvrages sur la musique et ouvrages didactiques."

452

Hofmeisters Handbuch der Musikliteratur. Bd. 1– . Leipzig, F. Hofmeister, 1844– .

Cumulation of *Jahresverzeichnis der deutschen Musikalien und Musikschriften* (no. 455).

Preceded by a similar work by Anton Meysel, Leipzig, 1817, listing music and music literature through 1815, with 10 supplements (2–8 by F. Hof-meister; 9–10 by C. F. Whistling) to 1827. Whistling issued a revised edition in 1828, with 3 supplements.

Title varies: Vols. 1–3 (to 1844): *C. F. Whistling's Handbuch der musika-lischen Literatur*. Vols. 4–6 (1844–67): *Handbuch der musikalischen Lite-ratur*. Vols. 4–18 (1844–1933): also called Ergänzungsband 1–15. Publication interrupted in Vol. 19 (1943) covering the years 1934–40, through the letter "L" in the alphabet.

The *Handbuch* is of greatest importance for its music (score) listings, but each volume contains an *Anhang* devoted to books and writings on music. The long life of the series, plus the leading position occupied by German music publishing during the period covered, make it one of the major reference tools.

See also nos. 455. The *Handbuch* is also cited under *Bibliographies of music* (no. 648) by virtue of its music listings.

453
Jahrbuch der Musikbibliothek Peters. V. 1–47. Leipzig, C. F. Peters, 1895–1941.

Most issues contain a section, "Verzeichnis der in allen Kulturländern erschienen Bücher und Schriften über Musik," edited at various times by Rudolf Schwartz, Emil Vogel, Eugen Schmitz, and Kurt Taut. Does not include periodical literature. The section, expanded to include periodical articles, has been continued as the *Bibliographie des Musikschrifttums*, published separately (no. 445).

454
Jahrbuch für Liturgik und Hymnologie. Bd. 1– . Kassel, Johannes Stauda-Verlag, 1955– .

Each volume contains an extensive "Literaturbericht," classified, frequently annotated, covering all aspects of liturgics and hymnology.

455
Jahresverzeichnis der Deutschen Musikalien und Muskschriften. Jahrgang 1– . Leipzig, F. Hofmeister, 1852– .

An annual listing which cumulates the material in the *Deutsche Musik-bibliographie*, no. 448, and is, in turn, cumulated in *Hofmeisters Handbuch der Musikliteratur* no. 452.

Title varies: Vols. 1–77 (1852–1928): *Verzeichnis der im Jahre . . . erschienen Musikalien*. Vols. 78–91 (1929–42): *Hofmeisters Jahresverzeichnis*.

Also cited as no. 649.

456

Journal of the International Folk Music Council. V. 1– . Published with the assistance of the International Music Council under the auspices of UNESCO, 1949– .

Each volume of this yearly publication contains a section, "Publications received," which gives a brief, authoritative survey of a wide range of publications in the field, including periodicals, recordings, and important articles.

457

Journal of Music Theory. V. 1– . New Haven, Yale School of Music, 1957– .

Each issue contains a "Bibliography of current periodical literature" covering articles related to music theory.

458

The Music Index; the key to current music periodical literature. V. 1, no. 1– . Detroit, Information Service, Inc., Jan. 1949– .

Currently indexes more than 225 periodicals by subject and author. Published in 12 monthly numbers, with an annual cumulation. Reviews are indexed under "Book reviews."

Review of 1954 annual cumulation by Richard Appel in *Notes*, 14 (1957) p. 364–65; of the 1955 and 1956 cumulations by James B. Coover in *Notes*, 16 (1958) p. 45–46. Review by Richard Schaal in *Die Musikforschung*, 10 (1957) p. 442–43.

459

Music Library Association Notes, a magazine devoted to music and its literature. 2nd ser. 1– . The Music Library Association, 1948– .

"Book reviews," a department compiled and edited chiefly by William Lichtenwanger and supplemented by a list of current publications on music is the most comprehensive listing of current music literature available. Since December, 1950, the list has been international in scope; classified by language.

460

Music Teachers National Association. Committee on Literature about Music. "Report." 1906– . In its *Proceedings* (annual) 1906– .

Classified lists of books on music in English, giving author, title, publisher, pagination, and price. Includes some translations, new editions, and reprints. Excellent listings of material in English; carefully selected, some annotations. Listed by authors and subjects.

461
Musica Disciplina. A yearbook of the history of music. V. 1– .
American Institute of Musicology, 1946– .
Title varies: Vol. 1, *Journal of Renaissance and Baroque music.*
Most of the volumes contain a bibliography of books, periodical articles
and editions related to early music, doctoral dissertations included. Com-
piled since 1958 by Wolfgang Schmieder.

462
"Musical Literature." In *The British catalogue of music.* London,
Council of the British National Bibliography, 1957– .
An annual listing, broadly classified, of all books about music published
in Great Britain. "Musical literature" appears first in the classified section.
Scores, however, occupy the greater part of the volumes. Indexed by
author and title.
See also no. 1321.

463
The Musical Quarterly. V. 1– . New York, G. Schirmer, 1915– .
The "Quarterly Book-List" in each issue is a selection of books of
musicological interest in all languages. Less comprehensive than the current
listings in *Notes* (no. 459 above). Compilers, successively, since 1936:
Edward N. Waters, Lee Fairley, Frank C. Campbell, Donald W. Krummel,
Carroll D. Wade, and Fred Blum.

464
The Musical Quarterly. Cumulative Index. 1915 thru 1959 [v. 1–45].
Compiled by Herbert K. Goodkind. New York, Goodkind Indexes
[1960]. 204 p.
Cumulative index supplement, 1960 thru 1962. New York, 1963.
The main volume indexes by author and subject in separate alphabets,
the *Supplement* in one alphabet. Indexes book reviews and "Current
chronicle" as well as articles.

465
Music and Letters. Index to volumes 1–40, 1920–59. London, Oxford
Univ. Press [1962]. 140 p.
An index compiled largely by Eric Blom before his death in 1959 and
completed by Jack A. Westrup. Two major sections. 1: articles (filed by
author and subject in one alphabet). 2: reviews (similarly treated). Reviews
of music are not indexed.

[113]

466

National Association of Schools of Music. A list of books on music. Cincinnati, 1935. 57 p.

Supplements 1–10, 1936–57.

Primarily an annotated listing of books in English, with smaller selections of foreign music literature, critical editions, contemporary American scores. Prices given through the 8th supplement. A cumulative index of the original list and the first 7 supplements was printed in 1952.

467

La Rassegna Musicale. Indice generale delle annate 1928–52 [v. 1–22]. Torino, Roggero & Tortia [1953]. 174 p.

An index, compiled by Riccardo Allorto, of articles, musical performances reviewed, book reviews, record reviews, and musical subjects.

468

Rivista Musicale Italiana. Indici dei volumi I a XX (1894–1913). Compiled by Luigi Parigi. Torino, Fratelli Bocca, 1917. 256 p.

Indici dei volumi XXI a XXXV (1914–28). Compiled by A. Salvatori and G. Concina. Torino, 1931. 195 p.

Both index articles, works reviewed, and subjects. The second volume contains a retrospective index of musical examples.

469

Royal Musical Association. Index to papers read before the members . . . 1874–1944. Leeds, Printed by Whitehead & Miller for the Royal Musical Association, 1948. 56 p.

A subject and an author index to the first 70 volumes of the *Proceedings* of the Association. Compiled by Alfred Loewenberg and Rupert Erlebach.

470

Svensk Tidskrift för Musikforskning. V. 1– . Stockholm, 1919– .

Since 1927 the *Tidskrift* has maintained an anual listing of "Svensk musikhistorisk bibliografi," compiled since 1946 by Åke Davidsson. Broadly classified. Indexes Swedish periodicals.

471

Vierteljahrsschrift für Musikwissenschaft. Ed. by Friedrich Chrysander & Philipp Spitta. V. 1–10. Leipzig, 1885–94.

Each volume contains a section, "Musikalische Bibliographie," compiled by F. Ascherson, which usually includes a listing of scholarly music books, critical editions, and the contents of current scholarly periodicals in all European languages.

472

Zeitschrift der International Musikgesellschaft. V. 1–15. Leipzig, 1899/1900–13/14.

Most issues contain departments under the headings, "Kritische Bücherschau" and "Zeitschriftenschau." The latter indexes approximately 84 periodicals, chiefly musical, in many languages. Vols. 1–11 by author only. Vols. 12–15 by subject with "see" references from the author.

473

Zeitschrift für Musikwissenschaft. V. 1–17. Leipzig, 1918–35.

Indexes once a year the periodical literature on music in some 200 journals, in many languages. 1914–18 covered retrospectively in the 1918 index, thus articulating with no. 472 above.

Lists of Music Periodicals

Probably the most comprehensive list of music periodicals is to be found in the article "Periodicals, musical," compiled by A. Hyatt King in the 5th edition of *Grove* (see no. 22). The best chronological survey is still offered by Freystätter (no. 483), but this has been supplemented and expanded in certain respects by the recent historical study by Rohlfs (no. 497).

474

Apel, Willi. "Periodicals, Musical." In his *Harvard dictionary of music.* Cambridge, Harvard Univ. Press, 1947. P. 567–68.

A selected list of historical music periodicals, current and recent titles classified according to countries, and musicological periodicals.

475

Blum, Fred. "East German music journals: a check-list." In *Notes*, 19 (1962) p. 399–410.

Lists 100 periodicals in alphabetical order (including secondary titles, former titles, and subsequent titles) as well as providing a critical description of a variety of East German music serials.

476

Campbell, Frank C. A critical annotated bibliography of periodicals. [New York, American Choral Foundation, 1962.] 14 p. (The American Choral Foundation. Memo no. 33. July 1962.)

Evaluates 44 periodicals that treat choral music and materials, giving pertinent details (address, price, emphasis, etc.).

[115]

477

Canadian Library Association. Union list of music periodicals in Canadian libraries. Compiled by a committee of the Canadian Library Association. Ottawa, 1964. 32 p.

Committee chairman: Jean Lavander.

Gives data on holdings in music periodicals of 66 Canadian libraries. Brief annotations on the nature and content of each periodical listed.

478

Clough, F. F. and G. J. Cuming. "Phonographic periodicals, a survey of some issued outside the United States." In *Notes*, 15 (1958). P. 537–58.

A critical description of some 30 foreign periodicals devoted to recordings, with additional comments on record coverage in general periodicals.

479

Coover, James B. "A bibliography of East European music periodicals." In *Fontes artis musicae* (1956) p. 219–26; (1957 p. 97–102; (1958) p. 44–45, 93–99; (1959) p. 27–28; (1960) p. 16–21, 69–70; (1961) p. 75–90; (1962) p. 78–80.

> This bibliography is an attempt at a comprehensive and authoritative listing of all music periodicals which have been and which are being published in the countries of Bulgaria, Czechoslovakia, Estonia, Finland, Hungary, Latvia, Lithuania, Poland, Rumania, the U.S.S.R., and Yugoslavia (Compiler's Introduction).

480

"Europäische Musikzeitschriften 1945-48." In *Jahrbuch der Musikwelt*. Bayreuth, J. Steeger, 1949–50. P. 111–23.

Organized by country. Information brief and inconsistent, with German periodicals given most complete coverage; Russian, Czech, and others very incomplete.

481

Fairley, Lee. "A check-list of recent Latin American music periodicals." In *Notes*, 2 (1945) p. 120–23.

Lists 23 periodicals from the collections of the Library of Congress and the Pan American Union, with brief comments on the general character of each. Covers publications established between 1940 and 1945.

482

Fredericks, Jessica M. [et al.]. "Music magazines of Britain and the U.S." In *Notes*, 6 (1949) p. 239–63, 457–59; 7 (1950) p. 372–76.

Lists 200 periodicals, arranged alphabetically by title, with a subject and type index. Brief descriptions of nature and contents.

483
Freystätter, Wilhelm. Die musikalischen Zeitschriften seit ihrer Entstehung bis zur Gegenwart. Chronologisches Verzeichnis der periodischen Schriften über Musik. München, T. Riedel, 1884. 139 p.
Unaltered reprint of the original edition by Frits A. M. Knuf, Hilversum, 1965.
Based on E. Gregoir's *Recherches historiques concernant les journaux de musique*, Antwerp, 1872.
A chronological listing, from 1722 to 1884, with extensive annotations as to content, editors, contributors, etc. Still invaluable as a source of information on early music periodicals.

484
Kallmann, Helmut. "A century of musical periodicals in Canada." In *The Canadian music journal*, 1:1 (1956) p. 37–43; 1:2 (1957) p. 25–36.
The last installment contains a section entitled "A check-list of Canadian periodicals in the field of music," p. 30–36.

485
McClellan, William M. A check-list of music serials in nine libraries of the Rocky-Mountain region. Boulder, Univ. of Colorado Libraries, 1963. 21 p. (typescript).
A project initiated by the Rocky Mountain Chapter of the American Musicological Society. An alphabetical listing of music serials with a precise statement of holdings in the libraries represented.

486
Malm, William P. "A bibliography of Japanese magazines and music." In *Ethnomusicology*, 3 (1959) p. 76–80.
Annotated bibliography of 25 Japanese periodicals related to music and the dance. Place, publisher, date of first issue, and price given.

487
Michałowski, Kornel. Bibliografia polskich czasopism muzycznych. V. 1– . Cracow, Polskie Wydawnictwo Muzyczne, 1955– .
A bibliography of Polish music periodicals; classified listings of their contents from 1820 to 1939. 10 v. to 1964.

488
"Music [Section]." In *Ulrich's Periodicals directory; a classified guide to a selected list of current periodicals, foreign and domestic.* 9th ed. . . . New York, R. R. Bowker Co., 1959. P. 526–31.

See also earlier editions.

Lists 123 periodicals, many of which are not included in the *Music Index* (no. 458). Gives full title, first year, frequency, price, publisher, and address. Also indicates the presence of illustrations, reviews, abstracts, or bibliographies, and where each journal is indexed.

489
Music Library Association. Northern California Chapter. A union list of music periodicals [published 1949–64] in the libraries of Northern California. Ed. by C. R. Nicewonger. [Pub. for the Resources Comittee, Northern Calif. Chapter, Music Library Association, 1965]. 141 leaves (typescript).

Covers the music periodical holdings of 24 Northern California libraries, including both public and academic institutions.

490
"Periodicals and Other Serial Publications." In *Reference works in music and music literature in five libraries of Los Angeles County.* Ed. by Helen W. Azhderian. Los Angeles, 1953. P. 213–39.

491
"Periodicals and Trade Publications." In *The musician's guide; the directory of the world of music, 1957 edition.* New York, Music Information Service, Inc., 1957. P. 640–55.

Basic information on 178 American and 153 foreign periodicals, some of which have ceased publication.

492
"Periodicals Indexed." In *The music index 1962 annual cumulation.* Detroit, Information Service, Inc., 1965.

A listing of more than 225 titles of periodicals currently covered by the *Index.* Addresses and subscription prices given. In its first year (1949) the *Music Index* treated only 81 titles. Since that time there has been a constant increase in the number of periodicals indexed.

493
"Periodicals, Musical." In *Grove's.* . . . 5th ed. v. 6, p. 638–65.

A list, compiled by A. Hyatt King, of over 1,000 music periodicals from all parts of the world, arranged by countries in chronological order of the date of first appearance.

See also the corrections and additions to the above list in the *Supplementary volume* (1961) to *Grove's*, p. 344–47.

494
"Periodische Schriften." In *Jahrbuch der Musikbibliothek Peters.* V. 1–47. Leipzig, C. F. Peters, 1894–1941.

A regular section of the annual "Verzeichnis . . . Bücher und Schriften über Musik," listing new periodicals and other serial publications that have been issued during the year. Compiled by a variety of editors. See no. 453.

495
"Revistas Musicales." In *Diccionario de la Música Labor.* Barcelona, Labor, 1954. V. 2, p. 1863–70.

An extensive listing of music periodicals, classified by country, with a short bibliography on musical journalism.

496
Riedel, A. Répertoire des periodiques musicaux belges. Bruxelles, Commission belge de bibliographie, 1954. 48 p. (Bibliographia belgica, 8.)

330 items, of which the first 130 are music serials; the remainder are periodicals in the usual sense.

497
Rohlfs, Eckart. Die deutschsprachigen Musikperiodica, 1945–57. Regensburg, G. Bosse, 1961. 108, 115 p. (Forschungsbeiträge zur Musikwissenschaft, 11.)

A source book of information about music periodicals, their history, bibliographical coverage, distribution, and subject emphasis. Not confined to German journals, as the title might suggest. The systematic bibliographic *Anhang*, p. 5–64, lists 589 periodicals in 12 categories. Indexed by chronology, place, title.

Review by Fred Blum in *Notes*, 19 (1961) p. 77–78.

498
Thoumin, Jean-Adrien. Bibliographie rétrospective des périodiques français de littérature musicale 1870–1954. Préface de Madame Elizabeth Lebeau. Paris [Éditions documentaires industrielles et techniques] 1957. 179 p.

An alphabetical listing of 594 French music periodicals. Chronological index; indexes of persons and places of publication.

[119]

499

"United States Music Periodicals." In *The music magazine/Musical courier: The Annual Directory of the concert world 1963.* Compiled and edited by Max D. Jones. Evanston, Summy-Birchard Co., 1963. P. 100–102.

A listing of 153 American music periodicals. A list of 224 "foreign music periodicals" is found on p. 154–57.

500

"Verzeichnis der Zeitschriften und Jahrbücher." In *Hofmeisters Jahresverzeichnis,* v. 100. Leipzig, F. Hofmeister, 1953. P. 334–39.

Lists more than 100 German and Austrian periodicals and yearbooks available in 1951. Since 1953, periodicals are listed annually in a subsection of the "Anhang: Musikschriften."

See also earlier issues of the *Jahresverzeichnis.*

501

"Zeitschriften." In Mendel's *Musikalisches Conversations-Lexikon,* v. 11. Berlin, Heimann, 1879. P. 443–62.

An early listing of music periodicals, but still useful for its detailed descriptions of the journals of the 18th- and early 19th-centuries.

502

"Zeitschriften." In *Repertorium der Musikwissenschaft.* Bearb. von Willi Kahl und Wilhelm-Martin Luther. Kassel, Bärenreiter, 1953. P. 23–39.

Lists 187 music periodicals, in all European languages, with their locations in German libraries. Selected for their musicological importance.

Special and Subject: Contemporary Music

503

Basart, Ann Phillips. Serial music, a classified bibliography of writings on twelve-tone and electronic music. Berkeley and Los Angeles, University of Calif. Press, 1961. 151 p. (University of California Bibliographic Guides.)

A classified bibliography of 823 items, treating the literature of 12-tone music, electronic music, the Viennese school (Schönberg, Berg, and Webern) and 20 other contemporary composers using serial techniques. Author and subject indexes.

Review by Dika Newlin in *Notes,* 19 (1961) p. 256–57; by James B.

Coover in *Journal of music theory*, 6 (1962) p. 316–17; by Donald Mitchell in *Tempo*, 63 (Winter, 1962–63) p. 46–48, and by Josef Rufer in *Die Musik-forschung*, 17 (1964) p. 315–16.

504
Bull, Storm. Index to biographies of contemporary composers. New York, Scarecrow Press, 1964. 405 p.

Indexes 69 sources of biographical information (dictionaries, Who's Whos, publishers' lists, etc.) and indicates if the composer under consideration is mentioned. No page references given.

505
Deliège, Celestin. "Bibliographie" [of serial and experimental music]. In *Revue belge de musicologie*, 13 (1959) p. 132–48.

Broadly classified bibliography, with an introduction surveying the literature of the field.

506
Edmunds, John and Gordon Boelzner. Some twentieth-century American composers, a selective bibliography. . . . With an introductory essay by Peter Yates. V. 1– . New York, The New York Public Library, 1959. 57 p.
V. 2 (1960): 55 p., with an introductory essay by Nicolas Slonimsky.

This bibliography has been made with the purpose of bringing together in a single body separately published writings by and about a representative group of 20th-century American composers . . . conservative, moderate, dodecaphonic, and experimental (Preface).

Vol. 1 includes bibliographies for 15 composers. Vol. 2, for 17, with two appendices: composers cited in one of 21 standard reference works, and composers not cited in these works but who are under 35 and merit some attention.

Both volumes are "reprinted with additions" from *The bulletin of the New York public library* (July-August, 1959; July, 1960).

Special and Subject: Dissertations

Doctoral dissertations, along with articles in scholarly periodicals, represent the growing edge of research activity in any field. We are currently well supplied with bibliographies of doctoral studies in music for the United States (no. 508) and for Germany (no. 517) but studies produced in other countries are less easy to locate. Included here are only those reference tools concerned exclusively with studies in music. There are a number of comprehensive national bibliographies of dissertations from which music titles can be extracted. For these, the user should consult Winchell's *Guide to reference books*, latest edition, and its *Supplements*. See also Keith Mixter's *General bibliography for music research* (no. 1333).

507
"Dissertations." In *Current musicology*, No. 1– . New York, The Music Department, Columbia University, 1965– .

A department in a recently established musicological journal; contains critical reviews of selected doctoral studies and listings of current European dissertations, completed or in progress.

508
Doctoral Dissertations in Musicology. 4th ed. Compiled by Helen Hewitt. Philadelphia, American Musicological Society, 1965. 152 p.

First published, 1951, in photo-offset from typed copy.

2nd edition, 1958, published jointly with the Music Teachers National Association. 3rd edition, 1961, by American Musicological Society.

Supplements to the 1951 list appeared in the May–June issue of *The American music teacher* (1953–56) and in *JAMS*, 7 (1954) p. 131–40; 8 (1955) p. 116–22; 9 (1956) p. 202–09. Supplements to the 2nd edition appeared in *The American music teacher*, 8 (1959) p. 10 ff., and in *JAMS*, 11 (1958) p. 217–26. Supplements to the 3rd edition, in *JAMS*, 16 (1963) p. 382–93; 17 (1964) p. 346–62.

The 1951 publication is still useful in its own right since it contains material deleted from later compilations (studies tangential to musicology in fields such as acoustics, psychology, and history, or pursued in departments other than music).

The 4th edition gives 1,204 entries for dissertations completed or in progress, grouped by historical periods under institutions, with additional classifications for nonhistorical studies. Indexed by authors and subjects. Those studies available for purchase on microfilm or microcard are identified.

509
Doe, Paul. "Register of theses on music." In *R.M.A.* Research Chronicle, No. 3. [Taunton, Barnicotts Ltd., for the Royal Musical Association]. 1963. P. 1–25.

Classified bibliography of music research studies, completed or in progress, for a variety of degrees in British universities. The major division separates studies of European music (excluding Great Britain) from British music. Within these divisions the listing is chronological, with added sections on "General subjects," "Non-European music," and "Acoustics."

510

Gillis, Frank and Alan P. Merriam. Ethnomusicology and folk music: an international bibliography of dissertations and theses. Middletown, Conn., published for the Society for Ethnomusicology by the Wesleyan University Press, 1966. 148 p. (Special series in *Ethnomusicology*, 1.)

An annotated listing which supersedes the bibliographies of theses and dissertations printed in *Ethnomusicology*, 4 (1960) p. 21–35, and 6 (1962) p. 191–214.

511

"Im Jahre . . . Angenommene Musikwissenschaftliche Dissertationen." In *Die Musikforschung*, v. 1– , 1948– .

A listing, annually or at more frequent intervals, of doctoral dissertations completed in German, Austrian, and Swiss institutions. Beginning with Vol. 18 (1965) the periodical has a special section devoted to reviews of selected dissertations.

512

Music Educators National Conference. Committee on Bibliography of Research Projects and Theses. Bibliography of research studies in music education, 1949–56. Compiled by William S. Larson. In *Journal of research in music education*, 5:2 (1957) 225 p.

Continuation of the above.

Lists all completed research studies in music education "which make a contribution to the teaching of music." Arranged alphabetically by state, university, and author. Gives degree awarded and date. Topical index.

513

Music Educators National Conference. Committee on Bibliography of Research Projects and Theses. Doctoral dissertations in music education, 1957–63. Compiled by Roderick D. Gordon. In *Journal of research in music education*, 12 (Spring, 1964) 112 p.

Continues the listings given in the preceding entries.

514

Music Educators National Conference. Committee on Research in Music Education. Bibliography of research in music education,

[123]

1932–44. Compiled by Arnold M. Small [et al.] [Iowa City] State University of Iowa Press, 1944. 55 p.

Theses and dissertations organized by state and school.

515
Music Educators National Conference. Music Education Research Council. Bibliography of research studies in music education, 1932–48. Compiled by William S. Larson. Chicago, Music Educators National Conference, 1949. 119 p.

This second edition of the preceding item contains more than 1,600 titles. A 4-page supplement with nearly 350 additional titles is provided as an insert.

Review by George Henderson in *Notes*, 7 (1949) p. 121.

516
Northwestern University (Evanston, Ill.) School of Music. Bibliography of research, School of Music, Northwestern University: theses, projects, dissertations. Edited by Hazel B. Morgan. Evanston, Illinois, 1958. 47 p.

517
Schaal, Richard. Verzeichnis deutschsprachiger musikwissenschaftlicher Dissertationen, 1861–1960. Kassel, Bärenreiter, 1963. 167 p. (Musikwissenschaftliche Arbeiten, hrsg. von der Gesellschaft für Musikforschung, 19.)

An alphabetical listing, by author, of 2,819 music dissertations in the German language. Publication data given for the works in print. Subject index.

Review by Erich Schenk in *Die Musikforschung*, 17 (1964) p. 421–23, giving numerous additional entries.

518
Texas Music Educators Association. Research in Music Education Committee. A bibliography of master's theses and doctoral dissertations in music completed at Texas colleges and universities, 1919–62. Houston, Texas Music Educators Association, 1964. 77 p.

Listings, chronological by institution, of research studies in music completed in 14 Texas colleges or universities. Subject and author indexes.

519
University Microfilms. Doctoral dissertations: music, 1959–64. Ann Arbor, Mich., University Microfilms, [1964?] 2 v.

[124]

One volume is by subject, the other roughly chronological by date of acquisition, of music dissertations available in photo duplication from University Microfilms. Prices given for film and Xerox copies. Originating institutions not identified.

520

"Verzeichnis der im Berichtsjahr . . . Bei der Deutschen Bücherei zu Leipzig Registrierten Musikwissenschaftlichen Dissertationen und Habilitationsschriften." [Compiled by Ortrun Landmann]. In *Deutsches Jahrbuch der Musikwissenschaft*. Leipzig, Peters, 1957– .

Continues a bibliography of dissertations originally published in the *Peters Jahrbuch*. Emphasizes East German institutions.

Special and Subject: Ethnomusicology

The field of ethnomusicology has attracted a great deal of interest and research activity in recent years. It developed as a discipline along scientific lines as "comparative musicology" in the first decades of the present century. It now supports its own journal, *Ethnomusicology*, see no. 450, and several specialized research organizations: The African Music Society, The International Folk Music Council, etc. No attempt has been made to list the many useful bibliographies appended to monographs, dissertations, and periodical articles in this field. The selection has been confined, with a few exceptions, to the major self-contained bibliographies of folk and primitive music.

See also under "Bibliographies of Music Literature: Current or Annual," nos. 440, 456; under "Bibliographies of Music Literature: Special and Subject, Dissertations," no. 510, and under "Discographies," nos. 1287–1295.

521

Bose, Fritz. Musikalische Völkerkunde. Freiburg, Atlantis-Verlag, 1953. 197 p. (Atlantis-Musikbücherei.)

"Bibliographie," p. 144–63. 393 items.

522

Densmore, Frances. "The study of Indian music in the nineteenth century." In *American Anthropologist*, 29 (1927) p. 77–86.

A survey of early studies in the field of American Indian music; generally valuable, although it contains some errors.

523

Emsheimer, Ernst. "Musikethnographische Bibliographie der nicht-slavischen Völker in Russland." In *Acta M*, 15 (1943) p. 34–63.

[125]

A bibliography of 433 items concerned with the music of the non-Slavic peoples of Russia. Classified according to ethnic groups. German translations for Slavic titles. Some editions of folk music cited, but chiefly concerned with periodical literature and monographs. Full bibliographical information.

524

Gaskin, Lionel. A select bibliography of music in Africa; compiled at the International African Institute by L. J. P. Gaskin under the direction of Prof. K. P. Wachsmann. London, International African Institute, 1965. 83 p.

525

Haywood, Charles. A bibliography of North American folklore and folksong. Second rev. ed. New York, Dover Publications, [1961] 2 v.

First published in 1 volume by Greenberg, New York, 1951.

Vol. 1, 748 p.: concerned with the non-Indian Americans north of Mexico. Vol. 2, p. 749–1,159: with the American Indians north of Mexico. Subdivisions in Vol. 1 include general bibliography, regional bibliography, ethnic and occupational bibliography. Vol. 2 is subdivided by cultural areas. Entries for folklore and for folk music are separated under each heading; recordings included. General index. End papers are maps of regional and cultural areas.

Review of first ed. by Duncan Emrich in *Notes*, 8 (1951) p. 700–701.

526

Henry, Mellinger Edward. A bibliography for the study of American folk-songs, with many titles of folk-songs (and titles that have to do with folk-songs) from other lands. London, Mitre Press [1937] 142 p.

Studies and collections of music interfiled in one alphabet. The emphasis is on the English-Scottish ballad and its derivatives.

527

Herzog, George. Research in primitive and folk music in the U.S., a survey. Washington, D.C., American Council of Learned Societies, 1936. 97 p.

Surveys U.S. resources for the study of primitive and folk music as of 1936. Record archives are described and their holdings tabulated; collections of primitive musical instruments listed. Bibliographies given for each of the main sections.

528

Kunst, Jaap. Ethnomusicology, a study of its nature, its problems, methods and representative personalities, to which is added a bibliography. 3rd ed. enl. The Hague, Nijhoff, 1959. 303 p.

First published in 1950 under the title *Musicologica*. . . . The 2nd edition, 1955, contains a selective bibliography.

Bibliography of the 3rd edition, p. 79–215, lists 4,552 items, most of them with location symbols referring to libraries in Western Europe. Entries which contain extensive bibliographies within themselves are marked with an asterisk. Portraits of ethnomusicologists.

Supplement to the 3rd edition, 1960, 45 p., adds some 500 items to the bibliography; new record listings through 1958, more portraits.

Review of the 3rd ed. by Bruno Nettl in *Notes*, 16 (1959) p. 560–61; of the *Supplement* by William Lichtenwanger in *Notes*, 19 (1961) p. 79.

Lawless, Ray McKinley. Folksingers and folksongs in America. . . . See no. 141.

529

Laws, George M. Native American balladry; a descriptive study and a bibliographical syllabus. Philadelphia, American Folklore Society, 1950. 276 p. (Publications of the American Folklore Society. Bibliographical Series, v. 1.)

530

League of Nations. International Institute of Intellectual Cooperation. Folklore musical; répertoire international des collections et centres de documentation avec notices sur l'état actuel des recherches dans les différents pays et références bibliographiques. Paris, Département d'Art, d'Archéologie et d'Ethnologie, Institut International de Coopération Intellectuelle [1939] 332 p.

Organization similar to the following item. Special section devoted to the international phonorecord archive in Berlin, Paris, and Vienna. P. 307–32: supplement of additions and corrections to the 1934 volume, below.

531

League of Nations. International Institute of Intellectual Cooperation. Musique et chanson populaires. Paris, Institut International de Coopération Intellectuelle, 1934. 257 p.

A reference book intended to establish an international listing of museums, archives, libraries, and other institutions, public and private,

[127]

concerned with research or collection in the field of popular music, with descriptions of their facilities. Contributions by leading specialists arranged alphabetically by country. Most of the essays contain bibliographies of studies and editions and a list of names and addresses of specialists.

532
Lomax, Alan and Sidney R. Cowell. American folksong and folklore, a regional bibliography. New York, Progressive Education Association, 1942. 59 p.

533
Merriam, Alan P. "An annotated bibliography of African and African-derived music since 1936." In *Africa*, 21 (1951) p. 319–30.

534
Nettl, Bruno. Reference materials in ethnomusicology. Detroit, Information Service, Inc., 1961. 46 p. (Detroit studies in music bibliography, 1.)
A narrative and critical discussion of the leading reference materials in the field, organized in terms of the structure of the discipline. P. 37–46: a list of publications cited, with full bibliographical information.
Review by William Lichtenwanger in *Notes*, 19 (1962) p. 428–30; by Marius Schneider in *Die Musikforschung*, 17 (1964) p. 88–89.

535
Nettl, Bruno. Theory and method in ethnomusicology. New York, The Free Press, 1964. 306 p.
Chapter 2 is a history of the field, focusing on bibliography. Each chapter is followed by a list of publications cited.
Review by David P. McAllester in *MQ*, 51 (1965) p. 425–28.

536
Thieme, Darius L. African music, a briefly annotated bibliography. Washington, D.C., Library of Congress, Reference Department, Music Division, 1964. 55 p. (typescript).

The present work lists sources discussing the music of sub-Saharan Africa. The work is divided into two main sections, the first listing periodicals and serial articles, the second listing books (Preface).

A bilibography of 597 items, with an author and linguistic area index.

537
Varley, Douglas H. African native music, an annotated bibliography. London, The Royal Empire Soc., 1936. 116 p.

Two sections of general bibliograhy followed by local bibliographies relating to 30 African countries. Special section on "African survivals in the New World." List of museums containing collections of African instruments. Author index. Brief but informative annotations.

538
Waterman, Richard [et al.]. "Bibliography of Asiatic musics." In *Notes*, 5:1–8:2 (Dec., 1947—March, 1951) 181 p. in all.

A classified bibliography, published serially, 3,488 books, monographs, article, sections of larger works, texts, transcriptions and recordings, arranged geographically and ethnologically. All European languages, including Russian and Romanized Turkish.

Special and Subject: Instruments

539
Graaf, G. A. C. de. Literature on the organ, principally in Dutch libraries. Amsterdam [1957] 71 p.

Lists over 1,250 titles of books, brochures, and reprints concerning the use, the history and the construction of organs. Does not include books on organ playing.

540
Heron-Allen, Edward. De fidiculis bibliographia: being an attempt towards a bibliography of the violin. . . . London, Griffith Farran & Co., 1890–94. 2 v.

Classified bibliography of literature on the violin in all its aspects. Full bibliographical data and copious annotations. The work was issued in parts, printed on recto only, and concludes with 4 supplements.

541
Hutschenruyter, Willem. Bijdrage tot de bibliographie der muziek-literatuur. Een zooveel mogelijk aangevulde samenvatting der boek- en tijdschrift-overzichten, die sedert 1885 zijn opgenomen in het *Viertel-jahrschrift für Musikwissenschaft*, het *Zeitschrift der Internationalen Musik-gesellschaft*, en het *Jahrbuch der Musikbibliothek Peters*. [v. 1] Instrumentale muziek, mechanische muziek, electrische muziek, klokken. Zeist, 1941. 513 p. (typescript).

Incomplete. A projected comprehensive bibliography of music literature that progressed only so far as to include writings on instrumental music, electrical music, and bells.

542

Miller, Dayton C. Catalogue of books and literary material relating to the flute and other musical instruments, with annotations. Cleveland, Prov. pr., 1935. 120 p.

Includes books and pamphlets, short magazine articles and newspaper clippings, concert programs, maker's catalogues and price-lists, index of poetical quotations, patent specifications, novels, etc.

Material on all wind instruments included; unclassified; brief annotations.

The literary portion of one of the largest collections ever assembled on the flute and related instruments. Now in the Music Division of the Library of Congress.

For a catalog of the instruments in this collection, see no. 1184.

543

Schlesinger, Kathleen. A bibliography of musical instruments and archaeology. . . . London, W. Reeves, 1912. 100 p.

Only the first 20 pages are devoted to works on musical instruments and the orchestra. Short sections on catalogs of instrument collections, and general works on music. The greater part of the volume is devoted to classical and medieval antiquities.

544

Torri, Luigi. La costruzione ed i costruttori degli istrumenti ad arco. Bibliografia liutistica storico-tecnica. 2a edizione. . . . Padova, G. Zanibon [1920] 43 p.

Brief critical and descriptive annotations. Alphabetically arranged, with a subject index.

Special and Subject: Jazz

545

Merriam, Alan P. A bibliography of jazz. With the assistance of Robert J. Benford. Philadelphia, American Folklore Society, 1954. 145 p. (Publications of the American Folklore Society, Bibliographical series, 4.)

3,324 numbered entries, arranged alphabetically by author, with subject emphasis indicated by a code system. List of 113 jazz periodicals. Subject index.

Review by Marshall W. Stearns in *Notes*, 12 (1955) p. 436–37.

546
    Reisner, Robert G. The literature of jazz; a selective bibliography. With an introduction by Marshall W. Stearns. New York, The New York Public Library, 1959. 63 p.

    A preliminary edition appeared in *The Bulletin of the New York Public Library*, March–May, 1954.

    Classified as to books on the subject, background books, a selective list of magazine references, magazines devoted wholly or principally to jazz.

    Review by William Lichtenwanger in *Notes*, 16 (1959) p. 398.

Special and Subject:
Medieval and Renaissance Music

547
    Gleason, Harold. Music in the Middle Ages and Renaissance. 2nd ed. Rochester, N.Y. Levis Music Stores, 1951. 158 p. (Music literature outlines, series 1.)

    The outline follows the organization of Reese's *Music in the Middle Ages*, but each section is accompanied by numerous bibliographical references to books, periodical articles, scores, and recordings.

548
    Reese, Gustave. "Bibliography." In his *Music in the Middle Ages*. New York, Norton [1940] p. 425–63.

    Lists books, periodical articles, facsimiles, and editions. Somewhat difficult to use because the material is grouped under chapter headings, but one of the most comprehensive bibliographies available for students of medieval music.

549
    Reese, Gustave. "Bibliography." In his *Music in the Renaissance*. Rev. ed. New York, Norton, 1959. P. 884–946.

    A comprehensive bibliography of monographs, editions, and periodical articles related to Renaissance music. Unclassified, alphabetical arrangement.

550
    Smith, Carleton Sprague and William Dinneen. "Recent work on music in the Renaissance." In *Modern philology*, 42:1 (Aug., 1944) p. 41–58.

    A bibliographical article in narrative style citing and evaluating research

[131]

and editorial activity in Renaissance music from about 1900 to date of publication.

551

Smits van Waesberghe, Joseph. "Die gegenwärtige Geschichtsbild der mittelalterlichen Musik." In *Kirchenmusikalisches Jahrbuch*, 46– . 1962– .

A narrative survey and discussion, under major topics, of the contributions on Medieval music in 19 current musicological and historical journals.

1: For 1957–60, in Jahrgang 46 (1962) p. 61–82. 2: For 1960–62, in Jahrgang 47 (1963) p. 11–38. 3: For 1963, in Jahrgang 48 (1964) p. 1–26. 4: For 1964, in Jahrgang 49 (1965) p. 9–33.

552

Suñol, Grégorio María. "Bibliographie générale." In his *Introduction à la paléographie musicale grégorienne*. Paris, Desclée, 1935. P. 511–65.

This bibliography first appeared in 1925 as part of the original Spanish edition of the author's work on Gregorian paleography.

317 items on medieval music with emphasis on plainchant. Listed in order of publication and broadly classified.

Special and Subject: Music Education

553

International Society for Music Education. International listing of teaching aids in music education. Edited by Egon Kraus. Cologne, International Society for Music Education. (Distributing agent: Möseler Verlag, Wolfenbüttel.) 1959. 52 p.

A classified bibliography of materials, since 1945, concerned with music instruction.

Review by Theodore Normann in *Journal of research in music education*, 8 (1960). P. 55–56.

554

Modisett, Katherine C. "Bibliography of sources, 1930–52, relating to the teaching of choral music in secondary schools." In *Journal of research in music education*, 3 (1955). P. 51–60.

A classified bibliography of 236 items, with a brief introductory survey of the field and its problems.

555
Music Educators National Conference. Committee on Bibliography. "Music education materials, a selected bibliography." Published as v. 7, no. 1 of the *Journal of research in music education*, 1959. 146 p.

A classified listing of materials. Major groupings are: elementary music education; junior high school; choral materials; instructional materials for . . . instrumental music; music appreciation guides and reference materials; music theory texts an workbooks; audio-visual aids; teacher training.

556
Music Educators National Conference. Curriculum Committee. Music education source book [number one]. Ed. by Hazel N. Morgan. Chicago, Music Educators National Conference, 1951. 268 p.

First printed in 1947.

Various sections contain brief bibliographies; the 1951 printing has an appendix of revisions and additions. Much of the bibliographical material of the first four printings is now out of date.

557
Music Educators National Conference. Music in American Education Committee. Music in American education. Music education source book, number two. Ed. by Hazel N. Morgan. Chicago, Music Educators National Conference, 1955. 365 p.

Brief bibliographies to various chapters and subchapters concerned with aspects of American public school music.

558
Music Educators National Conference. Selected bibliography, music education materials. [Prepared for the U.S. Department of State by a special committee of the MENC]. Chicago, Music Educators National Conference [1952]. 64 p.

Contains five bibliographies, classified, partially annotated: music education materials for elementary schools; collections for junior high; collections for senior high; instrumental music materials; textbooks on music education. Emphasizes school music performance materials.

Special and Subject: National Music

The first fifteen entries in this section call attention to a series of articles that have appeared in *Acta musicologica*, journal of the International Musicological Society, since 1957. These articles survey the bibliographical and research activities in music in various countries since the end of World War II. Most of them cite major scholarly publications, dissertations, and important music reference works.

Austria

559

Wessely, Othmar. "Die österreichische Musikforschung nach dem zweiten Weltkrieg," in *Acta M*, 29 (1957) p. 111–19.

Belgium

560

Clercx-Lejeune, Suzanne. "La musicologie en Belgique depuis 1945," in *Acta M*, 30 (1958) p. 199–214; with a supplement in v. 31 (1959) p. 130–32.

Finland

561

Ringbom, Nils-Eric. "Die Musikforschung in Finnland seit 1940," in *Acta M*, 31 (1959) p. 17–24.

France

562

Lesure, François. "La musicologie française depuis 1945," in *Acta M*, 30 (1958) p. 3–17.

Germany

563

Heckmann, Harald. "Musikwissenschaftliche Unternehmungen in Deutschland seit 1945," in *Acta M*, 29 (1957) p. 75–94.

Holland

564

Reeser, Eduard. "Musikwissenschaft in Holland," in *Acta M*, 32 (1960) p. 160–74.

Israel

565

Gerson-Kiwi, Edith. "Musicology in Israel," in *Acta M*, 30 (1958) p. 17–26.

Italy

566

Allorto, Riccardo e Claudio Sartori. "La musicologia italiana dal 1945 a oggi," in *Acta M*, 31 (1959) p. 9–17.

Japan

567

Nomura, Francesco Yosio. "Musicology in Japan since 1945," in *Acta M*, 35 (1963) p. 47–53.

Latin America

568

Devoto, Daniel. "Panorama de la musicología Latinoamericana," in *Acta M*, 31 (1959) p. 91–109.

Portugal

569

Kastner, Macario Santiago. "Veinte años de musicología en Portugal (1940–60)," in *Acta M*, 32 (1960) p. 1–11.

Scandinavia

570

Rosenberg, Herbert. "Musikwissenschaftliche Bestrebungen in Dänemark, Norwegen und Schweden in den letzten ca. 15 Jahren," in *Acta M*, 30 (1958) p. 118–37.

Switzerland

571

Schanzlin, Hans Peter. "Musikwissenschaft in der Schweiz (1938–58)," in *Acta M*, 30 (1958) p. 214–24.

United States

572

Goldthwaite, Scott. "The growth and influence of musicology in the United States," in *Acta M*, 33 (1961) p. 72–79; with a "Codetta: some details of musicology in the United States," by Jan LaRue, p. 79–83.

Yugoslavia

573

Cvetko, Dragotin. "Les formes et les résultats des efforts musicologiques yougoslaves," in *Acta M*, 31 (1959) p. 50–62.

574

Chase, Gilbert. Guide to Latin American music. Washington, D.C. The Library of Congress, Music Division, 1945. 274 p.

2nd ed., 1962, under the title *A Guide to the music of Latin America*. 411 p.

A general bibliography of 301 items, followed by listings related to individual Latin American countries; 2,699 items in all. Index of authors, and of names and subjects.

575

Correia de Azevedo, Luís H. [et al.]. Bibliografia musical brasileira (1820–1950). Rio de Janeiro, 1952. 252 p. (Ministerio da Educação e Saúde, Instituto Nacional do Livro, Col. BI, Bibliografia 9.)

1,639 titles under 13 subject sections. Includes writings by Brazilian authors on non-Brazilian music. Publications containing music only are omitted.

Review by A. Hyatt King in *Music and letters*, 35 (Jan., 1954) p. 67–68; by Charles Seeger in *Notes*, 11 (1954) p. 551–52.

576

Davidsson, Åke. Bibliografi över Svensk Musiklitteratur, 1800–1945. Uppsala, 1948. 215 p.

A classified bibliography of general works, general music histories, histories of music in Sweden, works on musicians of all nationalities, and theoretical works. Restricted to writings by Swedish authors except for subjects connected with Swedish music. 5,432 items in all. Index.

577

Historical Records Survey. District of Columbia. Bio-bibliographical index of musicians in the U.S.A. from Colonial times.

Washington, D.C., Library of Congress, Music Division, 1941. 439 p. (Pan American Union, Music Division. Music series, 2.)

Indexes biographical material in about 65 books, giving biographies of musicians in the U.S. P. 421–39: a list of special studies, biographies, and autobiographies pertaining to persons whose names appear in the index.

578

Kinscella, Hazel G. "Americana index to *The musical quarterly, 1915–57.*" Published as vol. 6:2 (1958) of *The journal of research in music education.* 144 p.

579

Lissa, Zofia. "Die Musikwissenschaft in Volkspolen (1945–56)." In *Die Musikforschung,* 10 (1957) p. 531–47.

Translated from the Polish by Werner Kaupert.

In narrative style with many titles quoted. Discusses the state and organization of Polish musicology since World War II.

580

Michałowski, Kornel. Bibliografia muzyczna polskich czasopism niemuzycznycn. V. 1– . Cracow, Polskie Wydawnictwo Muzyczne, 1962– .

A bibliography of writings on music in Polish nonmusical periodicals from 1800 to 1830.

581

Michałowski, Kornel. Bibliografia polskiego piśmiennictwa muzycznego. [Cracow] Polskie Wydawnictwo Muzyczne [1955] 280 p. (Materiały do bibliografii muzyki polskiej, 3.)

A classified bibliography of some 2,000 items of Polish music literature. Includes a list of music theses completed in Polish universities, 1917–54.

582

"Music Section." In *Handbook of Latin American studies, a guide to the material published in 1935–1948.* Nos. 1–14. . . . Cambridge, Mass., Harvard Univ. Press, 1936–51. 14 v.

583

Nef, Karl. Schriften über Musik und Volksgesang. Bern, K. J. Wyss, 1908. 151 p. (Bibliographie der schweizerischen Landeskunde, Faszikel V 6d.)

A classified bibliography of literature on Swiss music, its history and practice. Index of names.

584

Potúček, Juraj. Súpis slovenských hudobnín, a literatúry o hudobníkoch. Bratislava, Nakadateľstvo slovenskej akadémie vied a umnení, 1952. 435 p.

List of musicians, briefly identified, active in Slovakia to 1949 or mentioned in Slovak periodical literature. Bibliographies of works with Slovak texts, 1881 to 1949. Chronological index, classified index, name index.

585

Potúček, Juraj. Súpis slovenských hudobnoteoretických prác (knižné publikácie, štúdie, članky, kritiky a referáty). Bratislava, Vydavateľstvo slovenskej akadémie vied, 1955. 469 p.

Bibliography of music and books on music published in Czechoslovakia: classified bibliography of literary and theoretical works, including periodical articles, p. 15–216. List of theoretical works in chronological order, 1519–1853, p. 219–25. Biographical section, including under composer's name both publications of music and biographical or critical articles, p. 223–380. Classified list of music published 1950–52, p. 383–403. Chronological index of music, 1830–1953. General index.

586

Rajeczky, B. "Musikforschung in Ungarn 1936–1960 (Bibliographischer Bericht)." In *Studia musicologica*, 1 (1961) p. 225–49.

A brief survey of recent Hungarian musical scholarship, with a classified bibliography of music literature. Hungarian titles given with German translations. Sections on folk music, Hungarian music history, general music history, collective works.

587

Rocha da Silva Guimarães, Bertino D. Primeiro esboco duma bibliografia musical portuguesa, com uma breve notícia histórica de música no nosso país. Porto, 1947. 174 p.

P. 13–36: brief history of Portuguese music.

The bibliography includes works on music by Portuguese authors, works on music in Portugal by native or foreign authors, old Portuguese pedagogical works, special bibliographies (sacred music, villancicos, opera, etc.), and music periodicals.

588

Schaal, Richard. Das Schrifttum zur musikalischen Lokalgeschichtsforschung. Kassel, Bärenreiter [1947] 62 p.

A bibliography of works about music in various European cities and provinces, arranged alphabetically by place. Includes articles from a few leading periodicals. Very brief citations.

589
Sendrey, Alfred. Bibliography of Jewish music. New York, Columbia Univ. Press, 1951. 404 p.

A classified bibliography of 5,854 items concerned with writings on Jewish music and musicians. Includes periodical articles.

Part II of this work is entered as no.   .

Review by Milton Feist in *MQ*, 37 (1951) p. 432–35; by Ernst C. Krohn in *JAMS*, 7 (Summer, 1954) p. 150–52.

590
Vyborny, Zdenek. "Czech music literature since World War II," in *Notes*, 16 (1959) p. 539–46.

Translated from the German by William Lichtenwanger.

A classified bibliography, each section preceded by a brief descriptive statement. Titles given in Czech and English.

591
Woodfill, Walter L. "Bibliography." In his *Musicians in English society*. Princeton, N.J., Princeton Univ. Press, 1953. P. 315–61.

A substantial listing of the primary and secondary sources for the study of English music of the late 16th and early 17th centuries. Separated as to works before and after 1700.

The Woodfill bibliography is a particularly fine example of the kind of information to be expected in histories of national music, or monographs related to the music of a local school or development.

Special and Subject: Opera and Theatre Music

592
Baker, Blanch M. "Music." In *Theatre and allied arts, a guide to books dealing with the history, criticism, and technic of the drama and theatre and related arts and crafts*. New York, H. W. Wilson, 1952. P. 428–41.

Broadly classified and selective list. Annotated. Few entries have more than an indirect bearing on theater music.

593
Bustico, Guido. Bibliografia della storie e cronistorie dei teatri italiani. Milano, Bollettino bibliografico musicale, 1929. 82 p.

Subtitle: "Il teatro musicale italiano."

Part I (p. 19–27): a general bibliography of the Italian musical theater. Part II (p. 31–83): a bibliography of the musical theater in specific Italian cities, arranged alphabetically by place. Includes periodical articles. Some brief descriptive annotations.

594

Grout, Donald J. "Bibliographies, lexicons, guides, histories and other works dealing with opera. . . ." In his *A short history of opera*. 2nd edition. New York, Columbia Univ. Press, 1965. P. 585–768.

One of the most comprehensive bibliographies of literature on the opera. Includes both books and articles in leading European and American periodicals. Arranged alphabetically by author.

Special and Subject: Primary Sources [Early Music Literature]

The bibliographies in this section are concerned with writings on music that appeared before 1800. For further listings of early music literature, one should consult the general bibliographies compiled before 1840, such as Becker (no. 414), Forkel (no. 425), and Lichtenthal (no. 432). See also the narrative bibliography by Matthew (no. 435) and the catalogs of libraries with noteworthy holdings in early music theory, such as the U.S. Library of Congress (no. 1117), the library of the late Alfred Cortot (no. 1133), and the Paul Hirsch Library (no. 1135).

595

Bukofzer Manfred F. "Check-list of baroque books on music." In his *Music in the Baroque era*. New York, Norton [1947] p. 417–31.

Theory treatises, instruction books, and histories written between *c.* 1590 and 1770. Modern facsimiles and reprints indicated. Arranged alphabetically by author.

596

Coover, James B. "Music theory in translation; a bibliography." In *Journal of music theory*, 3 (1959) p. 70–95.

Includes only English translations of early theory works. An alphabetical listing, by author, of works from antiquity to the present day.

597

Davidsson, Åke. Bibliographie der musiktheoretischen Drucke des 16. Jahrhunderts. Baden-Baden, Heitz, 1962. 99 p. (Bibliotheca bibliographica aureliana, 9.)

A bibliography of 16th-century theory works; more than 600 titles, arranged alphabetically by author, with bibliographical references. Index of persons, including printers, editors, etc. Bibliography, p. 85–88. 25 facsimile plates.

Future volumes projected to cover the 17th and 18th centuries.

Review by Fred Blum in *Notes*, 20 (1963) p. 234.

598
Davidsson, Åke. Catalogue critique et descriptif des ouvrages théoriques sur la musique imprimés au XVIe et au XVIIe siècles et conservés dans les bibliothèques suédoises. Upsala [Almquist & Wiksells] 1953. 83 p. (Studia musicologica upsaliensia, 2.)

A union catalog of early works on music theory in Swedish libraries. 108 items fully described, with locations and references to relevant literature. P. 77–83: bibliography of works cited.

599
Farmer, Henry G. The sources of Arabian music: an annotated bibliography of Arabic manuscripts which deal with the theory, practice, and history of Arabian music from the eighth to the seventeenth century. Leiden, E. J. Brill, 1965. 71 p.

First issued privately by the author in 1940.

Entries arranged chronologically by century, preceded by a brief general discussion of Arabian music and its sources. Author index.

600
Mandyczewski, Eusebius. "Bücher und Schriften über Musik. Druckwerke und Handschriften aus der Zeit bis zum Jahre 1800." In *Geschichte der K. K. Gesellschaft der Musikfreunde in Wien....* Wien, 1912. V. 2, p. 55–84.

An extremely useful listing of pre-1800 writings on music, based on the holdings of the Gesellschaft der Musikfreunde in Vienna.

See no. 1104 for a full citation of the *Geschichte*.

601
Reese, Gustave. Fourscore classics of music literature; a guide to selected original sources on theory and other writings on music not available in English, with descriptive sketches and bibliographical references. New York, The Liberal Arts Press, 1957. 91 p.

80 works presented in chronological order, with illuminating commentary. This bibliography, sponsored by the American Council of

Learned Societies, was intended to stimulate new English editions and translations of important early theory works. Index of titles.

602

Riley, Maurice W. "A tentative bibliography of early wind instrument tutors." In *Journal of research in music education*, 6 (1958) p. 3–24.

The listing is chronological under the various instruments: flute, oboe, clarinet, bassoon, horn, trumpet, trombone, tuba, and related instruments. Annotated.

603

Smits van Waesberghe, Joseph, ed. The theory of music from the Carolingian era up to 1400. V. 1– . Edited by Joseph Smits van Waesberghe with the collaboration of Peter Fischer and Christian Maas. Descriptive catalogue of manuscripts. München, G. Henle Verlag [1961] 155 p. (International inventory of musical sources, ser. B, v. 3:1.)

Offers a description of all manuscripts in which are preserved Latin treatises— however small—dealing with the theory of music which was in use from the Carolingian era to 1400 (Preface).

Index of libraries; index of authors and of incipits of anonymous treatises.

Review by James B. Coover in *Journal of music theory*, 6 (1962) p. 314–15.

Special and Subject: Sacred Music

Bibliographies of writings on sacred music are surprisingly few. Additional references will be found in the various handbooks to hymnology (nos. 237–46). See also the current listings in the *Jahrbuch für Liturgik und Hymnologie* (no. 454) and Gregório Suñol's bibliography of works related to Gregorian chant. (no. 552).

604

Buszin, Walter [et al.]. A bibliography on music and the church. Prepared for the Commission on music, Dept. of Worship and the Arts, National Council of Churches of Christ in the U.S.A. New York, National Council of Churches of Christ, 1958. 16 p.

Bibliographies of Music

IN this category are listed bibliographies of *musical scores* as distinct from *writings about music*. This section lends itself to fewer subdivisions than the preceding "Bibliographies of Music Literature," the major approaches being that of the performer in search of music appropriate to his particular instrument or ensemble and that of the student of early music.

Not included here are the numerous listings of the works of individual composers, including the thematic catalogs. One of the best approaches to information of this kind is through the biographical dictionaries such as *Baker* (no. 51) and *Riemann* (no. 38), or such comprehensive encyclopedias as *MGG* (no. 6). For thematic catalogs, except for the most recent, a useful guide is found in the Music Library Association's *Check list of thematic catalogues* (no. 1359).

This section also excludes the catalogs of individual music publishing firms, except where their coverage extends beyond the output of a single business house.

General

Included are those bibliographies in which the intent of the compiler is to cover a large or hetrogeneous body of materials (performance being one of several possible interests), or music confined to a particular national group: Belgian, Swedish, Finnish, etc.

605
American Society of Composers, Authors and Publishers.
ASCAP symphonic catalog. Second edition, including 1966 supplement. New York, American Society of Composers, Authors and Publishers [1966] 369 p. (bound with *1966 Supplement*, 376 p.).

Alphabetical listing, by composers and arrangers, of symphonic literature controlled by ASCAP. Entries give instrumentation, duration, publisher. Supplementary list of publishers' addresses.

For a corresponding volume issued by Broadcast Music, Inc., see no. 611.

606

Aronowsky, Salomon. Performing times of orchestral works. Foreword by Percival R. Kirby. London, E. Benn, 1959. 802 p.

Covers both standard and minor composers of all countries and periods, with some emphasis on British names. Arrangements listed under both composer and arranger. Operas, orchestral versions of single songs, and opera excerpts appear frequently. No precise indication of edition or publisher, but lists of publishers and publishers' organizations are given. The work is a more lavish and expensive publication than seems warranted by its contents.

Review by Howard Mitchell in *Notes*, 17 (1960) p. 237–39.

607

Berkowitz, Freda P. Popular titles and subtitles of musical compositions. New York, Scarecrow Press, inc., 1962. 182 p.

Alphabetical listing of 502 works, by title, with brief accounts of the origins of their popular titles. Bibliography. Composer index.

608

Boll, André. Répertoire analytique de la musique française des origines à nos jours. Paris, Horizons de France [1948] 299 p.

Not as comprehensive as the title suggests. Part 1: a list of composers of the French school, with dates, arranged alphabetically within historical periods. Part 2: a classified list of published French secular music, alphabetical by composer, followed by a similar listing of sacred music. Publishers indicated. Indexed by works and by composers.

609

Boustead, Alan. Music to Shakespeare, a practical catalogue of current incidental music, song settings and other related music.... London, printed by Novello and Co., sole distributor, Oxford Univ. Press, 1964. 40 p.

Shakespearean works entered alphabetically, with music given under three headings: (1) incidental music; (2) songs; (3) other music. Minimum bibliographical information. Indexes of song titles and of composers. No key to publishers.

For other listings of Shakespeare music, see no. 613.

610

British Broadcasting Corporation. Central Music Library.
[Catalogues] London, British Broadcasting Corp., 1965– .

[1] Chamber music catalogue: chamber music, violin and keyboard, cello and keyboard, various. (1965) 1 v. various pagings.

[2] Piano and organ catalogue. (1965) 2 v. various pagings.

[3] Song catalogue. I. Composers A–K. (1966) 605 p.

These volumes, in process of publication, record the holdings of one of the world's great radio libraries. Each volume is devoted to a special category of materials. Entries include composer's full name, dates if known, title of the work, score or parts, duration, publisher. A bibliography of relevant reference works and a listing of the principal music publishers are given in each volume. The chief value of the set lies in the information it offers as a reference tool. The BBC Music Library is not a lending library.

Published under the supervision of John H. Davies, BBC Music Librarian; with an introduction by William Glock. Review by Donald Krummel in *Notes*, 23 (1966) p. 46–48.

611

Broadcast Music Inc. Symphonic catalogue. New York, Broadcast Music Inc. [1963] 132 p.

An alphabetical listing, by composer, of symphonic works the performing rights of which are controlled by Broadcast Music Inc. Entries give instrumentation, duration, and publishers of the works.

For a parallel volume issued by the American Society of Composers, Authors and Publishers, see no. 605.

612

Bryant, Eric T. Music librarianship; a practical guide. London, James Clarke; New York, Hafner [1959] 503 p.

Part II, p. 287–487, is a series of lists of recommended musical scores for libraries, classified under instrumental music, vocal music, miniature scores. Detailed annotations. The Bryant work is also entered as no. 1323.

613

"Catalogue of Musical Works Based on the Plays and Poetry of Shakespeare." Compiled by Winton Dean, Dorothy Moore, and Phyllis Hartnoll. In *Shakespeare in music*. London, Macmillan, 1964. P. 243–321.

Works listed under the titles of the plays, in three categories: opera, incidental music, song settings. Check list of composers. The bibliography of operatic settings, by Winton Dean, is also published in *Shakespeare survey*, No. 18 (1965) p. 75–93.

[145]

614

Centre Belge de Documentation Musicale. Catalogus van werken van Belgische componisten. Bruxelles, Centre Belge de Documentation Musicale, 1953–57. 20 numbers.

A series of paper-bound catalogs (11 in French, 9 in Flemish) averaging 20 pages each, devoted to contemporary Belgian composers and their works.

615

Cudworth, Charles. "Ye olde spuriosity shoppe or, put it in the *Anhang.*" In *Notes*, 12 (1954–55) p. 25–40, 533–53.

A lively discussion of the problems of plagiarism, hoaxes, misattribution, and the use of pseudonyms in the music field. The article contains three useful supplements: (1) spuriosities proper, listed under their supposed composers; (2) nicknamed and falsely titled compositions; (3) pseudonyms, altered forms of names, and nicknames.

For works covering similar material, see nos. 607, 627.

616

Cushing, Helen G. Children's song index, an index to more than 22,000 songs in 189 collections comprising 222 volumes. New York, H. W. Wilson, 1936, 798 p.

A dictionary catalog of children's song literature. Main entry is by song title, with subordinate entries under composer, author of the words, and subject. References from first line to title. Foreign titles given in the original language. There is a preliminary "catalog of collections indexed," and a "directory of publishers" at the end of the volume.

617

De Charms, Desiree and Paul F. Breed. Songs in collections, an index. [Detroit] Information Service, Inc., 1966. 588 p.

Indexes 411 collections of solo songs published between 1940 and 1957. Entries for more than 9,400 songs. Composed songs entered under composer, with anonymous and folk songs entered alphabetically by title under nationality. Separate sections for carols and for sea chanties. Complete title and first line index.

This work articulates with the Sears *Song index*, see no. 635.

618

Dedinsky, Izabella K. Zeneművek, 1936–40. Budapest, Kiadja az országos széchényi könyvtár, 1944. 286 p. (Az 1936–40. Evkör magyar szakkönyvészete.)

Classified bibliography of music published in Hungary, 1936–40. Includes both popular and serious music.

619

Deutscher Musikverleger-Verband. Bonner Katalog. Verzeichnis der urheberrechtlich geschützten musikalischen Werke mit reversgebundenem Aufführungsmaterial. Bonn, Musikhandel-Verlagsgesellschaft M.B.H. [1959] 326 p.

A listing, alphabetical by composer, of musical works protected by international copyright under the Bern Convention. Also includes copyright editions of works by early composers. Type of work indicated by symbol. Duration and publisher given.

An excellent source of information on published contemporary music.

620

"Documents du Demi-Siècle. Tableau chronologique des principales oeuvres musicales de 1900 à 1950 étabili par genre et par année. Numéro spécial." *La revue musicale*, no. 216 (1952) 146 p.

A listing, year by year, of the important musical works of the first half of the 20th century, together with miscellaneous information relating to music for each year. Catalogs of six publishers, with significant works issued by them between 1900 and 1950: Heugel, Costallat, Amphion, Ricordi, Choudens, Ouvrières. Minimal bibliographical information.

621

Föreningen Svenska Tonsättare. Nyare svenska orkesterverk samt instrumental- och vokalverk med orkester. Katalog. Swedish orchestral works (20th century) including instrumental soli and vocal works with orchestra. Stockholm, Society of Swedish Composers, 1956. 109 p.

Supplement, 1959. 15 p.

Earlier lists published in 1937 and 1944. Title varies: *Nyare svenska orkester- och vokalverk, katalog.*

Classified listings of works under composers' names in alphabetical order. Information includes publisher, instrumentation, timings.

622

Foster, Myles B. Anthems and anthem composers, an essay upon the development of the anthem from the time of the Reformation to the end of the 19th century; with a complete list of anthems (in alphabetical order) belonging to each of the four centuries. . . . London, Novello, 1901. 225 p.

[147]

623

Hofmeister, Friedrich. Verzeichnis der in Deutschland seit 1868 erschienenen Werke russischer Komponisten. Leipzig, Druck der Buchdruckerei Frankenstein, 1949. 253 p.

Alphabetical listing of composers, with their works in order of opus number. Detailed bibliographical information, including price, but lacking date of publication.

624

Leigh, Robert. Index to song books, a title index to over 11,000 copies of almost 6,800 songs in 111 song books published between 1933 and 1962. Stockton, Calif., Robert Leigh, 1964. 273 p.

Intended to supplement the Sears *Song index*, no. 635.

625

McCarty, Clifford. Film composers in America: a check-list of their work. Foreword by Lawrence Morton. Glendale, Calif., John Valentin [1953] 193 p.

163 names, with film scores listed by date. Index of film titles; index of orchestrators.

Review by F. W. Sternfeld in *Notes*, 11 (1953) p. 105.

Also entered as no. 142.

626

McColvin, Lionel R. and Harold Reeves. "Music: a comprehensive classified list." In their *Music libraries*. London, Grafton, 1937–38. V. 2, p. 1–209.

A guide to selection for music librarians. A classified list containing, for the most part, music in print at the time of compilation. Emphasis on British publishers, though some foreign material is included. This list has been superseded, to a large extent, by the one given in Bryant, see no. 612.

627

Mies, Paul. Volkstümliche Namen musikalischer Werke. Bonn, Musikhandel-Verlags [1960] 32 p.

Nicknames and popular titles for musical compositions, listed under composers with an alphabetical index of titles.

Similar compilations are cited as no. 607, 615.

628

The Music Trader's Guide to Works by Twentieth Century British Composers, together with the names of their publishers; comprising instrumental works, songs, text books and manuals up to and including June, 1955, compiled by L. D. Gibbin. London, Boosey & Hawkes [1956] 132 p.

Brief entries for works by 76 composers, listed alphabetically by title under the composers' names. Supplementary listing for "other British composers and their principal publishers."

629
National Jewish Welfare Board. Bibliography Committee. Bibliography of Jewish instrumental music. New York, National Jewish Music Council [1948] 16 p.
Addenda [1950] 7 leaves.
A selective list of the "best and most interesting works that are easily available . . . either in published form or through rental." Classified according to various combinations of instruments. Publishers indicated.

630
National Jewish Welfare Board. Bibliography Committee. Bibliography of Jewish vocal music. New York, National Jewish Music Council [*c*. 1948] 36 p.
Addenda [1950] 15 leaves.
A selective list of available Jewish vocal music, "in good taste, and . . . suited for programming." Classified by genre. Language or languages of text, and publishers, indicated.

631
Nordiska Musikförlaget. Swedish orchestral works. Annotated catalogue. [Commentary by Edvin Kallstenius] Stockholm, Nordiska Musikförlaget [1948] 85 p.

This catalogue is intended to guide conductors, members of programme committees and other music lovers who wish to learn something about Swedish composition (Foreword).

Selected works by 25 contemporary Swedish composers. Portraits and brief biographical sketches.

632
Pan American Union. Music Section. Latin American orchestral music available in the United States. Washington, Pan American Union [1956] 79 p.
Supersedes a shorter list issued in 1955.
Part I: classified list of Latin American music available through publishing houses and other agencies. Part II: Latin American music in the Edwin A. Fleisher Collection in the Free Library of Philadelphia.

[149]

633

Reddick, William. The standard musical repertoire, with accurate timings. Garden City, N.Y., Doubleday & Co., 1947. 192 p.

A classified list of overtures, orchestral works, works for piano and for violin, songs, and choral numbers, with timings to the nearest 5 seconds. Designed primarily for program directors of radio stations.

634

Säveltäjäin Tekijänoikeustoimisto Teosto. Catalogue of Finnish orchestral and vocal compositions. Helsinki, Teosto (Composers' copyright bureau) [1951] 88 p.

Lists works for 57 Finnish composers, giving titles, instrumentation, timings, publishers. Brief biographical sketches. English translations of Finnish titles.

635

Sears, Minnie E. Song index: an index to more than 12,000 songs in 177 song collections . . . New York, H. W. Wilson Co., 1926. 650 p.

Supplement: an index to more than 7,000 songs in 104 collections . . . 1934. 366 p.

Contains titles, first lines, authors' names, and composers' names in one alphabet. Each song is cited under title, with added entry under composer and author, and cross references for first line and variant or translated titles. Classified and alphabetical listings of the song collections indexed.

The work of Sears has been continued in *Songs in collections* by De Charms and Breed (1966). See no. 617.

636

Sendrey, Alfred. Bibliography of Jewish music. New York, Columbia Univ. Press, 1951. 404 p.

Part II, p. 209–339: a classified list of about 4,000 pieces of Jewish music, alphabetical by composer within classifications, giving scoring, author, and language of text. Publisher and year indicated for published works; some manuscripts also listed.

The first part of this work is entered as no. 589.

637

Simbriger, Heinrich. Werkkatalog zeitgenössischer Komponisten aus den deutschen Ostgebieten. Esslingen-Necker, Künstlergilde [1955] 203 p. *Ergänzungsband*, 1961. 151 p.

A classified bibliography of works by East German composers. Entries give title of the work, instrumentation, publisher if any, and timing. A preliminary section is devoted to biographical sketches of the composers.

638

Taylor, Jed H. Vocal and instrumental music in print. New York and London, The Scarecrow Press, 1965. 166 p.

A highly selective list, containing much material of purely pedagogical interest. Classified under instrumental and vocal headings. Entries give title of work, with English translation, medium, publisher, and price. Of limited value, although there is a useful list of publishers and dealers, with their current addresses.

639

Thompson, Leila Fern. Partial list of Latin American music obtainable in the U.S., and Supplement. 3rd ed., rev. and enl. Washington, D.C., Pan American Union, Division of Music and Visual Arts, 1948. 56 leaves. *Suppl.* 17 leaves (mimeographed).

The 1st and 2nd editions were prepared by Gilbert Chase, 1941 and 1942.

Concerned with concert music to the exclusion of popular and folk music. Classified by genre and country. Scoring, language of text, and publisher indicated. Indexed by country and composer.

640

U.S. Information Agency. Catalog of published concert music by American composers. Selected, compiled and prepared by the Music Branch, Information Center Service, under the direction and supervision of the music advisor, U.S. Information Agency. [Washington, D.C., for sale by the Superintendent of Documents, U.S. Govt. Printing Office] 1965. 175 p.

Supplement No. 1, July 1965. 74 p.

A good guide to contemporary American orchestra music in print.

641

Universal-Handbuch der Musikliteratur Aller Zeiten und Völker. Als Nachschlagewerk und Studienquelle der Welt-Musikliteratur. Wien, Pazdirek & Co. [1904–10?] 14 v.

The nearest thing to a comprehensive listing of "music in print" ever published. Primarily useful for 19th-century material in establishing the existence of and dates of editions. Arrangement under composer by opus number, if known; otherwise by title.

642

Upton, Raymond. Index of miniature scores: British availability. London, C. Jackson, 1956. 120 p.

[151]

Review by Betty Buyck in *Notes*, 14 (1957) p. 367.

643

Was Wir Singen. Katalog des in der Deutschen Demokratischen Republik Erschienenen Weltlichen Lied- und Chormaterials. Band I: 1945–58 Auswahl. Herausgegeben vom Zentralhaus für Volkskunst. Leipzig, Friedrich Hofmeister [1959] 255 p.

Title listing of 6,582 entries, supplemented by lists of collections and of cantatas and oratorios under composers. Indexed by subtitles or working titles, by voice combination and by affective theme, and by national character. Further indexes by writer of text and composer.

Current

The current music bibliographies listed below restrict their entries to music only. For a full coverage, one should be acquainted with the various national bibliographies in which music appears in company with listings from other fields. An excellent introduction to the use of these major bibliographical tools is an article by Donald W. Krummel and James B. Coover, "Current national bibliographies, their music coverage," in *Notes*, 17 (1960) p. 375–88.

See also the current listings and reviews in such periodicals as *Notes*, *Fontes artis musicae*, *Acta Musicologica*, and the *Music review*.

644

The British Catalogue of Music. 1– . London, The Council of the British National Bibliography, 1957– .

Published quarterly; the last issue of each year is a cumulated annual volume. Organized in two parts: a classified and an alphabetical section. There is also a section devoted to musical literature. Lists of music publishers with their British agents specified.

The classification scheme used in this catalog has been published separately; see no. 1321.

645

Brünn. Universita. Knihovna. Prírustky hudebnin v cesko. Slovenských knihovnách. Spracoval Zdeněk Zouhar. Praha, Statní Pedagogicke Nakladatelstvi, 1953– .

Joint accession list of ten principal music libraries in Czechoslovakia, listing 2,000–3,000 items per year. Classified by medium, without index.

646

Dansk, Musikfortengnelse. Udgivet af Dansk Musikhandlerforening. V. 1– . København, 1931– .

An index to music issued by Danish music publishers. Arranged alphabetically with composers and titles interfiled. Each volume ordinarily covers three years of publication.

647

Deutsche Musikbibliographie. Jahrgang 1– . Leipzig, F. Hofmeister, 1829– .

See no. 448 for full annotation.

648

Hofmeisters Handbuch der Musikliteratur. Bd. 1– . Leipzig, F. Hofmeister, 1844– .

See no. 452 for full annotation.

649

Jahresverzeichnis der Deutschen Musikalien und Musikschriften. Jahrgang 1– . Leipzig, F. Hofmeister, 1852– .

See no. 455 for full annotation.

650

Letopis' Muzykal'noĭ Literatury; organ gosudarstvennoĭ bibliografiĭ SSSR. Izdaetsia s 1931 goda; vykhodit 4 raza v god. Moskva, Izdatel'stvo vsesoĭuznoĭ knizhnoi palaty, 1931– .

Quarterly. Organization and content vary slightly. In 1960 a classified list of publications in musical notation. Includes literary works with musical supplements or extensive musical illustrations, and music issued in periodicals. Index by composer for each issue, and separate lists of books, magazines, newspapers containing music. Annual index of vocal works by title and first line, and by language of text. Entries give full bibliographical information, including complete contents, price, size of edition.

651

Materiały do Bibliografii Muzyki Polskiej. [Redaktor serii: Tadeusz Strumiłło. Kraków] v. 1– . Polskie Wydawnictwo Muzyczne [1954]– .

Tom I: Opery polskie, opracował Kornel Michałowski, 1954. 277 p. Polish operas and foreign operas with Polish settings or subjects, listed by title, giving composer, librettist, date and place of first performance. Composer, librettist, and chronological indexes.

Tom II: Piésni solowe S. Moniuszki, katalog tematyczny, opracował

Erwin Nowaczyk, 1954. 332 p. Thematic catalog of 304 songs by Moniuszki, giving authors of texts, lists of editions, etc.

See no. 581 for further volumes in this series.

652
U.S. Copyright Office. Catalog of copyright entries. Music. Third series, v. 1– , 1947– . Washington, D.C., Copyright Office, The Library of Congress, 1947– .

From 1891 to 1906, the quarterly copyright index was issued by the Treasury Department and musical compositions were included as part of the general series. In a new series, from 1906 to 1946, a music catalog was published separately. In 1946 it was subdivided into separate sections: Published music, Unpublished music, and Renewal registrations, with main entries by composer and a classified index. This arrangement was maintained until Vol. 11 of the Third series (1958), when the listings were grouped under "Current registrations" and "Renewal registrations," with the main entry under title and a name index for composers.

653
U.S. Library of Congress. Library of Congress catalog, music and phonorecords, a cumulative list of works represented by Library of Congress printed cards. Washington, D.C., The Library of Congress, 1954– .

Current music accessions, printed or sound recordings, of the Library of Congress and of libraries participating in its cooperative cataloging program. Includes purchased current or retrospective materials and a selection of recent copyright deposits. Entries are reproduced from the library's printed cards. Name and subject index. Semiannual, with annual cumulation.

Music for Performance

The reference tools listed here are designed for the musician who has a specific objective in view; namely, the selection of material for performance, for solo or ensemble use. The need for such tools is a perpetual one and has given rise to generous number of resources. Following is a summary classification of the items within this section:

Band—No. 667.
Chamber Ensemble—Nos. 656–61, 671, 683, 696.

Orchestra—Nos. 662, 666, 668, 680, 688, 700, 703.
Organ—Nos. 686, 689, 695, 701, 704, 710.

Piano—Nos. 663, 673, 675, 687, 692, 698, 699, 706.

Stringed instruments—Nos. 670, 671, 677.

  Violin—Nos. 665, 684, 707.

  Viola—Nos. 664, 684, 713.

  Cello—Nos. 691, 711.

  String bass—No. 676.

Voice, Solo—Nos. 669, 681.

Voice, Choral—Nos. 682, 685, 702, 709.

Wind Instruments—Nos. 690, 695 A.

  Bassoon—No. 697.

  Clarinet—Nos. 672, 692, 708.

  Flute—Nos. 674, 694.

  Recorder—Nos. 654, 655, 712.

  Ensemble—Nos. 678, 679.

654
Alker, Hugo. Blockflöten-Bibliographie. Aufführungs-praxis—Literatur—Spielgut. Wien, Universitätsbibliothek, 1960–61. 2 v. (Biblios-Schriften, 27–28.)

A source book of bibliographical information for performers on the recorder. Each volume contains a bibliography of writings on the instrument and its performance, including early accounts; a bibliography of instruction manuals; and a classified listing of modern editions of recorder music. Supplementary essays on history and performance practice. Facsimile plates from early methods.

655
Alker, Hugo. Literatur für alte Tasteninstrumente. Versuch einer Bibliographie für die Praxis. Wien, H. Geyer, 1962. 82 p.

The main division is between music for harpsichord and music for organ (without pedals). Brief entries, with publisher and editor given. Collections entered by title and filed in the same alphabet with composers. The emphasis is on music currently available in practical editions.

656
Altmann, Wilhelm. Handbuch für Klavierquartettspieler . . . Mit 237 Notenbeispielen. . . . Wolfenbüttel, Verlag für musikalische Kultur und Wissenschaft, 1937. 147 p.

Notenbeispiele in pocket at end of *Handbuch*.

A companion to a selective list of piano quartets, arranged chronologically by birthdates of the composers. German works curtailed in an effort toward international coverage. Brief descriptive and critical commentaries. Index of composers.

657
Altmann, Wilhelm. Handbuch für Klavierquintettspieler . . . Mit 343 Notenbeispielen. Wolfenbüttel, Verlag für musikalische Kultur und Wissenschaft, 1936. 178 p.

Notenbeispiele in pocket at end of *Handbuch*.
Similar to the above, with emphasis on piano quintets.

658
Altmann, Wilhelm. Handbuch für Klaviertriospieler; Wegweiser
durch die Trios für Klavier, Violine und Violoncell. Mit fast 400 Notenbeispielen. Wolfenbüttel, Verlag für musikalische Kultur und Wissenschaft, 1934. 237 p.

659
Altmann, Wilhelm. Handbuch für Streichquartettspieler. . . . Berlin,
M. Hesse, 1928–31. 4 v. (Hesses Handbücher, 86, 87, 92, 94.)
Vols. 1–2: string quartets; Vol. 3: string trios, quintets, sextets, octets;
addenda to quartets; Vol. 4: works for strings and winds.
A companion to quartet literature, giving brief descriptions and analyses
of works in the standard repertory, as well as for lesser known works.
Arrangement within each category is chronological.

660
Altmann, Wilhelm. Kammermusik-Katalog; ein Verzeichnis von
seit 1841 veröffentlichten Kammermusikwerken. 6. bis August 1944
ergänzte Auflage. Leipzig, F. Hofmeister, 1945. 400 p.
Succeeded by Richter's *Kammermusik-Katalog.* . . . See no. 696.
Chamber music published since 1841, separate works or works in
collections. Classified by medium, with composer indexes. International
coverage.

Altmann, Wilhelm. Katalog der seit 1861 in den Handel gekom-
menen theatralischen Musik. . . .
See no. 247.

661
Altmann, Wilhelm. Kleiner Führer durch die Streichquartette für
Haus und Schule. . . . Berlin/Halensee, Deutscher Musikliteratur-Verlag
[1950] 166 p.
An abridgement of the author's *Handbuch für Streichquartettspieler* (no.
659) concentrating on the classical literature for the ensemble, curtailing
all post-Brahms works.

662
Altmann, Wilhelm. Orchester-Literatur-Katalog; Verzeichnis von
seit 1850 erschienenen Orchester-Werken. . . . Leipzig, F. E. C. Leuckart,
1926–36. 2 v.

Orchestral music published since 1850, listing scores, miniature scores, parts, and arrangements. Vol. 2 gives, in addition, instrumentation and timing and contains a composer index to both volumes. Thematic quotations given for works whose serial numbers are often confused, e.g. Haydn's symphonies, Händel's concertos, etc.

663
Altmann, Wilhelm. Verzeichnis von Werken für Klavier vier- und sechshändig, sowie für zwei und mehr Klaviere. Leipzig, F. Hofmeister, 1943. 133 p.

Classified catalog of works for piano, 4 and 6 hands, and for 2 or more pianos, with and without other instruments. Original works and arrangements included. Alphabetical by composer within classifications. Index.

664
Altmann, Wilhelm und W. Borissowsky. Literaturverzeichnis vür Bratsche und Viola d'amore. Wolfenbüttel, Verlag für musikalische Kultur und Wissenschaft, 1937. 148 p.

Classified catalog, including solo works, duos, and other combinations in which the viola has the leading role. Lists some works in manuscript and all known editions of published works, with dates. Includes transcriptions as well as original works.

665
Baudet-Maget, A. Guide du violoniste; oeuvres choisies pour violon, ainsi que pour alto et musique de chambre, classées d'après leur dégré de difficulté. Lausanne, Paris [etc.] Foetisch Frères [n.d.] 295 p.

Selective list of violin, viola, and string ensemble music from mid-17th century to the present. Classified according to genre and degree of difficulty.

666
Beck, Georges H. Compositeurs contemporains: oeuvres d'orchestre. Paris, Heugel & Cie [1960] 35 p.

A descriptive listing of recent orchestral works by 27 composers, chiefly French. Brief biographies of the composers. Entries give instrumentation, timings. Scores and performance materials available on rental from Heugel.

667
Berger, Kenneth W. Band music guide; alphabetical listing of titles of all band music and composers of band music. 4th ed. Evanston, Ill., Instrumentalist Co. [1964] 350 p.

2nd edition in 1960.

[157]

668

Buschkötter, Wilhelm. Handbuch der internationalen Konzert-literatur. Berlin, Walter de Gruyter & Co., 1961. 374 p.

Compiled as a successor to Theodor Müller-Reuter's *Lexikon der deutschen Konzertliteratur* (no. 688). Works listed chronologically under composer. Information includes performance time, instrumentation, date of composition, performance, publisher.

Review by Richard Schaal in *Die Musikforschung*, 17 (1964) p. 84–85.

669

Coffin, Berton. Singer's repertoire. 2nd ed. New York, Scarecrow Press, 1960. 4 v.

First published in one volume, 1956.

Classified catalog of solo songs, each volume devoted to a particular voice range; information on subject, accompaniment, publisher.

Review by Arnold Caswell in *Journal of research in music education*, 9 (1961) p. 76.

670

Farish, Margaret K. String music in print. New York, R. R. Bowker Co., 1965. 420 p.

The work was first issued in a preliminary edition, 1963.

> *String music in print* is a guide to published music for the violin, viola, violon-cello and double-bass. It contains information on solo music, accompanied and unaccompanied; chamber music, including combinations of stringed instruments with wind instruments, keyboard instruments, harp, guitar, percussion and voice; methods and studies. To my best knowledge, all music listed was available on July 1, 1965 (Author's Preface).

Alphabetical by composer within each category; composers' dates given. Brief titles, with instrumentation. Publishers indicated by symbols, with a comprehensive list of publishers, p. 411–20.

Review of the preliminary edition by Joal H. Berman in *Notes*, 20 (1963) p. 229.

671

Feinland, Alexander. The combination violin and violoncello without accompaniment. [Paramaribo, Netherland Guyana, Printed by J. H. Oliviera, 1944] 121 p.

Classified catalog, including manuscripts, of music from the baroque to the present. Original publisher or location given. Biographical sketches of the composers represented.

672

Foster, Levin W. A directory of clarinet music. Pittsfield, Mass., Printed by A. E. Johnson & Son [1940] 128 p.

The work claims to list practically all the music known to be published for the clarinet. Classified arrangement, alphabetical by composer within each classification; publishers indicated. Some transcriptions and arrangements included, as well as more than 50 methods and studies.

673

Friskin, James and Irwin Freundlich. Music for the piano. A handbook of concert and teaching material from 1580 to 1952. New York, Rinehart [1954] 432 p. (The field of music, 5.)

Selective listing of standard works in the piano repertory. Classified arrangement. Remarks are concerned largely with the technical demands of the material and with its interpretation.

674

Girard, Adrien. Histoire et richesse de la flûte. Paris, Libraire Gründ, 1953. 143 p.

A handsome illustrated volume, printed in an edition of 1,500 copies. Chapter IV, "Les flûtistes," lists the principal performers from the 15th to the 20th centuries, with brief comments on each. Chapter V, "Littérature," is a chronological listing of the important composers of flute music, with their works, from Louis Couperin to the present, followed by an alphabetical listing, by composer, of works for solo flute accompanied by keyboard, harp, or orchestra. Manuscript works included.

675

Gratia, L. E. Répertoire pratique du pianiste . . . Préface de I. Philipp. Paris, Delagrave, 1931. 117 p.

A list of 2,500 piano pieces by 271 composers, arranged alphabetically by composer, with categories of varying degrees of difficulty. Four-hand pieces, p. 112–17.

676

Grodner, Murray. Comprehensive catalogue of available literature for the double bass. 2nd ed. Bloomington, Indiana, Lemur Musical Research, [1964] 84 p. (typescript).

First published in 1958.

Lists works in print, 1964. Solos and ensembles, for from 2 to 14 instruments, using string bass. Each entry gives composer, title, instrumentation, grade of difficulty, publisher, price, with occasional annotations as to availability. A short bibliography of works about the bass and bass playing. Index of names.

Review of the first edition by Darius Thieme in *Notes*, 16 (1959) p. 258.

677
Grünberg, Max. Führer durch die Literatur der Streich-instrumente ... Kritisches, progressiv geordnetes Repertorium von instruktiven Solo- und Ensemble-Werken. . . . Leipzig, Breitkopf & Härtel, 1913. 218 p. (Handbücher der Musiklehre . . . hrsg. von X. Scharwenka, 10.)

A listing of music for violin, viola, cello, and ensemble from the baroque through the 19th century, classified according to genre and degree of difficulty. Publishers, prices indicated. Bibliography, p. 207–209. Index.

678
Helm, Sanford M. Catalog of chamber music for wind instruments. Ann Arbor [The Author, University of Michigan School of Music] 1952. 85 p.

Chamber music for from 3 to 12 instruments employing at least one wind instrument. Classified according to size and instrumentation, giving publisher, date, and American agent for currently available editions. Composer index.

679
Houser, Roy. Catalogue of chamber music for woodwind instruments. 2nd ed. [Bloomington, Indiana] Indiana University, 1960. 158 leaves (typescript).

Supplement: Woodwind ensembles bibliography.

Material for from 3 to 10 instruments, classified according to ensemble. P. 147–48: A list of woodwind music found in the Moravian archives at Winston-Salem, North Carolina and at Bethlehem, Pennsylvania. P. 152–55: Selected publications from the catalog of the Donemus Foundation, Amsterdam.

680
International Music Council. Répertoires internationaux de musique contemporaine à l'usage des amateurs et des jeunes. I. Musique symphonique de 1880 à 1954. Frankfurt, New York, C. F. Peters, 1957– (v. 1, 63 p.).

A catalog of recently composed symphonic works suitable for young people's and amateur orchestras. Material listed alphabetically by country; publisher, date and instrumentation given. Indexes of composers, types of ensemble. List of publishers.

681

Kagen, Sergius. Music for the voice; a descriptive list of concert and teaching material. New York, Rinehart [1949] 507 p. (The field of music, 3.)

Selective list of works in the standard vocal repertory from the 17th century to the present. Classified arrangement. Each entry gives compass, type of voice required, and brief descriptive remarks.

682

Knapp, J. Merrill. Selected list of music for men's voices. Princeton, N.J., Princeton Univ. Press, 1952. 165 p.

Original works and arrangements, published and unpublished. Alphabetical by composer within main classification scheme. Each entry gives dates of composer, scoring, language, publisher, and editor. Index of composers.

Review by Archibald Davison in *Notes*, 10 (1952) p. 104–105.

683

Lemacher, Heinrich. Handbuch der Hausmusik. Graz, A. Pustet, 1948. 454 p.

The second part of the volume, p. 219 to end, lists works for solo instruments and various chamber ensembles. Many lesser known works included. Arranged alphabetically by composer within various categories. Publisher and brief description of works given. Bibliography, p. 435–39. Index.

684

Letz, Hans. Music for violin and viola. New York, Rinehart [1948] 107 p. (The field of music, 2.)

Selective, graded list of music for unaccompanied violin, or violin and piano (p. 1–94); followed by a similar list of music for the viola (p. 96–107).

685

Locke, Arthur W. and Charles K. Fassett. Selected list of choruses for women's voices. 3rd ed., revised and enlarged. Northampton, Mass., Smith College, 1964. 253 p.

First published in 1927; 2nd edition, 1946, edited by A. W. Locke.

Principal section is an alphabetical catalog, by composers, with titles of choruses, voice combination, publisher, or source in a collection. Foreign titles usually translated. Collections listed separately and their contents given. Indexes include a chronological list of composers, compositions by categories, authors and sources of texts, first lines and titles.

[161]

686

Lukas, Viktor. Orgelmusikführer. Stuttgart, Philipp Reclam Jun. [1963] 271 p.

A listener's guide to concert organ literature, quite selective and confined to European repertory. Brief biographies of the composers; numerous thematic quotations. Contains a section on the organ with other instruments, a glossary of organ terms, and a description of the mechanics of the instrument. Index of composers and works.

687

Moldenhauer, Hans. Duo-pianism; a dissertation. [Chicago, Chicago Musical College Press, 1951] 400 p.

Contains a list of original 2-piano music, arranged alphabetically by composer. Publishers indicated. The main part of the dissertation concerns itself with practical rather than historical aspects of the subject. Also contains a list of recorded two-piano music.

688

Müller-Reuter, Theodor. Lexikon der deutschen Konzertliteratur; ein Ratgeber für Dirigenten, Konzertveranstalter, Musikschriftsteller und Musikfreunde. Leipzig, G. F. Kahnt nachf., 1909. V. 1. 626 p.

Nachtrag zu Band I. Leipzig, Kahnt, 1921. 238 p.

The standard guide to orchestral and chamber music by the major composers of the romantic period, with detailed information as to date of composition, first performance, duration, instrumentation, relation to the composer's other works. Band I covers the following composers: Schubert, Mendelssohn, Schumann, Berlioz, Liszt, Raff, Wagner, Draeseke, Reinecke, Bruch, Gernsheim, and Richard Strauss. The *Nachtrag* is devoted to Beethoven, Brahms, and Haydn (symphonies only).

Buschkötter's *Handbuch* ... (no. 668) is intended to supplement Müller-Reuter and bring it up to date.

689

Münger, Fritz. Choralbearbeitungen für Orgel. Verzeichnis zu den Chorälen des Deutschen Evangelischen Kirchengesangbuches und des Gesangbuches der evang. -reform. Kirchen der deutschsprachigen Schweiz. Kassel, Bärenreiter [1952] 148 p.

Alphabetical listing by chorale text incipit, locating each in the German or Swiss chorale books and indicating the organ settings available in some 56 collections of chorale preludes.

690

National Association of Schools of Music. Solo literature for the wind instruments. 32 p. (The Bulletin of the National Association of Schools of Music, no. 31. January, 1951.)

Lists of solos, including concertos, for flute, oboe, clarinet, bassoon, French horn, cornet and trumpet, trombone. Graded as to difficulty; brief critical or descriptive annotations. Publishers indicated.

691

Nogué, Edouard. La littérature du violoncelle . . . Préface de M. Paul Bazelaire. . . . Paris, Delagrave, 1925. 151 p.

Lists nearly 2,000 works for violoncello, solo or with other instruments. Classified and graded, with short descriptions of most of the works. Publishers indicated.

692

Opperman, Kalmen. Repertory of the clarinet. New York, Ricordi [1960] 140 p.

Classified index of music for the clarinet, including methods, etudes, and music for the instrument as solo and in combination with other instruments. List of publishers given, and a short bibliography of books on the clarinet.

Review by Roger P. Phelps in *Notes*, 18 (1960) p. 63–64.

693

Parent, Charlotte F. H. Répertoire encyclopédique du pianiste; analyse raisonnée d'oeuvres choisies pour le piano, du XVIe siècle au XXe siècle, avec renseignements pratiques degré de difficulté, nombre de pages, éditeur et prix. . . . Paris, Hachette et Cie. (1900–1907) 2 v.

694

Pellerite, James J. A handbook of literature for the flute (a list of graded method materials, solos, and ensemble music for the flute). Bloomington, Indiana, Zalo Publications [1963] 96 p.

This listing of flute literature is specifically designed to familiarize the music teachers, music educators, and students of the flute with a portion of available materials presently appearing in publishers' catalogs (Foreword).

Graded and annotated.

695

Protestant Episcopal Church in the U.S.A. Joint Commission on Church Music. Service music and anthems for the nonprofessional choir. Greenwich, Conn., Seabury Press, 1955. 56 p.

Service music classified by liturgical use; anthems by the church year. Information includes degree of difficulty, number of parts, presence of solos, type of accompaniment, publisher, and number in series.

696

Richter, Johannes F. Kammermusik-Katalog. Verzeichnis der von 1944 bis 1958 veröffentlichten Werke für Kammermusik und für Klavier vier- und sechshändig sowie für zwei und mehr Klaviere. Leipzig, F. Hofmeister, 1960. 318 p.

Successor to Wilhelm Altmann's work of the same title (no. 660). Covers chamber music from 1945 through 1958. A classified bibliography, including chamber works with voice, piano 4-hands, etc. Alphabetical index of composers and titles of collections. List of publishers.

697

Risdon, Howard. Musical literature for the bassoon; a compilation of music for the bassoon as an instrument in ensemble. Seattle, Berdon [1963] 24 p.

698

Rowley, Alec. Four hands—one piano. A list of works for duet players. London/New York, Oxford Univ. Press, 1940. 38 p.

Classified list, with composer index, of original works for the medium, 1750 to date. Alphabetical arrangement with each class (the classics, the French school, etc.). Entries give composer's name and dates, title, usually in the original language, opus number, publisher.

699

Ruthardt, Adolf. Wegweiser durch die Klavier-Literatur. 10. Aufl. Leipzig, Zürich, Hug & Co., 1925. 398 p.

First published in 1888.

Selective list of keyboard music, including works for 4 or more hands, from the Renaissance to the early 20th century. Classified according to genre and degree of difficulty. Brief descriptions of lesser-known works. Bibliography of writings on keyboard music, p. 359–76. Index.

700

Saltonstall, Cecilia D. and Hannah C. Smith. Catalogue of music for small orchestra. Washington, D.C., Music Library Association, 1947. 267 p.

Selective list of works for orchestras with basic strings plus from 2 to 8 winds. Arranged by composer. Entries give movements, scoring, timing, and publisher. Many American compositions included. Indexed by title and by number of winds employed.

701
Sartorius, Richard H. Bibliography of concertos for organ and orchestra. Evanston, Ill., Instrumentalist Co., [1961] 68 p.
Includes primary sources as well as modern publications. Extensive annotations, biographical and descriptive of the music. Locations of original materials given. The list includes much material not exclusively for organ, i.e. concertos for "harpsichord or organ."

702
Schünemann, Georg. Führer durch die deutsche Chorliteratur. Wolfenbüttell, Verlag für musikalische Kultur und Wissenschaft, 1935–36. 2 v.
Vol. 1: Männerchor. Vol. 2: Gemischter Chor.
Classified according to type of composition. Entries give composer, title, publisher, grade of difficulty, number of parts, duration. Indexed by first line of text, title, composer and arranger, author of text. Includes both secular and sacred works.

703
Stein, Franz A. Verzeichnis der Orchestermusik von 1700 bis zur Gegenwart. Bern und München, Francke Verlag [1963] 126 p.
A pocket guide to orchestral literature. Selective list of composers and their principal orchestral works. Entries give title, instrumentation, date of composition, movements if a composite work. No publishers given.

704
Stellhorn, Martin H. Index to hymn preludes . . . and other organ compositions, based on hymns, chorales, and carols. A listing of 2,200 selections of various publishers according to key, difficulty, and length. St. Louis, Concordia Publishing House [1948] 151 p.

705
Swan, Alfred J. The music director's guide to musical literature (for voices and instruments). New York, Prentice-Hall, 1941. 164 p.
P. 117–64: A selected list of works from the early Middle Ages through the 20th century. Arranged chronologically, with subdivisions by genre and country. Occasional annotations. The earlier part of the book contains brief comments on the composers represented in the bibliography.

[165]

706

Teichmüller, Robert und Kurt Herrmann. Internationale moderne Klaviermusik, ein Wegweiser und Berater. Leipzig und Zürich, Hug & Co., 1927. 300 p.
Supplement, 1934.
Critical and selective bibliography of piano music from about 1890 to date of publication, arranged alphabetically by composer, with an index by country. Gives date of composition, opus number, title, publisher, price, grade, and critical comment.

707

Tottmann, Albert K. Führer durch die Violinliteratur. . . . 4. wesentlich vervollständigte, bis auf die Gegenwart seit 1901 forgeführte und neu bearbeitete Auflage von Wilhelm Altmann. Leipzig, J. Schuberth, 1935. 472 p.
Title varies: first published as *Führer durch den Violin-Unterricht*, 1873; 2nd ed., 1886; 3rd ed., 1902.
Classified bibliography, including etudes, solo or accompanied violin works, duos, trios, quartets, etc., for violins. Gives full bibliographical information and brief critical comments. Supplements Altmann's *Kammermusik-Katalog* (no. 660) for solo works.

708

Tuthill, Burnet C. "The concertos for clarinet," in *Journal of research in music education*, 10 (1962) p. 47–58.
Brief introduction to the history of the clarinet concerto and its literature, followed by annotated listing of such concertos from the 18th century to the present.

709

Valentin, Erich. Handbuch der Chormusik. Hrsg. im Auftrag der Arbeitsgemeinschaft deutscher Chorverbände. Regensburg, G. Bosse [1953–38] 2 v.
These volumes serve as general source books of information useful to choral directors. Special sections include a discography of choral music, listings of the contents of *Denkmäler*, writings on choral conducting. Major sections devoted to classified bibliographies of choral music, with full performance details. Each volume has a composer index.

710

Weigl, Bruno. Handbuch der Orgelliteratur. . . . Leipzig, F. E. C. Leuckart, 1931. 318 p.

Classified listing of compositions for organ solo or organ with orchestra, instruments, or voices. Original works and transcriptions listed separately. International coverage.

711

Weigl, Bruno. Handbuch der Violoncell-Literatur; systematisch geordnetes Verzeichnis der solo- und instruktiven Werke . . . 3. Auflage. Wien, Universal, 1929. 357 p.

Classified listing of compositions for cello and orchestra, cello and piano, cello solo, or accompanied by other instruments. Comparable in arrangement and content to his *Handbuch der Orgelliteratur* (above).

712

Winterfeld, Linde H. Von und Harald Kunz. Handbuch der Blockflöten-Literatur. Berlin/Wiesbaden, Bote & Bock, 1959. 139 p.

Listings of music for recorder, solo, ensemble, and in combination with other instruments. Publisher and price given. Composer and title index, and a short list of books on the recorder.

713

Zeyringer, Franz. Literatur für Viola: Verzeichnis der Werke für Viola-Solo, Duos mit Viola, Trios mit Viola, Viola-Solo mit Begleitung, Blockflöte mit Viola, Gesang mit Viola und der Schul- und Studienwerke für Viola. Hartberg, Oesterreich, Julius Schönwetter, 1963. 151 p. Ergänzungsband 1965. 82 p.

With indexes of publishers and composers.

Jazz and Popular Music

Within recent years the field of jazz and popular music has developed it own bibliographical resources. Some of the principal items in this area are listed below. Others will be found in the section on *Dictionaries and encyclopedias*, e.g. Leonard Feather's *The encyclopedia of jazz* (no. 138) or the Lewine and Simon *Encyclopedia of theater music* (no. 262). Still others are cited under *Collectors' guides to jazz recordings* (nos. 1279–1286) or belong in the category of early American popular song: see Dichter (no. 755), Sonneck (no. 800), or Wolfe (no. 809).

714

Burton, Jack. The blue book of Tin Pan Alley, a human interest encyclopedia of American popular music. Vol. 1: 1776—1860—1910. Watkins Glen, N.Y., Century House [1962] 304 p.

First published in 1951.

The 1962 publication is the first volume of an expanded new edition which, when completed, will carry the survey through the 1960s. The approach is chronological, with detailed listings of songs by the principal popular composers.

715

Charters, Samuel B. Jazz: New Orleans, 1885–1963, an index to the Negro musicians of New Orleans. Rev. ed., New York, Oak Publications, 1963. 173 p.
First published in 1958 by Walter C. Allen.
Brief descriptions of musicians and groups, under chronological periods. Discographical appendix; index to names of musicians and bands; to halls, cabarets, etc.; to tune titles. Illustrated.

716

Chipman, John H. Index to top-hit tunes (1900–1950) . . . with a foreword by Arthur Fiedler. Boston, Bruce Humphries [1962] 249 p.
An alphabetical index, by title, of the most popular American songs of the first half of the 20th century. Gives key, composer and author, publisher and original publication date, source in film or musical comedy. Chronological index; short bibliography.

717

Fuld, James J. American popular music (reference book) 1875–1950. Philadelphia, Pa., Musical Americana, 1955. 94 p.
Supplement . . . 1956. 9 p.
A bibliography of some 250 selected American popular songs. Detailed information as to first printing, copyright date, description of cover. 20 plates of song covers. An interesting attempt to approach American popular song with the methods of descriptive bibliography.

718

Fuld, James J. The book of world-famous music, classical, popular and folk. . . . Foreword by William Lichtenwanger. New York, Crown Publishers [1966] 564 p. Review by Ruth Hilton in *Notes*, 23 (1966) p. 56–57.

719

Mattfeld, Julius. Variety music cavalcade, 1620–1961; a chronology of vocal and instrumental popular music in the United States. . . . With an introduction by Abel Green. Revised edition. Englewood Cliffs, N.J., Prentice-Hall [1962] 713 p.
First published as *Variety music cavalcade, 1620–1950.* 1952.

[168]

Originally appeared in a modified form as *Variety radio directory*, 1938–39, supplemented in weekly issues of *Variety*.

A chronological bibliography of American popular music, with reference to parallel social and historical events for each year. Index of musical works by title, with dates of first publication.

Review by Irving Lowens in *Notes*, 20 (1963) p. 233–34.

Also entered as no. 390.

720

Shapiro, Nat. Popular music: an annotated index of American popular songs. [New York] Adrian Press, 1964–65. 2 v.

Vol. 1: 1950–59. Vol. 2: 1940–49.

The first two volumes of a projected series. Songs are listed alphabetically by title under each year of the decade. Each volume has its own index of titles and list of publishers.

Early Music in Modern Editions
(Including Collections and Monuments)

The purpose of the bibliographies listed in this category is to direct the user to new editions of old music, one of the most pressing needs of the performer, the teacher, and the music historian. Some of the items listed below are focused on the contents of the major critical editions (*Denkmäler, Gesamtausgaben*); others emphasize the more practical, performing editions of early music. In either case, listings of this kind are soon out of date. To keep abreast of new publications in this area, one should consult the music review sections of a variety of current periodicals: *Notes, Music and letters, Die Musikforschung, JAMS*, as well as such regular listings as may be found in *Fontes artis musicae*. See also the entries in this volume under "Guides to Systematic and Historical Musicology." Many of the works listed there have bibliographical supplements which cite and evaluate historical editions and monuments.

By far the most useful guide to the contents of the historical sets and critical editions is *Heyer*, no. 730, below.

721

Apel, Willi. "Editions, historical." In his *Harvard dictionary of music*. Cambridge, Mass., Harvard Univ. Press, 1947. P. 226–34.

Lists 31 important serial publications of early music, from plainsong through the 18th century. Contents of such large collections as the German and Austrian *Denkmäler* arranged alphabetically by composer.

722

Bukofzer, Manfred F. "A check-list of instrumental ensemble music before Haydn." In *Music Teachers' National Association Proceedings*, 1946. P. 470–79.

Includes only practical editions available through American publishers at the time of compilation.

723

Bukofzer, Manfred F. "List of editions [of Baroque music]." In his *Music in the Baroque era*. New York, Norton, 1947. P. 461–69.

A selective list organized under 4 main headings: (1) general anthologies; (2) historical collections; (3) smaller collections and performing editions; and (4) complete or collected editions of individual composers. Minimum bibliographical information.

724

"Denkmäler der Tonkunst" [by Wolfgang Schmieder] In *MGG*, v. 3, col. 164–92.

Lists 213 major editions, practical and scholarly, with contents given in considerable detail. Classified as to national or international coverage.

725

"Denkmäler und Gesamtausgaben." In *Repertorium der Musikwissenschaft* . . . bearb. von Willi Kahl und Wilhelm-Martin Luther. Kassel & Basel, Bärenreiter, 1953. P. 232–43.

140 entries for major historical sets. Full bibliographical information, but no listing of contents.

726

"Editions et Rééditions de Musique Ancienne (avant 1800)." In *Fontes artis musicae*, no. 1– . Paris, Assoc. Internationale des Bibliothèques Musicales, 1954– .

One of the few current listings of new editions of early music. International coverage. Full bibliographical information, including price.

727

"Editions, Historical." In *Reference works in music and music literature in five libraries of Los Angeles County*. Ed. by Helen W. Azhderian. Los Angeles, Univ. of Southern California, 1953. P. 116–37.

360 editions listed, both critical and practical. No detailed content analysis, but good coverage of the important sets.

728

Eitner, Robert. Verzeichnis neuer Ausgaben alter Musikwerke aus der frühesten Zeit bis zum Jahre 1800. Berlin, Trautwein, 1871. 208 p. (Monatshefte für Musikgeschichte. Beilage. 1871.)

Nachträge, published in Monatshefte, 9 (1877); "Register zu den Nachträgen" as its Beilage, 1877; and 10 (1878).

Still useful as a guide to the contents of early historical collections, including music in histories. *Abtheilung I:* annotated list of collections and literary works containing music; *Abtheilung II:* index of composers and their works, with separate listings of anonymous works and of German secular song through the 16th century.

729

"Gesamtausgaben" [by Wolfgang Schmieder] in *MGG*, v. 4, col. 1850–76.

A valuable discussion of the historical development of critical editions of the work of individual composers, followed by entries for 84 such editions, with detailed listings of contents.

730

Heyer, Anna H. Historical sets, collected editions and monuments of music, a guide to their contents. Chicago, American Library Association, 1957. 485 p.

A new edition of this work is in preparation as of 1966.

An indispensable guide to editorial work in the field of early music. Detailed listings of the contents of sets, including important publishers' series (e.g. Bärenreiter's *Hortus musicus*, Nagel's *Musik Archiv*, Kistner & Siegel's *Organum*, etc.). Numerous cross references. Comprehensive index of composers, editors, titles.

Review by Irene Millen in *Notes*, 15 (1958) p. 390–91; by Harriet Nicewonger in *The Library journal* (Sept., 1958) p. 2,380.

731

Hirsch, Paul and Kathi Meyer. "Sammelwerke und Gesamtausgaben." In their *Katalog der Musikbibliothek Paul Hirsch*. Bd. IV, Cambridge, England, Cambridge Univ. Press, 1947. P. 331–409.

Lists 90 complete editions and collections, with a detailed survey of their contents.

732

"Novae Editiones Musicae Classicae." In *Acta M*, v. 3– . Leipzig & Copenhagen, International Gesellschaft für Musikwissenschaft, Jan., 1931– .

Regular listing of the new editions of early music, arranged alphabetically by composer, giving title, scoring, editor, place, publisher, date, and price. Discontinued after 1952.

733
Schering, Arnold. "Ubersicht über die musikgeschichtlichen Sammelwerke und kritische Gesamtausgaben der Werke der grossen Meister der Musik aus dem Verlage von Breitkopf & Härtel." In his *Tabellen zur Musikgeschichte*. Leipzig, Breitkopf & Härtel, 1934. *Anhang*, 30 p.
A useful breakdown of the contents of the critical editions published by Breitkopf & Härtel. This supplement is omitted from the 1962 edition of the *Tabellen*.

734
Schiedermair, Ludwig. "Gesamtausgaben und Publikationsreihen in Ubersichten." In his *Einführung in das Studium der Musikgeschichte*. Bonn, F. Bümmlers Verlag, 1947. *Anhang*, p. 104–61.
Surveys the contents of the major sets and publishers' series.

735
Verzeichnis der Neudrucke alter Musik. Herausgegeben im Auftrage des Staatlichen Instituts für deutsche Musikforschung von Walter Lott. Leipzig, F. Hofmeister, 1937–43. 7 v.
An annual bibliography of new editions of music composed before 1800, covering the years of publication 1936–42. Includes separate works and contents of collections. German publications emphasized. Works listed by composer; medium and title index.

Primary Sources of Early Music:
Manuscripts and Printed Books

This section will direct users to bibliographies of original source materials, chiefly those prior to 1800. The list is highly selective. Nearly every dissertation or research study devoted to early music contains its bibliography of primary sources. Some of these bibliographies are of considerable value, but an attempt to cite them all would extend far beyond the scope of the present work. The user should be reminded that the major reference works such as *MGG* or Riemann's *Lexikon* contain abundant listings of primary sources. See, for example, the *MGG* articles on "Ars antiqua," "Ars nova," or "Chanson."

It should be obvious that one of the most direct approaches to primary sources will be found in the section devoted to "Catalogs of music libraries and collections." Another useful approach, although not employed here apart from one or two exceptions, is through the catalogs of antiquarian music and book dealers such as Leo Liepmannssohn, Otto Haas, Maggs Bros., etc.

See also the section "Histories and bibliographies of music printing and publishing" for bibliographies of the output of some of the major music publishing houses from the 16th through the 18th centuries.

736

Albrecht, Otto E. A census of autograph music manuscripts of European composers in American libraries. Philadelphia, Univ. of Pennsylvania Press, 1953. 331 p.

Lists 2,017 manuscripts now in America by 571 European composers, giving title, pagination, dimensions, and descriptive notes. Current and former owners indicated. Organized alphabetically by composer. Index of owners.

Review by Jack A. Westrup in *Music review*, 16 (1955) p. 84–85.

737

Apel, Willi. "Sources, musical, prior to 1450." In his *Harvard dictionary of music.* Cambridge, Mass., Harvard Univ. Press, 1947. P. 702–703.

A listing of some of the major sources of Gregorian chant, secular monophonic, and polyphonic music to 1450. Locations of the sources given; references to modern editions, if any.

738

Bäumker, Wilhelm. Das katholische deutsche Kirchenlied in seinen Singweisen, von den frühesten Zeiten bis gegen Ende des 17. Jahrhunderts. Freiburg, Herder'sche Verlagshandlung, 1883–1911. 4 v.

Reprinted from the original by Georg Olms, Hildesheim, 1962.

Bäumker's work is the basic study of the German Catholic church song. The main body of the work consists of quotations and discussion of the individual melodies, classified according to the church year or liturgical use. Each volume contains an extensive bibliography of early printed song collections, arranged chronologically. Entries cover the period from 1470 to 1800. Transcriptions from the prefaces of early song collections are given.

739

Becker, Carl Ferdinand. Die Tonwerke des XVI. und XVII. Jahrhunderts, oder systematisch-chronologische Zusammenstellung der in

[173]

diesen zwei Jahrhunderten gedruckten Musikalien. Zweite . . . Ausgabe. Leipzig, E. Fleischer, 1855.

First published in 1847.

An early classified bibliography of musical source materials, chronologically arranged under categories, with an index by composers and a chronological index to the whole. Attempts to list all musical compositions published in the 16th and 17th centuries to which actual or approximate dates could be assigned. An abridgement of Rimbault's *Bibliotheca madrigaliana* (no. 788) is included as a supplement.

740

Besseler, Heinrich. "Studien zur Musik des Mittelalters: 1. Neue Quellen des 14. und beginnenden 15 Jahrhunderts. 2. Die Motette von Franko von Köln bis Philipp von Vitry." In *Archiv für Musikwissenschaft*, 7 (1925) p. 167–252, and 9 (1927) p. 137–258.

Two articles that are basic source studies for the music of the late medieval period, containing numerous inventories and descriptions of *ars nova* manuscripts. They supplement the work of Ludwig covering the *ars antiqua* sources, see no. 779.

741

Bibliotheca Musico-Liturgica. A descriptive handlist of the musical and Latin-Liturgical mss. of the Middle Ages preserved in the libraries of Great Britain and Ireland. Drawn up by W. H. Frere . . . and printed for the members of the Plainsong and Mediaeval Music Society. . . . London, B. Quaritch, 1901–32. 2 v.

Vol. 1 (nos. 1–545): manuscripts at Lambeth and Oxford. Vol. 2 (nos. 546–1,031): manuscripts in cathedral chapter libraries and at Manchester, Dublin, Cambridge, etc. Full descriptions of the manuscripts. 17 plates. Indexes of service books, places, persons, and of Bodleian and Cambridge University Library manuscripts.

742

Bohn, Emil. "Bibliothek des gedruckten mehrstimmigen weltlichen deutschen Liedes vom Anfange des 16. Jahrhunderts bis ca. 1640." In the author's *Fünfzig historische Concerte in Breslau, 1881–1892*. Breslau, Hainauer, 1893. p. 77–188.

A bibliography of German printed secular polyphonic song. The collections are listed chronologically to 1625; the volumes containing works by a single composer are listed alphabetically by composer. Detailed bibliographical information, but contents not given. A useful guide to the printed sources of early German song.

[174]

743

Borren, Charles van den. "Inventaire des manuscrits de musique polyphonique qui se trouvent en Belgique." In *Acta M*, 5 (1933) p. 66–71, 120–27, 177–83; 6 (1934) p. 23–29, 65–73, 116–21.

An inventory of the manuscript sources of early polyphony in Belgian libraries. Detailed descriptions, with listings of contents, of manuscripts in the libraries in Brussels, Ghent, Liège, Louvain, Malines, and Tournai.

744

Breslauer, Martin (Firm, Booksellers, Berlin). Das deutsche Lied, geistlich und weltlich bis zum 18. Jahrhundert. Berlin, M. Breslauer, 1908. [304 p.] (Documente frühen deutschen Lebens. Reihe 1.)

An important dealer's catalog listing 556 items in the field of early German song. Full bibliographical entries with descriptive annotations. Numerous facsimiles of title pages. Prices given. Index of first lines of song texts, melodies, persons.

745

Bridgman, Nanie. "Musique profane italienne des 16e et 17e siècles dans les bibliothèques françaises," in *Fontes artis musicae*, 2 (1955) p. 40–59.

Full bibliographical descriptions of 32 16th- and 17th-century prints of Italian secular music in French libraries.

Also cited under FRANCE in the section "Catalogs of Music Libraries and Collections."

746

British Museum. Department of Printed Books. Hand-list of music published in some British and foreign periodicals between 1787 and 1848, now in the British Museum. London, The Trustees of the British Museum, 1962. 80 p.

Indexes the music, chiefly songs, in 12 periodicals. 1,855 entries arranged by composer.

This item also appears as no. 971.

Review by Richard Schaal in *Die Musikforschung*, 17 (1964) p. 423.

747

The British Union–Catalogue of Early Music Printed Before the Year 1801. A record of the holdings of over 100 libraries throughout the British Isles. Editor: Edith B. Schnapper. London, Butterworths Scientific Publications, 1957. 2 v.

One of the major reference tools for work with early printed sources of music, *The British Union-Catalogue* provides the key to the materials in British libraries. Brief bibliographical entries; locations established in more than 100 libraries in England, Scotland, Ireland.

Review by A. Hyatt King in *Music and letters*, 39 (1958) p. 77–79; by Richard S. Hill in *Notes*, 15 (1958) p. 565–68; by Richard Schaal in *Die Musikforschung*, 12 (1959) p. 367–69.

748

Brook, Barry S. La symphonie française dans la seconde moitié du XVIIIe siècle. Paris, Publications de l'Institut de Musicologie de l'Université de Paris, 1962. 3 v.

Vol. 1 is a study of the French symphony of the latter half of the 18th century, with important bibliographical supplements: *Annexe IV:* "Index thematique arrangé par tonalities et temps" (p. 511–73); *Annexe V:* "Index alphabetique des incipits transposés en do majeur ou do mineur et indiqués par les lettres" (p. 574–84); *Annexe VI:* "Inventaire sommaire de la symphonie et de la symphonie concertante françaises" (p. 585–633); *Annexe VII:* "Reeditions et enregistrements" (p. 634–39). Bibliography (p. 643–65); general index.

Vol. 2: "Catalogue thématique et bibliographique." Full descriptions of the works, location of sources. Short biographies of each composer.

Vol. 3: Scores of 6 previously unedited symphonies.

The work treats some 1,200 symphonies by 150 composers.

Review by Marc Pincherle in *Revue de musicologie*, 49 (1963) p. 131–33; by H. C. Robbins Landon in *Die Musikforschung*, 17 (1964) p. 435–39; by Jan LaRue in *MQ* (1963) p. 384–88.

749

Brown, Howard M. Intrumental music printed before 1600; a bibliography. Cambridge, Mass., Harvard Univ. Press, 1965. 559 p.

A bibliographical work of the greatest importance for students of early instrumental music. Chronologically arranged beginning with Michel de Toulouze's *L'Art et instruction de bien dancer* (148?) and ending with works printed in 1599. Full bibliographical descriptions incorporating much valuable commentary. Instrumental contents of each item listed. Includes references to works now lost.

P. 441–69: list of works cited. Indexes: (1) list of libraries and their holdings; (2) volumes described, arranged by types of notation; (3) volumes described, arranged by performing medium; (4) names; (5) first lines and titles.

750

Chaillon, Paule. "Les fonds musicaux de quelques bibliothèques de Province," in *Fontes artis musicae*, 2 (1955) p. 151–63.

A listing of libraries in 24 French provincial centers with a description of their catalogs, if any, followed by a list of *unica* or rare and unusual works in their collections.

751

Chevalier, Ulysse. Repertorium hymnologicum. Catalogue des chants, hymnes, proses, séquences, tropes en usage dans l'église latine depuis les origines jusqu'à nos jours. Louvain, 1892–1920. 6 v.

The standard bibliography of Latin rhymed poetic texts for liturgical use. A volume of additions and emendations was prepared by Clemens Blume under the title *Repertorium repertorii*, Leipzig, 1901.

752

Daschner, Hubert. Die gedruckten mehrstimmigen Chansons von 1500–1600. Bonn [Rheinische Friedrich-Wilhelms-Universität] 1962. 195 p.

A dissertation the greater part of which consists of a first-line index of polyphonic chansons from the printed collections of the 16th century. 4,273 chansons are entered.

P. 175–82: "Verzeichnis der Musikdrucke." P. 184–86: "Verzeichnis der anonymen Gedichtsammlungen." P. 187–95: "Literaturverzeichnis."

753

Davidsson, Åke. Catalogue critique et descriptif des imprimés de musique des XVIe et XVIIe siècles conservés dans les bibliothèques suédoises (Excepté la Bibliothèque de l'Université Royale d'Upsala). Upsala [Almquist & Wiksells] 1952. 471 p. (Studia musicologica upsaliensia, 1.)

A union catalog of early music in 18 Swedish libraries, excluding the University of Uppsala, which is treated elsewhere (see no. 1095). Full descriptions, contents, references. P. 455–71: bibliography of works cited.

754

Deakin, Andrew. Outlines of musical bibliography: a catalogue of early music and musical works printed or· otherwise produced in the British Isles; the whole chronologically arranged with descriptive and critical notes on the principal works. Birmingham, A. Deakin, 1899. 112 p.

This work was projected on a much larger scale, but not completed. P. 5–18: a listing of manuscript sources. P. 19–96: chiefly printed music of the 16th and 17th centuries, but with a few manuscripts included. The entries are not precise and the locations given are indefinite. Indexed by composer and title.

755

Dichter, Harry and Elliott Shapiro. Early American sheet music, its lure and its lore, 1768–1889 . . . including a directory of early American music publishers. . . . New York, R. R. Bowker Co., 1941. 287 p.

A cross-section of early American sheet music, classified according to subject content. Composer, main title, publisher, and date included. The directory of publishers is an alphabetical listing of firms active from 1768 to 1889 and carries their histories to 1940. Additional list of lithographers and artists active before 1870. Plates of illustrated title pages. Index.

756

Dichter, Harry. Handbook of American sheet music . . . first annual issue, 1947. Philadelphia, H. Dichter [1947] 100 p.

Second series, with Bernice Larrabee. Philadelphia, 1953.

Catalogs of early American sheet music for sale by the author. Full of useful bibliographical data. Classified under selected headings: topic, author, title. Prices given. No index. The 1947 volume lists over 2,000 items.

757

Draudius, Georg. Verzeichnisse deutscher musikalischer Bücher, 1611 und 1625. In originalgetreuem Nachdruck herausgegeben von Konrad Ameln. Bonn, Deutschen Musikverleger-Verband [1957].

Facsimile reprint of the music sections from the 1611 and 1625 editions of Draudius' *Bibliotheca librorum germanicorum classica*, one of the earliest bibliographies of music. ("Musikalischer Bücher" here means "scores.") Classified according to type of composition. Primarily of historical interest.

758

Duyse, Florimond van. Het oude Nederlandsche lied; wereldlijke en geestelijke liederen uit vroegeren tijd, teksten en melodieën, verzameld en toegelicht door Fl. van Duyse . . . 's-Gravenhage, M. Nijhoff, 1903–1908. 4 v.

First issued in parts, 1900–1908; unaltered reprint by Frits A. M. Knuf, Hilversum, 1965.

The standard reference book for the study of early Dutch song. Actually an edition of 714 melodies given with their variants and with an abundance of related information on the texts and music. Sacred songs treated in Vol. 3;

Vol. 4 contains indexes of names, of song titles, and of first lines of text.

759

Eitner, Robert. Bibliographie der Musik-Sammelwerke des XVI. und XVII. Jahrhunderts. Im vereine mit Frz. Xav. Haberl, A. Lagerberg und C. F. Pohl. Berlin, L. Liepmannssohn, 1877. 964 p.

Supplemented by additions and corrections published in the *Monatshefte für Musikgeschichte*, 14 (1882) p. 152–55; 161–64.

Reprint of the original edition by G. Olm, Hildeshiem, 1963.

A chronological bibliography of some 795 collections of music published between 1501 and 1700, with full descriptions, summary of contents, lists of composers represented, and library locations of individual copies. The second part of the work, p. 297–938, is a first-line index of the vocal texts arranged alphabetically by composer.

Eitner's *Sammelwerke* is one of the major bibliographical tools for historical research in music, although it has been superseded, in part, by the first volume of the *International inventory of musical sources*, see no. 774.

760

Eitner, Robert. Biographisch-bibliographische Quellen-Lexikon der Musiker und Musikgelehrten der christlichen Zeitrechnung bis zur Mitte des 19. Jahrhunderts. . . . Leipzig, Breitkopf & Härtel, 1898–1904. 10 v.

Supplemented by the *Miscellanea musicae bio-bibliographica*, no. 782, and by G. Radiciotti's "Aggiunte e correzioni ai dizionari biografici dei musicisti" no. 786.

Reprinted with supplements by Musurgia, New York, 1947. *Neuauflage* . . . Breitkopf & Härtel, Wiesbaden, 1959–60. "2. verbesserte Auflage," Graz, Akademische Druck- und Verlagsanstalt, 1959–60.

Eitner's *Quellen-Lexikon* remains the basic reference tool for locating primary sources of music before 1800. Both printed music and manuscripts are included, with their locations in European libraries. The work is badly out of date; much of the information, particularly as regards locations is no longer correct; but it will be a long time before it is superseded by the new *International inventory of musical* sources now in progress.

This work is also cited for its biographical treatment as no. 55.

761

Fischer, Kurt von. Studien zur italienischen Musik des Trecento und frühen Quattrocento. Bern, P. Haupt [1956] 132 p. (Publikationen der Schweizerischen Musikforschenden Gesellschaft, ser. 2, v. 5.)

A catalog of Italian secular music of the 14th and early 15th centuries. Text incipits, arranged alphabetically, for 177 madrigals, 25 cacce, and 423 ballate, with information as to sources and modern editions.

Review by Hans Tischler in *Notes*, 15 (1958) p. 405–406.

762

Fortune, Nigel. "A handlist of printed Italian secular monody books, 1602–1635," In *R.M.A. Research Chronicle*, No. 3. [Taunton, Barnicotts Ltd., for the Royal Musical Association] 1963. P. 27–50.

A "list of all publications containing at least one Italian secular monody, from the first in 1602 to 1635." Location symbols given for the scarcer volumes. The notes indicate contemporary reprints and modern editions where they exist. By far the most comprehensive listing of Italian monody books available.

763

Friedlaender, Max. Das deutsche Lied im 18. Jahrhundert, Quellen und Studien. . . . Stuttgart und Berlin, Cotta, 1902. 2 v. in 3.

Vol. 1:1, p. 1–62: a chronological listing of 798 German songbooks of the 18th century (1689–1799), followed by detailed commentary on the most important examples. Vol. 1:2: A collection of musical examples. Vol. 2: discussion of the poets, with indexes of names, text incipits.

764

Frost, Maurice. English and Scottish psalm and hymn tunes, *c.* 1543–1677. London, Oxford Univ. Press, 1953. 531 p.

P. 3–50: a bibliography of English-Scottish "Old Version" psalters from 1556 to 1677, with full descriptions and lists of contents. The main body of the work is an edition of 457 psalm tunes or harmonized versions thereof.

765

Geering, Arnold. Die Organa und mehrstimmigen Conductus in den Handschriften des deutschen Sprachgebietes vom 13. bis 16. Jahrhundert. Bern, P. Haupt [1952] 99 p. (Publikationen der Schweizerischen Musikforschenden Gesellschaft, ser. 2: 1.)

A study concerned with the sources of early polyphony in the German-speaking countries, with a listing of the relevant manuscripts and an inventory of the organum and conductus settings they contain.

766

Gennrich, Friedrich. Bibliographie der ältesten französischen und lateinischen Motetten. Darmstadt, Selbstverlag, 1957. 124 p. (Summa musicae medii aevi, 2.)

A bibliography of the 13th-century motet, serving also as a guide to the manuscript sources and a record of scholarly work done in this field. Gennrich expands the work begun by Friedrich Ludwig in his *Repertorium* (see no. 780). Motets are grouped under their respective tenors, with references to all known concordances and modern editions. Supplementary bibliographies of literature and of scripts, indexes of Latin and French tenors and of incipits to motettus and triplum parts.

Review by Hans Tischler in *Notes*, 16 (1959) p. 561–62.

767
Gennrich, Friedrich. Der musikalische Nachlass der Troubadours. Kommentar. Darmstadt, Selbstverlag, 1960. 176 p. (Summa musicae medii aevi, 4.)

A complete bibliography of the surviving musical settings of Troubadour songs, 302 in all, with information as to source, editions of text and music, verse forms, use of the melody as a contrafactum. Songs numbered consecutively but grouped under composer, with full bibliographical references to work done on the individual musicians. 25 manuscript sources described and discussed.

Vol. 3 of the series *Summa musicae medii aevi* (1958) is a musical edition of the surviving Troubadour melodies.

768
Göhler, Albert. Verzeichnis der in den Frankfurter und Leipziger Messkatalogen der Jahre 1564 bis 1759 angezeigten Musikalien. . . . Leipzig, C. F. Kahnt Nachf., 1902. [4 parts in 1 v., 20, 64, 96, 34 p.].

Unaltered reprint by Frits A. M. Knuf, Hilversum, 1965.

A bibliography of the music listed in the Frankfurt and Leipzig trade catalogs from 1564 to 1759. Works listed separately by century, under composer. Works identified by type.

769
Gröninger, Eduard. Repertoire-Untersuchungen zum mehrstimmigen Notre Dame-Conductus. Regensburg, Bosse, 1939. 163 p. (Kölner Beiträge zur Musikforschung, 2.)

An introductory essay of 59 pages, followed by tabulations, with concordances, of the polyphonic conductus compositions found in the four major Notre Dame sources.

770
Groppo, Antonio. "Catalogo di tutti i drammi per musica recitati ne' Teatri di Venezia dell'anno 1637, in cui ebbero principio le pubbliche

[181]

rappresentazioni de' medesmi fin all'anno presente 1745." In *Bollettino bibliografico musicale*. Nuova serie. Milano, 1952.

Published serially in 4 installments.

Lists 811 operas performed in Venice between 1637 and 1745, in chronological order, with title, librettist, composer, theater, and date of performance given. Title index in the last installment.

771

Hagopian, Viola L. Italian *ars nova* music, a bibliographic guide to modern editions and related literature. Berkeley and Los Angeles, Univ. of Calif. Press, 1964. 75 p. (University of California publications in music, 7.)

An organized, annotated bibliography treating the work done by scholars in the field of 14th-century Italian music.

772

Index to Early American Periodicals to 1850. E. SONGS. (Cards E1 to E11.) New York, Readex Microfilm Corp. [1965]. (Bibliographic aids in microprint.)

Microprint edition of the entries under "Songs" from an index of some 650,000 cards compiled by members of the English department of Washington Square College, New York University, with the aid of the WPA. Indexes some 340 early American magazines by authors, composers, anonymous titles, first lines.

773

International Association of Music Libraries. Radio Commission. Catalogue of rare materials, and first supplement. Editor: Folke Lindberg. Stockholm, 1959. 185 leaves.

Supplement I: leaves 175–85.

A list designed for the use of radio librarians in locating copies of rare material that can be used for performance purposes.

774

International Inventory of Musical Sources. Recueils imprimés XVIe—XVIIe siècles. Ouvrage publié sous la direction de François Lesure. I. Liste chronologique. München-Duisburg, G. Henle Verlag [1960–]. 639 p.

This volume is Part I of the systematic-chronological section of a comprehensive bibliography of musical sources currently being compiled under the joint auspices of the International Musicological Society and the International Association of Music Libraries. The present volume supersedes Eitner's *Bibliographie der Musik-Sammelwerke* (no. 759), and, when completed, the project will replace his *Quellen-Lexikon* (no. 760) as a modern, comprehensive reference tool for locating primary source materials for musical research.

This volume lists collections of music published between 1501 and 1700, with a summary of their contents and with the locations of copies in major European and American libraries. Index of editors and printers, and of titles and authors.

Review by Vincent Duckles in *Notes*, 18 (1961) p. 225–27; by Jack A. Westrup in *Music and letters*, 42 (1961) p. 76.

775

International Inventory of Musical Sources. Recueils imprimés XVIIIe siècle. Ouvrage publié sous la direction de François Lesure. München-Duisburg, G. Henle Verlag [1964] 461 p.

Volume B II of the series.

Cites about 1,800 collections printed between 1701 and 1801, giving basic bibliographic descriptions, composers represented, and locations of copies throughout the world. This volume is organized alphabetically by title rather than chronologically as in the preceding entry.

776

International Inventory of Musical Sources. Tropen- und Sequenzenhandschriften. Von Heinrich Husmann. München-Duisburg, G. Henle Verlag [1964] 236 p.

A volume of the *Inventory* set devoted to the manuscript sources of tropes and sequences. Sources grouped by country. Each entry gives information as to the signature, provinence, type of liturgical book, notation, structure of the source, contents, and related literature. Indexes of manuscripts arranged by libraries and by places of origin. Further indexes of places and subjects, names of saints, names of persons. Bibliography.

Review by Michel Huglo in *Revue de musicologie*, 51 (1965) p. 99–102.

777

Jander, Owen H. A catalogue of the manuscripts of compositions by Alessandro Stradella found in European and American libraries (Revised edition). Wellesley, Mass., Wellesley College, 1962. 72 leaves (typescript).

First issued in 1960.

A classified catalog of Stradella's works with locations of the manuscript sources. The principal divisions are: instrumental music, vocal music with sacred texts, vocal music with secular texts.

[183]

778

Linker, Robert W. Music of the Minnesinger and early Meistersinger, a bibliography. Chapel Hill, University of North Carolina Press [1961] 79 p.

A bibliography of German medieval song arranged alphabetically under the composers' names. A preliminary list gives 40 manuscript sources and 41 modern publications of literary history, music, and text editions.

Review by Walter Salmen in *Die Musikforschung*, 17 (1964) p. 432.

Loewenberg, Alfred. Annals of opera, 1957–1940. . . . See no. 263.

779

Ludwig, Friedrich. "Die Quellen der Motetten ältesten Stils." In *Archiv für Musikwissenschaft*, 5 (1923) p. 185–222, 273–315.

A basic source study of medieval polyphony, in which the author gives complete or partial inventories for some 50 manuscripts containing motets of the *ars antiqua* period.

This study has been reprinted as a supplement to Gennrich's edition of Ludwig's *Repertorium, Abteilung 2* (see below).

780

Ludwig, Friedrich. Repertorium organorum recentioris et motetorum vetustissimi stili. Band 1: Catalogue raisonné der Quellen. Abteilung 1: Handschriften in Quadrat-Notation. Halle, Niemeyer, 1910. 344 p.

Ludwig's *Repertorium*, although incomplete, is the starting point for all studies in the music of the *ars antiqua* period. It is essentially an inventory, with concordances, of the contents of the major manuscripts of the Notre Dame repertory.

Band 1, Abteilung 2: Handschriften in Mensuralnotation. Besorgt von Friedrich Gennrich. Langen bei Frankfurt, 1961. (Summa musicae medii aevi, 7.)

This portion of the *Repertorium* appeared in proof copy but was never published in Ludwig's lifetime. It consists chiefly of inventories of two major sources of the 13th-century motet, the *Montpellier Codex* and the *Clayette MS*. Included as a supplement to this volume is a reprint of Ludwig's study, "Die Quellen der Motetten ältesten Stils," which appeared in the *Archiv für Musikwissenschaft*, 5 (1925). See no. 779 above.

A "2. erweiterte Auflage" of *Band 1*, edited by Luther A. Ditmer, appeared in 1964 as a joint publication of the Institute of Mediaeval Music, New York, and Georg Olms, Hildeshiem.

Band 2: Musikalisches Anfangs-Verzeichnis des nach Tenores geordneten

Repertorium. Besorgt von Friedrich Gennrich. Langen bei Frankfurt, 1962. 71 p. (Summa musicae medii aevi, 8.)

A thematic catalog of 515 motets based on 50 tenors taken from the liturgy of the Mass. Reprinted, incomplete, from Ludwig's unpublished proof copy.

781
Meyer, Ernst H. "Quellennachweise." In his *Die mehrstimmige Spielmusik des 17. Jahrhunderts in Nord- und Mittel-Europa.* . . . Kassel, Bärenreiter, 1934. P. 128–258.

A bibliography of the sources of 17th-century chamber music of the North-European school. Partially thematic for the English sources. Locations given.

782
Miscellanea Musicae Bio-Bibliographica. . . . Hrsg. von H. Springer, M. Schneider und W. Wolffheim. 2., um einen Anhang vermehrte Auflage. New York, Musurgia, 1947. 435 p.

Originally published by Breitkopf & Härtel in quarterly issues, 1912–16, with annual index for each of the years covered. Provides corrections and additions to all the kinds of information in Eitner's *Quellen-Lexikon,* no. 760.

Reprinted in Vol. 11 of the Akademische Druck- und Verlagsanstalt *2. verbesserte Auflage* of the *Quellen-Lexikon,* which also contains marginal numerical references to the *Miscellanea.*

783
Musiker Handschriften. . . . [Band I] von Palestrina bis Beethoven; [Band II] von Schubert bis Strawinsky. Zürich, Atlantis Verlag [1960–61] 2 v.

Two handsome books made up chiefly of facsimile plates of autograph manuscripts by famous musicians, with brief descriptive commentary and identification of the sources. 159 plates in Vol. 1; 140 plates in Vol. 2. Editor: Walter Gerstenberg.

Review by Werner Neumann in *Die Musikforschung,* 17 (1964) p. 454–55.

784
Nisser, Carl M. Svensk instrumentalkomposition, 1770–1830. Nominalkatalog. Stockholm, Bokförlaget Gothia [1943] 467 p.

Swedish instrumental music, native composers or composers living in Sweden. Alphabetical listing by composer, with detailed bibliographical and analytical descriptions, including key, movements, time signature, measure count. Bibliographical references. Index of names and places.

785

Pillet, Alfred. Bibliographie der Troubadours. Erg., weitergeführt und herausgegeben von Dr. Henry Carstens. Halle, Niemeyer [1933] 518 p. (Schriften der Königsberger Gelehrten Gesellschaft. Sonderreihe, 2.)

Based on a bibliography of troubadour songs compiled by Karl Bartsch in 1872. Songs arranged alphabetically by first word of text, with inclusive numeration and subseries of numbers for works by individual authors. The emphasis is directed toward literary rather than musical scholarship.

786

Radiciotti, Giuseppe. "Aggiunte e correzioni ai dizionari biografici dei musicisti." In *Sammelbände der Internationalen Musikgesellschaft*, 14 (1914) p. 551–67; 15 (1915) p. 566–86.

Corrections and additions to Eitner's *Quellen-Lexikon* (no. 760) with special attention to Italian composers.

Reprinted in the Musurgia edition of the *Quellen-Lexikon*, and as Vol. 11 of the Akademische Druck- und Verlagsanstalt, *2. verbesserte Auflage*, 1960.

787

Radó, Polycarpe. Répertoire hymnologique des manuscrits liturgiques dans les bibliothèques publiques de Hongrie. Budapest, Stephaneum Nyomda, 1945. 59 p. (Az orságos széchenyi könyvtár kiadványai, 20.)

Alphabetical listing of 727 hymns found in 146 liturgical manuscripts in libraries in Hungary.

788

Raynaud, Gaston. Bibliographie des altfranzösischen Liedes. Neu bearbeitet und ergänzt von Hans Spanke. Erster Teil. Leiden E. J. Brill, 1955. 386 p.

The first part of a projected revision of Raynaud's *Bibliographie des chansonniers francais des XIIIe et XIVe siècles*. Paris, 1884. 2 v. This work serves as a guide to trouvère songs, similar to that offered by the Pillet (no. 785) or the Gennrich (no. 767) for the troubadour repertory. Lists more than 2,130 songs, arranged according to the rhyme word of the first stanza, with references to the manuscript source and to literary and musical studies concerned with the item. P. 1–32: a bibliography of the manuscript sources, and of modern editions and studies.

789

Riaño, Juan F. Critical and bibliographical notes on early Spanish music. . . . London, B. Quaritch, 1887. 154 p.

Manuscripts and printed music to 1600, classified, giving descriptions and library locations of manuscripts. Numerous facsimile plates.

790

Riedel, Friedrich W. Quellenkundliche Beiträge zur Geschichte der Musik für Tasteninstrumente in der zweiten Hälfte des 17. Jahrhunderts (vornehmlich in Deutschland). Kassel und Basel, Bärenreiter, 1960. 224 p. (Schriften des Landesinstituts für Musikforschung Kiel, 10.)

A "source study" concerned with late 17th-century prints and manuscripts of keyboard music, with emphasis on the German school. Numerous useful lists and inventories incorporated into the work, e.g. "Verzeichnis der von 1648–1700 im Druck veröffentlichen Musik für Tasteninstrumente" (p. 57–72); "Quellenregister" [Handschriften] (p. 219–24).

791

Rimbault, Edward F. Bibliotheca madrigaliana. A bibliographical account of the musical and poetical works published in England during the 16th and 17th centuries under the titles of madrigals, ballets, ayres, canzonets, etc. London, J. Smith, 1847. 88 p.

An early, and rather faulty, chronological list of vocal music published in England, 1588–1638, giving bibliographical descriptions and contents, source references. First line index of madrigals and songs. Composer index.

792

Sartori, Claudio. Bibliografia della musica strumentale italiana stampata in Italia fino al 1700. Firenze, L. Olschki, 1952. 652 p. (Biblioteca di bibliografia italiana, 23.)

Chronological list of instrumental music, collections of vocal music containing one or more instrumental pieces, or vocal music with one or more instrumental parts, published in Italy to 1700. Includes a few works by Italian composers published outside Italy. Excludes lute music and dramatic music. Complete bibliographical data, including dedications, prefaces, tables of contents. Composer index.

Review by Dragan Plamenac in *Notes*, 10 (1953) p. 616–19; by Harvey Olnick in *MQ*, 40 (1954) p. 98–1,021; by Willi Apel in *JAMS*, 7 (1954) p. 84–86; by Richard Schaal in *Die Musikforschung*, 7 (1954) p. 342.

793

Sartori, Claudio. "Finalmente svelati i misteri delle biblioteche italiane," in *Fontes artis musicae*, 2 (1955) p. 15–37; 3 (1956) p. 192–202.

A product of the work on the International Inventory in Italy, this article contains a summary report of the holdings of 40 Italian libraries and an alphabetical listing of early printed music newly discovered in these collections.

794

Schanzlin, Hans Peter. "Musik-Sammeldrucke des 16. und 17. Jahrhunderts in schweizerischen Bibliotheken." In *Fontes artis musicae*, 4 (1957) p. 38–42.

795

Schanzlin, Hans Peter. "Musik-Sammeldrucke des 18. Jahrhunderts in schweizerischen Bibliotheken (I)." In *Fontes artis musicae*, 6 (1959) p. 20–26; II. *ibid.*, (1961) p. 26–29.

Preliminary reports prepared by the Swiss office of the International Inventory of Musical Sources.

796

Scheurleer, Daniel F. Nederlandsche liedboeken; lijst der in Nederland tot het jaar 1800 uitgegevan liedboeken . . . 's-Gravenhage, M. Nijhoff, 1912. 321 p.

Erste supplement, 1923.

A bibliography of song books published in the Netherlands from 1487 to 1800, with or without music, arranged chronologically under main headings of sacred and secular music, with index by author, editor, publisher, main word of title. 3,887 titles in the main work, 660 in the supplement.

797

Schreiber, Max. Kirchenmusik von 1500–1600, Originaldrucke und Manuskripte chronologisch zusammengestellt. . . . [Regensburg] Druckerei St. Georgsheim Birkeneck, 1932. 88 p.

Chronological list of 16th-century sacred music, printed and manuscript sources. Entered alphabetically by composer under year of issue. Brief titles, and locations in British and continental libraries. Index of composers and classified index of forms.

798

Schreiber, Max. Kirchenmusik von 1600–1700, Originaldrucke und Manuskripte chronologisch zusammengestellt. . . . [Regensburg] Druckerei St. Georgsheim Birkeneck, 1934. 184 p.

Treats 17th-century sacred music as in the entry above.

799

Schünemann, Georg. Musikerhandschriften von Bach bis Schumann. Berlin, Atlantis Verlag [1936] 106 p. 96 plates.

[188]

Facsimiles of 96 autographs in the Berlin State Library, with extensive commentaries by the author.

800

Sonneck, Oscar G. T. A bibliography of early secular American music (18th century) . . . rev. and enl. by W. T. Upton. [Washington, D.C.]. Library of Congress, Music Division, 1945. 617 p.

First published in 1905. Reprinted, with a new preface by Irving Lowens, by Da Capo Press, New York, 1964.

A title list, with full bibliographical descriptions, including first lines of texts. Completely indexed, with lists of composers, first lines, publishers, etc.

Review of the 1964 reprint by Harry Eskew in *Anuario, Inter-American Institute for Musical Research*, 1 (1965) p. 134.

801

Stevenson, Robert. "Sixteenth and seventeenth century resources in Mexico." In *Fontes artis musicae*, 1 (1954) p. 69–78; 2 (1955) p. 10–15.

The first installment is concerned with the manuscript resources of the Puebla Cathedral music archive, comprising some 365 sacred works by 36 composers. Arranged alphabetically by composer. The second part is a description of a 16th-century manuscript of sacred music in the library of Canon Octaviano Valdés of Mexico City.

802

Thibault, Geneviève et Louis Perceau. Bibliographie des poésies de P. de Ronsard mises en musique au XVIe siècle. Paris, E. Droz, 1941. 121 p. (Publications de la Société Française de Musicologie, 2 sér., t. 8.)

Chronological bibliography, 1552–1629, of some 148 collections containing musical settings of lyrics by Ronsard. Full bibliographical citations of the collections, with Ronsard settings listed for each. Index of text incipits, and of collections and names.

803

Vogel, Emil. Bibliothek der gedruckten weltlichen Vocalmusik Italiens. Aus den Jahren 1500–1700. . . . Berlin, A. Haack, 1892. 2 v.

Partially revised and enlarged by Alfred Einstein, under running title "Italian secular vocal music," in *Notes*, 2 (1945)—5 (1948), 232 p. in all. Einstein's revision treats only the second part of Vogel's original work, namely, the collections containing works by two or more composers.

Unaltered reissue. Hildesheim, Olms, 1962. 2 v. This issue incorporates Einstein's revision as published in *Notes*.

Vogel's *Bibliothek* is the basic source of information concerning early printed secular vocal music in Italy. In two parts: the first gives publications of the work of individual composers, arranged alphabetically by composer; the second gives collections, listed chronologically from 1501 to 1697. Full bibliographical citations, lists of contents, locations in European libraries. Index of collections, of places and publishers, of authors of texts and persons to whom works are dedicated.

A complete revision of Vogel is badly needed. Einstein's emendations concerned only the section on collections. It is reported that such a revision is being undertaken by Claudio Sartori and François Lesure, and that the results of their work will be published as part of the series, *Bibliotheca musicae*, Milan.

804
Wackernagel, Philipp. Bibliographie zur Geschichte des deutschen Kirchenliedes im XVI. Jahrhundert. Frankfurt am Main, 1855. 718 p.

Unaltered reprint of the original edition by Georg Olms, Hildesheim, 1961.

A chronological listing of 1,050 editions of German sacred song published during the 16th century. Detailed bibliographical descriptions, with annotations. Transcriptions given of the introductions to 110 of the collections.

805
Walther, Hans. Initia carminum ac versuum medii aevi posterioris latinorum. Alphabetisches Verzeichnis der Versanfänge mittellateinischer Dichtungen. . . . Göttingen, Vanderhoeck & Ruprecht, 1959. 1,186 p. (Carmina medii aevi posterioris latina, 1.)

Not a music bibliography, but a most valuable reference tool for musicologists working in the field of medieval studies. An alphabetical index of text incipits for more than 20,000 medieval Latin lyrics, with references to manuscript sources and modern editions. Bibliography of literature; index of names and subjects.

806
Wiel, Taddeo. I teatri musicali veneziani del settecento. Catalogo delle opere in musica rappresentate nel secolo XVIII in Venezia (1701–1800). Venezia, Fratelli Visentini, 1897. 600 p.

Chronological listing of operas performed in the Venetian theater during the 18th century. 1,274 items. Entries give librettist, composer, place of performance, cast if known, ballet if included. Indexes of titles, librettists, composers, singers, dancers, etc. Introductory essay of 80 pages on the Venetian musical theater.

807

Winternitz, Emanuel. Musical autographs from Monteverdi to Hindemith. Princeton, N.J., Princeton Univ. Press, 1955. 2 v.

Reissued by Dover Publications, New York, paperbound edition, 1965. 2 v.

Vol. 1 is devoted to commentary on the plates, with two introductory chapters: "The written sign" and "The writing act." Vol. 2 contains 196 full-page plates of autographs.

808

Wolf, Johannes. Handbuch der Notationskunde. I. Teil: Tonschriften des Altertums und des Mittelalters. II. Teil: Tonschriften der Neuzeit, Tabulaturen, Partitur, Generalbass und Reformversuche. Leipzig, Breitkopf & Härtel, 1913–19. 2 v. (Kleine Handbücher der Musikgeschichte, 7.)

The Wolf *Handbuch* is cited here on the strength of its useful listings of early manuscript sources connected with the author's discussion of notational practices. For example: "Quellen der *ars antiqua*" (Vol. 1, p. 258–63); "Die *ars nova*" (Vol. 1, p. 351–54); "Handschriftliche Quellen des 15. und 16. Jahrhunderts" (Vol. 1, p. 444–65); "Verzeichnis einiger wichtiger deutscher Lautentabulaturen" (Vol. 2, p. 47–59); "Italienische Lautentabulaturen" (Vol. 2, p. 66–71); "Quellen französischer Lautentabulatur" (Vol. 2, p. 95–106); "Guitarretabulaturen" (Vol. 2, p. 209–18).

809

Wolfe, Richard J. Secular music in America, 1801–1825. A bibliography. Introduction by Carleton Sprague Smith. New York, New York Public Library, Astor, Lenox and Tilden Foundations, 1964. 3 v.

A major work of bibliography in the field of early American music. Prepared as a continuation of the Sonneck-Upton *Bibliography* (no. 800). The arrangement is alphabetical by composer. Brief biographies. Full bibliographical descriptions and locations of copies in American libraries and private collections.

Appendixes: (1) "Unrecorded 18th-century imprints located during the course of this work." (2) "A list of works in the Sonneck-Upton *Bibliography* which have been redated into the 19th century." (3) "Locations of newly discovered copies of works in the Sonneck-Upton *Bibliography*." Index of titles; of first lines; of publishers, engravers, and printers; of numbering systems. General index.

Review by James C. Downey in *Anuario of the Inter-American Institute for Musical Research*, 1 (1965) p. 122–24.

810
Wotquenne, Alfred. Table alphabétique des morceaux mesurés contenus dans les oeuvres dramatiques de Zeno, Metastasio et Goldoni. Leipzig, Breitkopf & Härtel, 1905. 77 p.

An alphabetical first-line index of aria and ensemble texts by Zeno, Metastasio, and Goldoni, citing volume and page numbers in the standard editions of their works and title of the work from which the incipit is derived. Table of librettos by the three authors.

811
Zahn, Johannes. Die Melodien der deutschen evangelischen Kirchenlieder aus den Quellen geschöpft und mitgeteilt.... Gütersloh, Bertelsmann, 1889–93. 6 v.

Reprint of the original edition by Olms, Hildesheim, 1963.

Zahn is primarily an edition, giving 8,806 melodies, derived from the earliest sources, for the German Protestant liturgy. Classified according to metrical form.

Vol. 5, p. 397–494: biographical notices of 463 chorale composers or editors of chorale collections. Index of composers; first-line index of texts.

Vol. 6: a bibliography of 1,408 items, listing the sources of the melodies, arranged chronologically from 1507 to 1892, with locations of copies in the principal European libraries. Further supplements give non-German sources and manuscript sources.

Folk Song and Ballad

This section should be used in conjunction with the section "Bibliographies of Music Literature . . . Ethnomusicology," which lists studies and monographs pertaining to folk song and ballad. Here, the emphasis is on the music itself. The user should bear in mind, however, that a work such as Haywood's *Bibliography of North American folklore and folksong* (no. 525) contains numerous entries for music, both printed and on sound recordings. Also relevant in certain respects are such bibliographies as Sears' *Song index* (no. 635), Fuld's *American popular music* (no. 717), and the bibliographies by Sonneck/Upton (no. 800) and by Wolfe (no. 809), which serve to bridge that uncertain gap between folk and popular song.

812

Bronson, Bertrand H. The traditional tunes of the Child ballads, with their texts, according to the extant records of Great Britain and America. V. 1- . Princeton, N.J., Princeton Univ. Press, 1959- .

Vol. 1: Ballads 1-53. Vol. 2: Ballads 54-113 (1962).

A monumental work of scholarship, in progress, in the field of the English-Scottish ballad. Based on the work of Francis J. Child, but far exceeding it in scope and authority. The literary and musical tradition of each ballad is discussed, together with a printing of all the known variants both literary and musical.

813

California. University. Department of Music. Check list of California songs. Archive of California folk music. Part I: texts in print. Berkeley, Calif., University of California, 1940. 160 leaves (typescript).

Published in connection with a WPA project supervised by Sidney H. Robertson.

A list, alphabetical by title, of more than 2,500 songs from texts either published or known to have circulated in California, with an index of first lines. P. 157-60: bibliography of songsters and broadsides.

814

Dean-Smith, Margaret. A guide to English folksong collections. . . . Liverpool, University Press of Liverpool, in association with The English Folk Dance and Song Society, 1954. 120 p.

Foreword by Gerald Abraham.

Indexes approximately 62 collections of English folk songs, 1822-1952. Main entry is by song title, with cross-references from text incipit. Chronological list of collections. Detailed annotations.

Review by Bertrand H. Bronson in *JAMS*, 8 (1955) p. 57-58.

815

Merwe, F. Z. van der. Suid-Afrikaanse musiekbibliografie 1787-1952. Pretoria, J. L. Van Schaik, 1958. 410 p.

A comprehensive bibliography of music related to South Africa (by South African composers wherever published, writings on South African themes or subject matter). The largest part of the citations refer to songs, marches, dance music of a popular nature, although a few studies and monographs are interfiled. Entries are unclassified, arranged alphabetically by composer or author. Index of South African composers and musicians. The language is Afrikaans.

[193]

816

Sidel'nikov, Viktor M. Russkaĩa narodnaĩa pesnĩa: bibliograficheskiĭ ukazatel' 1735–1945. Moskva, Izd. Akademiĭ Nauk SSSR, 1962.

At head of title: Akademĩa Nauk SSSR, Institut mirovoi literatury im. A. M. Gor'kogo.

Part I: texts of folk poetry and folk songs, published in journals, newspapers, etc., with or without music. Part II: books, articles, etc. about Russian folksong. Index of names.

816A

Simpson, Claude M. The British broadside ballad and its music. New Brunswick, N.J. Rutgers Univ. Press, 1966. 919 p.

An indispensable reference tool for students of English popular song from the 16th through the 18th centuries. Gives music for 540 broadside ballads and traces each melody from its earliest printed and manuscript sources. No ballad texts printed. The work takes its point of departure from William Chappell's *Popular music of the olden time* (1855–59, 2 v.) but far exceeds *Chappell* in coverage.

Review by Bertrand Bronson in *MQ*, 52 (1966) p. 384–87.

Catalogs
of Music Libraries and Collections

A KNOWLEDGE of the published catalogs of the major music libraries and collections is essential for locating source materials for study or research. There are at least two comprehensive listings of such catalogs in recent encyclopedia articles: (1) "Musikbibliotheken und Sammlungen," by Alfons Ott, in *MGG*, 9, col. 1034–78, and (2) "Libraries and collections," by Charles Cudworth, in *Grove's*, 5th edition, 9, p. 160–223. Extensive as these articles are, they do not supply full bibliographical information. The following list covers the catalogs of the principal music libraries and also includes a number of important exhibition catalogs and union lists. A few descriptive articles covering the holdings of certain libraries have also been cited. Excluded are the auction or sale catalogs of music collections that have been dispersed, with the exception of the famous Wolffheim catalog (no. 1138), a bibliographical tool of first importance.

It goes without saying that a great many musical source materials have never been listed in the special music catalogs, and must be sought in general library catalogs of early printed books and manuscripts. The music manuscripts in the Bodleian Library at Oxford, for example, must be extracted from the seven volumes of F. Madan's *Summary catalogue of Western manuscripts in the Bodleian library* . . . (1895–1953). Likewise, Cambridge University music manuscripts are to be found in the series of college library manuscript catalogs compiled by Montague Rhodes James. No attempt has been made here to cite general catalogs of this kind, but, in this connection, the reader's attention may be called to the invaluable guide to *Latin manuscript books before 1600, a list of the printed catalogues and unpublished inventories of extant collections* by Paul Kristeller. Rev. ed., Fordham Univ. Press, 1960.

In the following list the catalogs have been grouped, as far as is possible, by place. Place is ordinarily designated as a city followed by the appropriate country. Places within the United Stated are entered under the name of the city followed by the state. Certain national union catalogs, or articles on the holdings of several libraries within a country, are entered under the name of the country in capital letters (GERMANY, GREAT BRITAIN, SWEDEN, etc.). There remain a few catalogs of important collections that have been dispersed, or have changed their locations, in recent years (Hirsch, Cortot, Wolffheim, etc.). These are grouped in a special category at the end of this section.

Attention should be called to two recently issued series that are devoted to the publication of music library catalogs and bibliographies: (1) *BIBLIOTHECA MUSICAE; collana di cataloghi e bibliografie diretta da Claudio Sartori*. Milano Istituto Editoriale Italiano, 1962– (see nos. 819, 985, 1066); and (2) *CATALOGUS MUSICUS, a series of catalogues and bibliographies*, general editor, Harald Heckmann. Kassel, Bärenreiter [for the International Association of Music Libraries] 1963– (see nos. 820, 1110, 1219).

Most of the catalogs published as *Beilage* to the *Monatshefte für Musikgeschichte* in the late 19th century have become available again through the reprinting of this set by Annemarie Schnase, Scarsdale, New York.

For a useful survey of those European libraries and collections that have outstanding holdings in music, the reader should consult Richard C. Lewanski's *Subject collections in European libraries; a directory and bibliographical guide*. New York, R. R. Bowker, 1965. The report on the music collections is found on p. 499–514 of this work.

AARHUS, DENMARK

817

Statsbiblioteket. Fagkataloger [redigeret af Erling Winkel og Ingeborg Heilmann] 2. forøgede udg. Aarhus, Aarhuus Stiftsbogtrykkerie, 1946–57. 4 v.

Three volumes cover scores; one, music literature. Entries for scores include collections and separate publications, with contents given for collections.

[Afdeling] 3. Musikalier: 1. Udenlandsk musik. Del 1. Samlingsvaerker og musik for eet instrument, 1951. Del. 2. Kammermusik og orkestermusik, 1955. Del 3. Vokalmusik, dramatisk musik, folkemusik, 1957.

[Afdeling] 4. Musik: Musikfilosofi, musikteori, musikhistorie, biografi, 1946.

Aldrich, Richard. A catalogue of books relating to music. . . . See no. 867.

AMSTERDAM, HOLLAND

818

Vereniging voor Nederlandse Muziekgeschiedenis. Bibliotheek. Catalogus van de bibliotheek der Vereniging voor Nederlandse Muziekgeschiedenis. Amsterdam, G. Alsbach, 1919. 274 p.

Classified catalog, including both early and recent works. Contains a special section on manuscripts. Index of names and titles.

ASSISI, ITALY

819

La Cappella della Basilica di S. Francesco. Biblioteca. I. Catalogo del fondo musicale nella Biblioteca Comunale di Assisi, a cura di Claudio Sartori. Milano, Istituto Editoriale Italiano, 1962. 449 p. (Bibliotheca musicae, 1.)

Expands the work of Francesco Pennacchi published in the series *Associazione dei musicologi italiani* (see no. 938). Lists early printed music, books, and manuscripts separately. Most of the material is pre-1800, but some 19th-century manuscripts are included. Entries give contents of early items; locations for rarities. Descriptive annotations.

Review by Walther Dürr in *Die Musikforschung*, 18 (1965) p. 83–84.

AUGSBURG, GERMANY

820

Schaal, Richard. Das Inventar der Kantorei St. Anna in Augsburg. Ein Beitrag zur protestantischen Musikpflege im 16. und beginnenden 17. Jahrhundert. Kassel, Bärenreiter, 1965. 107 p. (Catalogus musicus, 3.)

Transcription of an inventory compiled in the early 17th century of the music collection of the Lutheran church and school of St. Anna in Augsburg. The collection itself is no longer intact.

821

Schletterer, Hans M. Katalog der in der Kreis- und Stadtbibliothek dem Städtischen Archive und der Bibliothek des Historischen Vereins zu Augsburg befindlichen Musikwerke. Augsburg, Fidelis Butsch Sohn, 1879. 138 p. (Monatsheft für Musikgeschichte. Beilage. Jahrgang 10 und 11, 1878–79.)

BADAJOZ, SPAIN

822

Monasterio de Guadalupe. Catálogo del archivo musical del Monasterio de Guadalupe, por El. P. Dr. Arcángel Barrado, O.F.M., Bibliotecario y maestro de capilla. Badajoz, 1945. 181 p.

Catalog of a collection of accompanied sacred vocal music, chiefly late 18th century. 947 entries, preceded by an historical study of the archive. Index of composers, and of musical forms.

[197]

BARCELONA, SPAIN

823

Diputación Provincial. Biblioteca Central. Catàlech de la Biblioteca Musical . . . per en Filipe Pedrell. Barcelona, Palau de la Diputació, 1908–1909. 2 v.

Classified catalog of 1,271 entries, including theory, history, practical music. Full bibliographical entries, collations, extensive notes, facsimiles, and musical quotations. Items listed by signature number, with an alphabetical index in volume 2.

824

Diputación Provincial. Biblioteca Central. La música española desde la edad media hasta neustros días; catálogo de la exposición histórica . . . por Higinio Anglés. [Barcelona] Diputación provincial de Barcelona, Biblioteca Central, 1941. 82 p.

Exhibition catalog commemorating the centennial of the birth of Filipe Pedrell. 171 items, manuscripts and printed books, associated with the history of Spanish music, assembled from a number of collections. Chronological arrangement, full entries, 52 facsimiles.

BASEL, SWITZERLAND

825

Universität. Bibliothek. Catalog der Schweizerischen Musikbibliothek. Herausgegeben von der Öffentlichen Bibliothek der Universität Basel. I. Musikgeschichtliche und theoretische Werke. Basel, E. Birkhäuser, 1906. 39 p.

A collection of music literature. The catalog of musical compositions, which was to form Vol. 2, was issued as Vol. 1 of the library's *Katalog der Musikabteilung der Öffentlichen Bibliothek* . . . (see next item).

826

Universität. Bibliothek. Katalog der Musikabteilung der Öffentlichen Bibliothek der Universität Basel und in ihr enthaltenen Schweizerischen Musikbibliothek. Band 1: Musikalische Kompositionen [hrsg. von Edgar Refardt] Basel, Universitäts-bibliothek, 1925. 141 p.

Works listed in alphabetical order by composer; important collections analyzed. Separate listing of collections, followed by a summary of the contents of several manuscript collections of music by Swiss composers. Index of editors, arrangers, librettists.

827
Universität. Bibliothek. Katalog der Musik-Sammlung auf der Universitäts-Bibliothek in Basel (Schweiz) . . . von Julius Richter. Leipzig, Breitkopf & Härtel, 1892. 104 p. (Monatshefte für Musikgeschichte. Beilage, Jahrgang 23 und 24.)

Full descriptions, contents, musical quotations, for manuscripts and early printed music in the university library.

828
Universität. Bibliothek. Thematischer Katalog der Instrumental-musik des 18. Jahrhunderts in den Handschriften der Universitätsbibliothek Basel. Von Edgar Refardt. Bern, P. Haupt, 1957. 59 p. (Publikationen der Schweizerischen Musikforschenden Gesellschaft, ser. 2, v. 6.)

The major part of the collection was assembled by the Basel silk manu-facturer Lucas Sarasin (1730–1802). Some 473 of the works cited were once part of his library. With these are incorporated the collection of the Basel *Collegium musicum* and that of the de Pury family. References made to 18th-century printings of the works here found in manuscript.

BELGIUM

Borren, Charles van den. "Inventaire des manuscrits de musique polyphonique aui se trouvent en Belgique."
See no. 743.

BEREA, OHIO

829
Baldwin-Wallace College. Riemenschneider Memorial Bach Library. Catalog of the Emilie and Karl Riemenschneider Memorial Bach Library. Edited by Sylvia W. Kenney. New York, Published for Baldwin-Wallace College by Columbia Univ. Press, 1960. 295 p.

Numbered catalog of 2,537 items, of which the first 520 are writings on Bach and his time. Nos. 521–31: music of contemporaries and sons of J. S. Bach; no. 532 to end: music of J. S. Bach. The principal grouping is by musical forms; manuscripts listed separately. Index of cantatas, general index.

Review by Walter Emery in *Music and letters*, 42 (1961) p. 376–77.

BERGAMO, ITALY

830
Biblioteca Civica. Il fondo musicale Mayr della Biblioteca Civica di Bergamo, nel secondo centenario della nascita di Giovanni Simone Mayr

(1763–1963). [By Arrigo Gazzaniga.] Bergamo, Edizioni "Monumenta Bergomensia," 1963. 149 p. (Monumenta bergomensia, 11.)

A classified catalog of works by Mayr and his contemporaries in the Biblioteca Civica in Bergamo. Chiefly manuscripts, including many autographs. 24 pages of facsimile.

BERKELEY, CALIFORNIA

831

University of California. Music Library. Autograph manuscripts of Ernest Bloch at the University of California. [Berkeley, University of California, 1962] 20 p.

Describes 35 autograph manuscripts bequeathed to the University of California Library from the estate of Ernest Bloch. The catalog was compiled by Minnie Elmer.

832

University of California. Music Library. Thematic catalog of a manuscript collection of eighteenth-century Italian instrumental music in the University of California, Berkeley, Music Library. By Vincent Duckles and Minnie Elmer. Berkeley & Los Angeles, University of Calif. Press, 1963. 403 p.

A collection comprising some 990 manuscripts containing works by 82 composers. The central figures are Giuseppe Tartini and Michele Stratico, and the collection itself has close connections with Tartini's school of violin playing at Padua. Preliminary chapters discuss the historical background of the collection and tabulate the handwritings and watermarks represented.

Review by Charles Cudworth in *Galpin society journal*, 18 (March, 1965) p. 140–41; by Denis Stevens in *Musical times*, 105 (July, 1964) p. 513–14; by Donald Krummel in *Notes*, 22 (1966) p. 1,025–26.

BERLIN, GERMANY

833

Die Amalien-Bibliothek. Musikbibliothek der Prinzessin Anna Amalia von Preussen (1723–87). Historische Einordnung und Katalog mit Hinweisen auf die Schreiber der Handschriften. [Von] Eva Renate Blechschmidt. Berlin, Merseburger, 1965. 346 p. (Berliner Studien zur Musikwissenschaft, 8.)

Reconstruction of the catalog of an important 18th-century collection formed by the youngest sister of Friedrich the Great. The bulk of the collection was acquired by the Joachimsthalsche Gymnasium in the late 18th century. The collection was dispersed for safe keeping in World War II, and since then parts of it have found their way to libraries in Tübingen, Marburg, and the Deutsche Staatsbibliothek in Berlin.

Blechschmidt's study treats the history of the collection and describes each item in detail, including both prints and manuscripts. Special attention is given to the identification of the scribes responsible for the manuscript copies.

834

Deutsche Staatsbibliothek. Die Bach-Handschriften der Berliner Staatsbibliothek, von Paul Kast. Trossinger, Hohner-Verlag, 1958. 150 p. (Tübinger Bach-Studien, 2/3.)

A catalog of manuscripts of music by members of the Bach family, once a part of the collection of the Prussian State Library and now distributed between the Westdeutsche Bibliothek in Marburg and the Universitäts-bibliothek in Tübingen. Essentially a finding list for one of the world's great collections of Bach sources now dispersed. Brief entries. Indexes of composers, scribes, and former owners of the manuscripts.

835

Deutsche Staatsbibliothek. Manuscrits de musique. Berlin, 1927. 45 p.

At head of title: Exposition internationale de musique, Genève, 1927. Preussische Staatsbibliothek.

P. 39–46: "La Section de musique de la Preussische Staatsbibliothek." [signed: Wilhelm Altmann.]

836

Deutsche Staatsbibliothek. "Die Musikabteilung," [von] Karl-Heinz Köhler. In *Deutsche Staatsbibliothek, 1661–1961.* Leipzig, 1961. Band I: Geschichte und Gegenwart, p. 241–74.

A narrative account of the founding of the music division of the Berlin State Library, the work of its successive directors, the growth of its collections up to the restoration of the music room after its destruction in World War II. The riches of the collection are summarized, particularly the Bach, Mozart, and Beethoven holdings. The author is director of the music division.

837

Internationale Musikleihbibliothek. Katalog. Berlin, 1952. 276 p.

Classified catalog of an international lending library of instrumental, vocal, and choral works. Includes parts for orchestral music. Strong in

[201]

works by Soviet composers, but other countries are also well represented. Composer index.

838
Joachimsthalsches Gymnasium. Bibliothek. Katalog der Musikaliensammlung des Joachimsthalschen Gymnasium zu Berlin. Verfasst von Robert Eitner. Berlin, T. Trautwein, 1884. 106 p. (Monatshefte für Musikgeschichte. Beilage, Jahrgang 16.)

This collection incorporates the library of Princess Anna Amalie, sister of Frederick the Great. Strong in 18th-century music of the North-German school. 627 numbered items, manuscripts, and early printed music. Author-composer index. See also no. 833.

839
Joachimsthalsches Gymnasium. Bibliothek. Thematischer Katalog der von Thulemeir'schen Musikalien-Sammlung in der Bibliothek des Joachimsthal'schen Gymnasiums zu Berlin. [By] Rudolf Jacobs, hrsg. von Robert Eitner. Leipzig, Breitkopf & Härtel, 1899. 110 p. (Monatshefte für Musikgeschichte. Beilgae, Jahrgang 30–31.)

The collection covers the period 1700–1800.

840
Königliche Hausbibliothek. Katalog der Musiksammlung aus der Königlichen Hausbibliothek im Schlosse zu Berlin. Verfasst und erläutert von Georg Thouret. . . . Leipzig, Breitkopf & Härtel, 1895. 356 p.

Supplemented by *Neue Erwerbungen der Königliche Hausbibliothek zu Berlin.* (Monatshefte . . . Beilage, Jahrgang 35, 1903.) 4 p.

Brief entries, alphabetical by composer. 6,836 items, printed and in manuscript, with a special section of works dedictated to members of the royal family and a supplementary section for military music.

BERN, SWITZERLAND

841
Schweizerische Landesbibliothek. Katalog der Schweizerischen Landesbibliothek. Musik Werke der Mitgleider des Schweizerischen Tonkünstlervereins veröffentlicht von 1848–1925, von Tonkünstlerverein und von der Landesbibliothek gemeinsam herausgegeben. [Ed. by K. Joss] Bern-Bümpliz, Buchdruckerei Benteli, 1927. 152 p.

About 5,000 titles, abridged to essential information, in a classified arrangement.

842
Archives of the Moravian Church. A catalogue of music by American Moravians, 1724–1842, from the Archives of the Moravian Church at Bethlehem, Pa. Bethlehem, Pennsylvania, The Moravian Seminary and College for Women, 1938. 118 p.
Short biographies and lists of compositions by 17 American-Moravian composers. Appendix of 24 plates of selected compositions and sample pages from the original manuscripts.

BLOOMINGTON, INDIANA

843
Indiana (State) University. School of Music. Latin-American Music Center. Latin American music available at Indiana University: score library, tape archive (art music), folk and primitive music. [Bloomington, Indiana] Indiana University, 1964. 101 leaves (typescript).

BOLOGNA, ITALY

Accademia Filarmonica. Archivio. See no. 926.

844
Accademia Filarmonica. Catalogo descrittivo degli autografi e ritratti di musicisti lasciati alla Reale Accademia Filarmonica di Bologna dall'Abb. Dott. Masseangelo Masseangeli. Compilato a cura degli Accademici Prof. Cav. Federico Parisini e Maestro Ernesto Colombani. Bologna, Regia Tipografia, 1896. 435 p.

845
Accademia Filarmonica. Mostra internazionale di musica in Bologna 1888. Catalogo con brevi cenni biografici e succinte discrizioni degli autografi e documenti de celebri o distinti musicisti posseduti da Emilla Succi, Accademica Filarmonica di Bologna. Bologna, Società Tipografica già Compositori, 1888. 179 p.
A collection of 886 items, chiefly letters of musicians of the 18th and 19th centuries, mostly autograph. Arranged alphabetically, with brief biographical notices and descriptions of the items.

Archivio di S. Petronio. See no. 926.

Biblioteca Ambrosini. See no. 926.

[203]

846

Biblioteca Universitaria. "Codici musicali della R. Biblioteca Universitaria di Bologna," [by Lodovico Frati] in *Rivista musicale italiana*, 23 (1916) p. 219–42.

A general description of the resources of the music collection, drawing attention to the major holdings in plainchant, early theory and polyphony.

847

Civico Museo Bibliografico Musicale. [Formerly designated Conservatorio di Musica "G. B. Martini"]. Catalogo della biblioteca del Liceo musicale di Bologna, compilato da Gaetano Gaspari, compiuto e pubblicato da Federico Parisini per cura del municipio. . . . Bologna, Libreria Romagnoli dall'Acqua, 1890–1943. 5 v.

Vols. 1–4 were reissued in photo-offset by Arnaldo Forni (Bologna, 1961) with corrections by Napoleone Fanti, Oscar Mischiati, and Luigi Ferdinando Tagliavini. A supplementary volume of materials recently added to the library is projected.

Vol. 1: music theory. Vol. 2: sacred vocal music (ed. Luigi Torchi). Vol. 3: secular vocal music and opera (ed. Luigi Torchi). Vol. 4: instrumental music and pedagogy (ed. Raffaele Caldolini). Vol. 5: libretti (ed. Ugo Sesini).

This catalog provides access to one of the richest collections of early music in the world, incorporating the library of the 18th-century scholar Padre Giambattista Martini. Full bibliographical descriptions, contents given for collections, transcriptions of numerous prefaces and dedications. Entries are alphabetical within each category. General index of names.

BONN, GERMANY

848

Beethoven-Haus. Katalog der Handschriften des Beethoven-Hauses und Beethoven-Archives Bonn. Bearbeitet von Dr. Joseph Schmidt-Görg. Bonn, Beethoven-Haus, 1935. 75 p.

275 numbered items, including letters, sketches, manuscripts and early editions of music by Beethoven and by his contemporaries.

849

Beethoven-Haus. Katalog der mit der Beethoven-Feier zu Bonn am 11.-15. Mai 1890 verbundenen Ausstellung von Handschriften, Briefen, Bildnissen, Reliquien Ludwig van Beethovens, sowie sonstigen auf ihn und seine Familie bezüglichen Erinnerungen. Bonn, Verlag des Vereins Beethoven-Haus, 1890. 75 p.

360 numbered items, including portraits, music, letters and other documents related to Beethoven and his contemporaries. Full transcriptions of numerous letters and excerpts from the "Conversationsheften."

850

Universitätsbibliothek. "Die musikalischen Autographen der Universitäts-Bibliothek Bonn," [by Theo Clasen]. In *Festschrift Joseph Schmidt-Görg zum 60. Geburtstag.* Bonn, Beethoven-Haus, 1957. P. 26–65.

The collection comprises 12 albums containing autograph letters, cards, sketches, etc. by 245 musicians. Material listed by author.

BORDEAUX, FRANCE

851

Bibliothèque Municipale. Catalogue des livres composant la bibliothèque de la ville de Bordeaux. Musique. [By I. Delas] Bordeaux, 1856. 127 p.

BOSTON, MASSACHUSETTS

852

Boston Public Library. Catalogue of the Allen A. Brown collection of music. Boston, Mass., 1910–16. 4 v.

A dictionary catalog of composers, titles, subjects, with explicit contents and analytics given for all collections. One of the first, and one of the few, printed catalogs for a major American music collection. Rich in operas and orchestral scores, primarily 19th-century editions.

BRANDENBURG, GERMANY

853

St. Katharinenkirche. Bibliothek. Die musikalischen Schätze der St. Katherinenkirche zu Brandenburg a.d. Havel. Ein Beitrag zur musikalischen Literatur des 16. und 17. Jahrhunderts [von Johann F. Täglichsbeck] Brandenburg, A. Müller, 1857. 50 p.

Manuscripts and printed works, 1564–1671, chronologically arranged, with full bibliographical information and descriptive notes.

BRASOV, RUMANIA

854

Honterusgymnasium. Bibliothek. Die Musiksammlung der Bibliothek zu Kronstadt, von Erich H. Müller. Kronstadt, J. Gött's Sohn, 1930. 176 p.

Manuscripts, printed music, and books. Brief biographical sketches of authors or composers. Publication dates, plate numbers.

BRESLAU, GERMANY and BRIEG, GERMANY
See Wroclaw, Poland

BRISTOL, ENGLAND

855

Public Libraries. Catalogue of music scores. Bristol, 1959. 305 p.

BRUSSELS, BELGIUM

856

Bibliothèque Royale de Belgique. Catalogue de la bibliothèque de F. J. Fétis, acquise par l'État belge. Bruxelles, C. Muquardt, 1877. 946 p.

The Fétis library was acquired by the Bibliothèque Royale in 1872, and contains many rarities. 7,325 items classified under two main headings: (1) "Bibliothèque générale," and (2) "Bibliothèque musicale."

857

Bibliothèque Royale de Belgique. Catalogue des imprimés musicaux des XVe, XVIe et XVIIe siècles. Fonds général. Par Bernard Huys. Bruxelles, Bibliothèque Royale de Belgique, 1965. 422 p.

446 numbered items. The catalog lists those works not part of the Fétis collection (above), although if another copy or a more complete copy is found in Fétis, this information is given. Contents listed for each item. Of particular interest is the listing of music excerpted from theoretical works such as Kircher, Clareanus, Zarlino, etc. Numerous facsimile pages. Liturgical books, except for Psalters, not included.

Review by François Lesure in *Revue de musicologie*, 51 (1965) p. 102.

858

Bibliothèque Royale de Belgique. Exposition de documents musicaux (Manuscrits—Imprimés—Estampes) 11–30 Septembre, 1955. [Brussels] Bibliothèque Royale de Belgique, 1955. 23 p.

An exposition catalog of 113 items assembled from the music collections of the Bibliothèque Royale. Prepared for the International Congress of Libraries and Documentation Centers held in Brussels in 1955.

859

Conservatoire Royal de Musique. Bibliothèque. Catalogue de la bibliothèque . . . par A. Wotquenne. Bruxelles, Coosemans, 1898–1912. 4 v.

Annexe I. Libretti d'opéras et d'oratorios italiens du XVIIe siècle. Bruxelles, O. Schepens, 1901. 189 p.

A classified catalog of one of the richest European collections. Prints and manuscripts interfiled.

BUDAPEST, HUNGARY

860

Országos Széchényi Könyvtár. "Catalogue raisonné der Esterházy-Opernsammlung, in chronologischer Ordnung der Premièren." In *Haydn als Opernkapellmeister; die Haydn-Dokumente der Esterházy-Opernsammlung.* Bearbeitet von Dénes Bartha und László Somfai. Budapest, Verlag der Ungarischen Akademie der Wissenschaften, 1960. P.179–403.

A chronological listing of the operatic works preserved in the Esterházy archive, now in the National Széchényi Library at Budapest. Each work is fully described, with special attention given to Haydn's annotations on works performed under his direction. An important new approach to Haydn research.

861

Országos Széchényi Könyvtár. Haydn compositions in the music collection of the National Széchényi Library, Budapest. Published on the occasion of the 150th anniversary of Haydn's death (1809–1959) [Edited by Jenö Vécsey . . .] Budapest, Publishing House of the Hungarian Academy of Sciences, 1960. 167 p. (Pubn. of the National Széchényi Library, 48.)

Also published in Hungarian and German.

A classified listing of 372 items, 72 of which are Haydn autographs. 42 facsimiles of Haydn manuscripts, prints, and other documents.

862

Országos Széchényi Könyvtár. "Die Musikalien der Pfarrkirche zu St. Aegidi in Bártfa." [By Otto Gombosi]. In *Festschrift für Johannes Wolf,* Berlin, 1929. P. 38–47.

The collection described here is now in the National Széchényi Library at Budapest. Gombosi discusses some 20 music prints of the 16th century and a number of important 16th and 17th century manuscripts.

863

Országos Széchényi Könyvtár. Zenei kéziratok jegyzéke. Budapest, Kiádja a Magyar Nemzeti Múzeum Orzágos Széchényi Kónyvtár,

1921–40. 2 v. (Catalogus bibliothecae musaei nat. hungarici. Musica, I and II.)

Vol. 1 (391 p.): Editor, Isoz Kálmán. Catalog of 1,449 autograph letters of musicians, including some of Haydn and Liszt. Vol. 2 (237 p.). Editor, Lavotta Rezső. Catalog of music manuscripts.

CAMBRAI, FRANCE

864

Coussemaker, Edmond de. Notice sur les collections musicales de la Bibliothèque de Cambrai et des autres villes du Départment du Nord. . . . Paris, Techener, 1843. 180, 40 p.

Concerned chiefly with 16 manuscripts and 4 printed collections in the Cambrai library. The descriptions are brief, faulty, and outdated.

CAMBRIDGE, ENGLAND

865

University. Fitzwilliam Museum. Library. Catalogue of the music in the Fitzwilliam Museum, Cambridge, by J. A. Fuller-Maitland and A. H. Mann. London, C. J. Clay & Sons, 1893. 298 p.

209 manuscripts, 196 printed books, and an important collection of Handel materials.

866

University. Peterhouse College. Library. Catalogue of the musical manuscripts at Peterhouse, Cambridge; compiled by Anselm Hughes. Cambridge, Cambridge Univ. Press, 1953. 75 p.

Important source materials for the study of English church music of the 16th and 17th centuries, comprising 4 Latin partbooks of c. 1540 and 2 sets of English partbooks c. 1630–40.

CAMBRIDGE, MASSACHUSETTS

867

Harvard University. Music Library. A catalogue of books relating to music in the library of Richard Aldrich. New York, 1931 [Printed at the Plimpton Press, Norwood, Mass.] 435 p.

A classified catalog of music literature, primarily of the 19th and 20th centuries, with a small collection of books printed before 1800 (p. 35–55). This library has been incorporated into the Harvard University music collection.

[208]

CARPENTRAS, FRANCE

868

Bibliothèque d'Inguimbert. Catalogue de la collection musicale J. B. Laurens donnée a la ville de Carpentras pour la Bibliothèque d'Inguimbert. Carpentras, J. Seguin, 1901. 151 p.

Classified catalog of music books and scores; a 19th-century scholar's library. Preceded by a biography of the donor, J. B. Laurens, archeologist, painter, writer, organist, composer, and musicologist.

CESENA, ITALY

869

Biblioteca Comunale. "Catalogo delle opere musicali a stampa dal'500 al'700 conservate presso la Biblioteca Comunale di Cesena." [By Sergio Paganelli] In *Collectanea historiae musicae*, 2 (1957) p. 311–38.

95 early prints of vocal and instrumental music; 6 theory works.

COIMBRA, PORTUGAL

870

Universidade. Biblioteca. Inventário dos inéditos e impressos musicais (subsídios para um catálogo). Fasc. I. Prefaciado por Santiago Kastner. Coimbra, Impresso nas oficinas da "Atlântida," 1937. 47 p. (Publicações da Biblioteca da Universidade.)

Separate alphabets for manuscripts and early printed works. Full descriptions.

871

Universidade. Biblioteca. Os manuscritos musicais n.os 6 e 12 da Biblioteca geral da Universidade de Coimbra (Contribuïçao para um catálogo definitivo). Por Mário de Sampayo Ribeiro. Coimbra, 1941. 112 p. (Publicäçōes da Biblioteca geral da Universidade de Coimbra.)

A detailed study of two manuscripts of polyphonic music in the university library at Coimbra.

COLOGNE, GERMANY

872

Domcapelle. Die Leiblsche Sammlung. Katalog der Musikalien der Kölner Domcapelle. [Von Gottfried Göller] Köln, Arno Volk-Verlag, 1964. 133 p. (Beiträge zur rheinischen Musikgeschichte, 57.)

A thematic catalog of a collection of 291 sacred choral works, chiefly early 19th century, including both manuscripts and printed books, formerly in the chapel of Cologne Cathedral. The collection is now in the Diözesanbibliothek of the Archbishopric of Cologne. It derives its name from Carl Leibl, Kapellmeister, 1826–63. Full bibliographical descriptions; numerous indexes.

873

Universitäts- und Stadtbibliothek. Katalog der in der Universitäts- und Stadtbibliothek Köln vorhandenen Musikdrucke des 16., 17., und 18. Jahrhunderts. [By Willi Kahl] Köln, 1958. 20 p.

118 items. Bibliographical references.

COPENHAGEN, DENMARK

874

Kommunebiblioteker. Katalog over dansk og udenlandsk musik og musiklitteratur. 2. udgave. København, B. Lunos Bogtrykkeri, 1932. 157 p.

First published in 1921. 72 p.

Tilvaext [supplement] 1932–39. København, B. Lunos, 1939. 53 p.

875

Kommunebiblioteker. Katalog over musik og musiklitteratur. København, Nordlunde, 1954–56(?) 5 v.

Del 1: Orkestermusik, Kammermusik, Enkelte Instrumenter, 1956. 72 p. Del 2: Klaver, Orgel, Harmonium, 1954. 65 p. Del 3: [Vokalmusik, 195?]. Del 4: Operaer, Operetter, Balletter, 1955. 46 p. Del 5: [Musikteori, Musikhistorie, Biografier, 195?].

CREMONA, ITALY

876

Biblioteca Governativa e Libreria Civica. Mostra bibliografica dei musicisti cremonesi: catalogo storico-critico degli autori e catalogo bibliografico. Cremona, Biblioteca Governativa e Libreria Civica, 1951. 149 p. (Annali della Biblioteca . . . 2.)

Catalog of an exhibition held in 1949. P. 1–106: biographical notices of Cremonese musicians; p. 107–45: exhibition catalog, arranged chronologically; about 140 items related to the history of music in Cremona.

CRESPANO VENETO, ITALY

877

Biblioteca Musicale del Prof. Pietro Canal in Crespano Veneto. Bassano, Prem. Stabilimento Tipogr. Sante Pezzato, 1885. 104 p.

A scholar's library of 1,152 items, of which the first 1,034 are books on music. Contains many rarities. The owner was a professor at the University of Padua and wrote studies of music in Mantua and Venice.

CZECHOSLOVAKIA

878

Plamenac, Dragan. "Music libraries in Eastern Europe, a visit in the summer of 1961." In *Notes*, 19 (1962) p. 217–34; 411–20; 584–98.

An illuminating account of present conditions in some of the major East-European music libraries, including those in Czechoslovakia. Locations of important bodies of source materials are cited.

879

Terrayová, Mária J. "Súpis archívnych hudobných fondov na Slovensku." In *Hudobnovedné stúdie*, VI. Bratislava, Vydavetel'stvo Slovenskej Akadémie Vied, 1960. P. 197–328.

Thematic catalog of the music manuscripts in two hitherto undescribed Czech archives: archive of the Pfarrkirche of Púchov (on deposit in the Musicological Institute of the Slovakian Academy of Sciences), and the archive of the Prílesky-Ostrolúcky family (on deposit in the Slovakian National Museum in Martin). The manuscripts are chiefly of late 18th-century instrumental and vocal music by Italianate Czech composers of the period.

The catalog is described as the beginning of a projected complete thematic catalog of early music in Czech archives.

See also no. 645 for a listing of the music accessions in ten major Czech libraries.

DAGENHAM, ENGLAND

880

Public Libraries. Catalogue of music; a complete catalogue of the scores, miniature scores, recorded music and books . . . in the Dagenham Public Libraries. Compiled by W. C. Pugsley & G. Atkinson. Dagenham [Essex] 1958. 299 p.

DANZIG.

See Gdansk, Poland

[211]

DARMSTÄDT, GERMANY

881

Hofbibliothek. "Musik-Handschriften der Darmstädter Hofbibliothek." [Beschreiben von F. W. E. Roth.] In *Monatshefte für Musikgeschichte*, 20 (1888) p. 64–73; 82–92.

117 items, 10th to 19th centuries. Brief descriptions.

882

Hofbibliothek. "Zur Bibliographie der Musikdrucke des XV. bis XVII. Jahrhunderts in der Darmstädter Hofbibliothek." [Von F. W. E. Roth.] In *Montshefte für Musikgeschichte*, 20 (1888) p. 118–25; 134–31; 154–61.

75 items, fully described.

883

Internationales Musikinstitut. Informationszentrum für zeitgenössische Musik. Katalog der Abteilung Noten. [Vorwort: Ernst Thomas] Pfungstadt, Jacob Helène, 1966. 293 p.

An international lending library, founded in 1948 to further the study and performance of contemporary music. Between 1949 and 1962 known as the *Kranichsteiner Musikinstitut*.

Catalog of some 12,937 scores of works by contemporary composers, entered under composer and sub-classified according to medium. P. 15–25: an international listing of publishers and distributors. The catalog is a useful tool for collection building.

See also the entry below.

DENTON, TEXAS

884

North Texas State College. Music Library. A bibliography of contemporary music in the Music Library of North Texas State College, March 1955. Compiled by Anna Harriet Heyer. . . . Denton, Texas, 1955. 128 leaves (typescript).

Alphabetical listing by composer, and by title under composer. Chiefly scores and chamber music with parts. No indexes.

Review by Dorothy A. Linder in *Notes*, 13 (1956) p. 656–57.

DRESDEN, GERMANY

885

Sächsische Landesbibliothek. Musikabteilung. Katalog der Musik-Sammlung der Kgl. öffentlichen Bibliothek zu Dresden (im Japanischen Palais). Bearb. von Robert Eitner und Otto Kade. . . . Leipzig, Breitkopf &

Härtel, 1890. 150 p. (Monatshefte für Musikgeschichte. Beilage. Jahrgang 21 and 22.)

Music manuscripts to the date of compilation; printed music and books on music to 1700.

886

Sächsische Landesbibliothek. Musikabteilung. Klaviermusik der sozialistischen Länder aus der Sächsischen Landesbibliothek. Bestandsverzeichnis zusammengestellt von Wolfgang Reich. Dresden, Sächsische Landesbibliothek, 1962. 79 p.

A list, grouped alphabetically by country, of keyboard music by East-European composers. Date, publisher, and pagination given for each entry.

EDINBURGH, SCOTLAND

887

L'Institut Français d'Ecosse. Hector Berlioz (1803–1869) an exhibition at l'Institut Français d'Ecosse on the occasion of the 1963 Edinburgh International Festival. Edinburgh, Institut Français d'Ecosse, 1963. 40 p.

An exhibition catalog compiled by Richard Macnutt. 127 items, arranged chronologically with respect to the composer's career. Fully annotated with connecting commentary.

888

University. Reid Library. Catalogue of manuscripts, printed music and books on music up to 1850 in the library of the Music Department of the University of Edinburgh (Reid Library), edited by Hans Gál. Edinburgh, Oliver and Boyd, 1941. 78 p.

Important for its holdings in 18th-century music, printed and in manuscript, from the private collection of John Reid, 1721–1807. Brief entries.

EISENACH, GERMANY

889

Richard Wagner-Museum. Katalog einer Richard Wagner-Bibliothek; nach den vorliegenden Originalien systematisch-chronologisch geordnetes und mit Citaten und Anmerkungen versehenes authentisches Nachschlagebuch durch die gesammte Wagner-Litteratur. [By Nikolaus Oesterlein.] Leipzig, Breitkopf & Härtel, 1882–95. 4 v.

Apart from being a bibliography of Wagner literature of the late 19th century, this work provides a catalog of a collection of Wagner documents formerly in Vienna but purchased by the city of Eisenach in 1895. Vols. 1 and 2 constitute the bibliography; Vols. 3 and 4, the catalog.

FERRARA, ITALY

Biblioteca Comunale. See no. 935.

890

Biblioteca Nazionale Centrale. Catalogo dei manoscritti musicali della Biblioteca Nazionale di Firenze. [By Bianca Becherini.] Kassel, Bärenreiter, 1959. 178 p.

144 numbered items; detailed descriptions, contents of collections. Indexes of text incipits, musicians, poets, and names mentioned in the descriptive notes.

Review by Frank L. Harrison in *Music and letters*, 42 (1961) p. 281; by Nanie Bridgman in *Fontes artis musicae*, 8 (1961) p. 31–33; by Walther Dürr in *Die Musikforschung*, 14 (1961) p. 234–35.

891

Biblioteca Nazionale Centrale. Mostra bibliografica di musica italiana dalle origini alla fine del secolo XVIII. Firenze, L. S. Olschik, 1937. 102 p.

An exhibition catalog. Preface signed: Anita Mondolfo.

Conservatorio di Musica "Luigi Cherubini" [formerly cited as R. Istituto Musicale]. See no. 928.

892

Conservatorio di Musica "Luigi Cherubini." Esposizione nazionale dei Conservatori Musicali e delle Biblioteche. Palazzo Devanzati, 27 Ottobre 1949—8 Gennaio 1950. Firenze, G. Barbèra, 1950. 121 p.

Exposition catalog celebrating the 100th anniversary of the founding of the conservatory. Includes manuscripts, printed music, and some musical instruments.

893

Conservatorio di Musica "Luigi Cherubini." "I manoscritti e le stampe rare della Biblioteca del Conservatorio 'L. Cherubini' di Firenze." In *La Bibliofilia*, 66 (1964) p. 255–99.

20 manuscripts and 21 early printed books "nuova catalogazione e reintegrazione."

A catalog compiled by Bianca Becherini for the purpose of giving full descriptions of those works in the collection that are most rare and most in demand by foreign scholars.

894

Conservatorio di Musica "Luigi Cherubini." Indice di alcuni cimeli esposti appartenenti alla Biblioteca del R. Istituto. [By Riccardo Gandolfi.] Firenze, Tipografia Galletti e Cocci, 1911. 32 p.

At head of title: "Nella commemorazione cinquantenaria dalla fondazione del R. Istituto Musicale 'Luigi Cherubini' di Firenze."

Brief descriptive entries for 30 manuscripts and 37 early printed books, 32 theory works and 4 "Curiosità diversi."

895

Galleria Degli Uffizi. I desegni musicali del Gabinetto degli "Uffizi" e delle minori collezioni pubbliche a Firenze. [By Luigi Parigi.] Firenze, L. S. Olschki [1951] 233 p.

A catalog of prints and drawings with musical content or subject matter: musicians, musical instruments, performance practice, etc. Indexed by instruments and by subjects.

896

Galleria Degli Uffizi. Mostra di strumenti musicali in disegni degli "Uffizi." Catalogo a cura di Luisa Marcucci con prefazione di Luigi Parigi. Firenze, L. S. Olschki [1952] 47 p.

An exhibition of 65 items from the Uffizi print collection; 25 plates.

897

Galleria Degli Uffizi. Gli strumenti musicali nei dipinti della Galleria degli Uffizi. [By] Marziano Bernardi e Andrea Della Corte. [Torino, Edizioni Radio Italiana, 1952] 177 p. 51 plates.

A handsome volume devoted to representations of musical activity in paintings in the Uffizi gallery. Index of artists and of instruments depicted.

898

Illustrazioni di Alcuni Cimeli Concernenti l'Arte Musicale in Firenze. . . . [Di Riccardo Gandolfi.] In Firenze, a cura della Commissione per la Esposizione di Vienna, 1892.

A lavish, illustrated catalog prepared for the Vienna exposition in 1892. Limited edition, elephant folio; 39 facsimile plates of Italian musical documents from the 11th to the 19th centuries. Historical introduction and notes on the plates.

FRANCE

899

Bridgman, Nanie. "Musique profane italienne des 16e et 17e siècles dans les bibliothèques françaises." In *Fontes artis musicae*, 2 (1955) p. 40–59.

A precise description of 32 rarities of the 16th and 17th centuries found in 5 public or private libraries in France.

900

Chaillon, Paule. "Les fonds musicaux de quelques bibliothèques de Province." In *Fontes artis musicae* (1955:2) p. 151–63.

Describes a group of source materials found in 24 French provincial libraries. These sources came to light in connection with work done in preparation for the RISM volumes.

FRANKFURT AM MAIN, GERMANY

901

International Exhibition "Music in the Life of the People." Catalogo della sezione Italiana. Roma, 1927. 161 p.

A separate listing of the Italian section of the exhibition below. 35 plates.

902

International Exhibition "Music in the Life of the People." Katalog der Internationalen Austellung "Musik im Leben der Völker," von Kathi Meyer. [Frankfurt am Main, Hauserpresse Werner U. Winter, 1927] 340 p.

Catalog of the large international music exhibition held June 11–August 28, 1927. Organized according to the systematic arrangement of the exhibition halls. Includes printed books, manuscripts, instruments, pictures, and other artifacts. 49 plates.

903

Lessing-Gymnasium. Bibliothek. Die musikalischen Schätze der Gymnasialbibliothek und der Peterskirche zu Frankfurt a.M., von Carl Isräel. Frankfurt a.M., Mahlau & Waldschmidt, 1872. 118 p.

Covers the period to about 1800; full bibliographical data.

904

Stadtbibliothek. Kirchliche Musikhandschriften des XVII. und XVIII. Jahrhunderts; Katalog von Carl Süss, im Auftrage der Gesellschaft der Freunde der Stadtbibliothek, bearb. und hrsg. von Peter Epstein. Berlin, Frankfurter Verlags-Anstalt [1926] 224 p.

Chiefly cantatas arranged alphabetically under composer, with a separate section of 834 works by G. P. Telemann. Entries give title, date if known, and instrumentation.

FREIBERG, GERMANY

905

Kade, Otto. Die älteren Musikalien der Stadt Freiberg in Sachsen. Leipzig, Breitkopf & Härtel, 1888. 32 p. (Monatshefte für Musikgeschichte. Beilage. Jahrgang 20.)

GDANSK, POLAND [formerly DANZIG]

906
Stadtbibliothek. Die musikalischen Handschriften der Stadtbibliothek und in ihrer Verwaltung befindlichen Kirchenbibliotheken von St. Katharinen und St. Johann in Danzig. [Von Otto Günther]. Danzig, 1911. (Katalog der Handschriften der Danziger Stadtbibliothek, Bd. 4: Handschriften, Teil 4.)

The surviving music manuscripts and early printed books of the Danzig Stadtbibliothek have been filmed and are listed in the catalog of music sources published by the Polish National Library in Warsaw, see no. 1116. Professor Plamenac in his articles on East-European music libraries (see no. 878 above), has given a summary listing of the major holdings of this collection.

GENOA, ITALY

Biblioteca Universitaria. See no. 933.

GERMANY

907
Deutsches Musikgeschichtliches Archiv. Katalog der Filmsammlung. Zusammengestellt und bearbeitet von Harald Heckmann. Band I, Nr. 1– . Kassel, Bärenreiter, 1955– (7 v. to Spring, 1965).

Title varies: Nr. 1, *Mitteilungen und Katalog.* . . . A series of catalogs, in progress, of the holdings of a microfilm archive of primary source materials for the study of German music history. Includes manuscripts and early printed books. For a description of this archive and its catalogs, see Harald Heckmann, "Archive of German music history," in *Notes,* 16 (1958) p. 35–39.

Kahl, Willi and Wilhelm-Martin Luther. Repertorium der Musikwissenschaft. . . .

For complete citation and annotation, see no. 428.

GLASGOW, SCOTLAND

908
Anderson's College. Library. Euing Collection. The Euing musical library. Catalogue of the musical library of the late Wm. Euing, Esq., bequeathed to Anderson's University, Glasgow. . . . Glasgow, Printed by W. M. Ferguson, 1878. 256 p.

Classified catalog. The collection is strong in theoretical works from 1487 and liturgical music of the Church of England, 16th to 19th centuries.

GÖTTINGEN, GERMANY

909

Niedersächsische Staats- und Universitäts-Bibliothek. Johann Sebastian Bach Documenta. Hrsg. . . . von Wilhelm Martin Luther zum Bachfest 1950 in Göttingen. Kassel, Bärenreiter [1950] 148 p.

545 numbered items from an exhibition illustrating J. S. Bach's influence from his own time to the present day; covers a wide area of Bach documentation. 54 plates.

910

Niedersächsische Staats- und Universitäts-Bibliothek. Die Musikwerke der Kgl. Universitäts-Bibliothek in Göttingen. Verzeichnet von Albert Quantz. Berlin, T. Trautwein, 1883. 45 p. (Monatshefte für Musikgeschichte. Beilage. Jahrgang 15.)

45 theoretical works and some 100 music prints of the 16th and 17th centuries; good representation of German composers.

GRANADA, SPAIN

911

Capilla Real. Archivo. "El Archivo de musica de la Capilla Real de Grenada." [By José lópez Calo.] In *Anuario musical*, 13 (1958) p. 103–28.

A small collection of manuscripts, early printed books, and documents. Lists full contents for polyphonic sources.

GRAZ, AUSTRIA

912

Neue Galerie. Bilder aus Beethovens Leben, aus der Beethoven-Sammlung G. L. de Baranyai. Ausstellung des Landes Steiermark und der Stadt Graz; Graz, Neue Galerie, 30. Juni–22 Juli 1962. [Graz] 1962. 77 p.

GREAT BRITAIN

913

Bibliotheca Musico-Liturgica. A descriptive handlist of the musical and Latin-liturgical mss. of the Middle Ages preserved in the libraries of Great Britain and Ireland. Drawn up by W. H. Frere . . . and printed for the

[218]

members of the Plainsong and Mediaeval Music Society. . . . London, B. Quaritch. 1901–32. 2 v.

Also entered as no. 741.

914

The British Union–Catalogue of Early Music Printed before the Year 1801. A record of the holdings of over 100 libraries throughout the British Isles. Editor: Edith B. Schnapper. London, Butterworths Scientific Publications, 1957. 2 v.

Also entered as no. 747.

GRIMMA, GERMANY

915

Königl. Landesschule. Bibliothek. Verzeichniss der in der Bibliothek der Königl. Landesschule zu Grimma vorhandenen Musikalien aus dem 16. und 17. Jahrhundert, von N. M. Petersen. . . . Grimma, [G. Gensel, 1861] 24 p.

The greater part of this collection is now in the Sächsischen Landesbibliothek in Dresden.

THE HAGUE, HOLLAND

916

Gemeentemuseum. Nederlandsche muziekleven 1600–1800. 's-Gravenhage, Gemeentemuseum, 6 Juni–6 September, 1936. 124 p.

Catalog of an exhibition on Dutch musical life of the 17th and 18th centuries. Includes printed books, manuscripts, musical instruments, and paintings with musical subjects. Illustrated. Introductions by D. J. Balfoort.

917

Muziekhistorisch Museum van Dr. D. F. Scheurleer. Catalogus van de muziek-werken en de boeken over muziek. 's-Gravenhage, M. Nijhoff, 1923–25. 3 v.

This catalog was preceded by two earlier compilations, one in 2 volumes in 1885–87, and one in 3 volumes, 1893–1910.

A classified catalog; volume 3 is a general index. Numerous facsimiles of early title pages. The Scheurleer collection is an outstanding working library in musicology, as well as containing many rarities. It is now the property of the city of The Hague, housed in the Gemeentemuseum and the Royal Library.

HALLE, GERMANY

918

Händel-Haus. Katalog zu den Sammlungen des Händel-Hauses in Halle. V. 1– . Halle an der Saale [Händel-Haus] 1961– .

1. Teil: Handschriftensammlung (1961) 330 p. 2. Teil: Bildsammlung, Porträts (1962) 288 p. 3. Teil: Bildsammlung, Städte- und Gebäudedarstellungen (1964) 380 p.

The first three volumes of a series projected to cover all of the collections of the Händel-Haus. *Teil 1* includes both musical and literary manuscripts. Rich in materials related to early 19th-century German song. Letters and documents transcribed in full. *Teil 2* is concerned with iconography: paintings, engravings, busts, and medals, with reproductions given for all items. Bibliography of Händel iconography: p. 283–88. *Teil 3* treats iconography with respect to places, cities, buildings, etc.

HAMBURG, GERMANY

919

Hamburger Musikbücherei. Oper, Operette, Singspiel. Ein Katalog der Hamburger Musikbücherei, 1965. [Hamburg] Herausgegeben von den Hamburger Öffentlichen Bücherhallen, 1965. 207 p.

A catalog of the theater holdings of the Hamburg Musikbücherei, comprising some 3,198 volumes, 1,590 titles. Full scores and vocal scores are indicated, with publishers and plate numbers. Chiefly 19th- and 20th-century works, but with some earlier items. Arranged alphabetically by composer, with indexes of Singspiele, of full scores, of titles. Annemarie Eckhoff, editor.

HEILBRONN, GERMANY

920

Gymnasium. Bibliothek. Alter Musikschatz, geordnet und beschreiben von Edwin Mayers. Heilbronn, C. F. Schmidt, 1893. 82 p. (Mitteilungen aus der Bibliothek des Heilbronner Gymnasiums, 2.)

HUNGARY

Radó, Polycarpe. Répertoire hymnologique. . . . See no. 787.

IOWA CITY, IOWA

921

University Library. An exhibit of music and materials on music, early and rare. Preface by Albert T. Luper. Iowa City, The Graduate

College and The University Libraries, State University of Iowa, April 1953. 39 p.

An annotated exhibition catalog of materials borrowed from the Library of Congress, The Newberry Library, The University of Illinois Libraries, The Sibley Musical Library, and private sources. Part I: autograph scores (13 times); Part II: early music editions and manuscripts (43 items); Part III: books on music, mainly 17th and 18th century (45 times).

922

University Library. Rare musical items in the libraries of the University of Iowa, by Frederick K. Gable. Foreword by Albert T. Luper. Iowa City, The University Libraries, University of Iowa, 1963. 130 p.

A carefully annotated catalog of 275 items. Part I: books on music; Part II: music scores. Index of names and of selected subjects. Selected bibliography.

ITALY

923

Associazione dei Musicologi Italiani. Catalogo generale delle opere musicali, teoriche o pratiche, manoscritti o stampate, di autori vissuti sino ai primi decenni del XIX secolo, esistenti nelle biblioteche e negli archivi d'Italia. . . . Parma, Freschig, 1911–38. 14 v.

The *Associazione* catalogs are of mixed quality and completeness, but in many cases they represent the best available listings of the holdings of important Italian libraries. Their coverage is confined to music and theoretical works written or published before 1810.

924

  i: 1. Città di Parma. [Compilatori: Guido Gasperini, Nestore Pellicelli] [1909]–11. 295 p.

925

  i: 2. Città di Reggio-Emilia. [Compilatore: Guido Gasperini, Nestore Pellicelli] 1911. 24 p.

926

  ii. Città di Bologna. [Compilatori: Alfredo Bonora, Emilio Giani] 1910–11–[38] 159 p.
  Archivio della R. Accademia Filarmonica (p. 1–43).
  Biblioteca dell'Avv. Raimondo Ambrosini (p. 47–66).
  Archivio di S. Petronio (p. 71–159).

927

iii. Città di Milano. Biblioteca Ambrosiana. [Compilatore: Gaetano Cesari] 1910–11. 20 p. (incomplete).

928

iv:1. Città di Firenze. Biblioteca del R. Istituto Musicale. [Compilatori: Riccardo Gandolfi, Carlo Cordara] 1910–11. 321 p.

929

iv:2. Città di Pistoia. Archivio capitolare della cattedrale. [Compilatore: Umberto de Laugier] 1936–37. 106 p.

930

v. Città di Roma. Biblioteca della R. Accademia di S. Cecilia. [Compilatore: Otello Andolfi] 1912–13. (incomplete).

931

vi:1. Città di Venezia. [Compilatore: Giovanni Concina] [1913?]–14. 382 p.
Biblioteca Querini Stampalia (p. 1–25).
Museo Correr (p. 29–113).
Pia Casa di Ricovero (p. 117–161).
R. Biblioteca di S. Marco. [Compilatori: Taddeo Wiel, A. d'Este, R. Faustini] (p. 169–382).

932

vi:2. Città di Vicenza. [Biblioteca bertoliana . . . de Sebastiano Rumor; Archivio della cattedrale . . . da Primo Zanini] 1923. 48 p.

933

vii. Città di Genova. R. Biblioteca Universitaria. [Schedatore: Raffaele Bresciano] [n.d.] 21 p.

934

viii. Città di Modena. R. Biblioteca Estense. [Compilatore: Pio Lodi] [1916–24] 561 p.

935

ix. Città di Ferrara. Biblioteca Comunale. [Compilatori: Emanuele Davia, Alessandro Lombardi] 1917. 40 p.

936

x:1. Città di Napoli. Archivio dell'Oratorio dei Filippini. [Compilatore: Salvatore di Giacomo] 1918. 108 p.

937

x: 2. Città di Napoli. Biblioteca del R. Conservatorio di S. Pietro a Majella. [Compilatori: Guido Gasperini, Franca Gallo] [1918]–34. 696 p.

938

xi. Città di Assisi. Biblioteca comunale. [Compilatore: Francesco Pennacchi] 1921. 45 p.

939

xii. Città di Torino. R. Biblioteca Nazionale. [Compilatore: Attilio Cimbro, Alberto Gentili] 1928. 38 p.

940

xiii. Biblioteche e archivi della città di Pisa. [Compilatore: Pietro Pecchiai] 1932–[35] 90 p.

941

xiv. Città di Verona. Biblioteca della Soc. Accademica Filarmonica di Verona. Fondo musicale antico. [Compilatore: Guiseppe Turrini] 1935–36. 54 p.

942

Rubsamen, Walter H. "Music research in Italian libraries." In *Notes*, 6 (1948–49) p. 220–33; 543–69; 8 (1950–51) p. 70–99, 513.

A narrative account of the author's experiences working in Italian libraries shortly after World War II. Contains useful inventories, partially thematic, of manuscript sources of early music in Italian libraries.

943

Smijers, Albert. "Vijftiende en zestiende eeuwsche muziek handschriften in Italie met werken van Nederlandsche componisten." In *Tijdschrift der Vereeniging voor Nederl. Muziekgeschiedenis*, 14 (1935) p. 165–81.

Describes a card file of compositions by Netherland composers of the 15th and 16th centuries in 50 manuscripts in Italian libraries. By means of collation the author has been able to clarify the attributions of numerous anonymous and misattributed works in these sources.

JENA, GERMANY

944

Universitätsbibliothek. Die geistlichen Musikhandschriften der Universitätsbibliothek Jena, von Karl Erich Roediger. Jena, Frommannsche Buchhandlung Walter Biedermann, 1935. 2 v.

[223]

Vol. 1: *Textband.* Vol. 2: *Notenverzeichnis.*

Primarily a study, with inventories, of 18 choirbooks containing music of the Burgundian-Netherland repertory in the University Library at Jena. Vol. 1 is a detailed study of the sources and their contents, with indexes of liturgical settings, of cantus fermi, of composers. Vol. 2 is a thematic catalog of the choirbooks.

Vol. 1, p. 111–14: a listing of 63 16th-century music prints in the Jena library.

KASSEL, GERMANY

Deutsches Musikgeschichtliches Archiv. See no. 907.

945

Landesbibliothek. [Katalog der Musikalien der Landesbibliothek, Kassel] durchgearbeitet und abgeschrieben [von] Wilhelm Lange. Kassel, 1920. 1 v. (various pagings).

An unpublished catalog, available on microfilm from the Deutsches Musikgeschichtliches Archiv, which supplements the printed catalog by Carl Israël, below, extending the coverage to 18th- and 19th-century materials. The Lange catalog describes 438 folio volumes, 247 quartos, 53 octavos, and a supplement of 32 items.

946

Landesbibliothek. Übersichtlicher Katalog der Musikalien der ständischen Landesbibliothek zu Cassel. Bearbeitet von Carl Israël. Cassel, A. Freyschmidt, 1881. 78 p.

Works from the 16th and 17th centuries, both manuscripts and printed books. Rich in German and Italian church and chamber music. For comparison with the Lange catalog, above, Israël describes 82 folios, 152 quartos, 6 octavos, and a supplement of 32 items.

KIEL, GERMANY

947

Hortschansy, Klaus. Katalog der Kieler Musiksammlungen; die Notendrucke, Handschriften, Libretti und Bücher über Musik aus der Zeit bis 1830. Kassel, Bärenreiter, 1963. 270 p. (Kieler Schriften zur Musikwissenschaft, 14.)

A catalog of the music in three libraries in Keil: Schleswig-Holsteinische Landesbibliothek; Bibliothek des Musikwissenschaftlichen Instituts des Universität; Universitätsbibliothek.

Review by Donald Krummel in *Notes*, 21 (1963–64) p. 129–31.

948

Staats- und Universitäts-Bibliothek. Bibliotheca Gottholdiana.
Die musikalischen Schätze der Königsberg in Pr., aus dem Nachlasse
Friedrich August Gotthold. Nebst Mittheilungen aus dessen musikalischen
Tagebüchern. Ein Beitrag zur Geschichte und Theorie der Tonkunst, von
Joseph Müller. Bonn, A. Marcus, 1870. 431 p.

Important collection, 55,000 volumes, with primary emphasis on 17th-
century church music, printed and in manuscript, and vocal music from the
16th to 19th centuries. Classified list of collections, with author index.
Works by various Königsberger Kapellmeister, such as Eccard, Stobaeus,
Sebastiani, and first editions of Beethoven, Haydn, Mozart. Full bibliographical citations.

949

Uniwersytet Jagiellónski. Bibljoteka. Ksiazki o muzyce w Bibl-
jotece Jagiellónskiej. Kraków, 1924–38. 3 v.

At head of title: Jósef Reiss.

950

Ritter-Akademie. "Katalog der in der Kgl. Ritter-Akademie zu
Liegnitz gedruckten und handschriftlichen Musikalien nebst den hymno-
logischen und musikalisch-theoretischen Werken." [By Robert Eitner.] In
Monatshefte für Musikgeschichte, 1 (1869) p. 25–39, 50–56, 70–76 (incomplete).

951

Ritter-Akademie. Die Musik-handschriften der Königl. Ritter-
Akademie zu Liegnitz. Verzeichnet von Ernst Pfudel. [Leipzig, Breitkopf
& Härtel, 1886–89] 74 p. (Monatshefte für Musikgeschichte. Beilage.
Jahrgang 18 & 21.)

952

Breitkopf & Härtel (Publisher). Catalogo delle sinfonie, partite,
overture, soli, trii, quattri e concerti per il violino, flauto traverso, cembalo

ad altri stromenti, che si trovano in manuscritto nella officina musica di Giovanni Gottlob Breitkopf in Lipsia. Leipzig, 1762–65 (six parts).

Supplemento I–XVI [1766–87].

An important 18th-century thematic catalog of instrumental music in manuscript in the Breitkopf archives. Useful in tracing or identifying works of the period.

Reprint projected by Dover Publications, New York, with an introduction by Barry S. Brook.

953

Breitkopf & Härtel. Katalog des Archivs von Breitkopf & Härtel, Leipzig, im Auftrage der Firma hrsg. von Wilhelm Hitzig. Leipzig, Breitkopf & Härtel, 1925–26. 2 v. in 1.

1. Musik-Autographe; –. Briefe.

348 autograph scores from Händel to Hindemith, fully described, with a composer index. Autograph letters are limited to persons born before 1780. Separate index to letters.

954

Musikbibliothek Peters (Publishers). Katalog der Musikbibliothek Peters, neu bearb. von Rudolf Schwartz. Band I: Bücher und Schriften. Leipzig, C. F. Peters, 1910. 227 p.

An earlier edition by Emil Vogel (1894) included both books and music.

Classified catalog of a large reference library of music literature maintained by C. F. Peters before the war. All publishers represented. Many early works, although the chief strength is in 19th-century literature. Entries give place and date of publication, but not publisher. Major classes: dictionaries, periodicals, music history, biographies and monographs, instruction, instruments, aesthetics, etc.

955

Musikbibliothek der Stadt Leipzig. Erst und Frühdrucke von Robert Schumann in der Musikbibliothek Leipzig. Leipzig, 1960. 64 p. (Bibliographische Veröffentlichungen der Musikbibliothek der Stadt Leipzig.)

The exhibition also included pictures, autographs, and Schumann literature.

956

Musikbibliothek der Stadt Leipzig. Quellenwerke zur Händelforschung: Katalog. Hrsg. anlässlich der wissenschaftlichen Konferenz zur

Händel-Ehrung der D.D.R. ,11–19 April, 1959, in Halle. [Leipzig, 1959] 29 p.

LENINGRAD, RUSSIA

957

Golubovskiĭ, I. V. Muzyakl'nyĭ Leningrad. Leningrad, Gosundarstvennoe Muzykalnoe Izdatel'stvo, 1958.

"Biblioteki i muzei," p. 351–411.

Describes in general terms the musical content of 14 libraries, 2 record libraries, and 12 museums. Lists manuscripts of Russian composers, and mentions a few examples of Western manuscripts and early books in various collections. Details as to organization, cataloging, circulation, etc.

LIÈGE, BELGIUM

958

Conservatoire Royal de Musique. Fonds Terry. Catalogue de la Bibliothèque du Conservatoire Royal de Musique de Liège. [Par] Eugène Monseur. Fonds Terry: Musique dramatique. [Liège, Conservatoire Royal de Musique, 1960] 75 p.

Opera scores in the collection of Léonard Terry, acquired by the Liège conservatory in 1882. Chiefly works from 1780 to 1880. Broadly classified as to full or vocal scores, and by language of the libretto—French or foreign.

959

Conservatoire Royal de Musique. Fonds Terry. . . . Musique instrumentale. [Liège, Conservatoire Royale de Musique, 1960] 51 p.

Instrumental music in the Terry collection; chiefly late 18th- and early 19th-century material, both printed and in manuscript.

LIEGNITZ, GERMANY.

See Legnica, Poland

LILLE, FRANCE

960

Bibliothèque. Catalogue des ouvragees sur la musique et des compositions musicales de la Bibliothèque de Lille. Lille, Imprimerie de Lefebvre-Ducrocq, 1879. 752 p.

2,721 items. The collection is particularly rich in late 18th- and early 19th-century French operas, which exist here in complete sets of per-

[227]

formance materials. Also a large collection of symphonies, overtures, chamber music.

LISBON, PORTUGAL

961

Biblioteca da Ajuda. Catálogo de música manuscrita ... Elaborado sob a direcçao de Mariana Amélia Machado Santos, directora da biblioteca. Lisboa, 1958–63. 6 v.

A collection of manuscripts, 3,617 items, entered alphabetically by composer and running consecutively through the 6 volumes. The collection is strong in 18th- and early 19th-century music, particularly opera.

962

Library of João IV, King of Portugal. Primeira parte do index de livraria de musica do muyto alto, e poderoso Rey Dom Joao o IV ... Por ordem de sua Mag. por Paulo Crasbeck. Anno 1649. [Edited by J. de Vasconcellos. Porto, 1874–76] 525 p.

Reprinting of a catalog, compiled in 1649 by Paul Crasbeck, for the royal library in Lisbon, which was destroyed in the earthquake of 1775. The catalog, although of a nonexistent collection, remains an important bibliographical tool for the study of early Spanish and Portuguese music.

LIVERPOOL, ENGLAND

963

Public Library. Catalogue of the music library. Liverpool, Central Public Libraries, 1954. 572 p.

Supersedes an earlier catalog, 1933. 374 p.

About 45,000 entries for books and music published for the most part after 1800. Brief entries.

LONDON, ENGLAND

British Broadcasting Corporation. Central Music Library. See no. 610.

964

British Museum. "Early Dutch librettos and plays with music in the British Museum." By Alfred Loewenberg. In *The Journal of documentation*, 2 (March, 1947) 30 p.

A catalog of 97 Dutch librettos of the 17th and 18th centuries. The list was projected as the first installment of a complete bibliography of librettos in the Museum, a project never carried out.

965

British Museum. Four hundred years of music printing. [By A. Hyatt King] London, Trustees of the British Museum, 1954. 48 p.

An exhibition catalog. Also entered as no. 1213.

966

British Museum. Henry Purcell, 1659(?)–1695; George Fredric Handel, 1685–1759; catalogue of a commemorative exhibition, May–August 1959. London, Published by the Trustees, 1959. 47 p.

66 items related to Purcell, 180 to Handel. Introduction; annotations; 8 full-page plates.

967

British Museum. Mozart in the British Museum. London, Published for the Trustees, 1956. 27 p. 12 plates.

Catalog of an exhibition of 196 prints, autographs, early editions, etc., drawn from various collections in the British Museum, including the Department of Prints and Drawings, the Burney collection, Maps, Hirsch, and Zweig collections.

968

British Museum. Department of Manuscripts. Catalogue of manuscript music in the British Museum, by A. Hughes-Hughes. London, 1906–1909. 3 v.

Vol. 1: sacred vocal music. Vol. 2: secular vocal music. Vol. 3: instrumental music, treatises, etc.

Entries are classified by genre or form, which means that the contents of manuscripts volumes are often separated and distributed through the three volumes of the catalog. Each volume indexed by author, title, first line of songs.

969

British Museum. Department of Printed Books. Catalogue of music. Accessions. Vol. 1– . [London, British Museum] 1884– .

An annual publication compiled from the printed catalog slips. It is ordinarily reserved for departmental use in the British Museum, but there are copies in the New York Public Library and the Library of Congress. Occasional volumes of special bibliographical interest have been given wider distribution. See nos. 292, 293.

970

British Museum. Department of Printed Books. Catalogue of printed music published between 1487 and 1800 now in the British

[229]

Museum, by W. Barclay Squire. London, Printed by order of the Trustees, 1912. 2 v.

First Supplement, 34 p., bound in. *Second supplement*, by W. C. Smith. Cambridge Univ. Press, 1940. 85 p.

Includes early music of all countries, but particularly rich in British sources. Early theory and some literary works on music included. Brief entries with dates, or estimated dates, of publication.

971

British Museum. Department of Printed Books. Hand-list of music published in some British and foreign periodicals between 1787 and 1848, now in the British Museum. London, The Trustees of the British Museum, 1962. 80 p.

Indexes the music, chiefly songs, in 12 periodicals. 1,855 entries arranged by composer. Printed from slips prepared for entry in the British Museum catalog.

This item also appears as no. 746.

Review by Richard Schaal in *Die Musikforschung*, 17 (1964) p. 423.

972

British Museum. Department of Printed Books. Hirsch Music Library. Books in the Hirsch Library, with supplementary list of music. London, The Trustees of the British Museum, 1959. 542 p. (Catalogue of printed books in the British Museum. Accessions, 3rd ser., Pt. 291B.)

A catalog of over 11,500 books on music, acquired by the British Museum in 1946 as part of the Paul Hirsch library. Brief entries printed from slips prepared for the Museum catalog.

Review by Richard S. Hill in *Notes*, 17 (1960) p. 225–27.

See also HIRSCH, PAUL. *Katalog der Musikbibliothek* . . . no. 1135.

973

British Museum. Department of Printed Books. Hirsch Music Library. Music in the Hirsch Library. London, The Trustees of the British Museum, 1951. 438 p. (Catalogue of printed music in the British Museum. Accessions, Pt. 53.)

About 9,000 entries listed in two sections: "Music printed before 1800," p. 1–112; "Music printed since 1800," p. 113 to end. Brief listings from the Museum's catalog slips.

See also the "Supplementary list of music" printed in the catalog of *Books in the Hirsch Library*, above.

Review by Vincent Duckles in *Notes*, 10 (1952) p. 281–82.

See also HIRSCH, PAUL. *Katalog der Musikbibliothek* . . . no. 1135.

974
British Museum. King's Music Library. Catalogue of an exhibition of music held in the King's Library, October 1953. [London, 1953] 52 p.

975
British Museum. King's Music Library. Catalogue of the King's Music Library, by William Barclay Squire and Hilda Andrews. London, Printed by order of the Trustees, 1927–29. 3 v.

Part I: The Handel manuscripts, by William Barclay Squire. 143 p., 5 facsimile plates. Part II: the miscellaneous manuscripts, by Hilda Andrews. 277 p. Part III: printed music and musical literature, by William Barclay Squire. 383 p.

The King's Music Library is now part of the permanent collection of the British Museum.

976
Historical Music Loan Exhibition, 1885. . . . A descriptive catalogue of rare manuscripts and printed books, chiefly liturgical . . . by W. H. James Weale. London, B. Quaritch, 1886. 191 p.

An exhibition held at Albert Hall, London, June–Oct., 1885.

Full bibliographical citations, with descriptive annotations, for 23 liturgical manuscripts, 73 liturgical books, 46 theory works, and some 56 items of early music. 14 plates; bibliographical notes.

977
Musicians' Company. An illustrated catalogue of the music loan exhibition held . . . by the Worshipful Company of Musicians at Fishmongers' Hall, June and July, 1904. London, Novello, 1909. 353 p.

Includes early printed music, manuscripts, instruments, portraits, concert and theater bills, etc. Descriptive annotations; numerous plates and facsimiles.

978
Plainsong and Mediaeval Music Society. Catalogue of the Society's library. Nashdom Abbey, Burnham, Bucks., 1928. 39 p.

A short title catalog; 4 facsimile plates. This collection is now on deposit in the Music Library of London University.

979
Royal College of Music. Catalogue of the manuscripts in the Royal College of Music, by William Barclay Squire, with additions by Rupert Erlebach. . . . [London, 1931] 568,216 leaves (typescript).

[231]

This catalog was never published. Typewritten copies are available in the major British libraries, and the catalog can be obtained on microfilm.

980

Royal College of Music. Catalogue of the printed music in the library of the Royal College of Music, by William Barclay Squire. . . . London, Printed by order of the Council . . ., 1909. 368 p.

This collection, rich in sources of early English music, incorporates the holdings of the Sacred Harmonic Society, below, and the library of Sir George Grove.

981

Sacred Harmonic Society. Catalogue of the library . . . new edition, revised and augmented. London, Published by the Society, 1872. 399 p.

First printed in 1862; *Supplement*, 1882.

Classified catalog of printed music, manuscript music, and musical literature. 2,923 numbered items. General index.

982

Westminster Abbey. Musik-katalog der Bibliothek der West-minster-Abtei in London. Angefertigt von William Barclay Squire. Leipzig, Breitkopf & Härtel, 1903. 45 p. (Monatshefte für Musikgeschichte. Beilage. Jahrgang 35.)

Broadly classified catalog, including both printed and manuscript music, sacred and secular.

LORETO, ITALY

983

Santa Casa di Loreto. l'Archivio Musicale. l'Archivio musicale della Cappella Laurentana. Catalogo storico-critico. [By Giovanni Tebaldini] Loreto, A cura dell'Administrazione di S. Casa, 1921. 198 p.

Printed music, 16th–18th centuries; manuscripts of the same period; an archive of manuscript scores by the Maestri della Cappella, anonymous works, etc. Full descriptions. Detailed history of the chapel. Index of composers.

LOS ANGELES, CALIFORNIA

984

University of California at Los Angeles. Library. The George Pullen Jackson collection of Southern hymnody (a bibliography). By

Paul J. Revitt. Los Angeles, University of California Library, 1964. 26 p. (UCLA Library occasional papers, 13.)

Review by Harry Eskew in *Anuario* of the Inter-American Institute for Musical Research, 1 (1965) p. 135.

LUCCA, ITALY

985

Biblioteca del Seminario. Catalogo delle musiche stampate e manoscritto del fondo antico. [By Emilio Maggini] Milano, Istituto Editoriale Italiano, 1965. 405 p. (Bibliotheca musicae, 3.)

Early printed music and manuscripts from the 16th to the early 19th centuries, with a small collection of writings on music. Contents of collections and locations of other copies listed. The library is rich in early 17th-century prints of sacred music.

986

Biblioteca del Seminario. "Il fondo di musiche a stampa della Biblioteca del Seminario di Lucca." [By Claudio Sartori] In *Fontes artis musicae*, (1955:2) p. 134–47.

A listing, alphabetical by composer, of the early music prints in the Seminary library, including, at the end of the list, 5 anthologies and 3 manuscripts.

987

Bonaccorsi, Alfredo. "Catalogo con notizie biografiche delle musiche dei maestri lucchesi esistenti nelle biblioteche di Lucca." In *Collectanea historiae musicae*, 2 (1957) p. 73–95.

Sources listed from 3 libraries in Lucca: the Seminario Arcivescovile; the Istituto Musicale "L. Boccherini"; and the Biblioteca Governativa.

988

Lucca All'esposizione Della Musica e del Teatro in Vienna Nel *1892*. Lucca, Dalla Tipografia Giusti, 1892. 50 p.

A rare exposition catalog of music from Lucca displayed at the exposition in Vienna in 1892. 37 facsimile plates, with detailed discussions, and a brief introduction on the history of music in Lucca.

LÜBECK, GERMANY

989

Stadtbibliothek. Katalog der Musik-Sammlung auf der Stadtbibliothek zu Lübeck. Verzeichnet von Carl Stiehl. Lübeck, Druck von Gebrüder Borchers [1893] 59 p.

[233]

990
Stadtbibliothek. Die Musikabteilung der Lübecker Stadtbibliothek in ihren älteren Beständen: Noten und Bücher aus der Zeit von 12. bis zum Anfang des 19. Jahrhunderts, verzeichnet von Wilhelm Stahl. Lübeck, 1931. 61 p.

991
Stadtbibliothek. Musik-Bücher der Lübecker Stadtbibliothek, verzeichnet von Prof. Wilhelm Stahl. Lübeck, Verlag der Lübecker Stadtbibliothek, 1927. 42 p.
Classified catalog of 19th- and 20th-century music literature.

LÜNEBURG, GERMANY

992
Ratsbücherei. Katalog der Musikalien der Ratsbücherei Lüneburg, von Friedrich Welter. Lippstadt, Kistner & Siegel, 1950. 332 p.
Music prints and manuscripts, theory and practical music to 1850. Rich holdings in 17th- and 18th-century instrumental music, particularly in the manuscript collections, which are listed separately. Numerous thematic incipits given.

LUZERN, SWITZERLAND

993
Theater- und Musik-Liebhabergesellschaft. Die Haydndrucke aus dem Archiv der "Theater- und Musik-Liebhabergesellschaft zu Luzern," nebst Materialien zum Musikleben in Luzern um 1800. Von Wilhelm Jerger. Freiburg in der Schweiz, Universitätsverlag, 1959. 45 p. (Freiburger Studien zur Musikwissenschaft, 7.)
Entries for 64 early Haydn editions, with a table of concordances with the Hoboken *Thematisch-bibliographisches Werkverzeichnis* of Haydn's compositions.

MADRID, SPAIN

994
Ayuntamiento. Biblioteca Musical Circulante. Catálogo. Ed. ilus. Madrid, Ayuntamiento, Sección de Cultura e Información, 1946. 610 p.
Apéndice 1, 1954. 213 p.
Music arranged in 16 classes, by instrument and form. Class T, "Bibliografía," contains books on music, almost exclusively in Spanish. No publishers or dates given for entries. Many light and popular works. No index.

[234]

995

Biblioteca Medinaceli. "Catalogue of the music in the Biblioteca Medinaceli, Madrid." By J. B. Trend. In *Revue hispanique*, 71 (1927) p. 485–554.

"The Medinaceli library is notable for possessing almost the entire corpus of Spanish (Castilian) madrigals." 34 items fully described, with inventories of contents and biographical sketches of the composers. Appendix: musical settings of famous poets.

996

Biblioteca Nacional. Catálogo músical de la Biblioteca Nacional de Madrid, por Higinio Anglés y José Subirá. Barcelona, Consejo Superior de Investigaciones Científicas, Instituto Español de Musicología, 1946–51. 3 v.

Vol. 1: Manuscritos (490 p., 27 facsimile plates). Vol. 2: Impresos: Libros litúrgicos y teóricos musicales (292 p., 12 facsimile plates). Vol. 3: Impresos: Música práctica (410 p., 13 facsimile plates).

Entries for 234 manuscripts, 285 liturgical and theoretical prints, 337 music prints. Full descriptions, with bibliographical references, lists of contents.

997

Biblioteca Nacional. Esposicion de música sagrada española. Catalog de los codices, manuscritos y libros musicales expuestos por Jaime Moll Roqueta. Madrid, 1954. 41 p. 120 items. 12 facsimile plates.

998

La Casa de Alba. La música en la Casa de Alba; estudios históricos y biográficos, por José Subirá. Madrid, [Establecimiento tipográfico "Sucesores de Rivadeneyra"] 1927. 374 p.

Not a catalog, but a mine of bibliographical information concerning the early music and books on music in the library of the Casa de Alba. Numerous early prints and manuscripts cited and described; 60 plates, chiefly facsimiles of bibliographical interest. This collection was a casualty of the Spanish Civil War.

999

Palacio Nactional. Capilla Real. Archivo de Música. Catálogo del Archivo de Música de la Real Capilla de Palacio. Madrid, Editorial del Patrimonio Nacional [19–] 361 p.

P. 13–149: listing of works by composer. P. 151–247: brief biographies of composers represented. P. 249–361: classified listing of works.

[235]

MAINZ, GERMANY

1000

Gutenberg-Museum. Tausend Jahre Mainzer Musik; Katalog der Ausstellung, 1957 [Text: Adam Gottron] Mainz, 1957. 32 p. (Kleiner Druck der Gutenberg-Gesellschaft, 63.)

An illustrated exhibition catalog of 138 items related to the history of music in Mainz.

1001

Stadtbibliothek. "Zur Bibliographie der Musikdrucke des XV.— XVIII. Jahrhunderts der Mainzer Stadtbibliothek." By F. W. E. Roth, in *Monatshefte für Musikgeschichte*, 21 (1889) p. 25–33.

A catalog of 45 early music prints, including both theory works and practical music. Full bibliographical citations for some items, otherwise references to citations in the catalogs of other collections.

MANNHEIM, GERMANY

1002

Hof- und Nationaltheater. Archiv und Bibliothek des Grossh. Hof- und Nationaltheaters in Mannheim, 1779–1839 . . . von Dr. Friedrich Walter. Leipzig, S. Hirzel, 1899. 2 v.

Band I: Das Theater-Archiv . . . Repertorium mit vielen Auszügen aus den Akten und Briefen, Inhalts-Ausgaben, usw.

Band. II: Die Theater-Bibliothek . . . Katalog der gedruckten Bücher, Manuskripte und Musikalien der älteren Periode, nebst einem Repertoire der Dalbergschen Zeit.

An important collection of theater history, in which music is well represented.

MECKLENBURG–SCHWERIN

See Schwerin, Germany.

MILAN, ITALY

Biblioteca Ambrosiana. See no. 927.

1003

Biblioteca Nazionale Braidense. La musica nelle biblioteche milanesi. Mostra di libri e documenti, Milano, 28 Maggio—8 Guigno 1963 . . . Milano, U. Allegretto di Campi, 1963. 55 p.

Compiled by Mariangela Dona.

1004

Cappella del Duomo. Archivio. La Cappella del Duomo di Milano. Catalogo delle musiche dell'archivio. [By Claudio Sartori] Milano, a cura dell Ven. Fabbrica del Duomo [1957] 366 p.

The archive, established in 1394, contains important manuscript holdings of the 15th century and sacred vocal works to the 19th century. Separate sections for manuscripts and printed music. Brief entries; contents for anthologies.

1005

Civica Raccolta delle Stampe e Dei Disegni. Castello Sforzesco. Ritratti di musicisti ed artisti di teatro conservati nella raccolta delle stampe e dei disegni. Catalogo descrittivo. [By] Paolo Arrigoni e Achille Bertarelli. [Milano] Tipografia del "Popolo d'Italia," 1934. 454 p.

Index, alphabetical by subject, of a portrait collection. Main alphabet includes musicians, singers, comedians, dancers; separate sections for acrobats, extemporaneous poets, child prodigies, etc. Entries give full names of subjects, descriptions of pictures, biographical information. Numerous indexes: names, places, theatrical performances, etc. 30 plates.

1006

Conservatorio di Musica "Giuseppe Verdi." Biblioteca. Indice generale dell'Archivio Musicale Noseda; compilato dal Prof. Eugenio de' Guarinoni . . . con una breve biografia del fondatore e con alcuni cenni intorno all'archivio stesso ed alla Biblioteca del R. Conservatorio di musica di Milano. Milano, E. Reggiani, 1897. 419 p.

First published in the *Annuario* of the R. Conservatorio di musica di Milano, 1889–96. 10,253 titles.

1007

Museo Teatrale alla Scala. Catalogo del Museo teatrale alla Scala. Edito a cura del Consiglio direttivo; compilato da Stefano Vittadini; pref. di Renato Simoni. Milano, E. Bestetti, 1940. 401 p.

An illustrated catalog of the musical-theatrical collection at La Scala. Bibliography: p. 375–93.

1008

Parigi, Luigi. La musica nelle gallerie di Milano. Con 21 illustrazioni in tavole fuori testo. Milano, F. Perrella, 1935. 71 p.

Paintings with musical subjects in the art galleries of Milan. Descriptions of each work and its subject-matter. 21 plates.

MODENA, ITALY

Biblioteca Estense. See no. 934.

1009
Biblioteca Estense. "Bibliografia delle stampe musicali della R. Biblioteca Estense." [By Vittorio Finzi] In *Rivista delle biblioteche* (1892–95) v. 3, p. 77–89, 107–14, 162–76; v. 4, p. 16–28, 174–85; v. 5, p. 48–64, 89–142. Full descriptions of 321 works. Index.

1010
Biblioteca Estense. "Repertorio dei libri musicali di S.A.S. Francesco II d'Este nell'archivio di Stato di Modena." [By E. J. Luin] In *La Bibliofilia*, 38 (1936) p. 419–45.
A catalog compiled in the late 17th century of the holdings of the music library of Francesco II d'Este. Much of the material has been incorporated into the collection of the Biblioteca Estense at Modena. Rich in late 17th-century opera, oratorio, cantata, etc. Includes both manuscripts and prints.

MONTECASSINO, ITALY

1011
Archivio Musicale. "L'Archivio musicale di Montecassino." [By Eduardo Dagnino] In *Casinensia*: miscellanea di studi Cassinesi publicati in occasione del XIV centenario della fondazione della Badia di Montecassino. V. 1 (1929) p. 273–96.
A summary account of the music holdings of the Montecassino archive, a collection of some 1,100 items, including more than 100 full scores of 18th-century operas, oratorios, etc. Four plates illustrating rarities from the collection.

1012
Archivio Musicale. "I manoscritti musicali gregoriani dell'archivio di Montecassino." [By Paolo M. Ferretti] In *Casinensia*: miscellanea di studi Cassinesi . . . v. 1 (1929) p. 187–203.
Detailed descriptions of 11 manuscripts of Gregorian chant in the Montecassino archive. The 11th consists of a group of fragments from various sources. Two facsimile plates.

MONTECATINI-TERME, ITALY

Biblioteca Antonio Venturi. See Pistoia, Italy.

[238]

1013

Lenaerts, René B. "Niederländische polyphone Musik in der Bibliothek von Montserrat." In *Festschrift Joseph Schmidt Gorg zum 60. Geburtstag.* Bonn, Beethovenhaus, 1957. P. 196–201.

Describes 6 manuscripts containing Netherlands polyphony: manuscript numbers 765, 766, 769, 771, 772, 778.

MOSCOW, RUSSIA

1014

Publichnaĭa Biblioteka. Otdel Rukopiseĭ. Sobraniĭa D. V. Razumovskogo i V. F. Odoevskogo. Arkhiv D. V. Razumovskogo. Opisaniĭa pod radaktsiei I. M. Kudriâvtseva. Moskva, 1960. 261 p.

Catalog of manuscripts, 15th–19th centuries, primarily of church music in various notations. The Razumovskii collection contains 135 manuscripts, the Odoevskii, 35. Description of biographical material, papers, letters, etc. in the Razumovskii archive. Chronological index; index of names and titles.

MÜNSTER, GERMANY

1015

Killing, Joseph. Kirchenmusikalische Schätze der Bibliothek des Abbate Fortunato Santini, ein Beitrag zur Geschichte der katholischen Kirchenmusik in Italien. Düsseldorf, L. Schwann [1910] 516 p.

A study based on the material in the Santini collection, a library of early music scored from the original partbooks by Fortunato Santini (1778–1862), and acquired by the University Library at Münster about 1856.

P. 455–67: "Verzeichnis der in der Bibliothek Santini enthaltenen Druckwerke." P. 469–516: "Verzeichnis von Musikwerken die in der Santinischen Bibliothek als Handschriften enthalten sind.

1016

Universitätsbibliothek. Die musikalischen Schätze der Santinischen Sammlung. Führer durch die Ausstellung der Universitäts-Bibliothek. . . . Münster, Westfälische Vereinsdruckerei, 1929. 32 p.

Exhibition catalog prepared by K. G. Fellerer.

MUNICH, GERMANY

1017

Bayerische Staatsbibliothek. Die musikalischen Handschriften der K. Hof- und Staatsbibliothek in München, beschreiben von Jul. Jos. Maier.

Erster Theil: Die Handschriften bis zum Ende des XVII. Jahrhunderts. München, in Commission der Palm'schen Hofbuchhandlung, 1879. 176 p.

278 items, chiefly anthologies, containing about 6,380 pieces of music. One of the richest collections of 16th-century music. A notable collection of 74 choirbooks belonging to the original Bavarian court chapel. "Inhalts Verzeichnis" of anonymous and attributed works.

1018

Städtische Musikbücherei. Kataloge der städtischen Musikbücherei München . . . Erster Band: Klavier. Bearbeitet von Bibliotheksrat Dr. Willy Krienitz. München, 1931. 407 p.

Catalogs the holdings in keyboard music of one of the major public music libraries in Germany. Some 40,000 items, classified. Includes works for piano solo, duet, and two pianos. Index of names.

1019

Theatermuseum. "Die vor 1801 gedruckten Libretti des Theatermuseums München." [By Richard Schaal] In *Die Musikforschung*, 10 (1957) p. 388–96, 487–94; 11 (1958) p. 54–69, 168–77, 321–36, 462–77; 12 (1959) p. 60–75, 161–77, 299–306, 454–61; 13 (1960) p. 38–46, 164–72, 299–306, 441–48; 14 (1961) p. 36–43, 166–83. Also published separately by Bärenreiter, Kassel, 1962.

983 librettos, listed alphabetically by title, with date and place of first performance, name of composer, etc.

NAPLES, ITALY

1020

Biblioteca Nazionale. "Il fondo musicale cinquecentesco della Biblioteca Nazionale di Napoli." [By Anna Mondolfi.] In *Collectanea historiae musicae*, 2 (1957) p. 277–90.

Describes 51 16th-century works.

Conservatorio di Musica S. Pietro a Majella. See no. 937.

1021

Conservatorio di Musica S. Pietro a Majella. Mostra autografi musicali della scuola napoletana . . . Settembre–Ottobre 1963. Napoli, Confederazione Fascista dei Professionisti e degli Artisti [1936] 58 p.

An exhibition catalog of musical autographs and portraits of musicians of the Neopolitan school.

1022
Conservatorio di Musica S. Pietro a Majella. Il Museo storico musicale di S. Pietro a Majella. Napoli, R. Stabilimento Tipografico Francesco Giannini & Figli, 1930. 153 p.

A collection of musicians' portraits, busts, autographs, musical instruments, medals, and photographs. 734 items. Special archives of material related to Vincenzo Bellini and Giuseppe Martucci.

Oratorio Dei Filippini. Archivio. See no. 936.

NEWCASTLE, ENGLAND

1023
Public Library. Handlist of miniature scores [in the] music section. 2nd ed. [Newcastle upon Tyne] 1958. 52 p.

NEW HAVEN, CONNECTICUT

1024
Yale University School of Music. Library. A temporary mimeographed catalog of the music manuscripts and related materials of Charles Edward Ives . . . Compiled by John Kirkpatrick in 1954–60. [New Haven, Conn., Yale School of Music] 1960. 279 p. (typescript).

NEW YORK CITY, NEW YORK

1025
Bartók Archives. The Béla Bartók archives, history and catalogue. By Victor Bator. New York, Bartók Archives Publication, 1963. 39 p.

Description of the Archives and of their founding, with summary inventories of materials in such categories as letters, books, articles, clippings, concert programs, printed music, photographs, recordings, as well as autograph and nonautograph manuscripts.

1026
New York Public Library. Music Division. Catalogue of Jos. W. Drexel's musical library. Part I: Musical writings. Philadlphia, King & Baird, 1869. 48 p.

This catalog contains only 1,536 of the more than 6,000 items in the Drexel collection. Especially rich in English printed music and manuscripts of the 16th, 17th, and 18th centuries.

1027
New York Public Library. Music Division. Dictionary catalog of the music collection, New York Public Library. Boston, G. K. Hall, 1965. 33 v.

Duplication by photo-offset of a catalog of some 522,000 cards, 21 cards per page, comprising the holdings of the Music Division of the New York Public Library. Books, pamphlets, and musical scores in one alphabet. The catalog includes numerous analytics for articles in Festschriften, periodicals, etc. A comprehensive reference tool based on the resources of one of the greatest music libraries in America.

1028
New York Public Library. Music Division. "Musicalia in der New York Public Library, mitgeteilt von Hugo Botstiber." In *Sammelbände der Internationalen Musikgesellschaft,* 4 (1902–1903) p. 738–50.

A summary account of some of the more interesting and important items in the Drexel collection. Gives a full inventory of the "Sambrook MS," with brief entries for other manuscripts and early printed books. Includes a listing of musicians' autographs.

OXFORD, ENGLAND

1029
University. Bodleian Library. [Catalog, in manuscript, of the music manuscripts in the Bodleian Library, with a list of books given to the University by Dr. Heather] 1 v., unpaged.

An unpublished, handwritten catalog made in the early 19th century, available for study in the Bodleian Library. Gives contents for some 303 "Music School" manuscripts dating from the early 17th century.

1030
University. Bodleian Library. Manuscripts of Byzantine chant in Oxford [by] N. G. Wilson and D. I. Stefanovic. Oxford, Bodleian Library, 1963. 56 p.

An exhibition catalog. Facsimiles. Bibliography, p. 5–6.

1031
University. Bodleian Library. Medieval polyphony in the Bodleian Library, by Dom Anselm Hughes. Oxford, Bodleian Library, 1951. 63 p.

Descriptions and inventories of contents for 51 manuscripts and fragments in the Bodleian. Index of text incipits and of composers and places of origin.

Review by Manfred Bukofzer in *JAMS,* 5 (1952) p. 53–65.

1032

University. Bodleian Library. "Seventeenth-century Italian instrumental music in the Bodleian Library," by Denis Stevens. In *Acta M*, 26 (1954) p. 67–74.

The author lists some 85 sets of parts of early Italian instrumental music in the Bodleian, by composer in alphabetical order, with essential bibliographical information. In an article in *Collectanea historae musicae*, 2 (1957) p. 401–12, he discusses 9 unica from the above collection.

1033

University. Christ Church College. Catalogue of music [manuscripts] in the library of Christ Church, Oxford, by G. E. P. Arkwright. London, Oxford Univ. Press, 1915–23.

Part I: Works of ascertained authorship, 1915. 128 p. Part II: 1: Manuscript works of unknown authorship. Vocal. 1923. 182 p. Part II: 2: [Manuscripts of instrumental music of unknown authorship] An unpublished catalog, completed in 1935, available for examination in the Christ Church College library.

1034

University. Christ Church College. Catalogue of printed music published prior to 1801, now in the Library of Christ Church, Oxford. Edited by Aloys Hiff. London, Oxford Univ. Press, 1919. 76 p.

A collection rich in Italian and English music of the 16th and 17th centuries. Alphabetical arrangement by composer, with analytics for collections.

PADUA, ITALY

1035

Basilica di San'Antonio. Archivio Musicale. . . . L'Archivio musicale della Cappella Antoniana in Padova; illustrazione storicocritico, con cinque eliotipie. Padova, Tipografia e Libreria Antoniana, 1895. 175 p.

Compiled by Giovanni Tebaldini.

P. 1–92: Historical essay on the chapel of St. Anthony. P. 93–149: partial catalog of manuscripts and prints. Complete lists of works for Vallotti, Sabbatini; thematic incipits for Tartini concertos.

1036

Biblioteca Capitolare. "Codici musici della Biblioteca Capitolare di Padova." [By Antonio Garbelotti] In *Revista musicale italiana*, 53 (1951) p. 289–314; 54 (1952) p. 218–30.

[243]

A summary description of the manuscript holdings of the Biblioteca Capitolare in Padua. Sources discussed chronologically by centuries. Both plainchant and polyphonic manuscripts considered.

PARIS, FRANCE

1037
Bibliothèque de L'Arsenal. Catalogue des livres de musique (manuscrits et imprimés) de la Bibliothèque de l'Arsenal à Paris, par L. de La Laurencie . . . et A. Gastoué. Paris, E. Droz, 1936. 184 p. (Publications de la Société française de musicologie, 2. sér., t. 7.)

Manuscripts and printed music arranged alphabetically by composer, or catchword of title if anonymous, under main divisions of sacred and secular. Manuscripts from the 10th century; printed works of the 16th–18th centuries. Exceptionally rich in editions of little-known French composers of the 18th century.

1038
Bibliothèque Nationale. Claude Debussy. Paris, Bibliothèque Nationale, 1962. 73 p.

An exposition catalog of 335 items celebrating the centennial of Debussy's birth. Arranged chronologically. 8 plates.

1039
Bibliothèque Nationale. Frédéric Chopin. Exposition du centenaire. Paris [Bibliothèque Nationale] 1949. 82 p.

234 items, 8 plates; documents arranged to parallel the chronology of the composer's life.

1040
Bibliothèque Nationale. Gabriel Fauré. Paris [Bibliothèque Nationale] 1963. 16 p.

An exhibition catalog of 100 items, with a chronology of the composer's life and work.

1041
Bibliothèque Nationale. Introduction a la paléographie musicale byzantine. Catalogue des manuscrits de musique byzantine de la Bibliothèque Nationale de Paris et des bibliothèques publique de France. [Paris, Impressions artistiques L. M. Fortin, 1928] 99 p. (Publications de la Société internationale de musique. Section de Paris.)

Compiled by Amédée Gastoué.

1042

Bibliothèque Nationale. Jean-Philippe Rameau, 1683–1764. Paris [Bibliothèque Nationale] 1964. 100 p.

Illustrated exhibition catalog celebrating the 200th anniversary of the death of Rameau.

1043

Bibliothèque Nationale. Mozart en France. Paris, [Bibliothèque Nationale] 1956. 76 p.

Illustrated exhibition catalog of 234 items related to Mozart's life in France. P. 67–76: a bibliography of early French editions of Mozart's music.

1044

Bibliothèque Nationale. La musique française du moyen âge à la révolution, catalogue rédigé par Amédée Gastoué [et al.] Paris, Édition des Bibliothèques Nationales de France, 1934. 196 p.

Illustrated catalog of 660 manuscripts, books, and works of art from major French public and private collections, displayed at the "Exposition de la musique française," 1933, in the Galérie Mazarine of the Bibliothèque Nationale.

1045

Bibliothèque Nationale. Départment des Imprimés. Catalogue du fonds de musique ancienne de la Bibliothèque Nationale. [By Jules Ecorcheville] Paris, 1910–14. 8 v.

Manuscripts, printed music, and theoretical and literary works on music not included in the general catalog of the library, to 1750. Partially thematic. Arranged alphabetically by composer, with collections analyzed. Brief bibliographical descriptions.

1046

Bibljteka Polska. Frédéric Chopin, George Sand et leurs amis. Esposition à la Bibliothèque Polonaise. Paris, 1937. 63 p.

An exposition of 638 items related to Chopin, George Sand, and their circle. Includes manuscripts, letters, portraits. Illustrated.

1047

Conservatoire National de Musique et de Déclamation. . . . Catalogue bibliographique . . . par J. B. Weckerlin, bibliothécaire. Paris, Firmin-Didot et Cie., 1885. 512 p.

Covers the period to about 1800. Includes only part of the early materials in the collection. Following a prefatory history of the library, three sections are given: early treatises, vocal music, early instrumental music of the French school.

1048

Conservatoire Nationale de Musique et de Déclamation. Fonds Blancheton. . . . Inventaire critique du Fonds Blancheton . . . Paris, E. Droz, 1930–31. 2 v. (Publications de la Société française de musicologie. 2. sér., 2:1–2.)

Compiled by Lionel de La Laurencie.

The Blancheton collection consists of 27 volumes containing some 300 instrumental compositions by 104 composers. It was assembled before 1750. Important source materials for the history of the symphony. Full descriptions, with critical and biographical notes on the composers.

1049

Opéra. Bibliothèque, Archives et Musée. Bibliothèque musicale du Théâtre de l'Opéra. Catalogue historique, chronologique, anecdotique . . . rédigé par Théodore de Lajarte. Paris, Librairie des Bibliophiles, 1878. 2 v.

A descriptive list of 594 stage works arranged in order of their first production at the Paris Opéra, 1671–1876. Classified by periods. Each period is concluded with a biographical section which lists composers and librettists alphabetically. Composer and title index to works in the repertoire.

PARMA, ITALY

Citta di Parma. See no. 924.

1050

Conservatorio di Musica "Arrigo Boito." "Biblioteche musicale in Italia: La Biblioteca del Conservatorio di Parma e un fondo di edizioni dei sec. XVI e XVII non compiese nel catalogo a stampa." [By Riccardo Allorto] In *Fontes artis musicae*, (1955:2) p. 147–51.

Describes a collection of 31 sets of 16th- and 17th-century partbooks acquired by the library in 1925.

1051

Conservatorio di Musica "Arrigo Boito." "Osservazione sulla Biblioteca Musicale di Parma." [By Mario Medici.] In *Avrea Parma*, 48 (May–August, 1964) p. 3–49.

Provides copious data on the library of the Conservatorio. Many of the rare manuscripts and printed books are cited in full, along with an account of the history of the institution and its administrative structure.

PHILADELPHIA, PENNSYLVANIA

1052

Free Library. Drinker Library of Choral Music. Catalog. [By Henry S. Drinker] Philadelphia, 1957. 116 p.

First published in 1947 by the Association of American Choruses, Princeton, New Jersey, with a *Supplement*, July, 1948.

Catalog of a lending library of choral materials, made available to members of the Association of American Choruses.

1053

Free Library. Edwin A. Fleisher Music Collection. The Edwin A. Fleisher music collection in the Free Library of Philadelphia; a descriptive catalogue. Rev. ed. Philadelphia, 1965– .

First published in 1933–45, 2 volumes, with a *Supplementary List*, 1945–55. (1956) 33 p.

Catalog of a loan collection of orchestral music, much of the material unpublished. Classified; information includes dates of composer, title of each work in the original language, with English translation, publisher, instrumentation, timing, date of composition, and information relating to first performance.

1054

Library Company. American song sheet, slip ballads and poetical broadsides, 1850–1870; a catalogue of the collection of the Library Company of Philadelphia, by Edwin Wolf 2nd. Philadelphia, 1963. 205 p.

A listing, alphabetical by title, of 2,722 American song sheets, ballads, and broadsides, with information as to author, composer, format, cover design, etc. Separate listing of 194 Confederate songs. Index of printers and publishers, of authors and composers, of singers.

PIACENZA, ITALY

1055

L'Archivio del Duomo. "L'Archivio del Duomo di Piacenza e il Liber XIII di Constanzo Antegnati." [By Claudio Sartori.] In *Fontes artis musicae*, (1957:4) p. 28–37.

Description of the collection and catalog of its early printed music. Special attention given to a unique copy of the *Liber XIII*, a collection of sacred and secular vocal music by C. Antegnati.

[247]

PIRNA, GERMANY

1056

Hoffmann-Erbrecht, Lother. "Die Chorbücher der Stadtkirche zu Pirna." In *Acta M*, 27 (1955) p. 121–37.

Detailed description of 8 choirbooks of polyphonic music of the mid-16th century. Partially thematic; summary inventories; 2 facsimile plates. These manuscripts are now in the Sächsischen Landesbibliothek in Dresden.

PISA, ITALY

Biblioteche e Archivi. . . . See no. 940.

PISTOIA, ITALY

Archivio Capitolare della Cattedrale. See no. 929.

1057

Biblioteca Antonio Venturi. "La collection Antonio Venture, Montecatini-Terme (Pistoia) Italie." [By Raymond Meylan.] In *Fontes artis musicae* (1958: 1) p. 21–44.

A private collection of late 18th-century vocal and instrumental music.

PITTSBURGH, PENNSYLVANIA

1058

Finney, Theodore M. A union catalogue of music and books on music printed before 1801 in Pittsburgh libraries. 2nd ed. Pittsburgh, Pa., University of Pittsburgh, 1963. 106 leaves (typescript).

First published in 1959. *Second edition supplement*, 1964. 42 leaves.

Lists the holdings in early music in 4 Pittsburgh libraries: the Carnegie Library, the University of Pittsburgh, St. Vincent's College, and the private library of the compiler. There is a strong emphasis on early English music.

Review by Donald Krummel in *Notes*, 21 (1963–64) p. 129–31.

PLASENCIA, SPAIN

1059

Catedral. Archivo. "El archivo de música en la catedral de Plasencia." [By Samuel Rubio] In *Anuario musical*, 5 (1950) p. 147–68.

A small collection of early manuscripts and printed music, fully described and contents listed.

POLAND

See *Warsaw, Poland,* **Biblioteka Narodowa.** No. 1116.
See also Dragan Plamenac's article in *Notes*, 19 (1962) cited as no. 878.

PRAGUE, CZECHOSLOVAKIA

1060

Cathedral. Catalogus collectionis operum artis musicae quae in
bibliotheca Capituli metropolitani pragensis asservantur. Composuit Dr.
Antonius Podlaha. Prague, Sumptibus S. F. Metropolitani capituli
pragensis. Typis Typographicae archiepiscopalis Prague, 1926. 85 p.

1061

Knihovna. Seznam hudebnin. [Část] 2–4. Praha, Nákladem obce
pražské, 1925–35. 3 nos. (Spisy Knihovny hlavního města Prahy, 4, 9, 19.)
   Část 2: Klavírní výtahy hudby scénické. Melodram. Harmonium.
Libretta. Část 3: Partitury. Komorní hudba ve hlasech. Část 4:
Housle.

1062

National Museum. Hudební sbírka Emiliána Troldy. [The music
library of Emilián Trolda.] [By Alesander Buchner] Prague, Národní
Museum, 1954. 132 p.

REGGIO–EMILIA, ITALY

Citta di Reggio-Emilia. See no. 925.

RIO DE JANEIRO, BRAZIL

1063

Biblioteca Nacional. "Estudio Brasilenos I. Manuscritos musicales en
la Biblioteca Nacional de Rio de Janeiro." [By Francisco Curt Lange.] In
Rivista de estudios musicales, 1 (April, 1950) p. 98–194.
   Chiefly 19th-century composers. A: works by European composers.
B: works by Brazilian composers or Europeans active in Brazil.

1064

Biblioteca Nacional. Música no Rio de Janeiro imperial 1822–1870.
[Rio de Janeiro.] Biblioteca Nacional, 1962. 100 p.
   At head of title: "Exposiçao comemorativa do primeiro decênio da
seçao de música e arquivo sonore."
   391 numbered items, chiefly Brazilian imprints of the period.

1065

Biblioteca Nacional. Rio musical: crônica de uma cidade. [Rio de Janeiro.] Biblioteca Nacional, 1965. 51 p.

At head of title: "Exposiçao comemorativa do IV centenário da cidade do Rio de Janeiro."

ROME, ITALY

1066

Bertini, Argia, ed. Roma, Biblioteca Corsiniana e dell'Accademia nazionale dei Lincei; catalogo dei fondi musicali Chiti e Corsiniano. Milano, Istituto editoriale italiano, 1964. 109 p. (Bibliotheca musicae, 2.)

The catalog covers printed music, printed theoretical works, and manuscripts. Rich in 17th and early 18th century vocal and instrumental music.

Biblioteca della R. Accademia di S. Cecilia. See no. 930.

1067

Collection of the Comtesse Doria-Pamphilj. "Die Musiksammlung der Fürsten Doria-Pamphilj in Rom." [By Andreas Holschneider.] In *Archiv für Musikwissenschaft*, 18 (1961) p. 248–64.

Description of the collection and inventory of its contents, classified under five headings: (1) collections, 16th and 17th centuries; (2) sacred music; (3) oratorios (early manuscripts); (4) operas (early manuscripts); (5) German instrumental music, 18th century.

1068

Vatican. Biblioteca Vaticana. Catalogo sommario della esposizione gregoriana aperta nella Biblioteca Apostolica Vaticana . . . 2. ed., riveduta e aumentata. Roma, Tipografia Vaticana, 1904. 74 p.

An exposition catalog devoted to material related to the chant.

1069

Vatican. Biblioteca Vaticana. "Die Sammlungen der Oratorien-libretti (1679–1725) und den restlichen Musikbestand der Fondo San Marcello der Biblioteca Vaticana in Rom." [By Andreas Liess.] In *Acta M*, 31 (1959) p. 63–80.

1070

Vatican. Cappella Sistina. Archivio. Bibliographischer und thematischer Musik-katalog des Päpstlichen Kapellarchives im Vatikan zu Rom . . . von Fr. X. Haberl. Leipzig, Breitkopf & Härtel, 1888. 183 p. (Monatshefte für Musikgeschichte. Beilage. Jahrgang 19/20.)

[250]

Descriptions of 269 items, manuscripts and early printed music, with a thematic catalog, by composer, of the early polyphonic works. Considerable documentary information about the Cappella Sistina and the musicians employed there. The catalog represents only part of the collection. See no. 1071 below.

1071

Vatican. Cappella Sistina. Archivio. Capellae Sixtinae Codices musicis notis instructi sivi manuscripti sive praelo excussi. Rec. J. M. Llorens. Roma, Città del Vaticano, Biblioteca Apostolica Vaticana, 1960. 555 p. 10 facsimile plates.

A catalog of the collection treated by F. X. Haberl, above, but much more complete, since Haberl covered only 269 of the 660 manuscripts and printed volumes present. Volumes listed by number, with detailed inventories of contents. Descriptive annotations in Latin. Thematic catalog for anonymous works, p. 477–98. Index of names and terms.

Review by Dragan Plamenac in *Notes*, 19 (1961) p. 251–52; by Peter Peacock in *Music and letters*, 42 (1961) p. 168–69; and by Glen Haydon in *MQ*, 48 (1962) p. 127–29.

SALT LAKE CITY, UTAH

1072

University of Utah. Library. A catalogue of books and music acquired from the library of Hugo Leichtentritt . . . Edited by Carol E. Selby. Salt Lake City, Univ. of Utah, 1954. 106 p. (Bulletin of the University of Utah, 45:10.)

A catalog divided in two sections: books (p. 9–46); music (p. 49–106). A scholar's working library of music books and scores; a few early editions, but chiefly 19th- and 20th-century material.

SALZBURG, AUSTRIA

1073

Mozart-Museum. Katalog des Mozart-Museums im Geburts- und Wohnzimmer Mozarts zu Salzburg. . . . 4. Aufl. Salzburg, Im Selbstverlage des obgenannten Stiftung, 1906. 62 p.

Describes the collection of Mozart memorabilia maintained in the composer's birthplace, room by room. The collection includes portraits, medals, letters, and music.

[251]

1074
Museum Carolino Augusteum. Die Musikaliensammlung im Salzburger Museum Carolino Augusteum, von Josef Gassner. Salzburg, 1962. 247 p.

Originally published in the Museum's *Jahresschrift*, 1961. Salzburg, 1962. P. 119–365.

The collection, founded in 1834, is rich in 19th-century editions. Manuscripts and printed music interfiled. Full bibliographical citations, with publishers' plate numbers given. Facsimile plates.

SAN FRANCISCO, CALIFORNIA

1075
San Francisco State College. Library. Frank V. De Bellis Collection. Orchestra scores and parts in the Frank V. De Bellis collection of the California State Colleges. [San Francisco State College] 1964. 24 unnumbered leaves (typescript).

A preliminary catalog of the orchestral portion of the De Bellis collection, a collection devoted exclusively to Italian music. Entries are alphabetical by composer, with early and modern editions interfiled. Parts specified.

SAN MARINO, CALIFORNIA

1076
Henry E. Huntington Library and Art Gallery. Catalogue of music in the Huntington Library printed before 1801. Compiled by E. N. Backus. [San Marino, Calif.] The Library, 1949. 773 p.

"Music publications and publications without music notation but of distinct interest to musicians and musicologists . . ." Excluded are manuscripts, song texts, opera librettos. Includes music published in periodicals. Entry is under composer, with anonymous works under title. Index to composers and editors, chronological index, first-line index of songs. The collection is strong in 17th- and 18th-century English music.

Review by Cyrus L. Day in *Notes*, 6 (1949) p. 609–10; by Harold Spivacke in *MQ*, 35 (1949) p. 640–42.

SANTIAGO, CUBA

1077
Hernandez Balaguer, Pablo. Catalogo de musica de los archivos de la catedral de Santiago de Cuba y del Museo Bacardi. La Habana, Biblioteca Nacional "Jose Marti," 1961. 59 p.

A catalog of works by Cuban composers in the archives of the cathedral at Santiago and in the Bacardi Museum in the same city.

SCHWERIN, GERMANY

1078
Grossherzogliche Regierungsbibliothek. Der musikalische Nach-lass der Frau Erbgrossherzogin Auguste von Mecklenburg-Schwerin ... alphabetisch-thematisch verzeichnet und ausgearbeitet von Otto Kade. Schwerin, Druck der Sandmeyerschen Hofbuchdruckerei, 1899. 142 p.

1079
Grossherzogliche Regierungsbibliothek. Die Musikalien-Samm-lung des grossherzoglich Mecklenburg-Schweriner Fürstenhauses aus den letzten zwei Jahrhunderten. Schwerin, Druck der Sandmeyerschen Hofbuchdruckerei, 1893. 2 v.
Compiled by Otto Kade.
Primarily 18th- and 19th-century manuscripts and printed music. Part I is a thematic catalog, alphabetical by composer, with a classified section under *Anonyma*. Part II: librettos. Part III: index of dedications, autographs, etc.

SEVILLE, SPAIN

1080
Biblioteca Colombina. "La musica conservada en la Biblioteca Colombina y en la Catedral de Sevilla." [By Higinio Anglés.] In *Anuario musical*, 2 (1947) p. 3–39.
88 manuscripts and prints from the Colombina library; 9 manuscripts and 22 prints from the cathedral archives. Bibliographical references and notes on all the items.

SORAU, GERMANY

1081
Hauptkirche. Musikalienkatalog der Hauptkirche zu Sorau N. L. Hergestellt von G. Tischer und K. Burchard. [Langensalza, H. Beyer & Söhne, 1902.] 24 p. (Monatshefte für Musikgeschichte. Beilage. Jahrgang 34.)
The collection contains 33 prints, chiefly 17th century, and a small group of manuscripts in which Telemann, Petri, and C. G. Tag are well represented.

[253]

STANFORD, CALIFORNIA

1082

Stanford University. Library. Catalogue of the Memorial Library of Music, Stanford University, by Nathan van Patten. Stanford, Calif., Stanford University Press, 1950. 310 p.

A collection of manuscripts, prints, inscribed copies of books and scores; the emphasis is on "association items." 1,226 items.

Review by Otto Albrecht in *Notes*, 8 (1951) p. 706–709.

STUTTGART, GERMANY

1083

Landesbibliothek. Die Handschriften der Württembergischen Landesbibliothek Stuttgart. Erste Reihe, erster Band: Codices musici (Cod. Mus. Fol. I 1–71) Beschreiben von Clytus Gottwald. Wiesbaden, Otto Harrassowitz, 1964. 184 p.

Describes 53 manuscripts in mensural notation and 18 plain-chant sources, giving concordances for texts and music, and index of text incipits, thematic catalog for anonymous works, and full bibliographical apparatus. An exemplary catalog.

1084

Landesbibliothek. Katalog über die Musik-Codices des 16. und 17. Jahrhunderts auf der K. Landesbibliothek in Stuttgart. Angefertigt von A. Halm. Langensalza, Beyer [1902–1903] 58 p. (Monatshefte für Musikgeschichte. Beilage. Jahrgang 34–35.)

Cites 70 manuscripts, with listings of contents for each. Index of text incipits under individual composers.

SWEDEN

The Swedish bibliographer, Åke Davidsson, has prepared union catalogs of early printed music, and of music theory works in Swedish libraries. See his *Catalogue critique et descriptif des ouvrages théoriques sur la musique imprimés au XVIe et au XVIIe siècles et conservés dans les bibliothèques suédoises.* No. 598; and his *Catalogue critique et descriptif des imprimés de musique des XVIe et XVIIe siècles conservés dans les bibliothèques suédoises. . . .* No. 753.

TENBURY WELLS, ENGLAND

1085

St. Michael's College. Library. The catalogue of manuscripts in the library of St. Michael's College, Tenbury, compiled by E. H. Fellowes. Paris, Éditions de l'Oiseau Lyre, 1934. 319 p.

Manuscripts in the library bequeathed to the College by Sir Frederick Ouseley. 1,386 items; rich in early English music. The library also incorporates the greater part of the "Toulouse-Philidor Collection," consisting of 290 volumes of manuscripts and 67 printed books devoted to the repertory of early 18th-century French opera. Composer index.

1086

St. Michael's College. Library. A summary catalogue of the printed books and music in the library of St. Michael's College, Tenbury. Compiled by E. H. Fellowes, 1934. 143 leaves (manuscript).

An unpublished catalog maintained at St. Michael's College covering the printed books and music in the collection. Intended as a companion volume to the manuscript catalog, above, but never printed.

TOKYO, JAPAN

1087

Nanki Music Library. Catalogue of the Nanki Music Library. Part I: Musicology. Tokyo, 1929. 372 p.

A reference library for the historical study of music. Much of the material came from the collection of W. H. Cummings.

1088

Nanki Music Library. Catalogue of the W. H. Cummings collection in the Nanki Music Library. [Tokyo] 1925. 70 p.

Includes the rarities of the Cummings library, acquired in its sale in 1918. About 450 items, including much important early English music.

TOLEDO, OHIO

1089

Museum of Art. The printed note, 500 years of music printing and engraving, January 1957. [Toledo, Museum of Art, 1957] 144 p.

Foreword by A. Beverly Barksdale.

A splendidly illustrated catalog of 188 items, on loan from major public and privaet collections throughout the country, related to the history of

[255]

music printing and engraving. Informative annotations. Bibliography of 67 items.

TOLEDO, SPAIN

1090

Biblioteca Capitolar. "Les manuscrits polyphoniques de la Bibliothèque Capitulaire de Tolede." [By René Lenaerts.] In *International Society for Musical Research, Fifth Congress, Utrecht, 1952.* p. 267–81.

Brief descriptions and discussion of the contents of approximately 30 sources of polyphonic music in the Toledo library.

TREVISO, ITALY

1091

Archivio Musicale del Duomo. La Cappella Musicale del Duomo di Treviso (1300–1633). [By Giovanni d'Alessi.] Vedelago, Tipografia "Ars et Religio," 1954. 272 p.

Historical study of the musical establishment of the cathedral at Treviso. Chapter 15, p. 169–218, deals particularly with the musical archive and its resources. Manuscripts are listed briefly; printed books, in greater detail.

TURIN, ITALY

Biblioteca Nazionale. See no. 939.

1092

Biblioteca Nazionale. "L'Intavolatura d'organo tedesca della Biblioteca Nazionale di Torino. Catalogo ragionato." [By Oscar Mischiati.] In *L'Organo, rivista di cultura organaria e organistica,* 4 (1963). P. 1–154.

A complete inventory of the contents of 16 volumes of German organ tablature in the National Library in Turin, the largest body of source material for German organ music known. The manuscripts contain 1,770 compositions on 2,703 written folios, and were compiled between 1637 and 1640. The inventory is followed by a set of appendices including palaeographic descriptions of the volumes, author lists added by later hands, watermarks, concordant prints, manuscripts and modern editions, and an index of composers.

1093

Biblioteca Nazionale. "La raccolta di rarità musicali 'Mauro Foa' alla Biblioteca Nazionale di Torino." [By Alberto Gentili.] In *Accademie e biblioteche d'Italia,* 1 (1927) p. 36–50.

A descriptive account of a collection comprising 95 volumes, manuscripts and printed books, founded by Count Giacomo Durazzo, Genoan ambassador to Venice in 1765. Includes autographs of Vivaldi and Stradella, as well as the German organ tablatures mentioned above.

1094

Biblioteca Nazionale. Manoscritti e libri a stampa musicali espositi dalla Biblioteca Nazionale di Torino. Firenze, L. Franceschini, 1898. 24 p.

Exposition catalog of 20 manuscripts and 36 prints, 16th–18th centuries.

UPPSALA, SWEDEN

1095

Universitet. Bibliotek. Catalogue critique et descriptif des imprimés de musique des XVIe et XVIIe siècles, conservés à la Bibliothèque de l'Université Royale d'Upsala; par Rafael Mitjana, avec une introduction bibliographique par Isak Collijn . . . Upsala, Impr. Almqvist & Wiksell, 1911–51. 3 v.

Vol. 1: Musique religieuse, I, par Rafael Mitjana (1911). Vol. 2: Musique religieuse, II, musique profane; musique dramatique; musique instrumentale; additions au Tome I, par Åke Davidsson (1951). Vol. 3: Recueils de musique religieuse et profane, par Åke Davidsson (1951).

Entries in Vols. 1 and 2 are arranged alphabetically within each category; Vol. 3 is arranged chronologically, with an index of the contents of the collections under composer. Index of printers and publishers, and a bibliography of works cited. Full bibliographical entries, with locations of copies of the works in other libraries.

See also no. 598.

1096

Universitet. Bibliotek. Catalogue of the Gimo Collection of Italian manuscript music in the University Library of Uppsala. By Åke Davidsson. Uppsala, 1963. 101 p. (Acta bibliothecae R. Universitatis Upsaliensis, 14.)

A catalog of 360 items, comprising both vocal and instrumental music of the 18th century. An introduction relates the history of the collection and discusses problems of compiling the catalog. There is a useful bibliography of sources and related literature.

Review by Minnie Elmer in *Notes*, 22 (1965) p. 715–16.

VALLADOLID, SPAIN

1097

Catedral. Archivo Musical. "El Archivo Musical de la Catedral de Valladolid." [By Higinio Anglés.] In *Anuario musical*, 3 (1948) p. 59–108.

[257]

20 manuscripts and 97 early printed books. Inventories given for the contents of the manuscripts, full bibliographical citations for the prints, references to Eitner and other bibliographies.

VENICE, ITALY

1098

Biblioteca del Palazzo Giustinian Lolin. Stampe e manoscritti preziosi e rari della Biblioteca del Palazzo Giustinian Lolin a San Vidal. [By Siro Cisiliano.] [Venezia] A cura del fondatore Dott. Ugo Levi sotto gli auspici dell'Ateneo Veneto [1966] 55 p.

At head of title: Fondazione Ugo e Olga Levi, Centro di Cultura Musicale Superiore.

Catalog of the library of a recently established musical foundation in Venice. 70 items listed, including printed books and manuscripts from the 16th to the early 19th centuries. Many of the manuscripts are composite in content. The collection contains important source materials for the study of 18th-century instrumental music.

Biblioteca Nazionale Marciana [formerly R. Biblioteca di S. Marco]. See no. 931.

1099

Biblioteca Nazionale Marciana. I codici musicali Contariniani del secolo XVII nella R. Biblioteca di San Marco in Venezia, illustrati dal Dr. Taddeo Wiel. Venezia, F. Ongania, 1888. 121 p.

The Contarini collection is a special library of manuscript scores of 17th-century Venetian opera, by such composers as Cesti, Cavalli, Pallavicino, Ziani, etc. 120 numbered items. Entries give information as to date of first performance, librettist, cast, general description of the work. Composer index.

Biblioteca Querini Stampalia. See no. 931.

Museo Correr. See no. 931.

Pia Casa di Ricovero. See no. 931.

VERCELLI, ITALY

1100

Archivio Della Cattedrale. "Il fondo musicale dell'archivio della Cattedrale di Vercelli." [By Claudio Sartori.] In *Fontes artis musicae*, 5 (1958) p. 24–31.

VERONA, ITALY

1101

Accademia Filarmonica. L'Accademia Filarmonica di Verona, dalla fondazione (Maggio 1543) al 1600 e il suo patrimonio musicale antico. [By Giuseppe Turrini.] Verona, "La Tipografica Veronese," 1941. 345 p.

A detailed history of the Accademia Filarmonica from its beginnings to 1600. Chapter 16 discusses the holdings of the library from 1565 to 1600 on the basis of early inventories. Chapter 17 continues the discussion to the first half of the 19th century. Chapter 18, p. 208–44, includes a catalog of the existing materials in the "Fondo musicale antico," some 217 prints and 21 manuscripts.

Accademia Filarmonica. See also no. 941.

1102

Biblioteca Capitolare. Il patrimonio musicale della Biblioteca Capitolare di Verona dal sec. XV al XIX. [By Giuseppe Turrini] Verona, "La Tipografica Veronese," 1952. 83 p. (Estratto dagli Atti dell'Accademia di Agricoltura, Scienze e Lettere di Verona, ser. IV, v. 2.)

Cites 57 manuscripts, 108 early printed books, 21 theoretical works, and 13 instruments of the 16th and 17th centuries. Composite indexes of the contents of the manuscripts. A chapter on the origin of the collections, with reference to some early inventories.

VICENZA, ITALY

Archivio della Cattedrale. See no. 932.

Biblioteca Bertoliana. See no. 932.

VIENNA, AUSTRIA

1103

Beethoven-Zentenarausstellung. Führer durch die Beethoven-Zentenarausstellung der Stadt Wien. "Beethoven und die wiener Kultur seiner Zeit." Wien, Selbstverlag der Gemeinde Wien, 1927. 248 p.

An exhibition catalog of 1,070 items, including letters, documents, pictures, musical instruments, scores, and prints related to Beethoven and his circle.

1104

Gesellschaft der Musikfreunde. Geschichte der Gesellschaft der Musikfreunde in Wien, 1912–27. (Fortsetzung der Festschrift zur Jahrhundertfeier vom Jahre 1912.) Wien, Gesellschaft der Musikfreunde, 1937.

Continues the documentation given in the following volume. Of particular interest is an account by Hedwig Kraus of "Die Sammlungen der Gesellschaft der Musikfreunde, 1912–1937," p. 1–42.

1105

Gesellschaft der Musikfreunde. Geschichte der K. K. Gesellschaft der Musikfreunde in Wien. . . . In einem Zusatzbande: Die Sammlungen und Statuten, von Dr. Eusebius Mandyczewski. Wien [Adolf Holzhausen] 1912. 2 v.

Vol. 1 is a history of the Gesellschaft, in two sections: 1812–70 and 1870–1912. Vol. 2, "Zusatz-Band," is not a true catalog but a summary listing of the holdings of the archive, library, and museum. Of particular value is the listing of "Bücher und Schriften über Musik. Druckwerke und Handschriften aus der Zeit bis zum Jahre 1800" (p. 55–84). Also, "Musik-Autographe" (p. 85–123).

1106

Hoftheater. Katalog der Portrait-Sammlung der K.V.K. General-Intendanz der K. K. Hoftheater. Zugleich ein biographisches Hilfsbuch auf dem Gebiet von Theater und Musik. Wien, Adolph W. Kunast, 1892–94. 3 v.

Catalogs a large collection of portraits and other graphic materials related to the theater; classified according to type of theater or kind of entertainment. *Gruppe III*, Vol. 1, p. 119–264, is concerned with pictorial documents on musicians: composers, librettists, concert singers, writers on music, etc.

1107

Internationale Ausstellung für Musik- und Theaterwesen. Fach-Katalog der Musikhistorischen Abtheilung von Deutschland und Österreich-Ungarn. . . . Wien, 1892. 591 p.

Catalog for a large and varied music exhibition held in Vienna in 1892. Includes prints, manuscripts, instruments, portraits, letters, and other documents, arranged roughly in chronological order from ancient times to the end of the 19th century.

See also no. 898.

1108

Künstlerhaus. Katalog der Ausstellung anlässlich der Centenarfeier Domenico Cimarosas. Wien, Verlag des Comités, 1901. 163 p.

Exhibition catalog of 524 items related to Cimarosa and his contemporaries; includes scores, portraits, medals, etc.

1109
Kunsthistorische Museum. Estensische Sammlung. Die Esten-
sischen Musikalien; thematisches Verzeichnis mit Einleitung [by Robert
Haas.] Regensburg, G. Bosse, 1927. 232 p.

Reissued 1957 as Bd. VII of *Forschungsbeiträge zur Musikwissenschaft.*
Regensburg, G. Bosse.

Catalog, largely thematic, of an important collection of 18th-century
instrumental music originating in northern Italy. Includes a small group of
cantatas and other vocal works. Classified within major sections of prints
and manuscripts. Index of names, text incipits.

1110
Minoritenkonvent. Das Musikarchiv im Minoritenkonvent zu Wien
(Katalog des älteren Bestandes vor 1784). [By Friedrich Wilhelm Riedel.]
Kassel [Bärenreiter, for the International Association of Music Libraries
and the International Musicological Society] 1963. 139 p. (Catalogus
musicus, 1.)

Catalog, broadly classified, of manuscripts and printed music, chiefly
of the 17th and 18th centuries. Strong in early keyboard music. Indexes of
composers, copyists, and former owners of the sources.

Review by Othmar Wessely in *Die Musikforschung*, 18 (1965) p. 204–206.

1111
Nationalbibliothek. "Die Musikbibliothek von Raimund Fugger
d.J.; ein Beitrag zur Musiküberlieferung des 16. Jahrhunderts." [By
Richard Schaal.] In *Acta M*, 29 (1957) p. 126–37.

Includes the catalog of the library copied from the original 16th-century
manuscript in the Staatsbibliothek, Munich. The bulk of the Fugger family
music collection is now in the Vienna Library.

1112
Nationalbibliothek. "Die Musiksammlung" [by Leopold Nowak.] In
*Die Osterreichische Nationalbibliothek. Festschrift herausgegeben zum 25.
Jährigen Dienstjubliäum des Generaldirektors Prof. Dr. Josef Bick.* Wien, H.
Bauer-Verlag, 1948. P. 119–38.

A description of the music collection and its growth, with references to
numerous articles and descriptive studies related to it.

1113
Nationalbibliothek. Richard Strauss Ausstellung zum 100. Geburt-
stag. Bearbeitet von Franz Grasberger und Franz Hadamowsky. Wien,
Österreichische Nationalbibliothek, 1964. 360 p.

Exhibition catalog of a rich collection of documents related to Richard Strauss. Illustrated.

1114

Nationalbibliothek. Tabulae codicum manuscriptorum praeter Graecos et Orientales in Bibliotheca Palatina Vindobonensi Asservatorum ... x. IX–X: Codicum musicorum, Pars I–II. Vindobonae, venum dat. C. Geroldi filius, 1897–99. 2 v. in 1.

Catalog, compiled by Joseph Mantuani, of the manuscripts numbered 15,501 to 19,500 and comprising the music holdings of the Vienna National Library. Introduction and descriptive notes in Latin. Each volume has an index of names, of subjects, and of text incipits.

1115

Nationalbibliothek, Photogrammarchiv. Das Archiv für Photogramme musikalischer Meisterhandschriften in der Musiksammlung der Österreichischen Nationalbibliothek in Wien. Widmung Anthony van Hoboken. Wien, Österreichische Nationalbibliothek, 1958. 39 p.

A pamphlet describing the nature and history of the archive of photocopies of composers' autographs founded in 1927 by Heinrich Schenker and Anthony van Hoboken. The collection emphasizes the autographs of the Viennese classic composers.

WARSAW, POLAND

1116

Biblioteka Narodowa. Katalog mikrofilmów muzycznych (Catalogue of musical microfilms) vol. 1– . Warszawa, Biblioteka Narodowa, 1956– .

A series of catalogs originating in the microfilm archive of the National Library at Warsaw. 3 volumes of a larger series (*Katalog mikrofilmow*) are concerned with music, Vols. 8, 9, and 12. The holdings of numerous Polish libraries are represented.

Vol. 1 (1956): chiefly manuscripts and printed materials of the 19th century. Vol. 2 (1962): musical documents of the 17th and 18th centuries. Vol. 3 (1965): historical source materials related to Polish music.

WASHINGTON, DISTRICT OF COLUMBIA

1117

U.S. Library of Congress. Music Division. Catalogue of early books on music (before 1800) by Julia Gregory. . . . Washington, D.C., Govt. Printing Office, 1913. 312 p.

[262]

Supplement (Books acquired by the Library, 1913–42) by Hazel Bartlett
. . . with a list of books on music in Chinese and Japanese. 1944. 143 p.

This catalog and its supplement provide access to the Library of Congress'
rich holdings in the field of early music theory. The citations conform to the
Library's printed catalog cards.

1118
U.S. Library of Congress. Music Division. Catalogue of first
editions of Edward MacDowell (1861–1908) by O. G. Sonneck. Washington, D.C., Govt. Printing Office, 1917. 89 p.

Includes works with and without opus numbers, compositions written
under pseudonyms, and works edited by the composer. Indexes of class,
titles, first lines of text, authors and translators, publishers.

1119
U.S. Library of Congress. Music Division. Catalogue of first
editions of Stephen C. Foster (1826–64) by Walter R. Whittlesey and
O. G. Sonneck. Washington, D.C., Govt. Printing Office, 1915. 79 p.

Works arranged by title; indexed by authors of text, publishers, first
lines. Detailed annotations.

1120
U.S. Library of Congress. Music Division. Catalogue of opera
librettos printed before 1800, prepared by O. G. T. Sonneck. Washington,
D.C., Govt. Printing Office, 1914. 2 v.

The Library's collection of librettos began in 1909 with the purchase of
the Schatz collection. By 1914 it contained 17,000 items and was particularly
strong in first editions of 17th- and 18th-century works. Vol. 1 is a title
listing, with notes giving date of first performance, place, name of composer
if known. Vol. 2 is an index by composer and by librettist, and of titles of
specific arias mentioned.

1121
U.S. Library of Congress. Music Division. Dramatic music.
Catalogue of full scores, compiled by O. G. T. Sonneck. Washington,
D.C., Govt. Printing Office, 1908. 170 p.

Full scores of operas in original editions, some manuscript copies
included, and some photocopies. Arranged alphabetically by composer.

1122
U.S. Library of Congress. Music Division. Orchestral music . . .
catalogue. Scores. Prepared under the direction of O. G. T. Sonneck.
Washington, D.C., Govt. Printing Office, 1912. 663 p.

Orchestra scores from about 1830 to date of publication. Main entries under composer, with a class index and title index.

1123

U.S. Library of Congress. Music Division. Elizabeth Sprague Coolidge Foundation. Coolidge Foundation program for contemporary chamber music; preliminary checklist of works available for loan (November, 1961). Compiled by Frances G. Gewehr. Washington, D.C., Library of Congress [1961] 38 p. (typescript).

Supplement, April 1963 (typescript).

A classified list of contemporary chamber music scores and parts which may be borrowed by qualified ensembles for study purposes. Entries give publisher and price; recordings, if available, are also cited.

U.S. Library of Congress. Music Division. Dayton C. Miller Flute Collection. See nos. 542, 1184.

1124

Washington Cathedral. Library. "The Douglas collection in the Washington Cathedral Library." In *The life and work of Charles Winfred Douglas*, by Leonard Ellinwood and Anne Woodward Douglas. New York, Hymn Society of America, 1958. P. 36–72. (Hymn Society of America. Papers, no. 23.)

A library of hymnology and liturgical music formed by one of the leading authorities in the field.

WOLFENBÜTTEL, GERMANY

1125

Herzog-August-Bibliothek. Die Handschriften nebst den älteren Druckwerken der Musikabteilung . . . Beschreiben von Emil Vogel 111 Wolfenbüttel, J. Zwissler, 1890. 280 p. (Die Handschriften der Herzoglichen Bibliothek zu Wolfenbüttel . . . 8 Abth.)

WROCLAW, POLAND [formerly BRESLAU, GERMANY]

1126

Bohn, Emil. Bibliographie der Musik-Druckwerke bis 1700 welche in der Stadtbibliothek, der Bibliothek des Acad. Inst. für Kirchenmusik, und der K. und Universitäts-Bibliothek zu Breslau aufbewahrt werden. . . . Berlin, A. Cohn, 1883. 450 p.

The three collections cataloged here are outstanding for their 16th- and 17th-century manuscripts and prints, particularly of liturgical and vocal music. P. 1–31: theoretical works; p. 32–351: practical works (music); p. 371–74: collections of chronological order; p. 374–400: continuation of practical works. Full bibliographical descriptions.

1127
Stadtbibliothek. Die musikalischen Handschriften des XVI. und XVII. Jahrhunderts in der Stadtbibliothek zu Breslau . . . von Emil Bohn. Breslau, Commissions-Verlag von J. Hainauer, 1890. 423 p.

356 items, with full inventories of contents. Numerous indexes and supplementary lists; first-line incipits of vocal texts, anonymous compositions, composer index, etc.

1128
Staats- und Universitäts-Bibliothek. Beschreibendes Verzeichnis der alten Musikalien-Handschriften und Druckwerke des Köniblichen Gymnasiums zu Brieg. Bearbeitet von Friedrich Kuhn. Leipzig, Breitkopf & Härtel, 1897. 98 p. (Monatshefte für Musikgeschichte. Beilage, Jahrgang 29.)

A collection placed in the library of Breslau University in 1890. 54 manuscripts and some 110 printed books, chiefly 16th century. Contents given for manuscript anthologies; full bibliographical description for prints. Index.

WUPPERTAL, GERMANY

1129
Stadtbibliothek. Musikalien-Bestand der Stadtbibliothek. Wuppertal, 1960. 117 p.

ZURICH, SWITZERLAND

1130
Allgemeine Musikgesellschaft. Katalog der gedruckten und handschriftlichen Musikalien des 17. bis 19. Jahrhunderts im Besitze der Allgemeinen Musikgesellschaft Zürich. Red. von Georg Walter. Zürich, Hug, 1960. 145 p.

A collection rich in 17th- and 18th-century instrumental music. Thematic incipits for works in manuscript.

Review by Donald Krummel in *Notes*, 19 (1961) p. 77; by Willi Kahl in *Die Musikforschung*, 16 (1963) p. 284.

1131
Zentralbibliothek. "Die Österreichische Musiküberlieferung der Züricher Zentralbibliothek." [By Erich Schenk.] In *Die Osterreichische*

[265]

Nationalbibliothek. Festschrift hrsg. zum 25. jährigen Dienstjubiläum des Generaldirektors Prof. Dr. Josef Bick. Wien, H. Bauer-Verlag, 1948. P. 576–81.

Consists chiefly of a listing of works by Austrian composers in the Zurich library, giving place, publisher and library signature. Special attention given to works not mentioned in Eitner.

ZWICKAU, GERMANY

1132

Ratsschulbibliothek. Bibliographie der Musikwerke in der Ratsschulbibliothek zu Zwickau, bearb. . . . von Reinhard Vollhardt. Leipzig, Breitkopf & Härtel, 1893–96. 299 p. (Monatshefte für Musikgeschichte. Beilage. Jahrgang 25–28.)

764 numbered items, manuscripts and printed books, including liturgical works, theoretical works, instrumental and vocal music. Chiefly 16th- and 17th-century materials.

Catalogs of Private Collections

In this section some of the catalogs of major private music collections are cited. Few of these remain intact. Some, like the Cortot or the Wolfheim collections, have been dispersed; others have changed location in recent years. No attempt has been made here to list the numerous catalogs issued in connection with auction sales, although some of these are of great bibliographical interest. Some indication of the information to be gained from the study of early music auction catalogs, a field very little explored as yet, can be found in A. Hyatt King's recent book on *Some British collectors of music, c. 1600–1960,* Cambridge University Press, 1963.

1133

Cortot, Alfred. Bibliothèque Alfred Cortot . . . v. 1. Catalogue établi par Alfred Cortot et rédigé par Frederik Goldbeck, avec la collaboration de A. Fehr. Préface de Henry Prunières. [Augenteuil, Sur les presses de R. Coulouma, 1936] 221 p.

Première partie (all published): Traités et autres ouvrages théoriques des XVe, XVIe, XVIIe & XVIIIe siècles.

The music theory holdings in the library of Alfred Cortot. Cortot's interests as a collector extended over a wide area of musical practice. The collection passed into the hands of a dealer at the owner's death in 1962.

1134
Heyer, Wilhelm. Musikhistorisches Museum von Wilhelm Heyer in Köln. Katalog von Georg Kinsky. Band 4: Musik-Autographen. Leipzig, Breitkopf & Härtel, 1916. 870 p.

1,673 items, one of the finest collections of musical autographs ever assembled. Dispersed and sold at auction in 1926 by the firm of Henrici and Liepmannssohn. Kinsky's catalogs of the Heyer collection are models of music bibliography, full of biographical and descriptive detail. 64 facsimile plates.

For other volumes of the Heyer *Katalog*, see no. 1156, 1157.

1135
Hirsch, Paul. Katalog der Musikbibliothek Paul Hirsch . . . Frankfurt am Main, herausg. von K. Meyer und P. Hirsch. . . . Berlin, M. Breslauer, 1928–47. 4 v. (V.4 has imprint: Cambridge Univ. Press.)

Vol. 1: Theoretische Drucke bis 1800. Vol. 2: Opera-Partituren. Vol. 3: Instrumental- und Vokalmusik bus etwa 1830. Vol. 4: Erstausgaben, Chorwerke in Partitur, Gesamtausgaben, Nachschlagewerke, etc. Ergänzungen zu Bd. I-III.

The Paul Hirsch Library, one of the great private music collections of the world, was removed from Frankfurt to Cambridge, England, just prior to World War II and was acquired by the British Museum in 1946.

See also nos. 972, 973.

1136
Koch, Louis. Collection. Katalog der Musikautographen Sammlung . . . Manuskripte, Briefe, Dokumente, von Scarlatti bis Stravinsky. Beschreiben und erläutert von Georg Kinsky. Stuttgart, Hoffmannsche Buchdruckerei F. Krais, 1953. 360 p.

An important collection of musical autographs. Strong in German music of the classic and romantic periods. 21 facsimile plates.

Review by Richard S. Hill in *Notes*, 11 (1953) p. 119–20.

1137
Meyer, André. Music Collection. Collection musicale André Meyer: manuscrits, autographes, musique imprimée et manuscrite, ouvrages théoriques, historiques et pédagogiques, livrets, iconographie, instruments de musique. Abbeville, F. Paillart [1960] 118 p.

Catalog compiled by François Lesure and Nanie Bridgman.

A collection of manuscripts and early printed music, particularly noteworthy for its holdings in iconography. Beautifully illustrated by 292 plates.

Review by Hans Hahn in *Die Musikforschung*, 17 (1964) p. 83–84.

1138
Wolffheim, Werner J. Library. Versteigerung der Musikbibliothek des Herrn Dr. Werner Wolffheim . . . durch die Firmen: M. Breslauer & L. Liepmannssohn. . . . Berlin, 1928–29. 2 v. in 4.

> One of the finest collections ever brought together by a private person . . . the 2-volume catalog compiled at the time of its sale will always rank as an indispensable work of reference (*Grove's*).

Classified catalog of a library that not only included rarities, but the standard reference books and editions as well. Full descriptions with copious notes. Numerous facsimile plates.

C*atalogs*

of Musical Instrument Collections

COLLECTIONS of musical instruments are frequently annexed to music libraries. The reader will note that a number of the catalogs in the preceding section are concerned, in part, with Western or Oriental instruments. In the section that follows, the catalogs of some of the major specialized collections of musical instruments are listed, along with a number of exhibition catalogs emphasizing this area of collecting activity.

For a comprehensive and historical view of instrument collections, see Alfred Berner's article, "Instrumentensammlungen," in *MGG*, 6, col. 1295–1310, There is also an illuminating paper by Georg Kinsky, "Musikinstrumentensammlungen in Vergangenheit und Gegenwart," in the *Jahrbuch Peters*, 27 (1920) p. 47–60. The article in *Grove's*, 5th edition, by Langwell (vol. 4, p. 509–15) provides the locations of the collections but no bibliographical information.

ANN ARBOR, MICHIGAN

1139

University of Michigan. Stearns Collection of Musical Instruments. Catalog of the Stearns collection of musical instruments, by Albert A. Stanley. 2nd ed. Ann Arbor, Mich., University of Michigan, 1921. 276 p.

First published in 1918.

A catalog of 1,464 instruments, Western and Oriental. 13 plates, descriptive annotations. Bibliography and indexes of makers, geographical distribution, names of instruments.

1140

University of Michigan. Stearns Collection of Musical Instruments. Stearns collection of musical instruments—1965. By Robert Austin Warner. . . . Ann Arbor, School of Music, University of Michigan [1965] 10 p.

A brief, informative survey of the history of the collection, its character and present condition. 3 plates.

BASLE, SWITZERLAND

1141

Historische Museum. Katalog der Musikinstrumente im Historischen Museum zu Basel. Von Dr. Karl Nef. Basel, Universitäts-Buchdruckerei von Friedrich Reinhardt, 1906. 74 p.

Bound with *Festschrift zum zweiten Kongress der Internationalen Musikgesellschaft*, Basel, 1906. 294 instruments listed and described. 12 plates.

BERLIN, GERMANY

1142

Institut für Musikforschung. Die Berliner Musikinstrumenten-Sammlung; Einführung mit historischen und technischen Erläuterungen von Alfred Berner. Berlin, 1952. 58 p.

Not strictly a catalog, but a guide to the principal types of instruments with reference to examples in the Berlin collection. 11 plates.

1143

Staatliche Akademische Hochschule für Musik. Führer durch die Sammlung alter Musik-Instrumente, von Dr. Oskar Fleischer. Berlin, A. Haack, 1892. 145 p.

Classified catalog, chiefly early Western instruments, with a few Oriental.

1144

Staatliche Akademische Hochschule für Musik. Sammlung alter Musikinstrumente bei der Staatlichen Hochschule für Musik zu Berlin; beschreibender Katalog von Curt Sachs. Berlin, J. Bard, 1922. 384 cols. 30 plates.

The collection contains some 3,200 items, of which about 250 are non-European instruments. Classified catalog. Entries give description of instrument, maker, date and place of manufacture. Index of instruments, places, makers, etc.

BOSTON, MASSACHUSETTS

1145

Museum of Fine Arts. Leslie Lindsey Mason Collection. Ancient European musical instruments . . . by N. Bessaraboff . . . Pub. for the Museum . . . by the Harvard Univ. Press, 1941. 503 p.

An authoritative catalog, well illustrated, 213 items. Provides a wealth of background information for the historical study of instruments. Bibliography, p. 453–69. Indexes of names and subjects. 16 plates and 72 illustrations in text. The collection of Canon Francis W. Galpin forms the basis of the Mason collection.

BRAUNSCHWEIG, GERMANY

1146

Städtische Museum. Verzeichnis der Sammlung alter Musikinstrumente im Städtischen Museum Braunschweig . . . Instrumente, Instrumentenmacher und Instrumentisten in Braunschweig . . . Braunschweig, E. Appelhans, 1928. 124 p. (Werkstücke aus Museum, Archiv und Bibliothek der Stadt Braunschweig, 3.)

At head of title: Hans Schröder.

The catalog occupies p. 5–34; lists 113 items, all European. The remainder of the volume is devoted to studies of local instrument makers and performers.

BRUSSELS, BELGIUM

1147

Conservatoire Royal de Musique. Musée Instrumental. Catalogue déscriptif et analytique du Musée . . . par Victor-Charles Mahillon, conservateur . . . 2nd ed. Gand, A. Hoste, 1893–1922. 5 v.

One of the great instrument collections of the world. More than 3,000 instruments of all cultures. Classified catalog. The descriptions include precise indications of each instrument's pitch, tuning, and range.

CAIRO, EGYPT

1148

Museum of Egyptian Antiquities. Catalogue général des antiquités égyptiennes du Musée du Caire. Nos. 69201–69852: Instruments de musique, par Hans Hickmann. Le Caire, Imprimèrie de l'Institut français d'archéologie orientale, 1949. 216 p. 116 plates.

Classified catalog of 651 ancient Egyptian instruments, or fragments thereof, with detailed descriptions and photo reproductions.

CINCINNATI, OHIO

1149

Art Museum. Musical instruments. [Collection of the Cincinnati Art Museum] Cincinnati, 1949.

[271]

An illustrated brochure listing 110 instruments, 60 European, 50 non-European.

COPENHAGEN, DENMARK
1150
Carl Claudius Collection. Carl Claudius' Samling af gamle musikinstrumenter. København, Levin ; Munksgaards Forlag, 1931. 423 p.

A rich private collection of musical instruments, now administered by the University of Copenhagen. The catalog describes 757 items.

1151
Musikhistorisk Museum. Das Musikhistorische Museum zu Kopenhagen: beschreibender Katalog von Angul Hammerich; deutsch von Erna Bobé. Mit 179 illustrationen. Kopenhagen, G.E.C. Gad; Lepzig, Kommissionsverlag von Breitkopf & Härtel, 1911. 172 p.

The Danish edition appeared in 1909.

Classified catalog of 631 items, 582 of which are instruments, Western and Oriental, followed by a short listing of liturgical manuscripts and prints, and miscellany.

EISENACH, GERMANY
1152
Bachmuseum. Verzeichnis der Sammlung alter Musikinstrumente im Bachhaus zu Eisenach, hrsg. von der Neuen Bach Gesellschaft. 4., erweiterte Aufl. Leipzig, Breitkopf & Härtel, 1964. 97 p. (Veröffentlichungen der Neuen Bachgesellschaft. Vereinsjahr 50, 1962.)

First issued in 1913.

Classified catalog of more than 230 items. Illustrated with line drawings.

FLORENCE, ITALY
1153
Conservatorio di Musica "Luigi Cherubini." Gli strumenti musicali raccolti nel Museo del R. Istituto L. Cherubini a Firenze. [By Leto Bargagna. Firenze, G. Ceccherini] [1911] 70 p.

A catalog of 146 instruments; 12 plates.

THE HAGUE, HOLLAND
1154
Gemeentemuseum. Europese muziekinstrumenten in het Haags Gemeentemuseum. [By A. W. Ligtvoet & W. Lievense.] 's-Gravenhaag, Gemeentemuseu, 1965. 160 p.

With 64 full page illustrations.

1155

Gemeentemuseum. Exotische en oude Europese muziekinstrumenten, in de muziekafdeling can het Haagse Gemeentemuseum; 25 afbeeldingen toegelicht. [By A. W. Ligtvoet.] 's-Gravenhage, Nijgh & Van Ditmar [1955] 51 p.

A general, popular introduction to the collection. 25 plates. Text in Dutch and English.

[Heyer Collection]

1156

Heyer Collection. Kleiner Katalog der Sammlung alter Musik-instrumente, verfasst von Georg Kinsky. Köln, 1913. 250 p.

An abridgement of the material in the following catalog; valuable because it contains entries for the wind instruments in the Heyer collection, not included in the larger catalog.

1157

Heyer Collection. Musikhistorisches Museum von Wilhelm Heyer in Köln. Katalog von Georg Kinsky. Leipzig, Breitkopf & Härtel, 1910–16. 2 v.

Two volumes of this catalog are concerned with the instrument collection. Vol. 1: Besaitete Tasteninstruments. Orgel und orgelartige Instrumente. Friktionsinstrumente. Vol. 2: Zupf- und Streichinstrumente. Vol. 3 (not published) was intended to cover the wind instruments. The Heyer instrument collection, one of the finest in the world, was trans-ferred to Leipzig in 1926, where it was destroyed in World War II.

Kinsky's catalog is a mine of information for the student of early instruments; copiously illustrated, rich in detail.

See also no. 1134.

HOLYOKE, MASSACHUSETTS

1158

Mount Holyoke College. The Belle Skinner collection of old musical instruments. . . . A descriptive catalogue compiled under the direction of William Skinner. [Philadelphia, New York, etc. Printed by the Beck Engraving Co.] 1933. 210 p.

Illustrated catalog of 89 instruments, including some particularly fine examples of keyboard instruments. Colored plates.

Since 1959 this collection has been on loan to Yale University.

[Lachmann Collection]
1159

Lachmann, Erich. Erich Lachmann collection of historical stringed musical instruments. Los Angeles, Allan Hancock Foundation, Univ. of Southern California, 1950. 53 p.

A handsome catalog of 42 items; noteworthy for its photographic illustrations by Irvin Kershner.

LEIPZIG, GERMANY

1160

Karl-Marx-Universität. Führer durch des Musikinstrumenten-museum der Karl-Marx-Universität Leipzig. Von Paul Rubardt. Leipzig, Breitkopf & Härtel, 1955. 84 p. 16 plates.

1161

Universität. Musikwissenschaftliches Instrumenten-Museum. Führer durch das Musikwissenschaftliche Instrumenten-Museum der Universität Leipzig. Hrsg. von Helmut Schultz. Leipzig, Breitkopf & Härtel, 1929. 85 p. 19 plates.

A classified catalog organized according to the ground plan of the display.

LONDON, ENGLAND

1162

Fenton House. Benton Fletcher Collection. Catalog of the Benton Fletcher collection of early keyboard instruments at Fenton House, Hampstead. London, Country Life, Ltd., for the National Trust, 1957. 26 p.

A descriptive brochure by Raymond Russell for a collection of early keyboard instruments maintained in playing condition in a late 17th-century house in Hampstead, London.

1163

Galpin Society. British musical instruments. August 7–30, 1951. [London, The Galpin Society, 1951] 35 p.

A classified exhibition catalog of instruments, chiefly of British make or use. Includes 151 woodwind, 61 brass, 27 keyboard, 62 of the violin family, 16 of the viol family, and 16 miscellaneous. Brief descriptions, with short introductions for each class of instruments.

1164

Horniman Museum. The Adam Carse collection of old musical wind instruments [now in the Horniman Museum, London.] London, Staples Press for the London County Council, 1951. 88 p.

A collection of 320 instruments, briefly described, with historical notes for each family. Illustrated by drawings.

1165

Royal College of Music. Catalog of historical musical instruments paintings, sculpture and drawings. [London, Royal College, 1952] 16 p.

Forward by George Dyson.

Contains the Donaldson collection of musical instruments. Brief inventory with minimum description.

1166

Royal Military Exhibition, 1890. A descriptive catalogue of the musical instruments recently exhibited at the Royal Military Exhibition, London, 1890. Compiled by Charles Russell Day. London, Eyre & Spottiswoode, 1891, 253 p.

An exhibition confined to wind and percussion instruments. 457 wind instruments (percussion not inventoried). Plates.

1167

South Kensington Museum. A descriptive catalogue of the musical instruments of the South Kensington Museum . . . By Carl Engel . . . London, Printed by G. E. Eyre and W. Spottiswoode for H.M. Stationery Office, 1874. 402 p.

Preceded by an essay on the history of musical instruments.

LUCERNE, SWITZERLAND

1168

Richard Wagner Museum. Katalog der städtischen Sammlung alter Musikinstrumente in Richard-Wagner-Museum, Tribschen, Luzern. Erstellt im Auftrag der Museums-Kommission von René Vannes . . . Luzern, Otto Dreyer, 1956. 40 p.

A catalog of 95 stringed instruments, 46 wind, 11 idiophones, 37 exotic instruments. 16 plates.

LUTON, ENGLAND

1169

Museum and Art Gallery. The Ridley collection of musical wind instruments in the Luton Museum. [Luton, the Corp. of Luton, Museum and Art Gallery, 1957] 32 p.

65 wind instruments. Historical note, p. 1–21. Plates.

[275]

MILAN, ITALY

1170

Conservatorio de Musica "Giuseppe Verdi." Gli strumenti musicali nel Museo del Conservatorio di Milano. Ed. E. Guarinoni. Milan, Hoepli, 1908. 109 p.

A collection of 278 instruments, 177 European and 91 non-European. Index of donors and of instruments.

1171

Museo degli Strumenti Musicali. Catalogo, a cura di Natale e Franco Gallini. [Milano] Castello Sforzesco [1963] 448 p.

An earlier catalog of the same collection issued in 1958 under the title: *Civico Museo di antichi strumenti musicali.* The 1963 catalog, completely reorganized, lists 641 items, well described and illustrated in 141 plates.

1172

Museo degli Strumenti Musicali. Mostra di antichi strumenti musicali della Collezione N. Gallini (Maggio, 1953). Milano, Villa Communale (Ex Reale) [1955] 43 p.

An exhibition catalog of 200 items dating from the time when the Gallini collection was in private hands. It has since become the property of the city of Milan, and its complete catalog appears above. Preface signed by Natale Gallini; 32 plates.

MUNICH, GERMANY

1173

Bayerische Nationalmuseum. Ausstellung alte Musik, Instrumente, Noten und Dokumente aus drei Jahrhunderten. Veranstaltet durch die Stadt München im Bayerischen Nationalmuseum, November–December, 1951. Katalog. München, Musikverlag Max Hieber, 1951. 71 p. 23 plates.

An exhibition devoted to music in cultural history. 636 items, of which the majority are early instruments.

NEW HAVEN, CONNECTICUT

1174

Yale University. Art Gallery. Musical instruments at Yale, a selection of Western instruments from the 15th to 20th centuries. Catalog by Sibyl Marcuse . . . [New Haven] Yale University Art Gallery [1960] 32 p.

An exhibition, Feb. 19–March 27, 1960, of 26 instruments, as well as paintings, drawings, prints, and manuscripts. Illustrated.

1175
Yale University. Morris Steinert Collection. The Morris Steinert collection of keyed and stringed instruments. New York, Tretbar [1893].

NEW YORK CITY, NEW YORK
1176
Metropolitan Museum of Art. Crosby Brown Collection. Catalog of the Crosby Brown collection of musical instruments of all nations . . . New York, Metropolitan Museum of Art, 1903–1907. 3 v. in 4.

Vol. 1: Europe (1904). Vol. 2: Asia (1903). Vol. 3: Instruments of savage tribes and semi-civilized people: Pt. 1, Africa (1907); Pt. 2, Oceanica (1907); Pt. 3, Historical groups (1905).

1177
Metropolitan Museum of Art. . . . Catalog of keyboard instruments. New York, Metropolitan Museum of Art, 1903. 313 p.

PARIS, FRANCE
1178
Conservatoire National. . . . Le Musée de Conservatoire National de musique. Catalogue descriptif et raisonné, par Gustave Chouquet. Nouvelle ed. Paris, Firmin-Didot, 1884. 276 p.

First published in 1875. Supplements by Léon Pillaut, in 1894, 1899, and 1903.

A catalog of 1,006 instruments, subdivided into European and non-European sections. Index of instruments and of names. Catalogers of musical instruments owe much to the classification established by Chouquet in this catalog.

SALZBURG, AUSTRIA
1179
Museum Carolino Augusteum. Alte Musik-Instrumente in Museum Carolino Augusteum Salzburg. Führer und beschreibendes Verzeichnis von Karl Geiringer. Leipzig, Breitkopf & Härtel, 1932. 46 p.

A catalog of 288 instruments, with an index of makers and 4 photographic plates showing 48 different instruments.

VIENNA, AUSTRIA
1180
Kunsthistorische Museum. Alte Musikinstrumente; die Sammlung des Kunsthistorischen Museums in der neuen Burg zu Wein. [By Victor Luithlen] Wein, H. Bauer, 1954. 28 p.

A brief, visitor's guide to the collection described below.

1181

Kunsthisthorische Museum. Die Sammlung alter Musikinstrumente. Beschreibendes Verzeichnis von Julius Schlosser. Wein, Anton Schroll, 1920. 138 p.

The catalog describes 361 instruments, most of which are illustrated in 57 plates. 31 Oriental and folk instruments. Western instruments are entered in chronological order, grouped according to type, with full descriptions and an informative introduction to each major section: i.e. "Das Orchester des 16. und 17. Jahrhunderts;" "Die Entwicklung des Instrumentenbaus seit dem 18. Jahrhundert." Much useful historical information given, as, for example, a supplement quoting the descriptions of 20 early instruments from Mattheson's *Neu eröffnetes Orchester* (1713).

1182

Museum für Völkerkunde. Aussereuropäische Musikinstrumente. Wein, Museum für Völkerkunde [1961] 89 p.

Foreword by Alfred Janata.

Illustrated, classified catalog of 654 non-European instruments.

WASHINGTON, DISTRICT OF COLUMBIA

1183

U.S. Library of Congress. Gertrude Clarke Whittal Foundation. The Stradivari memorial at Washington, the national capital, by William Dana Orcutt. Library of Congress, Gertrude Clarke Whittal Foundation [1938] 49 p.

Description of the matched set of Stravidarius instruments donated to the Library of Congress.

1184

U.S. Library of Congress. Music Division. Dayton C. Miller flute collection, a checklist of the instruments. Compiled by Laura E. Gilliam and William Lichtenwanger. Washington, D.C., Library of Congress, 1961. 113 p.

Lists 1,593 instruments of the flute type. Indexes by maker, type of instrument, trade name, system of fingering, etc. 8 plates.

See also no 542 for the Dayton C. Miller *Catalog of books . . . relating to the flute.*

Review by Anthony Baines in *Galpin Society Journal*, No. 15 (Mar., 1962) p. 100.

1185
U.S. National Museum [Smithsonian Institution]. Handbook of the collection of musical instruments in the United States National Museum. By Frances Densmore. Washington, D.C., Govt. Printing Office, 1927. 164 p. 49 plates. (Smithsonian Institution U.S. National Museum. Bulletin 136).

Histories

and Bibliographies of Music Printing and Publishing

INCLUDED here are bibliographies of the output of some of the major early music printers and publishers, such as Petrucci, Playford, Walsh, Ballard, etc.; studies of music publishing in particular regions or countries (England, Italy, Paris, Vienna, etc.); and a few works concerned with the technical processes of music printing or engraving. The most comprehensive bibliography on the history of music printing has been compiled by Ake Davidsson: see no. 1191, below.

1186

Bergmans, Paul. "La typographie musicale en Belgique au XVIe siècle." In *Histoire du livre et de l'imprimerie en Belgique des origines à nos jours*, 5 (Bruxelles, 1929) p. 47–75.

An illustrated account of 16th-century Belgian music printers and printing.

1187

Bobillier, Marie. "La librairie musicale en France de 1653 à 1790, d'après les Registres de privilèges." [Par Michel Brenet, *pseud.*] In *Sammelbände der Internationalen Musikgesellschaft*, 8 (1906–1907) p. 401–66.

An examination with extensive transcriptions from the archives in the Bibliothèque Nationale pertaining to licenses granted for the publication of music and books on music in Paris from 1652 to 1790. Thorough discussion of the inception of the royal *privelège*, with transcriptions of sample 17th-century *privelegés*. Supplemented by Cucuel, no. 1190 below.

1188

Castelain, Raoul. Histoire de l'édition musicale; ou, du droit d'éditer au droit d'auteur, 1501–1793. Préf de André Siegfried. Paris, H. Lemoine, 1957. 92 p.

Brief history of music publishing, with emphasis on legal aspects.

1189

Cohen, Paul. Musikdruck und Drucker zu Nürnberg im 16. Jahrhundert erschienenen Noten und Musikbücher . . . Nürnberg, H. Zierfuss, 1927. 63 p.

Also issued as a dissertation (Erlangen) under the title, *Die Nürnberger Musikdrucker im sechzehnten Jahrhundert*, 1927. Historical study, with brief accounts of the individual printers, followed by a chronological listing of 443 works published in Nürnberg from 1501 to 1600.

1190

Cucuel, Georges. "Quelques documents sur la librairie musicale au XVIIIe siècle." In *Sammelbände der Internationalen Musikgesellschaft*, 13 (1911–12). p. 385–92.

A further study of the archives related to the licensing of music publications in France, supplementing the article by Bobillier, no. 1187 above.

1191

Davidsson, Åke. Bibliographie zur Geschichte des Musikdrucks. Uppsala, Almquist & Wiksell, 1965. 86 p. (Studia musicologica Upsaliensia, Nova Ser. 1.)

A bibliography of 598 items related to the history of music printing and publishing, with a brief introductory survey of the literature. The expansion of a bibliography first issued as part of the author's *Musikbibliographische Beiträge*. See no. 1193, below.

1192

Davidsson, Åke. Danskt musiktryck intill 1700-talets mitt. Dänischer Musikdruck bis zur Mitte des 18. Jahrhunderts. Uppsala, [Almquist & Wiksell] 1962. 100 p. (Studia musicologica upsaliensia, 7.)

An historical study of early Danish music printing, with a chronological listing of Danish prints issued during the period under consideration. Bibliography and index of names.

Review by Martin Geck in *Die Musikforschung*, 18 (1965) p. 346–47.

1193

Davidsson, Åke. "Die Literatur zur Geschichte des Notendruckes." In his *Musikbibliographische Beiträge*. Uppsala, A. B. Lundequistska

Bokhandeln, 1954. P. 91–115. (Uppsala Universitets Arsskrift, 1954:9.)

A survey of writings on the history of music printing, with a bibliography of 268 items.

Superseded by the author's *Bibliographie zur Geschichte des Musikdrucks*, see no. 1191, above.

Review by Edward N. Waters in *Notes*, 12 (1955) p. 604; by Vincent Duckles in *The Library quarterly*, 26 (1956) p. 73–74.

1194

Davidsson, Åke. Studier rörande svenskt musiktryck före år 1750. Studien über schwedischen Musikdruck vor 1750. Uppsala [Almquist & Wiksell] 1957. 167 p. (Studia musicologica upsaliensia, 5.)

Part I (Allmän del) is a general survey of early Swedish music printing. Part II (Speciell del) is a bibliography of 124 Swedish imprints issued between 1585 and 1750, in chronological order. Text in Swedish, summary in German. General bibliography and index of persons.

Review by Rudolph Gjelsness in *Notes*, 15 (1958) p. 569–70.

1195

Day, Cyrus L. and E. B. Murrie. English song-books, 1651–1702; a bibliography with a first-line index of songs. London, Bibliographical Society, 1940 [for 1937] 439 p.

Lists and describes the contents of 252 secular song books published in England and Scotland. Arrangement is chronological, nonextant works included. First-line index of 4,150 songs by about 250 composers. Also indexed by composer, author of text, performer, tunes and airs, sources, titles of collections, printers, publishers, and book-sellers. A model of descriptive bibliography, particularly valuable for its coverage of the publishing activity of John and Henry Playford and their contemporaries.

1196

Deutsch, Otto E. Musikverlags Nummern. Eine Auswahl von 40 datierten Listen. Zweite, verbesserte und erste deutsche ausgabe. Berlin, Merseburger, 1961. 32 p.

Revision and expansion of a list originally published in the *Journal of documentation*, 1 (1946) under the title: "Music publishers' numbers, a selection of 40 dated lists, 1710–1900."

Treats 20 German, 14 Austrian, 3 Dutch, 1 English, 1 French, and 1 Swiss firm. Index of places and individual publishers. Supplemented by the author's "Musikverlags-Nummern, ein Nachtrag," in *Die Musikforschung*, 15 (1962) p. 155.

Review by Donald W. Krummel in *Notes*, 19 (1961) p. 76–77; by Richard Schaal in *Die Musikforschung*, 16 (1963) p. 389.

1197
Dona, Mariangela. La stampa musicale a Milano fino all'anno 1700. Firenze, Olschki, 1961. 167 p. (Biblioteca di bibliografia italiana, 39.)
Milanese music publishers given in alphabetical order, with chronological listings of their publications. Copies of rare works located in major European libraries. Index of composers and works, index of persons to whom works are dedicated.
Review by Richard Schaal in *Die Musikforschung*, 17 (1964) p. 183.

1198
Eitner, Robert. Buch- und Musikalienhändler, Buch- und Musikaliendrucker nebst Notenstecher, nur die Musik betreffend nach den Originaldrucken verzeichnet. . . . Leipzig, Breitkopf & Härtel, 1904. 248 p. (Monatshefte für Musikgeschichte. Beilage.)
Compiled as a by-product of the *Quellen-Lexikon*; limited to material before 1850. Alphabetical listing of publishers, printers, and dealers, their dates of location at various addresses, changes in name, branches if any. International coverage.

1199
Elvers, Rudolf. "Musikdrucker, Musikalienhändler und Musikverleger in Berlin 1750–1850." In *Festschrift Walter Gerstenberg zum 60. Geburtstag*. Wolfenbüttel, Möseler Verlag, 1964. p. 37–44.
Lists 155 Berlin music printers, dealers, and publishers active during the century under consideration.

1200
Fisher, William A. 150 years of music publishing in the U.S.; an historical sketch with special reference to the pioneer publisher, Oliver Ditson Co., 1783–1933. Boston, Oliver Ditson [1934] 156 p.
A revision and extension of portions of the author's *Notes on music in old Boston*. Boston, Mass., 1918.

1201
Gamble, William. Music engraving and printing; historical and technical treatise. . . . London, New York, Pitman, 1923 [1922] 266 p.
Discusses the technical processes of music printing and engraving, with emphasis on contemporary practices. Illustrated.

1202
Gericke, Hannelore. Der Wiener Musikalienhandel von 1700 bis 1778. Graz, H. Böhlaus Nachf., 1960. 150 p. (Wiener musikwissen-schaftliche Beiträge, 5.)

Contents: Wiener Buchhändler als Verkäufer von Musikalien; Privat-verkäufer; Kopisten; Kupferstecher; Verzeichnis der Wiener Musikdrucke von 1700–78; Liste der verbotenen Musikbücher; Zusammenfassung; Literaturverzeichnis.

Review by Donald W. Krummel in *Notes*, 18 (1961) p. 229–30.

1203
Goovaerts, Alphonse J. M. A. Histoire et bibliographie de la typo-graphie musicale dans les Pays-Bas. Anvers, P. Kockx, 1880. 608 p. (Extrait des Mémoires de l'Académie Royale de Belgique, Collection in 8; tome XXIX.)

Reprint issued by Frits A. M. Knuf, Hilversum, 1963.

Part I (historical): a chronological discussion of music publishing in the Netherlands from 1539. Part II (bibliographical): chronological list of 1,415 music publications from 1539 to 1841. Full descriptions. Index of personal names, titles, and places.

1204
Grand-Carteret, John. Les titres illustrés et l'image au service de la musique. Turin, Bocca, 1904. 269 p.

Première partie (p. 3–120): Le titre de musique sous la Révolution, le Consulat et le premier Empire (1500–1800). Deuxième partie: Le titre de musique et la lithographie, 1. 1817–30; 2. 1830–50.

Abundantly illustrated with facsimiles of title pages, printers' devices, and pages of music.

1205
Heartz, Daniel. "La chronologie des recueils imprimés par Pierre Attaingnant." In *Revue de musicologie*, 44 (1959) p. 178–92.

Brief survey of Attaingnant's activity as a music printer, followed by a chronological tabulation of all collections published by him from 1528 to 1537.

1206
Hill, Richard S. "The plate numbers of C. F. Peters' predecessors." In *Papers . . . of the American Musicological Society . . .* Dec. 29 and 30, 1938. [*c.* 1940] p. 113–34.

Surveys the publishing activities of F. A. Hofmeister and A. Kühnel,

[285]

1784–1814, with a detailed analysis of their production in 1801–1802, plate numbers 1–102.

1207

Hopkinson, Cecil. A dictionary of Parisian music publishers, 1700–1950. London, Printed for the author, 1954. 131 p.

Describes some 550 publishers, tabulating their name forms and addresses where they were active during specific periods. A useful tool for determining dates of undated French publications.

Review by Inger M. Christensen in *Notes*, 11 (1954) p. 660–51; by Vincent Duckles in *JAMS*, 8 (1955) p. 62–64.

See no. 1209 for another approach to the dating of 18th-century French music publication.

1208

Humphries, Charles and William C. Smith. Music publishing in the British Isles from the earliest times to the middle of the 19th century; a dictionary of engravers, printers, publishers and music sellers, with a historical introduction. London, Cassell and Co. [1954] 355 p.

Covers more than 2,000 persons and firms associated with British music publishing. An introductory essay of 42 pages gives an excellent survey of the field. Indexes of firms outside London and of makers and repairers of musical instruments. 25 plates.

This volume supersedes the *Kidson*, no. 1211, below.

Review by J. M. Coopersmith in *Notes*, 11 (1954) p. 549–50.

1209

Johansson, Cari. French music publishers' catalogues of the second half of the eighteenth century. Uppsala, Almquist & Wiksell, 1955. 2 v.

Vol. 1 (octavo): Textband. 228 p. Vol. 2 (folio): Tafeln. 145 facsimiles of catalogs by French music publishing houses.

The first volume analyzes and describes the contents of the catalogs and their use for dating purposes. Compare Johansson's method with that of Hopkinson, no 1207, above. Index of names, of titles, and of catalogs chronologically under name of firm.

Review by Donald W. Krummel in *Notes*, 17 (1960) p. 234–35; by A. Hyatt King in *Music and letters*, 37 (1956) p. 376–77; by Wolfgang Schmieder in *Die Musikforschung*, 10 (1957) p. 180–82.

1210

Kast, Paul. "Die Musikdrucke des Kataloges Giunta von 1604." In *Analecta musicologica, Veröffentlichungen der Musikabteilung des Deutschen Historischen Instituts in Rom*, Band 2 (1965) p. 41–71.

Transcribes the music portion of a general catalog issued by the Florentine music dealer and publisher, Giunta, in 1604. Contains masses, motets, and secular works of the late 16th century, as well as a small selection of instrumental and theory works.

1211
Kidson, Frank. British music publishers, printers and engravers . . . from Queen Elizabeth's reign to George IV, with select bibliographical lists of musical works printed and published within that period. London, W. E. Hill & Sons, 1900. 231 p.

The pioneer work on English music publishing. Not as comprehensive as the *Humphries and Smith*, no. 1208, above, but many of Kidson's entries are fuller and are accompanied by lists of publications. Entries arranged alphabetically by place. No index.

1212
King, A. Hyatt. "English pictorial music title-pages, 1820–1885, their style, evolution and importance." In *The Library*, ser. 5: 4 (1949?50) p. 262–72.

1213
King A. Hyatt. Four hundred years of music printing. London, Published by the Trustees of the British Museum, 1964. 48 p.

A short, well-written account of the history of music printing, with a selected bibliography of 29 items on the subject. Illustrated with facsimile pages of early music printing.

1214
Kinkeldey, Otto. "Music and music printing in incunabula." In *Bibliographical Society of America, Papers*, v. 26 (1932) p. 89–118.

For other discussions of music incunabula, see nos. 1227, 1254.

1215
Kinsky, Georg. "Beethoven-Erstdrucke bis zum Jahre 1800." In *Philobiblon*, 3 (1930) p. 329–36.

1216
Kinsky, Georg. "Erstlingsdrücke der deutschen Tonmeister der Klassik und Romantik." In *Philobiblon*, 7 (1934) p. 347–64.

Also printed separately by H. Reichner, Vienna, 1934.

[287]

1217
Kinsky, Georg. Die Originalausgaben der Werke Johann Sebastian Bachs; ein Beitrag zur Musikbibliographie. Wien, H. Reichner [1937] 134 p.

This and the two preceding items are contributions by one of the leading specialists in music printing of the 18th and 19th centuries.

1218
Krummel, Donald W. "Graphic analysis, its application to early American engraved music." In *Notes*, 16 (1959) p. 213–33.

Discussion of the history of early American music publishing in terms of the printing processes used, with special reference to the work of Blake and Willig. 7 plates.

1219
Layer, Adolf. Katalog des Augsburger Verlagers Lotter von 1753. Kassel, Bärenreiter, 1964. 44 p. (Catalogus musicus, 2.)

Facsimile edition of the 1753 catalog of the music publications of the firm of Johann Jacob Lotter in Augsburg. Lists some 370 titles by 170 composers of the late 17th and early 18th centuries. Index and "Nachwort" provided by the editor.

1220
Lenz, Hans U. Der Berliner Musikdruck von seinen Anfängen bis zur Mitte des 18. Jahrhunderts. . . . Kassel, Bärenreiter, 1933. 116 p.

Also issued as a dissertation, Rostock, 1932.

Discussion of the Berlin music printers, their output, their techniques. P. 27–35: chronological listing of 126 prints.

1221
Lesure, François et G. Thibault. Bibliographie des éditions d'Adrian le Roy et Robert Ballard (1551–98). Paris, Société française de musicologie, Heugel et Cie., 1955. 304 p. (Publications de la Société française de musicologie. 2 sér., t.9.)

An exemplary bibliography of 319 musical editions issued by the Le Roy-Ballard press, cited chronologically with full bibliographical descriptions, lists of contents, and locations in public and private collections. Brief historical introduction, and an anthology of the most important prefaces, dedications, and other documents. First-line index of texts, index of titles and personal names. 9 facsimile plates.

Review by Kenneth Levy in *JAMS*, 8 (1955) p. 221–23; by Vincent Duckles in *Notes*, 15 (1957) p. 102–03.

1222

Lesure, François et G. Thibault. "Bibliographie des éditions musicales publiées par Nicolas Du Chemin (1549–1576)." In *Annales musicologiques*, 1 (1953) p. 269–373.

Bibliography similar in scope and format to the preceding work. Covers 100 editions published by Du Chemin, with full descriptions, listings of contents, and locations of copies. Numerous facsimiles of title pages. First-line index of Latin and of French texts, and of titles and names.

1223

Littleton, Alfred H. A catalog of one hundred works illustrating the history of music printing from the 15th to the end of the 17th century, in the library of Alfred H. Littleton. . . . London, Novello, 1911. 38 p. 12 facsimile plates.

Includes both musical and theoretical works, grouped by nationality, with annotations directing attention to their interest as examples of music printing.

1224

Marco, Guy A. The earliest music printers of continental Europe, a checklist of facsimiles illustrating their work. The Bibliographical Society of the University of Virginia, 1962. 20 p.

An index of facsimile plates of the work of early music printers to be found in a variety of music histories, monographs, and other reference works. 101 printers from the late 15th century to 1599 are included.

1225

Meyer, Kathi and Inger M. Christensen. "Artaria plate numbers." In *Notes*, 15 (1942) p. 1–22.

1226

Meyer, Kathi and Eva J. O'Meara. "The printing of music, 1473–1934." In *The Dolphin*, 2 (1935) p. 171–207.

A well-illustrated sketch of the history of music printing. Includes a bibliography of works on the subject.

1227

Meyer-Baer, Kathi. Liturgical music incunabula, a descriptive catalog. London, The Bibliographical Society, 1962. 63 p.

257 entries, arranged alphabetically by title, treating of some 800 items. References made to the standard bibliographies of incunabula and to

locations of copies in major libraries. 12 plates illustrating types of notation. Chronological index, and index of printers and places.

See also the author's preliminary study, "Liturgical music incunabula in the British Museum," in *The Library*, 4th ser., 20 (1939) p. 272–94.

Review, *anon.*, in *The Times literary supplement*, Nov. 16, 1962, p. 880.

1228
Molitor, P. Raphael. "Italienische Choralnotendrucke." In his *Die Nach-Tridentinische Choral-Reform zu Rom*, v. 1, p. 94–119. Leipzig, 1901.

A general discussion of Italian printers of liturgical books of the later 15th and 16th centuries.

1229
Neighbor, Oliver and Alan Tyson. English music publisher's plate numbers in the first half of the 19th century. London, Faber, 1965. 48 p.

1230
Novello (Firm, Music Publishers, London). A century and a half in Soho; a short history of the firm of Novello, publishers and printers of music, 1811–1961. London, Novello [1961] 85 p.

A popular history of the music publishing house that has exercised a wide influence on public taste in England through the printing of inexpensive editions of the classics.

Review by Donald W. Krummel in *Notes*, 19 (1961) p. 60–61; by Richard Schaal in *Die Musikforschung*, 17 (1964) p. 183–84.

1231
Oldman, Cecil B. Collecting musical first editions. London, Constable, 1938. 29 p. (Aspects of book collecting.)

Reprinted from *New Paths in book collecting*, ed. by John Carter, London, 1934. P. 95–124.

An informal and inviting discussion of the pleasures of collecting early music. Bibliography, p. 120–24.

1232
Pattison, Bruce. "Notes on early music printing." In *The Library*, ser. 4, 19:4 (1939) p. 389–421.

1233
Redway, Virginia L. Music directory of early New York City; a file of musicians, music publishers and musical instrument makers listed in N.Y. directories from 1786 through 1835, together with the most

important New York music publishers from 1836 through 1875. . . .
New York, The New York Public Library, 1941. 102 p.

Three main sections: (1) musicians and teachers; (2) publishers, printers,
lithographers, and dealers, with names and addresses as they appeared in
successive years; (3) instrument makers and dealers. Appendices include
chronological list of firms and individuals, 1786–1811, and a list of musical
societies, 1789–99.

1234
Ricordi (Firm, Music Publishers, Milan). Casa Ricordi, 1808–1958;
profile storico a cura di Claudio Sartori. . . . Milano, G. Ricordi, 1958.
116 p. 48 plates.

16 of the plates are facsimile pages of composers' autographs; the
remainder are chiefly reproductions, in color, of cover designs for noteworthy Ricordi music publications.

Review by Donald W. Krummel in *Notes*, 17 (1960) p. 400–401.

1235
Robert, Henri. Traité de gravure de musique sur planches d'étain et
des divers procédés de simili gravure de musique . . . précédé de
l'historique du signe, de l'impression et de la gravure de musique. 2nd éd.
Paris, Chez l'auteur, 1926. 151 p.

First published in 1902.

A rather sketchy historical survey of music writing, printing, and
engraving, followed by a description of the technical processes involved
in preparing engraved plates.

1236
Sartori, Claudio. Bibliografia delle opere musicali stampate de
Ottaviano Petrucci. Firenze, Olschki, 1948. 217 p. (Biblioteca di biblio-
grafia italiana, 18.)

Chronological bibliography of Petrucci's work, with full descriptions,
contents of each publication. Index of titles, lists of libraries and their
holdings of Petrucci prints. Bibliography.

1237
Sartori, Claudio. Dizionario degli editori musicali italiani (tipografi,
incisori, librai-editori). Firenze, Olschki, 1958. 215 p. (Biblioteca di
bibliografia italiana, 32.)

Italian music printers, editors, and publishers from the 16th century to
the present. Some bibliographical references given. The principal issues of

the publishers are noted, but no complete catalogs given. Index of names, but no chronology. 8 plates of early title pages.

Review by Dragan Plamenac in *Notes*, 16 (1959) p. 242–43; by Gerhard Croll in *Die Musikforschung*, 12 (1959) p. 255–56.

1238

Schmid, Anton. Ottaviano dei Petrucci da Fossombrone, erste Erfinder des Musiknotendruckes mit beweglichen Metalltypen, und seine Nachfolger im sechzehnten Jahrhunderte. . . Wien, P. Rohrmann, 1845. 342 p.

Schmid's work on Petrucci has long since been superseded, but the discussion of his successors in Italy, Germany, France, and the Netherlands (p. 111 to end) is still valuable.

1239

Smith, William C. A bibliography of the musical works published by John Walsh during the years 1695–1720. London, The Bibliographical Society, 1948. 215 p. 38 plates.

622 Walsh publications cited for the period under consideration, with numerous descriptive annotations. Index of titles and works, and general index.

Review by J. Coopersmith in *Notes*, 7 (1949) p. 104–106; by A. Hyatt King in *Music and letters*, 30 (1949) p. 273–76.

1240

Steele, Robert. The earliest English music printing; a description and bibliography of English printed music to the close of the 16th century. London, Printed for The Bibliographical Society, 1903. 102 p. (Illustrated monographs, 11.)

Brief introduction covers methods of printing, and includes a chapter on early English printers of music. The bibliography of 197 items is arranged chronologically from 1495 to 1600, giving full title and collation, library locations, and notes on typography. Bibliography of 34 items on music printing.

Reprinted, London, 1965, with a new appendix of *addenda* and *corrigenda*.

1241

Stellfeld, J. A. Bibliographie des éditions musicales plantiniennes. [Bruxelles, Palais des Académies, 1949] 248 p. (Academie royale de Belgique. Classe des beaux-arts. Memoires in 8°, T. 5, fasc. 3.)

Brief historical account of the Plantin press, with detailed bibliographical description and discussion of the 21 music items printed by the press at Antwerp and at Leiden. 21 plates.

Toledo (Ohio). Museum of Art. The printed note. . . .
See no. 1089.

1242
Tyson, Alan. The authentic English editions of Beethoven. London, Faber and Faber, 1963. 152 p.

An important work, one of the first to apply detailed bibliographical analysis to early 19th-century music printing. The author is able to make significant revisions in the chronology of Beethoven's works.

Review by Dagmar von Busch-Weise in *Die Musikforschung*, 17 (1964) p. 443–44; by Albi Rosenthal in *Music and letters*, 45 (1964) p. 256–58.

1243
Vol'man, B. Russkie pechatnye noty XVIII veka. Leningrad, Gosudarstvennoe muzykal'noe izdatel'stvo, 1957. 293 p.

Russian printed music of the 18th century.

1244
Weinmann, Alexander. Beiträge zur Geschichte des altwiener Musikverlages, 1948– .

A series of studies related to Viennese music publishing of the late 18th and early 19th centuries. They appear under varied imprints and in two subseries: Reihe 1, *Komponisten*; Reihe 2, *Verleger*. The volumes are listed below in series order.

1245
Reihe 1, Folge 1: Verzeichnis der im Druck erschienenen Werke von Joseph Lanner, sowie Listen der Plattennummern der Originalausgaben für alle Besetzungen. . . . Wien, Leuen [1948] 31 p.

Tables listing the work of Lanner (1801–43) in opus number order, with plate numbers of the first editions. Alphabetical index of works by title.

1246
Reihe 2, Folge 1: Verzeichnis der Verlagswerke des Musikalischen Magazins in Wien, 1784–1802. "Leopold Kozeluch." Ein bibliographischer Behelf. Wien, Österreichischer Bundesverlag [1950] 31 p.

Works without plate numbers, and with questionable plate numbers, in chronological order; works with plate number in numerical order, followed by an alphabetical list, by composer, of Kozeluch's catalog, 1800.

1247

Reihe 2, Folge 2: Vollständiges Verlagsverzeichnis Artaria & Comp. Wien, Ludwig Krenn [1952] 179 p.

A history of the Artaria firm, with a classified list, chronological within classifications, of its publications, giving in most cases exact dates of publication. Index by composers.

Review by Richard S. Hill in *Notes*, 10 (1953) p. 449–50.

1248

Reihe 2, Folge 3: "Vollständiges Verlagsverzeichnis des Musikalien des Kunst- und Industrie Comptoirs in Wien, 1801–1819." In *Studien zur Musikwissenschaft; Beihefte der DTOe*, 22 (1955) p. 217–52.

Contains a listing of 802 plate numbers in numerical order, with composer, title, and date of publication of the corresponding works. Composer index.

Review by William Klenz in *Notes*, 14 (1956) p. 117.

1249

Reihe 2, Folge 4: "Verzeichnis der Musikalien des Verlages Johann Traeg in Wien, 1794–1818." In *Studien zur Musikwissenschaft; Beihefte der DTOe*, 23 (1956) p. 135–83.

Lists all works published by the firm, in chronological order.

1250

Reihe 2, Folge 5: Wiener Musikverleger und Musikalienhändler von Mozarts Zeit bis gegen 1860; ein firmengeschichtlicher und topographischer Behelf. Wien, Rohrer, 1956. 72 p. (Österreichische Akademie der Wissenschaft . . . Veröff. der Kommission für Musikforschung, 2.)

Lists and discusses 38 music dealers and publishers, and 19 related general book dealers and publishers. Tables showing early and existing addresses of the firms. Useful in dating Viennese musical imprints.

Review by Richard S. Hill in *Notes*, 15 (1958) p. 396–97.

1251

Reihe 2, Folge 6: Verzeichnis der Musikalien aus dem K. K. Hoftheater-Musik-Verlag. Wien, Universal [1961] 130 p. (Wiener Urtext Ausgabe.)

Brief history of the firm and biographical notes on the men associated with it. List of publications from 1796 to *c.* 1820, with plate numbers and dates of issue if known.

Review by Donald W. Krummel in *Notes*, 19 (1961) p. 76.

1252

Reihe 2, Folge 7: Kataloge Anton Huberty (Wien) und Christoph Torricella. Wien, Universal, 1962. 135 p.

Brief histories of the firms, followed by detailed listings of their publications, giving composer, title, date of publication if known, location of copies in European libraries.

Review by Richard Schaal in *Die Musikforschung*, 18 (1965) p. 83.

1253

Reihe 2, Folge 8: Die wiener Verlagswerke von Franz Anton Hofmeister. Wien, Universal, 1964. 252 p.

Contains a biography Hofmeister; a dated list of plate numbers; entries, largely thematic, for all of the firm's publications; brief historical discussions of aspects of the firm's history.

1254

Wolf, Johannes. "Verzeichnis der musiktheoretischen Inkunabeln mit Fundorten." In Caza, Francesco, *Tractato vulgare de canto figurato*. . . . (Veröffentlichungen der Musik-bibliothek Paul Hirsch, 1.) Berlin, M. Breslauer, 1922. P. 64–92.

Wolf lists 104 incunabula in the field of music theory, with locations where copies are preserved, as a supplement to his edition of Caza's treatise.

1255

Zur Westen, Walter von. Musiktitel aus vier Jahrhunderten; Festschrift anlässlich der 57 jährigen Bestehens der Firma C. G. Röder. Leipzig, [1921] 116 p.

A study of musical title pages from the Renaissance to the end of the 19th century, with 96 facsimile illustrations.

Discographies

WITHIN the last few decades the field of recorded sound has given rise to an abundance of documentation of interest to librarians, teachers, research scholars, and private collectors. It is an area that has a particular attraction for the collector, whether his interests lie in early vocal discs or cylinders, or in jazz recordings. There has been a proliferation of record reviews, listeners' guides, manufacturers' catalogs and numerical lists, and journals devoted almost exclusively to discography. Some indication of the scope and variety of the bibliographical coverage is suggested by "A bibliography of discographies," by Carl L. Brunn and John Gray in *Recorded sound, Journal of the British Institute of Recorded Sound* (Summer 1962, p. 206–13). A field of this kind requires its own guide to reference materials. No effort has been made here to list more than a few representative examples of the major types of reference tools available to the specialist in recorded sound.

In the organization following, "Encyclopedias of recorded music" have been distinguished from "Collectors' guides." The distinction is perhaps an arbitrary one, but it is intended to separate the few comprehensive discographies from those directed toward the interests of collectors of classical music, jazz records, or early discs.

Encyclopedias of Recorded Music

1256
Clough, Francis F. and G. J. Cuming. The world's encyclopedia of recorded music. London, Sidgwick & Jackson, 1952. 890 p.

First Supplement (April, 1950 to May–June, 1951) bound with the main volume.

Second Supplement (1951–52) London, 1952. 262 p.

Third Supplement (1953–55) London, 1957. 564 p.

The World's encyclopedia is an indispensable reference tool for record specialists. Arrangement is alphabetical by composer, with a subclassification of works under prolific composers. Full information given as to content and labels. Special section for anthologies.

Review by Philip Miller in *Notes*, 10 (1952) p. 94–95; of the *Third Supplement* by Richard S. Hill in *Notes*, 14 (1957) p. 357–59.

1257

Gramophone Shop, Inc., New York. The Gramophone Shop encyclopedia of recorded music. New York, The Gramophone Shop, Inc., 1936. 574 p.

Compiled by R. D. Darrell. 2nd ed., New York, Simon & Schuster, 1942; George C. Leslie, Supervising editor. 558 p. 3rd ed., rev. and enl., New York, Crown, 1948; Robert H. Reid, Supervising editor. 639 p.

The prototype for all encyclopedias of recorded music in its organization and coverage. Works arranged alphabetically under composer and partially classified. Brief biographical accounts of composers. All three volumes must be consulted, since the later editions are not fully cumulative. Coverage restricted to 78 rpm discs.

1258

Johnson, William W. The gramophone book, a complete guide for all lovers of recorded music. London, Hinrichsen [1954] 169 p.

A compendium of miscellaneous information useful to record collectors. British emphasis. Lacks an index.

1259

Myers, Kurtz and Richard S. Hill. Record ratings, the Music Library Association's index of record reviews. New York, Crown Publishers, 1956. 440 p.

> *Record ratings* is essentially a guidebook pointing the way to a tremendous body of critical writing about recordings (Preface).

Two main sections: (1) composer and subject list; (2) composite releases. By means of a system of symbols, the user is given a summary of critical opinion concerning the discs. Full descriptions of each recording, including composer, title, label, number, and price. Contents list for composite recordings. The editors have taken great pains to clarify and verify information about the discs and their contents. This is a major reference work in the field of discography. See also the current listings which appear in each issue of *Notes* under the heading, "Index of record reviews." (See no. 1298.)

Collectors' Guides to Classical Music

Books of this kind, of which there are an increasing number, can be described as compilations of brief record reviews in which observations on the technical quality of the recordings are combined with comments on the work recorded and on its performance. The listings below are confined to the more comprehensive English-language works in this category. Specialized collectors' guides are available in abundance. See, for example, the useful set of paperback editions published by J. B. Lippincott in the series, *Keystone books in Music* including: Cornelius G. Burke, *The collector's Haydn* [1959] 316 p.; John Briggs, *The collector's Tchaikowsky and the five* [1959]; Harold C. Schonberg, *The collector's Chopin and Schumann* [1959] 256 p., etc.

1260

Coover, James B. and Richard Colvig. Medieval and Renaissance music on long-playing records. [Detroit, Information Service, Inc.] 1964. 122 p. (Detroit studies in music bibliography, 6.)

A well organized guide to the recorded resources in Medieval and Renaissance music. 322 anthologies are analyzed, with numerous discs containing works by individual composers. Performer index. *First supplement*, bound in, extends the coverage through 1961.

1261

The Guide to Long Playing Records. New York, Knopf, 1955. 3 v.

Vol. 1: Irving Kolodin. *Orchestral music.* 268 p. Vol. 2: Philip L. Miller. *Vocal music.* 381 p. Vol. 3: Harold C. Schonberg. *Chamber and solo instrument music.* 280 p.

1262

Hall, David. The record book, a music lover's guide to the world of the phonograph. New York, Smith & Durrell, 1940. 771 p.

Supplement. 1941. (Continuing pagination, 777–886.)

Second supplement. 1943. (Continuing pagination, 887–1,013.)

Complete edition. New York, Citadel Press, 1946. 1,063 p. Incorporates the two preceding supplements.

1263

Hall, David. The record book. International edition. New York, Durrell, 1948. 1,394 p.

1264

Hall, David. Records: 1950 edition. New York, Knopf, 1950. 524 p. Hall's books are addressed to the private collector with an interest in serious music. In the earlier editions the material is classified by medium. Beginning with the *International edition* (above) the arrangement is alphabetical by composer. Much general information for the record collector is included. The 1950 edition is the first to direct attention to long-playing discs.

1265
Kolodin, Irving. A guide to recorded music. Garden City, N.Y., Doubleday, 1941. 495 p.

1266
Kolodin, Irving. New guide to recorded music. Rev. ed. Garden City, N.Y., Doubleday, 1947. 512 p.

1267
Kolodin, Irving. New guide to recorded music. International edition. Garden City, N.Y., Doubleday, 1950.
Kolodin has adhered to an alphabetical arrangement by composer, with classification by form and medium under composer. Index of performers and performing groups.

1268
Sackville-West, Edward and D. Shawe-Taylor. The record guide. London, Collins, 1951. 763 p.

1269
Sackville-West Edward and D. Shawe-Taylor. The record guide . . . with Andrew Porter and William Mann. Rev. ed. London, Collins [1955] 957 p.
Supplement [1956] 191 p.

1270
Sackville-West, Edward and D. Shawe-Taylor. The record year, a guide to the year's gramophone records, including a complete guide to long playing records. Assisted by Andrew Porter. London, Collins [1952] 383 p.
The Sackville-West guides are designed for British record collectors. The commentary is literate and well informed. The discs are arranged by composer, with special sections devoted to collections, and a performer index.

1271

The Stereo Record Guide. By Edward Greenfield, Ivan March, and Denis Stevens. London, The Long Playing Record Library, Ltd., 1960–63. 3 v.

The main arrangement for each volume is by composer, followed by special sections devoted to concerts, recitals, light music, etc. Vol. 1 contains a selection of 50 outstanding records for 1958/59; Vol. 2, a selection of 100 outstanding records for 1960/61. The third volume supplements the two preceding, but it re-lists the important recordings from the earlier books, with page references to earlier commentary. The guide is distinguished by its intelligent, highly readable annotations. A fourth volume is projected.

Collectors' Guides to Early Recordings

The field of discs and cylinder recordings of the period from 1898 to 1925 has long been the province of private collectors. Emphasis is usually placed on the performer, particularly the vocalist, rather than on the composer. Recently the importance of collecting in this area has been recognized on a larger scale by libraries and research institutions throughout the world, as, for example, The New York Public Library, The Library of Congress, The British Institute of Recorded Sound, The Stanford University Archive of Recorded Sound, etc.

1272

Bauer, Robert. The new catalogue of historical records, 1898–1908/09. London, Sidgwick and Jackson [1947] 494 p.

Recordings listed under performer, grouped under label and year of pressing. Serial numbers given. Brief entries for composer and title of work.

1273

Bennett, John R. Voices of the past, a catalogue of vocal recordings from the English catalogues of The Gramophone Company 1898–99, The Gramophone Company Limited 1899–1900, The Gramophone & Typewriter Company Limited 1901–1907, and the Gramophone Company Limited 1907–25. [V. 1, pt. 1.] [Lingfield, Surrey, The Oakwood Press, 1955?–] 48 p.

Projected as the beginning of a series intended to cover the complete catalog of H. M. V. vocal recordings of 1898–1925.

1274

Deakins, Duane D. Cylinder records; a description of the numbering systems, physical appearance, and other aspects of cylinder records made

[301]

by the major American companies, with brief remarks about the earliest American companies and the foreign record manufacturers. [2nd ed.] Stockton, Calif. [1958] 35 p.

1275
Girard, Victor and Harold M. Barnes. Vertical-cut cylinders and discs; a catalogue of all "hill-and-dale" recordings of serious worth made and issued between 1897–1932 circa. London, British Institute of Recorded Sound, 1964. 196 p.

A major contribution to the discography of early recordings. Arranged in three major categories: (1) vocal recordings; (2) speech recordings; (3) instrumental and orchestral records; with appendices devoted to complete operas and to anonymous Pathé discs. Approach is mainly by performer.

1276
Hurst, P. G. The golden age recorded. New and revised edition. The Oakwood Press, 1963. 187 p.

First published by Sidgwick and Jackson, London, 1946.

A manual for private collectors. General discussions of record collecting, followed by biographical notices of the major artists classified by voice. Appendix, p. 147–87: a selected list of important early recordings, by performer.

1277
Moses, Julian M. Collector's guide to American recordings, 1895–1925; foreword by Giuseppe de Luca. New York, American Record Collectors' Exchange [1949] 199 p.

Discs arranged under performers by serial or matrix number. P. 172–95: numerical guide, Columbia and other labels. Index of operas, and instrumental index.

1278
Moses, Julian M. Price guide to collectors' records. New York, American Record Collectors' Exchange [1952] 31 p.

Discs identified by matrix number under performer, with estimates of value on the current market. Designed to accompany the preceding work.

Collectors' Guides to Jazz Recordings

The jazz record collector lives in a world of his own and is well equipped with reference tools designed to meet his needs. The impetus toward documentation has come from European rather than American enthusiasts: see Delaunay and

Panassié below. Most of the periodicals devoted to popular music include jazz record reviews and print occasional discographies of jazz musicians.

1279
Carey, David A. and Albert J. McCarthy. The directory of recorded jazz and swing music. London, Cassel, 1950– .
Cover title: *Jazz directory.* Vols. 2–4 have appeared in 2nd editions, 1955–57.
An alphabetical listing of performers and ensembles, with detailed information as to their recorded output. Informative annotations.
The work has progressed through 6 volumes (as of 1957), paged continuously through p. 1,112, as far as the entry "Longshaw."

1280
Delaunay, Charles. New hot discography, the standard dictionary of recorded jazz. Edited by Walter E. Schaap and George Avakian. New York, Criterion, 1948. 608 p.
First published in France in 1936.
Separates the "pioneers of jazz" from "post-1930 jazz." Subdivided by region. An elaborate classification system groups recordings by major jazz personalities. Complete index of names.

1281
Harris, Rex and Brian Rust. Recorded jazz. [Harmondsworth, Middlesex.] Penguin Books, 1958. 256 p. (Pelican Books A417.)

> It must not be regarded as a comprehensive discography, but nevertheless the authors have presented a reasonable cross-section of real jazz, together with biographical notes of performers and a critical assessment of the records listed (Preface).

1282
Lange, Horst H. Die deutsche Jazz-Discographie. Eine Geschichte des Jazz auf Schallplatten von 1902 bis 1955. Berlin, Bote & Bock, 1955. 652 p.
One of several recent European compilations of jazz records. Includes a number of English and Continental performers.

1283
McCarthy, Albert J. Jazz discography 1: an international discography of recorded jazz, including blues, gospel, and rhythm-and-blues for the year January–December 1958. London, Cassell, 1960. 271 p.
The first volume of a projected yearbook to cover all jazz recordings issued throughout the world. New releases are listed alphabetically by

country. Full contents of each disc listed, with personnel, place, and date of recording if known.

1284

Panassié, Hughes. Discographie critique des meilleurs disques de jazz. Paris, Robert Laffont [1958] 621 p.

An earlier edition, Paris, Corrêa, 1951. 371 p.

The author is a prolific writer on jazz and one of the first important discographers in the field. Arrangement is by performer, with an analytical index by medium and an index of names.

1285

Rust, Brian. Jazz records A–Z, 1897–1931. 2nd ed. [Hatch End, Middlesex, Eng., 1961] 736 p.

Jazz records: A–Z; 1932–1942. 1965. 680 p.

Performers and ensembles listed alphabetically, with their recordings identified by matrix numbers and titles. Introduction and preliminary listing of record labels. Index of names.

1286

Smith, Charles E. The jazz record book . . . with Frederic Ramsey, Jr., Charles Payne Rogers and William Russell. New York, Smith and Durrell, 1942. 515 p.

P. 1–125: a survey of the history of jazz in its various regional styles. P. 130–508: record listings by major performers and ensembles, with critical and descriptive commentary. Selected bibliography of jazz; index of bands.

Ethnic and Folk Music

The use of recorded materials is basic to the techniques of modern ethnomusicology. Here the scholar is concerned less with commercially recorded discs and tapes than he is with recordings made in the field by research institutions and by individual collectors. The problem of bringing these diverse materials under "bibliographical control" is a difficult one. A good start has been made with the cooperation of UNESCO in two series published under the general title, *Archives of recorded music.* Series B is concerned with Oriental music; *Series C*, with ethographical and folk music. (*Series A*, not under consideration here, is devoted to Occidental music, and has produced a general discography of the works of Frederic Chopin.)

1287
**Archives of Recorded Music (Archives de la Musique Enregistrée).
Series B: Oriental Music.** A catalogue of recorded classical and tradi-
tional Indian music. General discography and introduction by Alain
Danielou. Paris, UNESCO [1952] 236 p.

The main organization is by region, subdivided by instrumental and
vocal music, and listed under the performing artists. Chapter V is devoted
to the songs of Rabindranath Tagore. Index of names. Bilingual (English–
French).

1288
**Archives of Recorded Music. . . . Series C: Ethnographical and
Folk Music.** 1. Collection Phonothèque Nationale (Paris). Catalogue
prepared by the International Commission on Folk Arts and Folklore.
Paris, UNESCO [1952] 254 p.

Lists 4,564 discs in groups as acquired by the Phonothèque. Recordings
for any particular national group are scattered throughout the volume.
There is an index of countries, however. Bilingual (French–English).

1289
**Archives of Recorded Music. . . . Series C: Ethnographical and
Folk Music.** 2. Collection Musée de l'Homme (Paris). Catalogue pre-
pared by the International Commission on Folk Arts and Folklore. Paris,
UNESCO [1952] 74 p.

Catalog of a collection of 1,007 recordings, chiefly made in the field in
various parts of Asia and Africa. Grouped under the name of the collector
or expedition.

1290
**Archives of Recorded Music. . . . Series C: Ethnographical and
Folk Music.** 3. Katalog der europäischen Volksmusik im Schallarchiv
des Instituts für Musikforschung Regensburg . . . Bearbeitet von Felix
Hoerburger. Regensburg, Gustav Bosse [1952] 189 p.

Material grouped by country and province.

1291
**Archives of Recorded Music. . . . Series C: Ethnographical and
Folk Music.** 4. International catalogue of recorded folk music. . . . Edited
by Norman Fraser, with a preface by R. Vaughan Williams and introduction by Maud Karpeles. Prepared and published for UNESCO by the
International Folk Music Council in association with Oxford Univ. Press,
1954. 201 p.

[305]

Part I: "Commercial records," a listing of the commercially recorded discs of ethnic and folk music, arranged by continent and by country. Part II: "Recordings held by institutions," a survey of the major collections of ethnic and folk music in libraries and research institutions throughout the world. Statistical summary of their holdings; addresses, names of chief administrators.

1292

Hickmann, Hans et Charles Grégoire Duc de Mecklembourg. Catalogue d'enregistrements de musique folklorique Égyptienne. Strasbourg, Heitz, 1958. 78 p. (Collection d'études musicologiques, 37.)

Description and analysis of the contents of a recorded collection of Egyptian folk music assembled in 1955. 211 items. Preceded by a discussion of the music and instruments employed.

1293

Lumpkin, Ben G. and N. L. McNeil. Folksongs on records. . . . Issue three, cumulative, including essential material in issues one and two. Boulder, Colorado, Folksongs on Records, 1950. 98 p.

Lists 700 commercially recorded discs and albums of folksong and folk music, chiefly American. Contents of discs given, with informal annotations. Useful indexes to English and Scottish ballads, spirituals, work songs, Irish songs, Mexican and Latin-American songs; numerical list of albums.

1294

U.S. Library of Congress. Division of Music. Archive of American Folk Song. Check-list of recorded songs in the English language in the Archive . . . to July 1940. Washington, D.C., Library of Congress, Division of Music, 1942. 3 v. in 1.

A guide to the holdings of one of the world's great folk song collections. Songs listed by title, with name of singer, collector, and date of recording. The 3rd volume is a geographical index.

1295

U.S. Library of Congress. Music Division. Recording Laboratory. Folk music: a catalog of folk songs, ballads, dances, instrumental pieces, and folk tales of the United States and Latin-America on phonograph records. Washington, D.C., Library of Congress [1964] 107 p.

Earlier listings of the same nature appeared in 1948, 1953 and 1959.

A catalog of recordings available for purchase from the Archive of

American Folk Song at the Library of Congress. Presents a sampling of American folk music and tales recorded for the most part of their native environment.

Current or Annual

Current listings and record review are in abundant supply. There are periodicals, such as *High fidelity*, the *American record guide*, and *The Gramophone*, devoted exclusively to the interests of record collectors. Other literary or professional journals, such as *The Saturday review*, *The Nation*, and the *Library journal*, have regular departments of record reviews and comment. See the list of periodicals indexed in *Record ratings*, no. 1259. For a description of some 30 foreign periodicals devoted to recordings, see no. 478.

1296
Gramophone Shop, Inc., Record Supplement. V. 1:1 (Jan., 1938)—v. 17:2 (Feb., 1954).

Title varies: 1939, *Record reviews*. (Cover title: *Record supplement*.)

Extensively annotated listing of the major releases in the field of serious music. Confined chiefly to 78 rpm discs. A monthly publication.

1297
High Fidelity Record Annual. 1955– . Edited by Roland Gelatt. Philadelphia, J. B. Lippincott, 1955– .

Title varies: from 1957, *Records in review*. Great Barrington, Mass., The Wyeth Press. Editor, 1957: Joan Griffiths. Editor, 1958–60: Frances Newbury.

A yearly compilation of reviews from *High fidelity* magazine. Recordings arranged alphabetically by composer, with a section on "Collections and miscellany." Signed reviews by *High fidelity* contributors.

1298
"Index of Record Reviews, with symbols indicating opinions of reviewers." In *Notes*, 5—(March, 1948)— .

Since its inception, a regular feature of *Notes*. Compiled chiefly by Kurtz Myers with the assistance of various specialists from time to time. One cumulative volume appeared in 1956 (see no. 1259). A valuable guide to record selection for libraries and for private collectors.

1299
Polart Index to Record Reviews. Detroit, Polart, 1960– .

An annual publication indexing all record and tape reviews published

[307]

in the major journals. No evaluations, but the length of the review is indicated. Main entries under composer, with separate sections for collections, and for "pop and jazz" recordings.

1300

Schwann Long Playing Record Catalog, monthly guide to mono and stereo records. [Boston, Mass., W. Schwann, Inc.] 1949–   .

The standard guide to long playing records currently available for retail purchase. The May issue of each year is an "Artist's issue" in which the entries are under performers; otherwise the entries are under composer, with special sections devoted to collections, spoken and miscellaneous, musical shows, folk music, popular music, etc.

Specialized Discographies

1301

American Music on Records. A catalogue of recorded American music currently available. Prepared in cooperation with the Committee on Recordings of American Music of the National Music Council. New York, American Music Center [1956] 39 p.

A composer listing in alphabetical order, with references to published scores and parts if available.

1302

American Society of Composers, Authors and Publishers. 40 years of show tunes, the big Broadway hits from 1917–57. New York, ASCAP [1958] 149 p.

Chronological list of recorded show tunes arranged alphabetically under year of production. Composer, publisher, performing artist, and record number given. Title index.

1303

Cohn, Arthur. The collector's twentieth-century music in the Western Hemisphere. Philadelphia, Lippincott [1961] 256 p. (Keystone books in music, KB-23.)

One of the best discographies of contemporary music. Well annotated; full coverage for American composers.

1304

Cohn, Arthur. Twentieth-century music in Western Europe, the compositions and the recordings. Philadelphia & New York, J. B. Lippincott [1965] 510 p.

Part I, p. 3–345: discussion of the compositions of 30 contemporary European composers. Part II, p. 349–510: entries for the recordings of the works discussed in the preceding section. The records are graded from "poor" to "exceptional" in performance quality. The annotations in this section are devoted almost entirely to observations on performance.

1305
Davies, Hugh. A discography of electronic music and musique concrète. In *Recorded sound, journal of the British Institute of Recorded Sound,* No. 14 (April, 1964) p. 205–24.

Fully annotated listings of records and tapes; addresses of distributors and index of compositions.

1306
International Roman Catholic Association for Radiodiffusion and Television. Catalogue du disque de musique religieuse. Préf. de J. Schneuwly; introd. de Jean-Michel Hayoz. Edité par UNDA, Association catholique internationale pour la radiodiffusion et la télévision. Freibourg [1956] 300 p.

Yearbooks

PUBLICATIONS appearing under the title "Yearbook" can take a variety of forms. They may be annual volumes issued by learned societies, as, for example, the Spanish *Anuario musical*, the British *Proceedings of the Royal Musical Association*, the Swiss *Schweizerisches Jahrbuch für Musikwissenschaft* or the *Jahrbuch für Liturgik und hymnologie*. They may be annual volumes issued by music publishing houses such as C. F. Peters, Simrock, or Breitkopf & Härtel; or they may be publications of societies devoted to the work of a particular composer, as, for example, *Bach Jahrbuch*, *Handel Jahrbuch*, *Mozart Jahrbuch*, or *Haydn Jahrbuch*. Finally, they may be directories or compilations of factual information covering a specific year. Works of this kind have been emphasized in the following, highly selective list. Yearbooks in this sense are often useful for reference purposes, since they provide data on current musical activities and personalities difficult to find elsewhere.

1307
Annuario del Teatro Lirico Italiano, 1940– . Pubblicazione ufficiale della Federazione Nazionale Facista dei Lavoratori dello Spettacolo. Milano, Edizioni Corbaccio, 1940– . (737 p.)

A compendium of facts related to the Italian lyric theater, including opera companies, legal aspects, theaters, artists (with portraits), index of interpreters for the standard repertory, instrumentalists, statistics on performances.

1308
Hindrichsen's Musical Year Book, 1944– . London, Hinrichsen Edition Ltd., 1944– . 11 vols. to 1961.

A series of volumes edited by Max Hinrichsen, issued at irregular intervals, remarkably varied in content. The articles range from trivia to substantial contributions by recognized authorities. Most of the volumes contain bibliographies of current music publications, as well as numerous lists, illustrations, chronologies. More recent volumes have been organized about some central theme, i.e. Vol. 8, "The organ of Bach and matters related to this subject" (1956); Vol. 9, "John Gay and the Ballad Opera"

[311]

(1956); Vol. 10, "Organ and choral aspects and prospects" (1958). Vol. 11 (1961) contains the papers read at the Joint Congress of the International Association of Music Libraries and the Galpin Society, Cambridge, 1959.

1309
Jahrbuch der Musikwelt. The yearbook of the music world. Annuarie du monde musical. 1. Jahrgang, 1949–50. Bayreuth, Verlag Julius Steeger, 1949. 696 p.

Only one volume published. Contains a vast amount of information regarding musicians and musical institutions throughout the world. Contents include a classified listing of German music dissertations, 1885–1948, a chronology of music dictionaries and encyclopedias, a list of European music periodicals, 1945–48, a bibliography of German music and writings on music, etc.

1310
Musical America. [Annual directory or annual booking edition] New York, Music Publications, Ltd.

A special annual issue devoted chiefly to advertising performing artists, but editions in recent years contain many special articles and lists.

1311
The Musician's Guide; the directory of the world of music. 1954– . New York, Music Information Service.

A classified directory of names connected with all phases of commercial music activity.

Review of the 1957 issue by Richard S. Hill in *Notes,* 14 (1957) p. 111–13.

1312
The Music Magazine/Musical Courier. The annual directory of the concert world. 1963– . Evanston, Ill., Summy-Birchard Co.

Editions for 1957–61 published as the mid-January issue of *Musical courier,* with title: *Directory issue of the musical arts and artists.*

The 1963 issue, edited by Max D. Jones, contains pertinent information on American and foreign music organizations, artist and concert managers, artist availability, current series and associations, orchestras, opera booking organizations, festivals, foundations, schools of music, publishers, periodicals, recording firms, and music dealers.

1313
Opera Annual. Edited by Harold Rosenthal. No. 1– . London, Jahn Calder, 1953/54– .

Articles on aspects of the opera world during the current year. Attention focused on developments in Great Britain.

1314
Pierre Key's Music Year Book, the standard music annual, 1924–38. New York, Pierre Key, Inc., 1925–38. 6 v.
A directory of musical organizations and musicians, chiefly performers; issued irregularly over a period of 13 years. The earlier volumes are international in scope, the later are restricted to U.S. coverage.

1315
The Purchaser's Guide to the Music Industries. Annual edition, 1897– . New York, The Music Trades, 1897– .
Title varies: after 1958, *Directory issue.* . . .
Annual classified directory of instrument manufacturers, music publishers, engravers and printers, retail music stores, dealers in music merchandise, etc. Excludes performers and performing groups.

1316
The Year in American Music, 1946/47—1947/48. New York, Allen, Towne & Heath [1947–48] 2 v.
1946/47 edited by Julius Bloom; 1947/48, by David Ewen.
The first part of each volume is a chronological survey of the important musical events of the year; this is followed by a miscellany of factual information, biographical and bibliographical.

1317
The Year's Work in Music, 1947/48—1950/51. Edited by Alan Frank. London, New York, Published for the British Council by Longmans, Green & Co., 1948–51. 3 v.
Each volume contains a series of essays by various specialists on aspects of British musical life during the year: musical research, the making and playing of instruments, the British Broadcasting Corporation and contemporary music, etc. Contains an annual bibliography of published music and musical literature compiled by A. Hyatt King.

Miscellaneous
Bibliographical Tools

IN this section the few existing bibliographies of music bibliography are listed, together with a selected group of statements concerning the nature and current status of the field of music bibliography. The principal codes for cataloging music have been included, as well as the major guides to music library practice. Among the remaining miscellany will be found several works concerned with the vexing problem of music copyright. See nos. 1362, 1364, 1365.

1318

Allen, Warren D. "Bibliography of literature concerning the general history of music in chronological order." In his *Philosophies of music history.* New York, American Book Co., 1939. P. 343–65. Also issued in paperback, New York, Dover, 1962.

317 titles arranged chronologically from 1600 to 1939. Not all can be described as histories in the modern sense, but they have bearing on the development of music historiography.

1319

Besterman, Theodore. "Music." In his *A World bibliography of bibliographies* . . . 4th ed. Lausanne, Societas Bibliographica, 1965–66. vol. 3, col. 4052–4123. The entries under "Music" in this great standard bibliographical tool are particularly illuminating. The user should also consult entries under "Musical instruments," "Opera" and "Song" as well as the names of specific musicians.

1320

Bobillier, Marie (Michel Brenet, *pseud.*). "Bibliographie des bibliographies musicales." In *L'Année musicale*, 3 (1913) p. 1–152.

One of the first, and still one of the few, specialized bibliographies of music bibliography. Outdated but still useful. Lists general works, including periodical articles, by author; individual bibliographies; catalogs of libraries; catalogs of dealers and publishers.

1321

The British Catalogue of Music Classification. Compiled for the Council of the British National Bibliography, Ltd., by E. J. Coates. Published by the Council of the British National Bibliography, Ltd., British Museum, London, 1960. 56 p.

The classification scheme developed for use in *The British Catalogue of Music*. See no. 644.

1322

Bryant, Eric Thomas. Music. [London] Clive Bingley [1965] 84 p.

A short, practical guide to music documentation and reference work; designed for English students preparing to take a degree in librarianship.

1323

Bryant, Eric Thomas. Music librarianship; a practical guide. London, James Clarke [1959] 503 p.

Part I, p. 3–285: discussion of the administration, services, and technical processes of music libraries. Part II, p. 289–450: a series of annotated bibliographies of basic materials, chiefly scores, for a public library collection. The emphasis is on British practices.

Review by Rita Benton in *Notes*, 17 (1960) p. 397–98.

1324

Code International de Catalogage de la Musique. I. Der Autoren-Katalog der Musikdrucke. The author catalog of published music. [By] Franz Grasberger. Trans. by Virginia Cunningham. Frankfurt/London, C. F. Peters, 1961. 53 p.

Review by Richard S. Angell in *Notes*, 15 (1957) p. 110–11.

1325

Code International de Catalogage de la Musique. II. Code restreint. Redigé per Yvette Féderov. Kurzgefasste Anleitung. Limited code. Ubersetzung von Simone Wallon. Trans. by Virginia Cunningham. Frankfurt/London, C. F. Peters, 1961. 53 p.

This and the preceding volume are the result of the work of the Commission on Music Cataloging of the International Association of Music Libraries. Later volumes projected include a complete code and a code for cataloging music manuscripts.

Review of Vol. II by Minnie Elmer in *Notes*, 19 (1961) p. 247–49; by Richard Schaal in *Die Musikforschung*, 17 (1964) p. 295–6.

[316]

1326
Coover, James B. "The current status of music bibliography." In *Notes*, 13 (1956) p. 581–93.

A survey of the accomplishments, progress, and lacunae in the field of music bibliography as of 1956. The paper takes its point of departure from A. Hyatt King's statement in *The Library* (1945). See no. 1344, below.

1327
Coover, James B. Music lexicography, including a study of lacunae in music lexicography and a bibliography of music dictionaries. Denver, Bibliographical Center for Research, Denver Public Library, 1958, 126 p.

The 2nd edition of the author's *A bibliography of music dictionaries.* Denver, 1952.

The most comprehensive bibliography available of music dictionaries. 1,335 items, including all known editions of the works cited. Preceded by a general discussion of the history of music lexicography and of existing lacunae.

Review by Irene Millen in *Notes*, 16 (1959) p. 383–84.

1328
Currall, Henry F. J. Phonograph record libraries, their organization and practice . . . with a preface by A. Hyatt King. Hamden, Conn., Archon Books, 1963. 183 p. (Pub. for The International Association of Music Libraries.)

Review by Donald L. Leavitt in *Notes*, 20 (1963) p. 648–50.

1329
Detroit Studies in Music Bibliography. No. 1– . Detroit, Information Service Ic., 1961– .

A series of manuals, diverse in character and content, but each concerned with some aspect or area of music bibliography.

1330
No. 1: *Reference materials in ethnomusicology,* by Bruno Nettl. 1961. 46 p.

A bibliographic essay on primitive, oriental, and folk music, which organizes, describes, and evaluates books and articles on the subjects. Also entered as no. 534.

Review by William Lichtenwanger in *Notes*, 19 (1962) p. 428–30.

1331
No. 2: *Sir Arthur Sullivan: an index to the texts of his vocal works,* by Sirvart Poladian. 1961. 91 p.

A comprehensive index of first lines, titles, and refrains to the composer's vocal works, sacred and secular.

Review by William Lichtenwanger in *Notes*, 19 (1962) p. 428–30.

1332

No. 3: *An index to Beethoven's conversation books*, by Donald W. MacArdle. 1961. 46 p.

Review by Fred Blum in *Notes*, 20 (1963) p. 225–27.

1333

No. 4: *General bibliography for music research*, by Keith E. Mixter. 1962. 38 p.

Surveys the nonmusical aids to musical research, with emphasis on such reference works as general bibliographies of bibliography, national and trade bibliographies, general dictionaries, encyclopedias, union lists, and library catalogs.

Review by Fred Blum in *Notes*, 20 (1963) p. 225–27.

1334

No. 5: *A handbook of American operatic premieres, 1731–1963*, by Julius Mattfeld. 1963. 142 p.

Also entered as no. 265.

1335

No. 6: *Medieval and Renaissance music on long-playing records*, by James B. Coover and Richard Colvig. 1964. 122 p.

Also entered as no. 1260.

1336

No. 7: *Rhode Island music and musicians, 1733–1850*, by Joyce Ellen Mangler. 1965. 90 p.

Also entered as no 143.

1337

No. 8: *Jean Sibelius, an international bibliography on the occasion of the centennial celebrations, 1965*, by Fred Blum. 1965. 114 p.

P. 1–11: Books and dissertations devoted to Sibelius; p. 13–45: books partially devoted to Sibelius; p. 47–71: music journals; p. 73–94: non-music journals. Index of names. 1429 items in all.

1338

Deutsch, Otto E. "Music bibliography and catalogues." In *The Library, ser. 4*, 23: 4 (Mar., 1943) p. 151–70.

1339
Duckles, Vincent, ed. Music libraries and librarianship. *Library Trends*, 8 (April, 1960) p. 495–617. [Published by the University of Illinois, School of Librarianship.]

15 specialists discuss various aspects of music librarianship, covering the areas of training for the profession, bibliography and selection, cataloging, services, and administration.

Review by Vladimir Fédorov in *Fontes artis musicae*, 8 (1961) p. 30–31.

1340
Fischer, Wilhelm. "Verzeichnis von bibliographischen Hilfswerken für musikhistorische Arbeiten." In Adler, Guido, *Methode der Musikgeschichte*. Leipzig, Breitkopf & Härtel, 1919. P. 200–222.

Classified list, including general bibliographical works, general musical works, and bibliographies of single aspects of music history. Some inaccurate dates and incomplete titles for French and English works, which are less well covered.

1341
Hoboken, Anthony van. "Probleme der musikbibliographischen Terminologie." In *Fontes artis musicae*, 1958: 1. P. 6–15.

A discussion centered in the difficulties of establishing music bibliography as an "exact science" in view of the variety and complexity of the materials with which it is concerned.

1342
Hopkinson, Cecil. "The fundamentals of music bibliography." In *Fontes artis musicae*, 1955: 2. P. 122–31.

An attempt to stimulate discussion of some basic points as to the nature, content, and procedures of music bibliography as it serves the needs of collectors, musicians, and historians.

1343
International Association of Music Libraries. Deutsche Gruppe. Systematik der Musikliteratur und der Musilakien für öffentliche Musikbüchereien. Erarbeitet von der Kommission für Musiksystematik bei der Arbeitsgemeinschaft für Musikbüchereien in der Deutschen Gruppe der Association Internationale des Bibliothèques Musicales (AIBM) [Reutlingen] Bücherei und Bildung, 1963, 39 p.

A system of music classification devised for German public library practice.

[319]

1344

King, A. Hyatt. "Recent work in music bibliography." In *The Library*, 26: 2 (Sept.–Dec., 1945) p. 99–148.

Surveys the accomplishments in music bibliography during the period just prior to, and during, World War II.

1345

King, A. Hyatt. Some British collectors of music. Cambridge, Cambridge Univ. Press, 1963. 178 p. (The Sandars Lectures for 1961.)

A pioneer study of the activity of private collectors of music in England, with an appendix containing classified lists of collectors from the mid-17th century to the present.

Review by Albi Rosenthal in *Music and letters*, 45 (1964) p. 258–59.

1346

Krohn, Ernest C. "The bibliography of music." In *MQ*, 5 (1919) p. 231–54.

One of the first surveys of the state of music bibliography by an American scholar. Useful as a statement of the accomplishments in the field at the time of writing. Incomplete citations. Narrative style.

1347

Krummel, Donald W. and James B. Coover. "Current national bibliographies, their music coverage." In *Notes*, 17 (1960) p. 375–88.

Surveys the music coverage in the national bibliographies in the Western Hemisphere, Western and Eastern Europe, Africa, Asia, and Oceania.

1348

Laforte, Conrad. Le catalogue de la chanson folklorique française. Québec, Les Presses Universitaires Laval, 1958. 397 p. (Publications des archives de folklore, Université Laval.)

Demonstrates a method for establishing an alphabetical catalog, by title, of French folk songs, with appropriate cross-references to permit the grouping of variants under a common title. Based on material in Canadian archives and collections.

1349

Luther, Wilhelm-Martin. "Bibliographie . . . Literatur." In *MGG*. Kassel, Bärenreiter, 1949– . V. 1, col. 1837–39.

Recounts the history and surveys the concepts of music bibliography, with an extensive listing of titles pertaining to the field.

1350
McColvin, Lionel R. and Harold Reeves. Music libraries, including a comprehensive bibliography of music literature and a select bibliography of music scores published since 1957. . . . Completely re-written, revised and extended by Jack Dove. London, Andre Deutsch, 1965. 2 v.

First published in 1937–38.

Vol. 1 is made up of a series of chapters on various aspects of music library administration and practice: staff, binding, classification, cataloguing, etc. There are chapters devoted to British public libraries, British university and special libraries, overseas libraries, etc.

Vol. 2 consists of bibliographies and indexes of music literature and scores which are cited elsewhere. See nos. 433, 626.

1351
Mixter, Keith E. An introduction to library resources for music research. Columbus, Ohio, School of Music, College of Education, Ohio State University, 1963. 61 p.

A practical list of music books and editions for use in courses in music bibliography at the college or university level. Selective. A minimum of annotations.

1352
Music Library Association. Code for cataloging music and phono-records. Prepared by a Joint Committee of the Music Library Association and the American Library Association, Division of Cataloging and Classification. Chicago, American Library Association, 1958. 88 p.

The five major divisions of the code are: entry, description, phono-records, simplified rules, and filing rules for conventional titles. Glossary and index.

1353
Music Library Association. MLA index series. Ann Arbor, Michigan, Music Library Association Executive Office, 1964– .

A series of short, self-contained bibliographies or indexes prepared under the supervision of the Publications Committee of the Music Library Association. The five volumes published to date are as follows:

1354
No. 1: An alphabetical index to Claudio Monteverdi *Tuttie le Opere*. Edited by the Bibliography Committee of the New Chapter MLA. (1964).

[321]

1355

No. 2: An alphabetical index to Hector Berlioz *Werke*; edited by the Bibliography Committee of the New York Chapter MLA. (1964).

1356

No. 3: A checklist of music bibliographies (in progress and unpublished); compiled by the Publications Committee MLA [n.d.]

1357

No. 4: A concordance of the thematic indexes to the instrumental works of Antonio Vivaldi, by Lenore Coral. (1965).

1358

No. 5: An alphabetical index to Thomás Luis de Victoria *Opera Omnia*. Edited by the Bibliography Committee of the New York Chapter MLA. (1966).

1359

Music Library Association. Committee on Information and Organization. Manual of music librarianship. Ed. by Carol June Bradley. Ann Arbor, Michigan, Music Library Association Executive Office, 1966. 150 p.

A symposium of 13 papers devoted to various aspects of music librarianship: materials, plant, personnel and budget, acquisitions, classification and cataloging, binding and circulation, sound recordings, special materials, friends of music, community relations, and museum aspects of the library. The contributors are all practising American music librarians.

1360

Music Library Association. Committee on Thematic Indexes. A check-list of thematic catalogues, prepared by a Committee of the Music Library Association. New York, The New York Public Library, 1954. 37 p.

Reprinted from the *Bulletin of the New York Public Library*. (Jan.–March, 1953). Preface signed: Helen Joy Sleeper.

350 numbered entries, including thematic catalogs of 129 individual composers, 63 collections, 22 libraries, and 13 publishers.

Index of composers, and general index.

Review by Vincent Duckles in *Notes*, 11 (1954) p. 552–53; by Scott Goldthwaite in *JAMS*, 8 (1955) p. 58–59.

Queens College supplement (1966) to the Music Library Association's check

[322]

list of thematic catalogues (1954). Flushing, N.Y., Queens College, 1966. 45 p. (typescript)

This supplement not only brings the original list up to date, but extends its scope to include many unpublished thematic catalogs. It also gives a bibliography of 55 items on the literature of thematic catalogs. Introduction signed by Barry S. Brook.

1361

"Music . . . Musicology." In *The bibliographic index,* a cumulative bibliography of bibliographies. New York, H. W. Wilson, 1937– . P. 1087–97, and in subsequent issues.

1362

New York Public Library. Reference Department. Music subject headings, authorized for use in the catalogs of the Music Division. Boston, G. K. Hall, 1959. 512 p.

Reproduced from cards in the subject heading file of The New York Public Library. An important tool for music catalogers, since it represents the practice of one of the great American music libraries.

1363

Ott, Alfons. "Die Musikbibliotheken." In Fritz Milkau's *Handbuch der Bibliothekswissenschaft,* 2nd ed. 1958. v. 2, p. 222–42.

A comprehensive discussion of music documentation, bibliography, cataloging, and administration of music libraries. One of the best international surveys of the field.

1364

Pohlmann, Hansjörg. Die Frühgeschichte des musikalischen Urheberrechts (*ca.* 1400–1800). Neue Materialien zur Entwicklung des Urheberrechtsbewusstseins der Komponisten. Kassel, Bärenreiter, 1962. 315 p. (Musikwissenschaftliche Arbeiten. Hrsg. von der Gesellschaft für Musikforschung, 20.)

One of the few studies in the history of music copyright practice treating the sociological and psychological aspects of composers' rights, plagiarism, the history of honoraria for composers. An appendix gives 31 original documents in transcription.

Review by Werner Braun in *Die Musikforschung,* 17 (1964) p. 298–99.

1365

Regeln zur Katalogisierung der in der Deutschen Bücherei eingehenden Musikalien. Entwurf. Leipzig, Deutsche Bücherei, 1959. 35 p.

Cataloging rules developed for German libraries.

Review by Virginia Cunningham in *Notes*, 16 (1959) p. 567.

1366

Rothenberg, Stanley. Copyright and public performance of music. The Hague, Martinus Nijhoff, 1954. 188 p.

A survey of the current status of music copyright and performers' rights in the United States and in Europe.

1367

Schulze, Erich. Urheberrecht in der Musik. Dritte, neubearbeitete Auflage. Berlin, Water De Gruyter, 1965. 474 p.

First published in 1951.

A source book of information on music copyright practice. European orientation. 37 appendices of codes and other documents related to copyright. The bibliography, p. xii–xxiv, provides an international listing of performer's rights organizations.

1368

U.S. Library of Congress. Subject Cataloging Division. Classification. Class M: music and books on music. 2nd ed., with supplementary pages. Washington, 1963. 157, 101 p.

First issued in 1904, revised 1917.

Largely the work of L. G. Sonneck, this classification schedule has been accepted, with various modifications in a great many American music libraries, chiefly in colleges and universities.

"Additions and changes to July 1962," occupy the last 101 pages.

1369

U.S. Library of Congress. Subject Cataloging Division. Music subject headings used on printed catalog cards of the Library of Congress. Washington, D.C., Govt. Printing Office, 1952. 133 p.

1370

Wollon, Simone. "Musicologie," in L. N. Malclés, *Les sources du travail bibliographique*. Tome II: Bibliographies spêcialisées (Sciences humaines). Genéve, E. Droz, 1952. p. 536–52.

Basic but highly selective list of music reference works; classified and well annotated.

1371
   Winchell, Constance M. "Music." In her *Guide to reference books*. 7th ed. Chicago, American Library Association, 1951. P. 346–56.
   See also the appropriate sections in later supplements.

Addendum

1372
Dufourcq, Norbert, ed. La musique: les hommes, les instruments, les oeuvres. Tome premier: La musique des origines à la mort de Rameau. Paris, Larousse, 1965– .

This work is projected in two volumes, designed along lines similar to *La musique des origines à nos jours* (above) expanded and brought up to date. The first chapter deals with non-Western music. 42 contributors. P. 361–76: "Glossaire des instruments." P. 381–84: bibliography. General index.

1373
Krautwurst, Franz. Das Schrifttum zur Musikgeschichte der Stadt Nürnberg. Nürnberg, Stadtbibliothek, 1964. 68 p.

A bibliography of 824 items related to the history of music in Nürnberg; including books, periodical articles, dissertations. Indexed by persons, places, and subjects.

BIBLIOGRAPHIES OF MUSIC

1374
Diehl, Katharine Smith. Hymns and tunes—an index. New York, Scarecrow Press, 1966. 1,185 p.

Analyzes the contents of 78 hymnals. Indexes: (1) first lines and variants; (2) authors and first lines; (3) tune names and variants; (4) melodies, a systematic index. Glossary, and an analysis of the reference content of the hymnals treated.

1375
Rasmussen, Mary. A teacher's guide to the literature of brass instruments. Durham, New Hampshire, Brass Quarterly, 1964. 84 p.

General discussions of music available for brass ensembles and solos, each followed by extensive listings giving publisher, price, instrumentation and grade level of the works cited.

1376
Burton, Jack. The index of American popular music; thousands of titles cross-referenced to our basic anthologies of popular songs: *Blue book of Tin Pan Alley, Blue book of Broadway musicals, Blue book of Hollywood musicals, The melodies linger on.* Watkins Glen, N.Y., Century House, 1957. 1 vol. (unpaged)

1377
Spink, Ian. "Sources of English song, 1620–1660: a survey." In *Miscellanea musicologica, Adelaide studies in musicology,* 1 (March 1966) p. 117–136.

Treats the printed sources in summary fashion, but gives brief descriptions, with bibliographical references, of 21 manuscript sources, 1615–1660.

CATALOGS OF MUSIC LIBRARIES AND COLLECTIONS

1378
Internationales Musikinstitut. Katalog. [Vorwort: Dr. Wolfgang Steinecke] Darmstadt, Kranichsteiner Musikinstitut, 1956.

Classified catalog in expandable looseleaf format of the collection of contemporary music at the Kranichsteiner Musikinstitut. Chiefly scores and performance materials, but with a small collection of books on music. This catalog has been superseded, as far as content is concerned, by the entry above, but it is still useful because of its classified arrangement.

1379
Musikbibliothek der Stadt Leipzig. Handschriften der Werke Johann Sebastian Bachs in der Musikbibliothek der Stadt Leipzig. [Bearb. von Peter Krause. Leipzig] 1964. 62 p.

1380
Guildhall Library. Gresham Music Library: a catalogue of the printed books and manuscripts deposited in Guildhall Library. London, Corporation of London, 1965 [i.e., 1966] 93 p.

1381
Vatican. Biblioteca Vaticana. Monumenti vaticani di paleografia musicale latina. [by H. M. Bannister] Lipsia, O. Harrassowitz, 1913. 2 v. (130 plates) (Codices e vaticanis selecti, v. 12).

A volume of commentary and a volume of plates containing excerpts from Vatican manuscripts, assembled for the purpose of paleographical study. Contains a vast amount of information on manuscript sources of plainchant in the Vatican Library.

MISCELLANEOUS BIBLIOGRAPHICAL TOOLS

1382
Davies, John H. Musicalia: sources of information in music. Oxford, New York, Pergamon Press, 1966. 218 p.

A useful manual of music documentation addressed to a variety of interests, including the ordinary listener, performers in various categories, the musicologist, the music librarian, the broadcaster, record collector, etc. Illustrated with facsimile pages from the major music reference works. Appendix I: principal music collections, formerly in private hands, and now to be found in institutions and libraries of Great Britain. Appendix IIA: music publishers and agents. Appendix IIB: music publishers' organizations. Appendix IIC: performing rights societies.

INDEX OF AUTHORS,
EDITORS, AND REVIEWERS

[335]

[341]

INDEX OF SUBJECTS

INDEX OF TITLES

[353]

Encyclopedie van de Muziek (Arntze-nius), 20
Encyklopädie der evangelischen Kirch-enmusik (Kümmerle), 233
Encyklopädie des Geigenbaues (Jalovec) 173
English and Scottish Psalm and Hymn Tunes (Frost), 764
"English Pictorial Music Title-Pages, 1820-1885" (King), 1212
English Song-Books, 1651-1702 (Day & Murrie), 1195
Entsiklopedicheskiĭ Muzykalnyĭ 'Slovar' (Keldysh), 21
Erich Lachmann Collection of Historical Stringed Musical Instruments, 1159
Erst und Frühdrucke von Robert Schu-mann in der Musikbibliothek Leipzig, 955
"Erstlingsdrucke der deutschen Ton-meister der Klassik und Romantik" (Kinsky), 1216
Esposicion de Música Sagrada Española. Catalog de los Codices, Manuscritos y Libros Musicales (Moll Roqueta), 997
Esposizione Nazionale dei Conservatori Musicali e delle Biblioteche (Florence, Italy), 892
Essai de Terminologie Musical (Vannes), 226
Essaie sur la Musique Ancienne et Mo-derne (Laborde), 347
Die Estensischen Musikalien; thema-tisches Verzeichnis (Haas), 1109
"Estudio Brasilenos I. Manuscritos Mu-sicales en la Biblioteca Nacional de Rio de Janeiro "(Lange), 1063
Ethnomusicology, a Study of Its Nature, Its Problems, Methods and Repre-sentative Personalities (Kunst), 528
Ethnomusicology and Folk Music: an International Bibliography of Disser-tations and Theses (Gillis & Merriam), 510
Ethnomusicology. Journal of the Society for Ethnomusicology, 450

Etude Music Magazine, 56
The Euing Musical Library. Catalogue [Glasgow], 908
"Europäische Musikzeitschriften 1945-48," 480
European Composers Today (Ewen), 59
Europese Musiekinstrumenten in het Haags Gemeentemuseum (Ligtvoet & Lievense), 1154
Die evangelische Kirchenmusik (Blume), 299
Everyman's Dictionary of Music (Blom), 5
An Exhibit of Music and Materials on Music, Early and Rare (Luper), 921
Exhibition. British Musical Instruments [Galpin Society], 1163
Exhibition. Claude Debussy, Biblio-thèque Nationale, Paris, 1038
Exhibition. Frédéric Chopin, Biblio-thèque Nationale, Paris, 1039
Exhibition. Frédéric Chopin, George Sand et Leurs Amis, 1046
Exhibition. Gabriel Fauré, Bibliothèque Nationale, Paris, 1040
Exhibition. Jean-Philippe Rameau, Bib-liothèque Nationale, Paris, 1042
Exhibition. Mozart en France, Biblio-thèque Nationale, Paris, 1043
Exotische en Oude Europese Muziekin-strumenten in de Muziekafdeling van het Haagse Gemeentemuseum (Ligt-voet), 1155
Exposition de Documents Musicaux [Brussels 1955], 858

Fach-Katalog der Musikhistorischen Ab-theilung von Deutschland und Öster-reich-Ungarn, 1107
Fachwörterbuch der Musik (Gerigk), 208
Fagkataloger [Staatsbiblioteket Aarhus], 817
Famous Musicians of Jewish Origin (Saleski), 110
De Fidiculis Bibliographia: Being an Attempt Towards a Bibliography of the Violin (Heron-Allen), 540

[365]